A Marriage Sabbatical

A MARRIAGE SABBATICAL

Sabina Shalom

illustrated with photographs

DODD, MEAD & COMPANY   *New York*

Published by Dodd, Mead & Company, Inc.
79 Madison Avenue, New York, N.Y. 10016
Distributed in Canada by
McClelland and Stewart Limited, Toronto
Manufactured in the United States of America
Designed by Claire Counihan

2 3 4 5 6 7 8 9 10

Library of Congress Cataloging in Publication Data:

Shalom, Sabina.
    A marriage sabbatical.

    1. Shalom, Sabina. 2. Wives—United States—
Biography. 3. Marriage—United States—Case studies.
4. Self-realization—Case studies. 5. Voyages around the
world—Case studies. I. Title.
HQ759.S4615   1984   306.8'1'0924   84–1474
ISBN 0–396–08365–X

For Marco

and
in memory of my parents
Elsie and Joseph Prepsler
and
my most beloved sister
Audrey

Contents

Acknowledgments

In prefacing this book with acknowledgments my feelings are those of total inadequacy.

I can never thank enough my mentor, my confessor, and my most loyal friend, Peggy Mann. She not only encouraged me to write this book, but maintained faith in me at times when I lost faith that it would ever be completed.

I am particularly grateful to my knowledgeable editor, Evan Marshall, whose guidance and experience enabled us to work harmoniously together to produce the final work. To Kay Radtke goes my admiration for her tireless and conscientious efforts on my behalf, and to William Ashworth I am especially indebted for the excellence of his intuition and discernment. No less do I owe my sincere thanks to everyone at Dodd, Mead for their gracious and warm welcome to me during my extended working visit at their offices.

Throughout my lengthy travels many doors were opened to me as a complete stranger. These kind persons, too many to name individually, offered me a bed, sometimes a typewriter or a telephone, and that most precious gift of all, their sincere friendship. I mention with an especially grateful heart Marilyn and Norman Glubok; Vera, Daniel, and Serga Nadler; Marjorie and Alan Kwawer; and Sarina and Albert Shalom.

Nor can I ever forget Lena Rosen and Karen Messer, who took me in off the street, totally unknown, when, short of funds, I had no place to stay on the last lap of my journey home.

My sincere appreciation to the Polaroid Corporation of Cambridge, Massachusetts, which gave me not only cameras for my trip but also so much assistance in the development of my film.

To my two sons, Anthony and Michael, my deepest love. To Tony, for being my greatest champion from beginning to very end, and to Michael and his wife Elyse, for their unwavering support and encouragement that enabled me to continue writing during a most painful time of my life as the course of this book proceeded.

And last, but really first, all my love and thanks to my husband Marco for accepting the chaos I created, the erratic hours I labored, and my absolute indifference to everything about me other than the sheer necessities of shared living quarters. I must also thank him for his assurance that I am not only the best, but so far the only, wife he says he has ever had or wants.

Let me not pray to be sheltered from dangers
but to be fearless in facing them.
Let me not beg for the stilling of my pain
but for the heart to conquer it.
Let me not look for allies in life's battlefield
but to my own strength.
Let me not crave in anxious fear to be saved
but hope for the patience to win my freedom.
Grant me that I may not be a coward, feeling
your mercy in my success alone;
But let me find the grasp of your hand in my failure.

—RABINDRANATH TAGORE, "Fruit-Gathering"

A Marriage Sabbatical

1

The Last Straw

The last straw came that morning when, as I shuffled off to the kitchen to make Marco's breakfast, he watched my exit and non-chalantly remarked, "You know, darling, you really are disgusting. You are getting so fat, but so-o-o fat, that if you don't do something about it, you'll soon be quite obese."

I stopped dead. "Well, ducky, you didn't say that last night."

"Didn't I?"

"No, you damn well didn't. You said I was full and gorgeous and sexy and quite wonderful."

"Ah, well, last night was last night, if you know what I mean."

I knew only too well what he meant, and I was angry because I knew he was right. Marco is *always* right. Damn it, even when he is wrong he is right. It makes me sick sometimes.

I had reached a stage in my life where somehow I didn't care much about anything anymore. I didn't even care to think about not caring, so I distracted myself during the day by watching an endless, inane variety of television programs. The refrigerator was always full of yummy—and fattening—things to munch on, and what with the odd telephone call, and a little sleep later on, the day was soon over. Even when the beds went unmade, the dishes and clothes went unwashed, and the whole place went to pot, the day still seemed to be over before it had begun.

Often there was barely enough time to throw myself into some clothes, spruce up my appearance, and commence feverish preparations for the evening meal. Marco's dinner was the one conscientious project I accomplished each day. Without exception, it was imaginatively put together and attractively served. It was an act of love.

"Darling," he used to say in earlier days, "you have such a way of presenting things. I swear you could serve up cats' tails and people would think they were eating a gourmet dish."

Nowadays, nothing I placed before him drew forth comment or even acknowledgment. It didn't really matter—much. We had been married nearly thirty years and I no longer thought about compliments or thanks. I knew Marco generally enjoyed his meals, though there were the odd occasions when the silence of his approval might be shattered with a groan: "Oh, no, I had this for lunch."

One cannot always win.

Marco is not an ogre. He is not ill-natured. He is simply indifferent. I expect he'd best be classified as being a Typical Man. I mean the long-married kind. The kind that comes home from the office with a briefcase full of papers and addresses the peg upon which he hangs his jacket with a "Hi. What's for dinner? I'm starving."

From that point on, all further conversation between us ceases for the rest of the evening, until a "G'nite, hon," or, once we were in bed, a sleepy grunt.

As for me, perhaps I was the typical long-married woman. I had recently read an article on depression. Among other gloomy prognoses, it said there was a period in midlife called involution melancholia. Well, whatever that was, I was sure I had it. The empty-nest syndrome, menopause, the lot. Face it, you are just getting old. Better resign yourself to that which Fate has in store for you. A steady downhill slide from now on. At the rate I was going, it looked more like a fast downhill run.

What had happened to all those resolutions we had made when we moved to Florida eighteen months ago? Complete retirement had not been in our plans, for we were not of ample means and knew that some income would need to be found. Besides which, Marco, at fifty-five, was too young and energetic to remain inactive.

We had talked of living a simpler life and spending more time together, as Tony, our elder son, and Michael, our other boy, had left home some time ago, and our responsibilities toward them had

2

lessened considerably. Those earlier, rough years were over, and Marco's freely admitted addiction to work a thing of the past.

We had spoken of the walks on the beach we would take, the plays and concerts we would attend. Marco even promised, no matter what business he got into, a free day, midweek, as a "Just-for-Sabina Day," like the doctors who took Wednesdays off to play golf.

I never expected he would become so obsessively involved with a small business as to exclude almost all manner of relaxation. My offer to help in the office was turned down. "Not necessary at this stage, honey." I respected his wish to accomplish the job alone, certain that our leisure hours together would be the more enhanced.

It was not to be. His complete absorption left precious little time for me and absolutely none at all for making new friends or seeking other recreational outlets together.

Our lives assumed an all-too-familiar pattern. Instead of taking things a little easier, Marco lived to work instead of working to live. My hopes of finding the companionship for which I had waited so long quietly died.

I became restless, bored, and frustrated. I resented piddle-paddling around the house. It wasn't even a house—it was a very small apartment. Actually, it was a very small prison.

It hadn't seemed so bad at first, because I had thrown myself into getting the place together. After five weeks I had done as much as was necessary, and within the economic limits we had determined, I managed to create a harmonious atmosphere and a comfortable home.

Our lives adopted the character of the pleasant, unobtrusive, and practical pieces of furniture by which we were surrounded. We existed for each other's convenience.

Marco slipped into the old eat-work-and-sleep routine with no trouble at all. I headed into one that augured plenty of trouble: namely, total mental and physical disintegration.

My lack of recent work experience made suitable jobs hard to find; moreover, they were poorly paid, and I had no car. Twice a week I did volunteer social work, the satisfaction of which was much diminished by the lengthy wait in scorching heat and humidity for two changes of bus, both there and back. The rest of the time I spent at home in quiet desperation. I preferred loneliness to the risk of making friends with other tenants in the building, fearing curiosity, gossip, and unannounced visitors dropping by at all hours of the day.

When the telephone rang, I jumped out of my skin, since it happened so rarely. It was nearly always Marco, and invariably he would ask, "What's the matter with your voice? You sound hoarse." Hoarse it was for lack of speaking to someone all day and often most days of the week.

The recent loss of my mother heightened my sense of aloneness. There were times when sadness engulfed me with such profundity that I felt dragged down into a complete vacuum.

Those were the days I stayed in bed all day, oblivious of time, until the lengthening shadows indicated a waning sun and a closing office. Dressed and attentive to Marco, I gave the impression of having had a productive day. As questions were rarely asked, I had little fear that my inactivity would be noticed.

Consolation came by way of food, and I slowly ate my way into near obesity, aware that in so doing I was inviting serious illness as a possible consequence. Insanely I reasoned that Marco would then notice me more, fuss over me, talk to me. But nothing happened, and I remained in my usual strong-as-a-horse, big-as-a-house condition.

I knew it was sheer suicide to carry on this way. Periodically I tried crash diets, the more bizarre the better. But after a few days of strenuous effort all was wasted when I indulged in a mammoth gourmet binge. I read all the self-help books I could find, but they only told me things I knew or had already tried and failed at. Frustrations mounted. Anger at myself increased and turned inward to further self-punishment. The most ironic part of it all was the impression I gave on chance encounters with the doormen of our building, attendants in stores, or the occasional visitors to Miami with whom we'd spend an hour or two. All seemed to find me conversational, cheerful, and often quite humorous. Even Marco never suspected—or if he did, he chose not to acknowledge —the blackness of my despair.

Resentments piled up. Depression set in with a vengeance. I felt doomed to disaster. Worse, I resigned myself to the inevitable calamity I was convinced would sooner or later overtake me and relieve me of all responsibilities, especially the one to myself.

Never could I have dreamed that my whole life was to undergo a drastic change, a change brought about by so simple an event as a phone call from Harry.

Harry Hemsworth was an old school friend of Marco's who had gone to live in Australia. Once, during his single days, he paid us a visit when we lived in Detroit. Now he and his wife were passing through New York and called us from their suite at the Plaza.

"When are you two going to pay us a visit?" he asked. "I've been asking you for the last ten years, you know."

I had picked up the phone in the kitchen, waving to Marco to pick up in the living room as I said, "Careful, now, Harry, we just might take you up on that."

"Hold it," he bellowed, "let me put Liz on." The volume could probably have put Liz out, but there she was on the end of the line. "Hi there. We really mean it. We've plenty of room. Stay as long as you like; you're most welcome."

Harry again, "Well, you heard it. How about it, eh?"

"Thanks, old chap," Marco said on the extension, walking toward me as he tried to unravel the wormed-up cord. "Big trip. Afraid it's not on this time. But how're you doing, Harry? It's good to hear your voice. How've you been?"

"Fine, fine. Look, if you both can't make it, how about Sabina, then?"

"Have to think about it," Marco said. "Can't just say 'yes' like that, Harry. Awfully nice of you, thanks. We'll have to see." He was raising anguished eyes to the ceiling and giving me the "what-else-can-I-say?" look, completely ignoring my excited gestures as I pointed to myself and mouthed that I'd be glad to go.

Further pleasantries were exchanged. The phone call terminated. Marco dismissed the entire conversation with, "Who on earth would want to go to Australia, anyway?" No reply was expected, nor could I have made one, for at that moment I was unable to marshal my thoughts coherently. In those brief seconds I had sensed a break in the clouds of doom that had been gathering volume over the past twelve months. It was someone we knew offering somewhere I could go. Who cared where?

"Well, I'd like to go," I burst out, "and I'm going." I thrust out my chin determinedly. "Can I? Please, darling?"

"Oh, c'mon now, are you crazy?" Marco was a trifle impatient.

"No one ever goes to Australia. What on earth would you do there? Look, I'm tired. I'd like a cup of tea. Any more of that cake left? Got a lot of things to do tomorrow. Must get to bed."

Before turning out the light, he sleepily addressed the bedcovers, "Huh, Australia!"

The matter rested there for the time being, but it was not forgotten as far as I was concerned. My thoughts kept churning around for days. Harry's phone call had triggered all kinds of wild ideas, best kept to myself for the time being.

Marco had lately taken to the habit of coming home for lunch a couple of times a week. He said it was as quick to do so as it was for a waitress to bring him his order.

For my part, it obliterated one of my favorite television programs. The guests on the show were nearly always people who were doing something about living their lives. I did not dare confess that I preferred the charms of Phil Donahue at one-thirty in the afternoon to the rapture of watching my husband eat a lunch that was "much better and far less expensive than any meal in a restaurant, honey."

In my depressed state, the normal lethargy of the mornings was abruptly terminated by the need to jump into action to prepare these occasional midday meals. Unfortunately, after Marco's departure I would revert to an even deeper gloom, worrying about what on earth I could make for dinner that night, now that I had just served it for lunch.

Such were the limits of my horizon. In fact, it was all pretty sickening when I came to think about it. My first thought upon awakening, and generally my last upon retiring, was what to make for meals. The whole domestic scene was a downright crashing bore. After all, there were only the two of us now. Our older son, Tony, was teaching in Spain, and Michael, the younger, was working in San Francisco. Why, then, did I seem to be chained more than ever to the sink and stove? It wasn't fair. Why wasn't I doing things like those women on the Donahue show? I made "if only" my best excuse. It became a refuge in which I indulged excessively.

If only I had a car, I would get out a lot more. Eat a lot less. Get a job—maybe. If only Marco didn't come home for lunch. If only I were thinner. It was always "if only," and then—an idea began to take shape. It had started to germinate in the back of my mind after Harry's phone call. Marco would never agree. Still, it was worth a try. What had I to lose? Why not?

Of course, I hadn't taken Harry's invitation too seriously. People were always tossing out invitations like that. Just the same, it was Liz who had said, "We really mean it. We've plenty of room. Stay as long as you like." Surely they *must* have meant it? Even Marco had believed the invitation was genuine. He just couldn't imagine anyone ever wanting to go so far away. "Why, it's right off the map," he had said.

The idea obsessed me simply because it *was* right off the map. It became an excuse, not a reason, for getting away. I didn't even care if I never got to Australia. I just wanted to go as far away as possible. The greater the distance, the more desirable it seemed. Such a journey meant a long absence from home, from meals, from dishes, from everything. Everyone? Yes, everyone. Even Marco? Was this what I really wanted?

I gave the matter some hard and painful thought. Deep inside, my honest feelings told me that yes, this was indeed what I wanted. I longed to be free of duties and obligations. Free of thinking, worrying, protecting, mothering. Free of feeling everyone's burdens and making them mine. How could I make Marco understand this? I did not want freedom from my marriage per se. I loved my husband deeply and couldn't bear the thought of hurting him. I just wanted to be on my own for a while, that was all.

How I might manage to make out alone seemed far less of a worry than how Marco would get along. All our married life he had never lifted a finger to do a thing for himself. In the early years I had happily baked, cooked, and made jams, jellies, and pickles. Creating a relaxed atmosphere and a tasty meal ready for a tired husband at the end of a long day had been a challenge. Marriage was a serious job, as was being a good wife and mother. A change of careers. I had been determined to be as successful in my new role as I was in my previous, single, one. Alas, I had spoiled Marco rotten! Nowadays, with an electric stove we both had to get used to, he would squint and fiddle with the dials, singeing his hands before he knew which burner had been turned on. Just putting the kettle on was an ordeal of domesticity for which he had no patience whatsoever. Not only was he used to being waited upon hand and foot—he loved it. Worse, he made it clear that he had no intention of changing.

The prospect of a smooth domestic withdrawal from the scene looked slim. On the other hand, I reasoned optimistically, he would be relieved of guilt by bringing home piles of work. He would be spared my silent, disapproving looks. Who knows? Perhaps he would enjoy being alone. There would be nothing to disturb his concentration. He might even feel a sense of freedom too.

Besides, what happens when a man is left a widower? He has to manage then. There are no guarantees as to who will leave this world first. We push away all thoughts of death: it is something that happens to others, not us. Must we learn the painful way, when the inevitable happens? Why not a temporary separation? Not of divorce, bitterness, or hostility; not of tears and the sorrow of bereavement. A special kind of parting, born of joy and trust and friendship. An experience to be shared and laughed over later while we still had each other. It could enhance a marriage, strengthen and nurture that precious time when reunited. It could also remind us to prepare ourselves for that sad day, which lies ahead for all of us, when we will be truly alone.

I cautioned myself to make little mention of such thoughts to Marco. He would not like that kind of talk at all. I could just hear him say, "Another of your crazy ideas. You're not a kid anymore. You can't just traipse off alone to the ends of the world like that. What if you became ill? Wait a little, honey. We'll go away together one of these days, I promise you."

I didn't want to wait for one of those days. I felt I had been waiting for them most of my married life. Days just to spend time with him. Time for companionship, walks, talks, and time for love. Now, when I was middle-aged and lonely, they were getting fewer and fewer. The tomorrows were here and now and suddenly today. Could I really "go it alone"? It would be a challenge. It would be a chance to find the old me. The me I felt was slipping away forever.

Saturday night was our big night out. That is to say, our night off. What it usually meant was that Marco did not pore over his papers. It could be that we would do no more than settle down to watch a movie on television. This attraction might be forgone or combined with an evening walk, depending on the weather or the quality of the movie.

On this particular Saturday we chose to take a stroll that terminated at the back of our apartment building and beyond the pool area, where we could sit and face the ocean.

We had rented a small apartment on Collins Avenue in Miami Beach. Our building would have been labeled modest by comparison with the imposing glass-steel-and-concrete edifices that were our neighbors on both sides. For the two of us, our place seemed just right. Our hopes, originally directed toward semiretirement, favored this temporary arrangement. It was a convenient step until we decided what we were going to do and where we might ultimately wish to live—the latter being a decision I hoped to postpone for some time, since all my windows looked out on the ocean, the tranquilizing effects of which were a source of great comfort to me.

We were sitting now, facing the sea. It was about ten o'clock. The night air was damp but not chilly. We were quite alone. Other than the gentle lapping of the waves, the caprice of the tide did little to disturb the stillness that lay between us.

Conversation seemed out of place, for our senses were succumbing to the magical feeling that steals over one when contemplating the infinity of that vast body of water stretching out ahead.

I gazed into the darkness. Beyond the smudgy line of the far horizon lay England and all of my family, which I had left behind when we had emigrated twenty-five years ago. I thought of Europe and in my mind's eye conjured up visions of treelined boulevards and outdoor cafés. I saw square-shaped tram cars and double-decker buses. I could even see myself running to catch one. Perhaps now was the moment to speak. After all my years of marriage, I was surprised to find I was quite nervous.

"You know something?" It wasn't really a question and I didn't wait for a reply. "Since we moved to Miami, all I seem to do is run back and forth to the supermarket in order to make the kind of meals you pick at; and you stay thin, while I pig out and grow fat."

Without turning to face me, Marco mumbled, "What did you say?"

"I said there should be more to my life than just making meals."

"Yes, darling." Marco's gaze and attention were completely

"at sea." I knew he hadn't heard a thing I said. I tried again. "Mung . . ." (I rarely call him Marco; no one ever does. He is so conservatively British that the name Marco never seemed to fit. It's usually Mark, "Co" to members of his family, some of whom live in the States. I have a variety of names, Mung being the one most often used.) "Mung," I went on, "would you say that for the last twenty-eight years I've been a good wife?"

There was no reply. I repeated my question a little louder. "Have I been a good wife for the last twenty-eight years, Mung?"

"Yes, darling," came the instant and unhesitating reply. (He never calls me by name either.)

Well, at least he'd heard. So far, so good. "And would you say that when difficult choices had to be made, I always put you and the boys first?"

"Yes, darling, I would." His tone of voice was that of humoring a wayward child. He was still half-dreamily contemplating the ocean as he spoke.

Undaunted by the risk of plugging away too much, I ventured, "So would you say, then, that over the years I've done a good job?"

"Yes, I would, I would, but what's all this leading up to? Come on, what have you gone and done? Let's have it."

"I haven't done anything—yet." I took a deep breath and plunged on. "I was just thinking that with the boys away, and you happy with what you're doing, at my time of life I should be doing something I also enjoy."

"Well, that's all right. Go ahead and do it. Like what, for example?"

I dropped the bombshell. "Like going to Australia and visiting Liz and Harry."

"What?" In a flash he turned to look at me. "You're not serious?"

"Yes, I am. Quite serious."

"It's out of the question. I thought you understood that weeks ago when we spoke to them." He floundered on, perplexed. "I know you're feeling a bit low lately. Maybe you do need a little break somewhere, but Australia! No, it's just not possible."

Tears stung my eyes. I felt a surge of anger. "I don't want 'a little break somewhere.' I've let myself slide into a terrible state. I feel I'm going to pieces. You said yourself how fat I am, and it's

10

true. I've just got to do something about myself, and the best thing would be to go away—but *really away.*"

There was a long silence. At last, very slowly, he spoke. "Honey, I expect I do forget how rough the struggles have been over the years. Now, with your mom gone, no friends, I admit we do lead a pretty dull life. It's just that a trip to Australia would be an enormous expense."

"It wouldn't have to be. There are all kinds of bargains these days. I made a few inquiries already. Pan Am even offers an around-the-world fare for less than a thousand dollars. Of course, there are all kinds of conditions, but if I really looked into it, I'm sure I could come up with something that would be quite reasonable."

"Now wait a minute. You've just sprung this on me. Surely you don't expect an answer here and now? After all, there are other considerations to be taken into account."

"Like the wedding anniversary present I'm still waiting for?"

"Oh, well, I never know what to get you, and you nearly always take things back to exchange in any case."

"I wouldn't take back the secondhand car you've been promising me for I don't know how long now."

"That's different. A lot more money is involved there."

"Not much difference between a car and a trip to Australia, I would think."

"Now look." Marco showed signs of impatience. "Don't start badgering me. The whole idea is absurd. Besides, I'm not so sure of your welcome out there. They probably didn't mean it anyway."

Marco's irritation triggered a like response. I found myself replying testily, "They certainly did. I could tell from the way Liz spoke. You heard her yourself. I'll bet she is also very lonely out there." Suddenly I burst into tears. "How would you know? You have your work, you see people, you have your brothers and sisters over here to talk to or see. Whom have I got? What do I do except wait around all my life to be at your convenience?" All the pent-up feelings, so long repressed, now spilled out. I sobbed uncontrollably. "You're not even aware of what's going on inside me. You don't see, you don't think, you don't care."

Marco was aghast. "How can you say such things? Of course I care. Yes, I am wrapped up in the business. It has only just got

11

going; otherwise, I'd love to go somewhere *with* you. Not Australia, mind you." He gave me a searching look. "Why do you want to go so far away, all alone, without me? Is there more to this than you want to say? Something you are hiding? Someone, perhaps?"

I smiled through my tears at the thought. "Of course not, silly. I don't know how to explain it or if you'd understand, but I need to be on my own for a while. It's because Australia *is* so far away that I want to go there. Too far for complaining phone calls to make me feel guilty, and make me rush home. I want to feel free to do what I want without having to ask all the time."

Marco looked puzzled. "I've never stopped you from doing what you want, have I?"

"No, because it relieved your guilt at never doing much *with* me. Be honest. Hasn't your convenience always come first no matter what I've done?" My voice was steadier. I felt much more composed now.

"Yes, that's true. But a trip to Australia would hardly be a convenient week or two, would it?" Marco sounded almost conciliatory. I began to feel hopeful and mentally searched for ammunition to further my cause. "If time is to be a factor, then you should bear something else in mind as well as the money."

"Now what?"

I hesitated. This would really set the sparks flying. I mustered myself for battle. "Maybe you don't know, but the going rate for a domestic to clean house is between twenty-five and thirty dollars a day, and a live-in maid would be entitled to two free days—time off with pay—every week. Now, I think that after all these years of good service, to say nothing of the fringe benefits you've enjoyed, I am entitled to the same consideration you would have to give a maid. In other words, you owe me two days a week in time and money for every week we have been married."

There was a roar of laughter. I did not wait for further acknowledgment and went on, "So you figure out what you owe me in time and money for twenty-eight years."

"You're talking nonsense; it is utterly ridiculous," Marco exploded. "Why, fifty dollars a week for fifty-two weeks comes to, let me see, about twenty-six hundred dollars, and for twenty-eight years that would be—oh, heck, I don't know, maybe fifty or sixty thousand dollars. As for time off, two days a week is one hundred and four days a year, times twenty-eight . . . oh, this is preposterous. I need my calculator. We're speaking of thousands of dollars and four or five years. You're out of your mind. You don't really think I can take all this seriously, do you?"

"No, I never expected you to. But one day a week with pay—retroactive, mind you—would be a reasonable proposition, and even on that I am quite willing to make a compromise. I'll settle for less. How about that?"

"You mean like three years in time off and, say, a paltry thirty thousand dollars?"

I could see he was joking about it now, and I felt I was losing ground. "It's all very well your treating this humorously. Why shouldn't housewives get paid? You'd have to pay a stranger to come in and wash, cook, and clean for you. Nowadays women are asking for social security for the homemaker. What's wrong with that?"

"All right, enough already. Don't start giving me a women's lib speech."

"I'm not. I am only asking for recognition of a job well done. An around-the-world ticket with a year's time off would do very nicely, thank you."

"A year?" Marco was flabbergasted. "First it's Australia, then all this nonsense about time off with pay. Now a ticket around the world and a year—honey, that's like forever. I mean, even if I agreed—and I'm not saying I will—a year is quite ridiculous. Who would look after me? What would I do for food?"

"What would you do for food?" I gasped incredulously. "Your only concern is *food*? I don't believe this. Here we are, talking of thousands of dollars and days, and you can only think of food! Now, if you had asked me what would you do for, say, a little horizontal refreshment—! Well, I don't quite know how I would answer you. But food—really, aren't you ashamed of yourself?"

He had the grace to grin sheepishly. "I suppose I am spoiled. What with your cooking and everything, I've never really had to do anything for myself. Honestly, darling, I really don't know how I'd manage without you. Let's forget the whole stupid idea." Marco got to his feet and pulled me up. He put his arm around my shoulder and we started to walk slowly back to the apartment.

I suppose over the years one learns a thing or two about the marriage business. There are times when one feels needed and times when one feels taken for granted. There are also the times when it is wiser to let matters take their natural course. I made only occasional references to what I called my marriage sabbatical, but meanwhile quietly set about making extensive inquiries.

A lot of answers had to be found if, one of these sunny Miami Beach days, I was going to spread my wings and fly as free as a bird.

It was after dinner ten days later. Marco was sitting on the couch drafting a letter, a few books at his side. I was clearing the dishes from the table. With feigned nonchalance and without lifting his head, he called out, "Honey, where was that place you said you wanted to go to?"

My heart skidded. His tone of voice was so matter-of-fact. He must be referring to some restaurant, I thought. I froze ever so slightly and answered as lightly as I could. "What did you say?"

"I had a business inquiry today for some goods made in Hong Kong."

"Oh, yes?" My head began to reel. The way he casually threw the words out, as if asking me to pass him a beer. Very slowly I put the plates down on the table. "Hong Kong, eh?"

"Yes, it would be a terrific piece of business if I could bring it off. I can't leave the office, so I got to thinking that maybe you could stop there on your way to Australia and—"

My shriek of "What?" all but shattered the windows and completely drowned out the remainder of his sentence. A grin spread across his face as I threw myself onto the couch beside him. The books slid to the floor. I kicked them to one side and hugged him so fiercely that we toppled off the couch. We rolled over on the carpet, Marco's legs across mine, his glasses knocked off his nose, and my head narrowly missing the edge of the coffee table.

Breathlessly I said, "You mean you're going to let me go?"

Straightening up, but still on the carpet, Marco took my face between his hands. "Yes, darling, you can go. I've given it a lot of thought. I never got you a car, and when this inquiry came in and I remembered that Hong Kong was one of the places you said an around-the-world ticket covered, it all seemed to fall into place."

A tinge of disappointment cut into the elation I felt. "You mean you wouldn't have let me go if this hadn't come up?"

"I might not have decided quite so soon. I don't know. Are you complaining? Come on, don't be silly. You'll be my representative, and it will all work out beautifully, both to my advantage and to yours."

"You're right, Mung. You're always right." I kissed him to add emphasis, chiding myself for being such a fool as to question his motives. I could go. I could go. Wasn't that the main thing? A new wave of excitement swept over me, cut short by Marco's caution-ary words. "Now, I want you to make a list and write down every expense you think you'll have. We will have to work this out very carefully, so be realistic. Hotels, meals, everything. It's a big trip, and it's going to cost a lot of money."

"I will, I will. It won't cost so much. I'll economize on every-thing. You'll see. I don't have to stay in posh hotels. Other than the ticket and the expenses in Hong Kong, I bet I can do it on a thousand dollars. It will be a shoestring budget, I promise you. As for meals, I'll not be eating that much anyway. I need to lose weight."

"Ah, well, I was just coming to that." Marco was now back on the couch. I was still sitting on the floor, looking up at him. I felt like a little girl listening to Daddy as he administered words of wisdom.

"There is one condition," he continued.

"Oh. What's the condition?"

"You've got to lose some weight before you can go. I'm not getting into the expense of a whole new wardrobe for you. If you are representing me and conducting business for me, you've got to look decent. Apart from business, I want you to look good for yourself. The way you were before we came to Miami."

My heart sank. Hope receded rapidly. "You mean I can't go if I don't lose enough weight? How much? How soon? I'll do it, I'll do it."

"Well, you really must try hard. You used to look terrific at a hundred and twenty pounds. I'm not saying you have to weigh that before you go. There'll be a few weeks of correspondence first, no doubt. There's no immediate urgency for the trip. You've got time, but you must make a concentrated effort to stay with it. I'll stick to my part. I'm willing to let you have the kind of ticket you want, and we'll discuss the amount of time you might reason-ably need. You said you wanted a thousand dollars? You've got it, though I doubt you'll manage on that. We can talk about it later, but *no new clothes,* okay?"

"Okay, Mung. Yes, Mung. Whatever you say, Mung, and I love you very much."

"And I love you too. For all your nutty ways, you are my darling wife and very precious to me. I'm always so busy, I just don't realize how empty the days must be for you. We have to put an end to this awful depression of yours, all right? I want you to feel good, get ready, and go away free and lighthearted and have a wonderful time."

A big lump rose in my throat. Suddenly I wasn't so sure that I wanted to go away. "If you think there's a chance we could go together, even if it means waiting awhile, maybe I won't go after all, Mung. What do you think?"

"No, sweetheart, there isn't an earthly chance, and I do want you to go."

"Are you sure? You really don't mind my taking off?"

"That's right. Come here, you funny thing." He pulled me up and sat me down on the couch beside him. "Now listen carefully and repeat after me. 'Munga says I can take off.' Again, slowly. 'Munga—says—I—can—take—off.' All right?"

I nodded my head and smiled a misty smile. I didn't speak.

I had a lot to think about. There were now so many things to do—one of which was not to eat for the next six weeks.

Taking off is not so easy when one is thirty pounds overweight.

2
Taking Off

My proposed trip firmly established, I now had to decide upon an itinerary. Pan Am had been most cooperative, but until I was able to tell them where I wanted to make stopovers, they could not quote me a fare. I had picked up a few leaflets at the travel agencies, but they all seemed to describe package deals of limited duration. This would not do at all. Out came the huge *National Geographic* map of the world.

The kitchen table was cleared from breakfast. The dishwasher was stacked. Marco was not coming home for lunch, and the evening meal was partially prepared. The whole day lay ahead of me. Gone were those morning hours of indifference and apathy. The television had not even been turned on for the early news.

The map was too big for the kitchen table, so I spread it out on the one in the dining room. It was very quiet and still, except for the mounting excitement I felt as I settled down with a pencil and a paid of lined foolscap paper to make notes.

I looked at the map. It was mind-boggling. Going to Australia via Hong Kong and a westward route would take me halfway around the world, but going eastward and never turning back would take me all around it. Strange places I had heard of now revealed their geographic locations. Exotic, distant countries leaped off the page, beckoning. The more remote they were, the more they appealed to me. I became so engrossed and my imagination so fired that I found myself throwing in this country and that, as if I were adding condiments to a meat stew.

First I could stop off and see family and friends in England and

France, and my son Tony, who was on a teaching assignment in Spain. Switzerland, Italy, Yugoslavia, and Greece would follow— naturally! Turkey? Why not? India? Of course! Thailand was still en route, as was Malaysia. Hong Kong had already been decided upon, and Manila, on the map, looked only an inch or so away. Throw it in! Now, Papua New Guinea would be a most exciting country to visit, even though cannibalism was still rumored to exist. Probably not true nowadays. Right, put it down! After Australia? New Zealand is right next door, as it were—might as well go there; the South Island is said to be very beautiful. And then, and then, oh, my God! The whole of the vast South Pacific Ocean and its hundreds of islands lay stretched out before my eyes, right there on the dining-room table.

I stared in a dreamy hypnotic way at all those famed, faraway places. Could I really go there? New Caledonia, the Solomon Islands, Samoa, Tonga, Fiji, Tahiti, and then where? Back to the United States via Honolulu? No, that's a place Marco and I could perhaps travel to one day. But if I kept on going due east I would get to Easter Island, and *that* is somewhere I would never be able to go to under normal circumstances. That tiny speck of land was surely the remotest spot in the entire world, a place where the great monolithic figures had mystified archaeologists for decades. A fascinating civilization of centuries past known to me only from books, one I had never dreamed I could ever personally explore. Easter Island, the land of mysteries, burned in my brain. I simply had to go there.

I looked up and caught sight of the clock. I must have been lost in contemplation of this totally improbable journey for hours. Yet why should I not make it? As a mother, I had always told my sons, "Believe in yourselves. There is nothing you cannot do. The sky is the limit." This metaphor could now come true for me.

That endless, unfathomable ocean. That timeless, enveloping sky. Both were mine. Marco had said I could go. A voice within me clamored, "Go, do it. You may never have the chance again."

Gone was my depression. There was too much work to be done. All my thoughts were now concentrated on preparing for this gigantic, almost unrealistic journey. I couldn't sleep at night. Instead of counting sheep, I made lists in my head of all the countries I hoped to go to. At this stage I decided against telling Marco about all my plans, since I was unsure whether a trip of

18

such dimensions could really be undertaken. With an excitement I could hardly contain, I took my proposed itinerary to a travel agent.

To my consternation, not one travel agency would take me seriously. They stared at me with frank disbelief; one clearly regarded me as a loony lady. Some politely, some indifferently, suggested I leave my list with them and they would try to work something out. Others said they were rather busy just then and such a trip required weeks of work; perhaps I could give them a call in a month. I felt quite crushed. I was not prepared to wait all that time. Marco might change his mind.

Less ebulliently, I called Pan Am again, this time with more encouraging results. A most helpful young man was detained on the telephone for at least one hour. He took my itinerary quite seriously, even enthusiastically, but dashed my hopes of a cheap fare by explaining that such a journey would have to be based on mileage rather than the point-to-point construction on already-established routes. "You see, ma'am, we don't fly to all those places, and this is where your add-on fares will mount."

"What if I went by train or bus on some of the sections? Wouldn't that keep the price down?"

"Lady, you can even go by camel, but once you deviate from our routes, it's going to add to the cost."

Despite the growing impatience in his voice, I had to battle on. Marco wanted to know how much this trip was going to cost, and I had to get an approximate fare. "Yes, I do understand. If I keep to a Pan Am route, then, how much will my ticket be?"

"We have a basic, round-the-world economy fare of one thousand nine hundred and ninety-nine dollars."

"And approximately how much more would it be if I went to all the places I gave you originally?"

My insistence must have worn him down, but not quite out. He responded coldly, "Madam, when you have decided on the exact date of your departure and can give me the dates of your ongoing flights, then we can quote you a fare."

"But I don't know right now just how long I might want to stay in some of my stops." I was beginning to feel desperate.

"You must understand, ma'am, that we have to use other carriers where we have no service, and this becomes quite involved.

19

Just give us a call when you have your departure date, and Pan Am will take good care of you, believe me."

I did believe him. I just had the feeling he didn't quite believe me.

How was I ever going to arrive at dates when it looked as if no one wanted to take me where I wanted to go? It would certainly be cheaper and easier to fly the direct route Pan Am offered, but that meant giving up all those exotic places I had fantasized about. No, I wasn't going to—not yet, at any rate. Somehow or other I would find a way.

I called another airline, but the results were not much better. If anything, matters became even more complicated. In consultation with their *Official Airline Guide*, they pointed out that any flights currently in effect could well be inoperative by the time I reached some of my destinations. "We cannot say what the schedules will be in three or four months' time. We are now in February; the summer timetables are always changed."

I felt quite defeated. It was like a conspiracy. At this rate I would never get organized. Marco had asked me for a list of all my expenses, and all I had written down so far was a string of countries.

If no one was going to help me work out my trip, I would just have to try and do it myself. Maybe I could get hold of one of these *Official Airline Guides*. I could look up the stops, give random dates (even if I changed them later on), choose any flight for that matter, and thus I could obtain a fare. I had to make a start somewhere in calculating what my expenses were going to be.

As it turned out, travel agencies regarded these guides as their bible, and not one agency would allow one out of its sight. I remembered an acquaintance who had taken a travel agent course in night school but had not found the part-time work she had hoped for. We met occasionally at the Lighthouse, a facility for the blind where I used to read for those deprived of sight.

Her instructor at school was in the travel business, and my friend offered to borrow a guide from him if at all possible. He did not lend her one in current use, but gave her a back month's copy that she could keep. This she was kind enough to let me have, together with her class notes and some explanatory leaflets. I eagerly settled down to what I expected would be a long, but not difficult, task.

20

No wonder the agents and airlines had balked at my inquiries! What I thought might be a tedious job turned out to be a horrendous nightmare. The *Official International Airline Guide* was a monster of a reference book. It took me days to learn how to read and understand it, and then days of agonies in grappling with the cross-references and code indications. From the early hours of the morning until late at night I stuck with it, poring over the pages until my back ached with fatigue and my eyes stung hot and tired. By eleven-thirty, Marco, long since in bed, would call out, "C'mon to bed, honey. Why don't you give the trip to a travel agent to work out?" I had not yet told him the extent of my journey and that no one had wanted to undertake this mammoth exercise. He assumed I obstinately wanted to plan the journey for my own pleasure.

At last I felt ready to tackle Pan Am again. They had asked for dates. I gave them dates. They had asked for my stopovers. I gave them stopovers. If I changed dates and flights later on, it would make no difference in the price of my ticket. I impatiently awaited their return call after I had given them the information they needed to quote me a fare.

"It looks as if we are talking about thirty-five hundred dollars, Mrs. Shalom. It's the add-on fares, you see." I held the phone in stunned silence. I had hoped the $2,000 figure mentioned earlier might be increased by no more than the $500 or $600 to cover my additional stopovers. They had all seemed fairly en route as I looked at them on the map.

My arguments to this effect met with a sympathetic but firm response. "I'm sorry, madam, but for where you want to go, it's impossible. We simply do not have service there, and this is where you run into the expense of other carriers."

"All right, then I shall just have to make stricter economies with all my accommodations. Do you have any literature on hostels, pensions, and places like that?" It was just as well that our discussion was over the telephone, for it spared me the possible embarrassment of seeing a pained expression. It was the lengthy silence that suggested to me this probable reaction. I imagined him struggling to regain his composure. His guarded tone of voice conveyed courtesy but utter dismay that it should be his misfortune to have to deal with some crazy lady. The Hilton and Hyatt hotels were probably all he ever recommended, and here was this woman intent on making a journey that he most likely would never make himself or plan for anyone else, and she was arguing about hotel expenses. I felt he was wondering whether I was a lonely woman who passed away the time of day in making useless inquiries.

"No, madam, I do not." His cold reply terminated the conversation. I quickly thanked him, said I would be in touch shortly, hung up, sat down, and felt quite dejected. There had to be ways of keeping all the incidental expenses down. I *would* find hostels and pensions, and perhaps I *could* do parts of the journey by train or bus. Maybe ferries or boats? Heavens!—it hit me like a blast of cold air. I could *hitchhike!* Why not? Just because I was older then the youngsters who always hitchhiked around, why should it make any difference? To hitchhike, that was the thing. Meanwhile, I had other hurdles to overcome.

One of the first was to arrive at a figure for the entire trip. How much would I need for a modest hotel in Delhi? What should I reckon on spending in Hong Kong? How did other travelers calculate their daily expenses? Once again I called the travel agencies, picking at random from the Yellow Pages and avoiding those I had already spoken to earlier.

This time I got a snappy rule-of-thumb answer to most of my questions. "We generally advise tourists who want to do things on their own that they will need at least one hundred dollars a day. Of course, there are excellent package deals that take care of your hotels, meals, and all sightseeing for much less. Why don't you come in? We'd be glad to discuss your plans."

I wasn't interested in package deals, and I had no intention of spending $100 a day. It was certainly no figure to present to Marco. I rejected it outright, cut it ruthlessly in half, and unashamedly decided to lie through my teeth. It was bad enough that I now had to outline my journey to him and mention the fare, but to speak of $100 a day might be enough to make him change his mind about the trip altogether. I was a nervous wreck as I faced him after dinner to apprise him of my plans. "A travel agent said that some people need fifty dollars a day, others require more, but I am quite prepared to stay in less-than-posh hotels and I'm sure I can get by on thirty dollars tops. There's nothing wrong with pensions and YWCAs, you know."

"Maybe not, but you don't have to go to such extremes. What

22

about the fare? Have you an approximate idea now as to what you'll be spending?"

I gritted my teeth and plunged in. To my great surprise, it was not the cost of my ticket that upset him, but the list of some of the places I wanted to visit. "Madrid, London, Paris, Geneva," he repeated. "Very nice. Italy, Yugoslavia, Greece, Turkey? Why Turkey?" He looked at me quizzically and went on. "India, Papua New Guinea? You can't go there—it might be dangerous. New Zealand, Tonga, Fiji, Tahiti, Easter Island? Darling, what are you thinking of? You are going to the ends of the earth." He shook his head incredulously as I tried to explain.

"Mung, you said I should feel free to do as I please. Going to some of these underdeveloped countries, traveling in a simple way, perhaps staying with a family and really getting to know the people and their way of life, this is something I could never do with you. You wouldn't want to, would you?"

"No, certainly not. When I get a break, I want a little luxury. I want to relax in a comfortable hotel, or I'd rather not go away at all."

"I understand, and that's fine. Being alone and free to go where I want offers me an experience of a different kind. There's no challenge in staying at smart hotels, where all I shall probably hear is the English language and meet people who are only concerned with the tourist spots, home-style meals, gift shops, rest stops, and a package-deal outlook. Going away like this, being away from you and the comforts of our home, has to have much more meaning than just a vacation. I was a social worker once, remember?"

"Yes, and I know how deeply you feel about such things. I'm just a little nervous that some of these places could be unsafe for a woman alone. Anyway, we'll talk about that later. Meanwhile, what about your incidental expenses? Hotels, meals, restaurants, that sort of thing."

"For a start, I'll not be eating much," I replied dramatically. "You know very well that when I'm on my own I hardly eat a thing. It's only when I make tasty meals for you that I weaken and eat so much. Every overweight person knows how hard it is to avoid nibbling and snacking when one is alone in the house a great deal, and depressed into the bargain. You simply don't understand how hard it is to diet because you've never had a weight problem.

23

When I'm away, it will be easy not to eat. I'll have maybe one good meal a day. Not only will it keep expenses down, but I'll lose a lot of weight too. You'll see."

"I'm waiting to see you lose a bit of weight *before* you go. Have you managed to fit into any of your clothes? You'll need a few warm things. It will be cold in Europe for several more months, you know."

I knew, all right. I knew utter despair when I ransacked the closets to see what clothes might serve for the trip. Dresses, skirts, blouses, and slacks were strewn all over the place. I squeezed, pushed, tugged, and strained. Nothing I tried on fit my fat frame. I hastily crammed this devastating evidence of failure into large plastic bags and hid them before Marco came home. It was no use. I had better get started on a diet—and now!

Out came all the diet books. I raked through them for the fastest possible weight-reduction plan. The more bizarre the better if the results were quick. I chose the Stillman liquid diet, which recommended drinking eight glasses of water a day. I doubled it! I couldn't imagine any harm could come from an excess of water, and surely there was no need to check with a doctor (which all diet books suggest as a prerequisite) about drinking water, for goodness' sake! One hundred and twenty-eight ounces of clear water were quite an effort to get through in one day. Needless to say, I spent a great deal of time in the bathroom and, of course, never went out of the house on my "water days."

Other times I left the house early and stayed out until the last possible moment, eating nothing, but absolutely nothing, all day long. I often went to the library on those days. I read whatever literature was available on some of the countries I intended to visit. I also made copious notes about cities that had visitors' information bureaus and jotted down addresses and telephone numbers of YMCAs where available.

There were days when hunger so gnawed at my stomach that I had to cross the street or an aisle in a store so as to avoid the sight or smell of food. Peanuts, candies, even canned goods made direct assaults upon my senses. It was stupid and even dangerous, but I felt I had to do it. How else could I lose the weight in the short time I had set for myself? After all, I reasoned, what's a little fainting now and then, compared to those lost pounds? And yes, I had at last begun to lose them.

Strangely enough, Marco seemed to lose enthusiasm as I lost weight. Correspondence with the manufacturers in Hong Kong had been less than encouraging, and there seemed a strong possibility of a business opportunity failing to materialize. I did not ask for details when Marco briefly mentioned his disappointment at the way things were going. He had not yet said a visit to Hong Kong was out, but the acceptance he had shown when first agreeing to my trip was now not as much in evidence.

My own feelings were also ambivalent. When he responded indifferently to my questions, I felt some of the old resentments and told myself I was glad to be going away. Yet a remark as to how much he was going to miss me threw me into a tizzy of guilt and made me feel I should stay. All kinds of doubts would then beset me. How long could I take? How long was long? How would I manage for money? I had sworn it would be on a shoe-string budget. Was it wise, safe, sensible to go off all alone? I had said I wanted to be free of fixed dates and a fixed itinerary. With only three stops along the way where I would see or stay with friends or family, I had no accommodations in mind, nor could I be reached until I arrived in Australia.

A "marriage sabbatical" sounded fine, but could I really undertake such a journey, or had I set myself an impossible challenge out of sheer bravado?

In Europe, even with the strictest economy, accommodations would be adequate, and the countries were civilized. I could not imagine any situation that might lead to a real disaster. Quite another story was a middle-aged woman traveling alone and on the cheap in countries where hygiene, life-styles, and a woman's place altogether implied backward, even primitive, conditions. Apart from such simple considerations as to where I would stay, what about the dangers my ignorance of local customs might precipitate? Without the aid of the language, how would I fare alone? Disturbing though these thoughts were, I kept them to myself.

About this time our younger son, Michael, had moved out West to San Francisco from Oklahoma. It had been quite some time since we had heard from him. He had dropped out of college, and we were concerned that he should not drop out of our lives. We were most thankful to receive a phone call from him, and in a mutual exchange of conversation I told him about my trip. Half-expecting him to commiserate with his father about being left alone, I was delighted when he responded enthusiastically to my news.

"Say, Mom, that's just great. You've no kids to look after. It's your turn now." My gender underwent a rapid change as he continued. "Yeah, I'm all for you doing your thing, man. Say, would you like my backpack? It's a real beauty. I can send it to you with no trouble at all."

"Well, I hadn't really thought about luggage yet, darling. A backpack is quite a good idea. Keep yours, though, you might need it. But I'll certainly think about one."

"Are you crazy?" Marco shook his head in dismay. "You have some mad ideas, but really, this is the end. A backpack at your age?"

"What, pray tell, has my age to do with it?" My advancing years are a highly sensitive area (I invariably lie). "I think it's a terrific idea, as it happens."

"Well, I prefer that you look and travel like a lady. Next you'll be saying you're going to wear blue jeans, God forbid."

"Not at all—at least not unless I am much slimmer."

The remark mollified him, and the conversation ended there, but the idea of a backpack appealed greatly to me, and I quietly resolved to look into this alternative to the luggage problem, as yet not faced. I recalled many occasions when youngsters had "crashed" with us. They all had backpacks, sleeping bags, and wore jeans. It was standard uniform. They seemed to need so little as they moved around. Why should I need so much more? Who said I had to wear a matching outfit, with purse and shoes in coordinating colors? Why couldn't I also take a few T-shirts and a couple of skirts if slacks were to be ruled out? With the reduced capacity of a backpack I would *have* to limit my clothing to the absolute essentials. So much the better. I had little enough to start with. A backpack would be great if I was going to hitchhike. The image of a chubby, middle-aged woman, dressed in a polyester double-knit two-piece suit, standing on the road with suitcases, trying to hitch a ride, made me wince. Besides, how could I hop a bus, run to catch a ferry, clamber onto a train or up into a truck with suitcases? A backpack it was going to be. If I looked a little eccentric, too bad. Better to be regarded as a loony but harmless creature than as a seasoned traveler with plenty of cash!

With this new image in mind I felt highly pleased. My appearance was also a source of great satisfaction: the weight was going down beautifully. I could not wait to get on the scales each morning, and sure enough, the needle reassured me daily. There were occasional lapses, however, during this truly strenuous dieting. The absence of something sweet created a craving that took every ounce of willpower, which sometimes quite deserted me. An excellent help was my Sego Bar, a diet product that I had come across in the supermarket and that, unlike most, did not taste like sawdust. I had decided to take some with me but had been eating them occasionally as a meal replacement. They were crunchy, sweet, low in calories, and, when eaten with a cup of coffee, satisfied me. The three boxes I had bought were finished, and I could not find any more anywhere. I was desolate. The empty packet gave the name of the manufacturer, so I put in a long distance call to the product manager and asked for help in locating a source of them in my area. I mentioned my trip and that I wanted to take some Sego Bars with me both to curtail meal expenses and to enable me to go on dieting.

If he thought my story a little wild at first, by the time we had finished chatting he had not only promised to look into the matter but said he would send me a box of Sego to tide me over. Within a week, three boxes arrived. All different flavors. Twelve cartons to a box, a total of 228 Sego Bars! A little note mailed separately expressed his good wishes for my trip and wished me luck with my dieting. In no small measure did the consumption of these bars throughout my trip contribute to a steady weight loss, thirteen pounds of which I managed to lose in the six weeks prior to setting out upon it.

One other unexpected gesture of goodwill came from the Polaroid Corporation of Cambridge, Massachusetts. I had been wondering what to do about a camera. The only one we had was twenty-one years old. It still worked fine, but the lever was broken, it had no case, and it weighed a ton. I didn't want to ask Marco to buy me one. I didn't want him to buy me anything.

I managed to increase my "stealing" from the housekeeping money. I was quite adept at this, having had many years of practice. It was not a well-kept subterfuge, and Marco probably guessed the exact amount. I simply hated to ask for money and preferred to think such measures were a game. With the extra dollars in hand, I took a look at the cameras in the stores. It was not only the cost but the gadgets that put me off purchasing one. It was during such window shopping that I met a young lady who was the area representative of the Polaroid Corporation.

I told her a little about my trip and my need for a simple camera, whereupon she enthusiastically encouraged me to tell her company about it, giving me the name of the person in Public Relations/Consumer Affairs. My call was received with courtesy and great interest, and an immediate offer to lend me a Polaroid instant camera. It arrived within a few days, complete with carrying case. Little did I realize then what a wonderful friend this would prove to be. It even prompted Marco to comment upon my need for a 35-millimeter camera "as well as that toy thing." I was delighted; everything seemed to be going smoothly. Letters had been dispatched to family and friends in Europe. Tony called from Spain to say how much he was looking forward to seeing me.

The first ripple of discontent was caused by a typically unfavorable comment, from a visiting relative, about me "gadding about." Marco came home from the office that night, visibly disgruntled. At first he made no reference to the visitor or the comments, and I was at a loss to understand his complaints.

"I don't know what I'm going to do about meals. I expect I shall lose a lot of weight. Probably end up with a bad stomach as well. I suppose the only solution is eating out, and that will get expensive too."

His mumblings went on and on. My guilty reaction grew and grew. No doubt about it, his style of eating in restaurants would, on a permanent basis, make a sizable dent in the bank account. He is a soup, salad, meat, potato, and vegetable man, with dessert, fruit, and cheese to finish. Nuts, chocolates, cake, and tea often follow within an amazingly short time. He *never* seems to stop eating. It fills me with black rage sometimes that he stays forever thin.

If only I could "train" him to make a few simple meals. At first he flatly refused. "You're not getting me to mess around with pans and things." Slowly, grudgingly, he agreed to watch me make an omelet.

28

"You melt a little butter in the pan, Mung. Don't let it burn, of course. Then you put in the beaten eggs."

"What beaten eggs? I always manage to push my thumb through the damn shell, and it runs all over the place leaving nothing to beat."

"All right, darling." I made sympathetic clucks so as to maintain his interest. "Let's forget the eggs for now."

"They're forgotten, all right. I'll not have eggs until you come back."

Undaunted and with a great show of enthusiasm, I had another try the following evening. "Now, Mung, tonight, imagine I've gone and there's nothing prepared. There's plenty of fresh salad, and those tender, pink lamb chops that you bought the other day are groaning to be grilled."

With barely concealed impatience Marco barked, "Look, I'm in no mood for trial runs. I'm tired and hungry, and I'm not fooling around with that grill thing. What's for dinner?"

"Actually, the lamb chops were, and I only wanted to show you how to cook them. Of course, if you prefer them raw . . . ?"

My attempts at humor were not appreciated. "I'm not waiting for you to start cooking now. Let's have a can of something."

Obligingly I produced a can of soup and a can opener. "Here you are. I take it you know how to operate the instrument?"

With irritation Marco complied, grabbed the first pan he saw, and was shocked when I relieved him of it. "That's not the right pan. I use it for boiling milk or puddings. *This* is the one for soup or vegetables. Oh, and please use only the black-handled knives for onions or garlic. The brown-handled ones are for fruit or sweet things. Try and remember, darling."

"No, I won't try, because I'll not be using any of them. You can just put all your pans and knives away and lock them up, because I shall be eating out and that's that. Now let's eat something. I don't care what as long as it's fast."

"All right, my dear. I can see I shall have to take a season's ticket out for you at the local deli or Burger King."

I learned the best lesson myself. One doesn't try to teach someone how to cook when he is starving. Subsequent attempts met with much more success. With patience on my part, Marco conquered the intricacies of the toaster oven. He made exquisite toast. I praised him glowingly when he actually fried an egg. He even felt proud of his boiled hot dog. My appreciative comments encouraged him to tackle a steak one night. He insisted on being in charge of the whole operation. I was delighted, though not left in ignorance as to his progress. He treated me to a running commentary. "Do I put salt and pepper on now or later?" and "Damn thing seems to splutter a lot of fat, doesn't it?" A four-letter expletive, more appropriate to the bathroom than the kitchen, resounded with a roar, followed by, "Hell, the thing's on fire!"

I flew in to see flames leaping and Marco flailing the dishcloth about wildly. He had tried to pour off some of the grease and had done a good job of coating the red-hot electric coils. I grabbed salt and then flour to douse the fire. Marco reached over to turn off the stove and burnt his hand. The flour stuck to the rings and smelled vile. It was a mess. In smothering the flames, all future hopes of culinary prowess were smothered as well. I knew this was the first and last time he would ever attempt to prepare a mouth-watering, sizzly, meaty treat. His diet would just have to consist of cold things, or hot dogs, toast, and fried eggs.

"Phew," he said, "that has really put me off."

"Yes," I remarked grimly. "It nearly put you out too."

"Look, you can't expect to make a silk purse out of a sow's ear." I could not quite figure that one out. I assumed he meant he was no *cordon bleu* apprentice.

I decided that the best solution would be to stock up the house with a good variety of canned foods. My efforts were a model of market research. If only I could inculcate a little imagination, Marco could easily combine a few cans with vegetables or a salad and have a reasonably satisfactory meal with very little trouble.

I made time to cook and bake some of his favorite things, not to be found in the stores. These I wrapped and labeled, some with instructions on defrosting and heating, and all carefully stacked in the freezer clearly visible to the eye. Marco is too lazy to go looking and pushing aside undistinguishable frozen lumps to find what he wants.

I stocked the house with every conceivable household need and toiletry. He would not need to shop for these for months. The toilet rolls alone filled one entire closet. The only thing I could not do for him in advance was the washing and ironing. Surprisingly, he learned beautifully—a few mishaps and the loss of his best white shirt for not following my instructions about mixing colored things with white items. The ironing was a bit tricky, but the only calamity was a small shriveled patch on one garment made of a synthetic fiber. Not at all bad for a beginner, and I made sure to congratulate him warmly.

He dismissed what he considered flattery by saying he was only doing these things to please me. "You surely don't think I'm getting into this malarkey every time I need a clean shirt, do you? Hell, no. I'll wear them crumpled, that's all." Considering that I always avoid ironing if smoothing down did the job, I thought this attitude augured well for my prolonged absence. No doubt about it—on the domestic scene, Marco had made good progress. My guilts lessened. I felt a great weight was gradually easing from my shoulders. I only wished more had eased from other parts of my anatomy.

Despite the visible difference in my shape, I still had the problem of what to wear. Europe would be cold for months yet, and I had no heavy warm coat. My old raincoat was tight, even without the lining, and the few warmer garments I had saved from our colder days up north looked skimpy and out of style. My heart sank, for I had half-counted on these when I so resolutely affirmed that I didn't need a thing.

I suddenly remembered a resale shop. Inspiration prompted me to take in all the slinky clothes I had been saving and hoping one day to wear. Getting rid of them might bring in a few dollars with which I could buy something new. My clothes were welcomed, and luck had it that I came across a fine wool-and-polyester skirt that fit me beautifully. It was beige and would go with several sweaters I had at home. This modest outlay of seven dollars solved the problem of something warm to wear while in Europe. Good. Done. Wrap it up. What next? By the time I reached India it would be warm enough for some of the lightweight garments I already had. To be on the safe side, I purchased from a department store a cheap but good-looking cotton-and-dacron outfit in a serviceable, smart khaki color. It was a three-piece, consisting of a safari-type jacket, a skirt, and slacks. I didn't want the trousers, so I asked the sales girl if it would be cheaper without them. "No, it's already been reduced." At the sale price of $26.95 for the complete outfit, I had no complaints. "Right, I'll take it."

What to do for shoes? Sneakers might be necessary in Papua New Guinea and on the stony terrain of Easter Island. I had never owned a pair in my life. Now, thanks to Sears Roebuck's on-sale leftovers, I found some at $2.65. Ordinary walking shoes I had, only the backs were open. They would have to do; besides, my feet could swell when walking, and the slingback would allow an extra measure of comfort. This, together with two additional pairs of open-toe-and-heel leather sandals, completed the footwear I felt would be sufficient. How much underwear should I take? Makeup? The less, the better. A sorry sight I would look in humid Singapore with rivulets of black mascara around my eyes or makeup streaking down a perspiring face. Medications? Ah, that was something else. I wasn't going on an Antartic expedition, for goodness' sake. Sticking with essentials was not easy. Lomotil had top priority. It was to help me cope with a problem, not resolve a possible future one. Aspirin, sore-throat remedies, thermometer, shampoo, and soap for personal use and clothes washing. A few clothespins and some nylon string for hanging laundry and tying up baggage should it let me down.

What *was* I going to do about baggage? The very thought of lugging suitcases around made me feel hot and sweaty. Why *not* a backpack? It really did seem the most practical. I'll just keep it from Marco until the last moment. From whom can I borrow one? And having done so, how to secure it against pilferage? The answer was found in an Army and Navy store: a huge army-type duffle bag. The pack could be easily slipped inside, and I could zip it up and padlock it. Now it could be consigned to a checkroom whenever the occasion arose, the contents having some measure of protection against theft. At the same store I also bought a tin mug, a canteen, a camper's knife, fork, and spoon set, and a multipurpose can opener. To this, from home, I added a small paring knife and a wad of tinfoil. Wherever my water-heating gadget would work, I could now make a hot drink in my tin mug. With packets of instant soup, tea, and dried milk, supplemented by my Sego Bars, I felt all set for camping, not jetting. Who knew where I could end up, and like a good girl scout, I wanted to be prepared for any eventuality.

All this was carefully hidden from view, for I knew Marco would be horrified to see that I had resorted to such innovations in order to keep within the strict money limitations I had boasted about. I was living in a state of suspense not only on this account but because I had a nagging feeling that for some reason or other the whole trip might be called off. It was only three weeks away and I began to go through a "what if" phase.

What if Marco or one of the boys became ill? What if the business deal Marco was negotiating fell through and he felt that he could not cope with the expense of my journey after all? Apart from the "what ifs," I lay awake many a night thinking that perhaps I was, after all, a rotten wife to go off and leave my poor husband to fend for himself.

Fortunately, these misgivings were instantly dispelled the moment Marco complained, "How come I've no socks?" (Because you just dropped them on the floor for the last seven days, I said to myself.) "Where's my blue sweater, honey?" (Where you left it—underneath the wet towels you're always strewing around the place.) No, on the whole, I didn't feel so bad when I came to think about it. Marco would simply have to learn to do things for himself for once, and as most men do always. Well, sometimes. It was no big tragedy. I cannot always be his mother.

Preparations went on, full steam ahead. There seemed to be a million things to do. I began to feel very pressured; my hollow eyes and the black shadows beneath them revealed the sleepless nights I was having. I had to broach Marco about money, as I needed to get traveler's checks. He sat, patient and quiet, as I ran through my calculations. "I estimate that fifteen to twenty dollars a day will be all I shall spend if I find YMCAs. If I have to stay in proper hotels, I propose to use the American Express card. This will keep down the amount of cash I need to carry. The bulk of it should be in checks, don't you agree?"

Marco didn't answer me. He looked away from my face and out of the window. My stomach dropped. I knew immediately that something was wrong. What had happened?

"Darling," he started to say and hesitated. "Darling, the Hong Kong thing has fallen through. I've known for a couple of days, but I hadn't the heart to tell you."

"Tell me what?" I knew. I had tried to prepare myself for this a week ago. All along I had had a feeling that something was going to go wrong. I didn't wait for his reply. I could see he was distressed to say what I already knew. "You mean I can't go now? Is that it?"

"Oh, honey, I don't know what to say. I feel so bad about it."

I didn't know what to say either. All my plans were made. My ticket was written up and waiting to be picked up. Replies from Liz and Harry, family, and friends, all looking forward to seeing me. My small purchases, clothes, camera, film, Sego Bars, everything, all so neatly arranged on the bed in the spare room. I felt such a letdown. Unbidden, the tears welled up. "I wouldn't be spending any more than a secondhand car would cost. You don't know, because I didn't want to tell you, but I'm taking all kinds of things with me to enable me to economize. Snack meals, drinks I can make myself. I intend to buy only fruits, cheese, and vegetables to supplement the things I am taking from home. You cannot imagine how cheaply I am going to live. Please believe me, I shall do it on a thousand dollars and not a penny more."

Marco looked at me in amazement. "You really think you can?"

"*I know I can.* You simply have to have faith in me. You've forgotten our hard-up years. You always marveled at how I managed the housekeeping."

"Darling, it's true. You were, you still are, terrific."

"So have confidence in me now."

"I have, but I also don't want you to skimp like that. In India, for example, I'd like you to stay in the best hotel available. I haven't forgotten my years in India. True, I was in the army, but I saw what conditions were like. When I say the best hotel, I mean *the best.* Do you understand?"

I understood. I listened. I heard. I promised. I fell asleep, however, still not knowing whether my trip was on or off.

Saved by the bell! And indeed it was a bell. The telephone's insistent ringing woke both of us from a deep sleep at one o'clock in the morning. It was our son Michael calling from San Francisco.

"I waited until the cheap rates to call you guys. Hope you weren't asleep? Guess you'll be leaving soon, Mom. Wanted to know how you're doing."

He really wanted to tell us how he was doing, and that was not very much at all. He was down to his last few dollars; "doing his thing" had not worked out. I was overjoyed! In a sympathetic tone of voice I suggested what I was sure he wanted to hear.

"Well, darling, I'm supposed to be off in a couple of weeks. I'm not absolutely sure right now if I'll make it. I would love to see you before I go. How about coming home? You'd be great company for Daddy, besides which, I know you'd look after him for me. You know how he is about his meals. He says he's going to eat out until I come back."

"Yeah, I know Pop and his meals. He'll eat a lot of junk stuff as well."

"Not if you come home; but in any case, I'm longing to see you."

"I sure would love to see you too, Mom."

"All right then, what are you waiting for? Get moving."

"Dig it! I'm on the way. Say, Mom, you can have my backpack, too."

Long of hair, smooth of cheek, loaded down with backpack, guitar, and the string bag essential to all young people's attire, he emerged from airport baggage claim grinning, happy, and adorable. My little boy of six feet had come home.

My heart lifted, my spirits soared. It was Fate. Surely this meant I would be able to go. I knew with Michael's homecoming Marco would feel altogether different. He would now have Michael to talk to instead of the walls. Best of all, Michael is a terrific cook, albeit a vegetarian who believes only in natural foods, and would make all the meals.

My instincts proved correct. Marco kept his word. Several days later he quietly placed a bulky envelope on the kitchen table and, with the barest twinkle in his eye, said, "I thought you might be needing this."

It was my ticket. Like a concertina, it fell open in my hands, the coupons unfolding on and on. England, France, Switzerland, Yugoslavia, Spain, Italy, Greece. I couldn't quite believe it. India, Thailand, Hong Kong? "I can go to Hong Kong after all?"

"Why not? Forget about the business thing. Maybe you can make a phone call or two, but it really doesn't matter, honey. What the heck, on a trip like this you might as well make the most of it. You'll not get a second chance, you know!"

I looked at my ticket. Manila, Papua New Guinea, Australia, New Zealand, Tonga, Fiji, Tahiti, Easter Island, Chile, Peru, Ecuador, Colombia—I swallowed hard, it was so exciting. My ticket to unlimited freedom, my ticket to adventure, my ticket to who knew what? It was scary, it was beautiful. I was speechless.

Michael's excitement seemed greater than my own. His enthusiasm and high spirits infected all of us. There was too little time

35

to enjoy him as I became frantic with the packing. Michael watched with amusement as I stuffed, squashed, and pushed odds and ends into every crevice of the backpack, and there still remained a huge pile to be packed. I looked at it with dismay. "Oh, Mike, what on earth shall I do?"

"In the first place, Mom, you're not doing it right. In the second place, your pack is just not big enough. Why not take mine? It's stronger, bigger, and will probably hold everything, especially if I pack it for you."

"Will you, darling? I'd be glad to take your pack."

"Right, then. Where's your list?"

"List? Oh, yes, I was just going to make one."

"So make one. You gotta have a list or how else can you check things off as you pack them away. Dig it?"

I dug it. I dug the way Michael managed to fit everything in. Garments were first laid out, folded, rolled up, and then plastic-bagged into the smallest of bundles.

"You see, Mom, certain things you put into side pockets and other things only at the bottom. Now take these shoes. Oh, man, what are you taking shoes like these for?" He held up my high-heeled black patent-leather sandals.

"Well, you never know, Mike. I might need to dress up a bit. There are one or two smart things I'd like you to put in." I held up a silk-jersey black-print dress, a sheer black blouse, and a metallic multicolored sweater.

"Ma, c'mon. You're backpacking. You won't need stuff like that."

"But I do have a couple of special stops, honey. The people I'll be staying with would expect me to be dressed in more than a denim skirt. As a matter of fact, but don't tell Daddy, I'm even taking some of my jewelry."

"You're what?" Michael's eyes widened in dismay. "You're crazy to take real jewelry. That's asking for trouble."

"On the contrary, who would ever think a woman with a backpack would be going around with jewelry?"

"Well, I dunno. Anyway, remember shoes go in here like this —okay?"

"Okay." But was it? The fancy lady's backpack wardrobe. It did seem a little incongruous. Never mind, I reasoned to myself,

I had to have a few things suitable for any occasion. I was going to be away a long time, and you just never knew!

With Michael's expertise (he is a graduate backpack packer), everything seemed to fit in. I was delighted. This was some pack. My satisfaction was cut short by Michael's order. "Right now, Mom, let's see you put it on."

I gingerly took the straps in my hands, trying first to assess the weight and get a feel of the thing. It didn't move. I pulled a face. "I'm not sure how to do this, Mike. You seem to swing it up so easily. I've watched you so many times, but now I don't remember how you do it. You'll have to show me." The pack lay on the floor in the bedroom. We were alone, as Marco was working in the living room.

"Right, Mom. Bend down. Get on the floor on your knees. That's right. Now, sit on your haunches and twist your right shoulder back far enough to be able to slide your arm through this strap. You got it. Fine. Now do the same with the other arm and slip it into the left strap. Easy does it. Great, you got it! Now, just stand up."

That was all. Just stand up. Easy.

I leaned forward to get on my knees. The weight almost crushed me! How could I stand up? I could hardly lift my head up. I attempted to bring a leg out from under me. I couldn't. I simply could not move a muscle. I was cemented to the floor.

"Go on, Mom, you're doing fine."

"Fool, how can I be doing fine? I'm not doing anything. I'm stuck. I can't move a thing. I can hardly move my eyes!"

"Now, Mom, don't give up. You're really doing fine, just fine. Easy now, easy. First one leg, then the other. It's really quite simple. Do you think you've got it now?"

Got it? I'd got it, all right. A stab of pain shot across my back as I made a superhuman heave to move. I toppled over on my right side, my left leg spread-eagled to one side, the pack on top of me, as I lay struggling with its weight pinning me down to the floor. "Michael, I've broken my back. I'm telling you, my back is broken. I'll not be able to go now. I can't move, Mike. Help me up."

"S'all right, Mom. You're okay. You're just not used to it, that's all. The next try'll be better."

37

"What next try? You must be kidding. That was my last try. I'm telling you, I've broken my back. I can feel it."

"Naw, c'mon, Ma. You've gotta give yourself a chance to get used to it."

"Idiot. How can I get used to it, when I can't even get up with it? It's no good, honey. I can't go with a backpack after all. Help me up and take the damn thing off me."

Michael obliged, and I shakily got up and sat on the bed. I moved my shoulders up and down. My back didn't seem to feel quite so broken now.

"I know what. How about trying to put it on from the bed? You'd probably be lifting it from a waist-high level anyway." Michael tried so hard to encourage me, I had to show willingness.

"All right, son, let's have another go." I still felt a dull ache in the lower part of my back, but I braced myself for another attempt.

I placed my arms inside the straps the way Michael had shown me. I bent backward a little and found I had accomplished this without difficulty. So far, so good; I felt heartened. The next thing to do was to straighten up and stand up. I felt the pressure against my back, but that was all right, since my arms were inside the straps and these felt comfortable around my shoulders. I thought a slight rock on my heels might just give me the leverage to straighten up.

I couldn't rock. I couldn't straighten up. I couldn't muster a twitch anywhere. I decided to ease myself against the pack, thinking a swaying motion might do the trick. I promptly fell backward onto the pack and onto the bed, my legs raised in the air. Michael roared with laughter, and I could not help joining him. We were convulsed. Our shrieks and peals brought Marco striding into the room. When he took in the scene and realized what I had been trying to do, he admonished Michael and reproved me.

"How *could* you let your mother put that thing on her back? And you, haven't you any more sense in that feather-brained head of yours? Give me the thing. My God! It must weight fifty pounds. Are you mad? You're not going with any backpack. The whole idea is absolutely insane. Forget it." He returned to his papers, and Michael and I looked at each other with woeful grins. The matter was settled. I hastened to get into a hot bath. I was sure I had really strained my back and didn't dare say a word of this to anyone.

As if to bury any possible resurrection of the backpack idea, Marco came home the very next evening with a brand new suitcase and a set of luggage wheels. "Now you'll be able to wheel your case without effort and travel like a lady."

"Thank you, darling," I replied weakly. "They are certainly very sturdy."

Another unexpected surprise was the 35-millimeter camera Marco bought me. "It would be a shame not to have good photographs on such a trip. We needed a new camera anyway. Don't go and lose it now." He seemed so much happier these last few days. I was sure that Michael's being home was largely responsible. At any rate, he had stopped saying, "What am I going to do without you, honey?" The two of them were constantly reminding me of the few days I had left. "Only a week to go." "In five days you'll be off." "Three days, honey; are you packed?"

I was packed but not at all happy about it. The thought of pushing a smart case on wheels, perhaps on dirt roads in some primitive place, was all wrong. Wheels and suitcases suggested smart hotels, porters, bellboys, tips, and being dressed in a chic, casual way that everyone knows cost a fortune to put together. "Well, Mike, it looks as if the backpack is out, eh?"

"Not if you don't want to, Mom. I still think for this kind of trip, a backpack is the only way to go. If you could just reduce everything drastically, you'd really lighten the load."

"Maybe Pop is right though, Michael. I mean, I could look a bit ridiculous carrying that flaming orange backpack on my shoulders."

"That's it, Mom. That's the answer. Don't you see? You'll take the orange pack, not mine. It's as light as a feather, half the size of mine, and if you'll take the nylon zippered bag for the presents and the extras, and we sling out a few things, we can do it. Oh, man, that would be great."

"I'll do it, Mike, I'll do it." With feverish excitement we got to work. Over the next two days we packed and dumped everything out and started over again five or six times. Dried milk came out of tinfoil bags and went into plastic ones; coffee, tea, instant soups were reduced by half. Clothing was trimmed; everything—underwear, toiletries, medications—was carefully surveyed and ruthlessly discarded if in doubt. With Michael's patience and help, we somehow managed to get everything in. It was a work of art. A resounding triumph. It was a professional backpack packer's pack! It still weighed more than a feather, but I was able to get it hoisted without giving myself a hernia and with nothing more from Michael than words of praise and cheer.

"You did it, Mom. You really did it. You look great."

I was not so sure how I looked, but I certainly felt great. I pranced—well, no, I walked, a little hunchbacked, I'll admit—around the living room. Then I walked from the living room to the bedroom. I took the nylon bag in one hand, put my shoulder bag on my shoulder, and got all set to go on my bedroom-to-living-room-and-back-to-bedroom hike. All of thirty-five yards. I was a proper backpacker. First class. I had graduated.

I whooped with delight, and Michael celebrated the occasion with a blast of full-volume acid rock music on his tape deck. We felt like Eliza Doolittle and Professor Higgins when the refinements of English speech had been perfected by the recalcitrant student of Shaw's *Pygmalion*. We had "simply gone and done it."

"Oh, Mike, what on earth is Daddy going to say about not using his lovely suitcase and wheels?"

"Don't worry, Mom. I'll fix it. When you gotta do your thing, you just gotta do it, man, that's all. I'll make Pop see it's the only way you could go. Gosh, I wish I were going with you. We'd have a great time together."

"Darling, we always have great times together, and there will be a time. Right now you don't know how thankful I am that you are here with Pop. You know, Mike, you are my son, but Daddy is my baby."

"Don't I know it, Mom, and it's time he got weaned as well. I think it's just great for you to get away, and I think it's good for Daddy, too. And don't you worry about a thing. I'll take care of him, you bet."

"I know you will. I'm only sorry that I can't delay my departure and be with you a little longer, but the friend I'm staying with in Paris can only receive me at this time. You do understand?"

Michael hugged me reassuringly. "Sure I do. Say, have you ever made bean sprouts? Dead easy, and they're great in salads. Look, I've brought my screens, I'll show you." I fully expected him to produce something five feet by three feet and made of wire mesh. He referred to plastic screw-on jar caps with perforated holes of different dimensions through which some funny-looking snail-like things eventually produced green shoots. Michael is great fun to be with. I was so thankful that he would be home with his father.

After the initial disappointment, Marco reacted quite well when Michael broke the news about the backpack. He shook his head sadly and said, "I think you're making a big mistake. I wish you luck and hope you know what you're doing, that's all."

I had no *idea* what I was doing. I hardly knew what time of day it was. I felt so disorganized. I couldn't believe I was leaving *tomorrow*. There had to be a million things I had forgotten, but what were they? I hadn't even decided what to wear for the journey. Leaving from a hot climate and arriving in a cold one would be a hassle if I dressed with all my warm things from here. In Miami's heat and on the plane, too, I would roast.

In agonies of indecision, I eventually settled on a wool skirt and a lightweight dacron blouse. Pantyhose, a sleeveless wool pullover, and my cashmere sweater could travel in my shoulder bag, to be put on before landing. Without the lining, my old poplin raincoat now fit me, and it would just have to do. With all my wool extras I would surely be warm enough; anyway, it was too late to do anything about it now.

I checked over my papers. Passport, ticket, the little book in which I had written down all the information and tips I had gleaned from the library, and the table of dollar conversions. (I really am going to miss you, Mung, when it comes to currency exchange.) Ah, my traveler's checks, a thousand dollars' worth of them, and the cash. What was I going to do about the cash?

Marco had given me $300 in single bills. To this I added $200 I had secretly saved from housekeeping. This was in twenty-, ten-, five-, and one-dollar bills and made a thick wad. I felt that the one- and five-dollar bills could come in very handy if local currency was not readily available, but it was a lot of bills and too bulky to put in my wallet. Marco's cautionary words also troubled me. "You're such a scatterbrain. Remember where you put your money. Don't keep it all together. Write things down as you go along, and listen, honey, if you run short, don't be foolish now. Just pick up the telephone and call me."

"I won't run short. I'll manage. Yes, I will write everything down, and no, I won't be calling you. I made you a promise, remember?"

"I remember, but all that is forgotten. I don't know how I could have hesitated. I'm really very happy for you, but I'm still worried about some of your stops. How can I reach you once you've left Paris?"

"You can't, except to the *Post restante*s at American Express. Don't worry. I'll be writing constantly. You'll hear from me even if I don't hear from you."

There suddenly seemed to be a million things we had to say to each other. Surely there were dozens of details I might have overlooked. I felt slightly panic-stricken. This time tomorrow, I would be gone.

That night, sleep eluded me. The minutes ticked away until I had to get up. Marco was right; I was a scatterbrain. I decided I would make a little body belt into which I could put most of my money. I took a piece of fine, tightly woven nylon, cut two squares, and sewed them by hand to make a flat smooth pouch. To this I attached enough elastic to encircle my waist. Most of the larger bills could go in here. The rest I would split up and distribute among the contents of my purse and shoulder bag. Now to get some sleep. I was not too optimistic. I felt strangely ill at ease. Perhaps it was just excitement, or could it be that I felt a little afraid of what lay ahead?

I stood at the darkened windows of the living room. All was quiet and still. The lights of the pool deck outside illuminated the breaking surf as it crashed against the shore. Was it there, at water's edge so few weeks ago, watching that mighty ocean surrender her white-crested chargers, I had asked Marco to let me go? My mind went back to other partings, some of such sorrowful finality.

Life is like the waves, I thought. They heave and part in birth to deliver us to shore. There we tarry, bearing the ebbs and flows as best we can. High or low, our tide of life comes nigh. A force beyond our ken casts our restless souls on high to toss in storms of weightless space and time. And so we drift, and drift, till at last we reach that other shore . . . Eternity.

I closed my eyes and had a few private words with God.

*   *   *

The ride to the airport passed in silence. Marco seemed remote, and I was hardly bubbling over with rapt conversation either. Only Michael was in high spirits. He thought everything was just "great."

Later, Marco confessed he felt bewildered. He simply could not believe that in six short weeks I had lost enough weight to look presentable, that I had managed to pull together a journey of such dimensions, or that I was even undertaking one at all!

"I guess I've been so damn busy in the office, I never realized how the time sped by. It seems like yesterday that we spoke of it and now you're off. I really do have some misgivings about it all, darling." He wasn't the only one. I was full of them, and insisted that we buy an insurance policy to cover my entire trip. We took the largest one that was offered. "If anything should happen to me, Mung," I said in a very firm but matter-of-fact tone, "I want you to promise me that you'll spend every penny of it to enjoy life with your second wife, and do all those things we always planned to do together and for which you never found the time."

"Must you be so damn realistic? Nothing's going to happen to you. Just take care of yourself, that's all. And write, do you hear, write."

Michael wanted to take photographs of me wearing the pack before I checked it in. Quite a few people stared curiously at the neatly dressed middle-aged woman with a bright orange backpack hoisted across her shoulders. It must have presented a strange sight. The hippy-looking young man with the long hair, the jeans, and the bare feet was taking the photographs, yet it was the woman in the smart black-and-white blouse, beige skirt, and sling-back shoes who wore the pack! It was odd; shouldn't it have been the other way around? Michael loved the stares and smiles. Marco bore them stoically. I didn't care one way or the other. My mind seemed to be a complete blank.

The moment of parting was at hand. "Darling—" Marco held my face between his hands, looking at me anxiously—"you really are very brave and courageous, but I honestly don't know if it's right of me to let you go off alone like this."

"Mung," I said, my voice trembling, "I don't think I'm brave at all. In fact, right now I think I'm quite stupid." Privately I thought, What kind of an idiot goes off at my age this way? What sort of dangers, problems of security, bodily safety, or health am I going to be facing alone?

We stood at the security checkpoint. It was a very emotional scene for all of us. Marco held me close. When he released me, I saw that his eyes were misty, and I began to cry.

"Oh, Mung, God bless you, and God bless you, Michael darling. I love you both so much." I gulped and sobbed. "Oh, dear, I do hope you'll be all right."

That made us all laugh a little. I had only hoped that *they'd* be all right!

"You funny, funny thing," Marco said. "What about yourself? We only want *you* to be all right. You will be; God will protect you and bring you back safely. I know."

Michael hugged me tightly and said in a husky voice, "Don't worry about us. Everything here will be okay. I love you, Mom. You're the greatest, and you're going to be just fine. Don't I know my Mom?"

It was an unreal scene. Perhaps this is how soldiers feel, I thought, as they say good-bye to their loved ones before going off to battle. They must wonder if they will ever come back to see them again. They are obliged to go; I wasn't. Here I was, about to embark upon a journey that for me had neither time nor geographic limitations, intent on going to strange and distant lands. I was about to leave the only ones in the world I really cared for, not at all sure in my mind that I might ever be returned to them. Who knew what might befall me?

We embraced a second time, Marco's arms around Michael and me. We stood in close communion. Silent. Still. All three of us share a deeply felt religious belief. There is a spiritual tie that, especially in moments of great emotion, binds us together with an inspirational feeling of comfort and strength. It was transmitted now between us. I felt better for this silent farewell. My heart felt lighter. I was able to smile. There were no more tears.

I passed through the security barrier and collected my shoulder bag and nylon bag. I stepped to the side as I started to walk down the long concourse, so that on turning I could see them unobstructed. They were there, waving. I waved back. I turned around several times to wave, until I could no longer distinguish their shapes. Even then I turned and waved in case they were still standing there.

I waved myself out of their lives, as I had waved them out of mine.

But only for a while, I said. God willing . . . .

3

It's Never the Same

An international airport and no lineup for customs? Well, this was a nice change. How trusting of the British to allow one to walk straight through with one's baggage to the exit marked Nothing to Declare.

No, I had nothing to declare except my high spirits. I felt an elation that even the gray dull greeting of a typical English day could not dispel.

I marched purposefully ahead to the welcome of a Cockney porter's cheery, "Cor luv a duck, miss, watcha got on yer back? D'yer need a hand?" It was music to my ears.

"No, thanks, me old cock sparrer." (I slipped into the vernacular with gusto. I love hearing and speaking it.)

Salt of the earth are those Cockneys. I used to be a London girl myself once, before I was married. There had never been enough time to take advantage of all the wonderful things to be seen and done in this gracious capital city.

The whirl of society often graced by royalty and causing such a fuss and such a flurry. . . . The rich, cultural life, so full and varied. Where in the world could one stroll around or sit and munch one's sandwiches except in the Royal Albert Hall during the Promenade concert season? Here, high up in the "Gods" (the uppermost balcony), music lovers of all ages and walks of life would unite in their quest for the cheapest seats and the greatest music.

And the parks. London's lovely parks, scattered like sixpence across a concrete carpet. Ten stolen minutes of a busy day, or the lunchtime break from office, to find brief respite from the clamor and din that magically vanish among nature's greenery or the sight of God's small creatures. Feathered, crumb-fed, and hopping, or flat-beaked, downy, and gliding along the glistening waters of St. James's, Regent's, or Kensington parks. An escape that refreshed the senses and restored the strength to flagging spirits or tired feet.

The lumbering red double-decker buses that would take you from one end of this vast city and three hours later deposit you at the other. From the windows of the upper deck one could have the best sightseeing bargain in the whole world.

Piccadilly, and Fortnum and Mason's for tea and strawberries out of season, specially flown in from Cannes. Harrods, in genteel winding Knightsbridge, where dowager ladies in furs and pearls would dither over the purchase of a hatpin for sagging brimmed bonnets.

And what of The City, where once pulsed the financial heart of the world, where the bowler hat and furled umbrella were as much a part of the scene as the wigs and robes of the Old Bailey, the great criminal courts.

And the Lane. Who could forget Petticoat Lane, where just about everything under the sun was sold, bartered, bargained, and sometimes given away and an experience not to be missed.

Ah, London. London. It was the biggest city in the world, and I had loved her fiercely.

I stepped out of Heathrow Airport and turned toward the bus depot. My hoisted pack collided with someone's back, and I hastily swung around to apologize, almost tripping over a pile of luggage. My outstretched hands were caught to steady me and a man's voice was saying, "Sabina Shalom, well I'll be darned."

I looked up into the eyes of Dick Ellinson, an old friend from our New York days. "Dick! Dick, for heaven's sake! I don't believe it. How are you? Is Nan with you? Did you get our Christmas card? Are you still with the American Embassy in Bogotá? It's ages since we've heard from you; what's been happening to you all?"

"Hold it!" he said, laughing. "We're all fine. Life's been hectic because we were transferred from Colombia to Tehran. Nan is there now and very happy because she's from there, you know, and we have a new baby now, too. What about you? How's Mark? Is he with you? And what on earth have you got on your back?"

"Oh, Dick, don't laugh. I'm on a world trip. It's a sabbatical from Mark, or from marriage if you like. No, he's not with me—he wouldn't be seen dead with me and a backpack. You know Mark. I'm trying to do this on a strict budget, as simply as possible and with only what I can carry on my back."

"Sabina, you are incorrigible. Say, if you are on such an open-ended trip, why not trip our way? Nan would be thrilled to see you. How about it?"

"I don't know, Dick. Thank you. I'd love to, but I'm on to Paris next, and I'm not sure after that, because I've left all my ongoing flights open."

"Fine, couldn't be better—you only need to drop us a line, or better yet, give us a call and say when you're arriving and we'll meet you."

I stood dazed. Another excitement beckoned, but I was too bewildered to give an answer then and there. "In any case, Dick, I wouldn't stay with you, not now, with a new baby. Maybe if you could find me a modest place nearby? I couldn't just plunk myself on you like that. How does Nan manage with three little ones? She must have her hands full."

"She does, but we have help, and don't forget, Nan's entire family is there. Don't worry, we can always find you a place. Nan would be so happy to see you. Tehran is on a direct route to India, you know—it's really no problem. Look, I have to run." He scribbled something on a piece of paper and thrust it into my hand. "Here, drop us a line, or call us. We're expecting you now. Okay? Mustn't miss my plane. Bye, see you soon."

The sliding doors closed behind him. I stood as one in a trance, thinking what a small world it sometimes really is. No wonder we hadn't heard from them recently. Fancy their living in Tehran; it would certainly be an interesting place to visit. Maybe I could check into the routing on my ticket and see. But for now, where was the bus terminal?

Like soldiers of the Queen's Guard, the red buses awaited mobilization. Isolated from the harassment of passengers in his little cabin up front, the driver of one of them seemed about ready for action. His uniformed mate, his peaked cap pushed back on his head, took a last drag of his cigarette, flipped it casually into the air, and jumped aboard the rear platform.

I hastened toward him. "Please, do you go anywhere near Euston Station?"

"Near enough, but you'll 'ave to change buses."

"Right then, conductor, I'll go with you. Can I leave this here?" I indicated my pack, meanwhile pushing it underneath the stairs into the specially designed well for receptacles that all double-deckers are equipped with.

I clambered upstairs and seated myself right at the very front, where the large windows offered an excellent view. The bus was quite empty, and I looked forward to the ride with great anticipation.

"That'll be seventy-five p., miss."

"Seventy-five what?"

"Seventy-five pence. You're English, aren't cha?"

"Mm, yes. I've been away from England for a long time. Can't quite understand this new decimal system, actually."

I proffered a ten-shilling note. It was one of two that, with three single-pound notes, were relics of a dollar exchange with a visitor some time ago.

"Sorry, miss, that's not enough. A real foreigner, aren't cha? I s'pose it'll take yer awhile to get used to the new pence."

What? I thought. Ten shillings is not enough for a seventy-five-pence ride? "You mean it's more than ten bob? It used to be only half a crown."

"Cor, you've been away a long time, not 'arf. A quid [one pound] only buys me and me mate a couple of pints at the local these days." He jerked his head in the direction of the driver and gave me a pitying look. Feeling completely alien, I fished in my purse and reluctantly tendered a single-pound note, for which I received a ticket, two large silver coins that used to be worth two shillings each (once called a florin), and a small silver coin (in the old days called a shilling or a bob). My puzzled look betrayed confusion.

"Yer see, mate, the old bob's worth five pence now. The florin is ten pence. So wot you've got there is twenty-five pence. Seventy-five pence yer ticket and twenty-five pence yer change. See?"

"Yes, I see," I said, though for the life of me I didn't. All that was clearly apparent was the need for an imminent stop at a bank to exchange some money. My two remaining pound and ten-shilling notes were obviously not going to get me very far.

The bus swung away from the construction going on all about the vicinity of the airport into a multilaned divided highway. It was all very new to me and greatly changed. What a lot of traffic, and in comparison to the States, how tiny all the cars seemed to be. A bus approaching from the opposite direction bore the name Uxbridge as its destination. Thirty-five years flashed by in seconds.

It was wartime England and everyone seemed to be following exciting, vital-to-the-war occupations. I was too young to be accepted into the women's armed services and felt too old to be still studying. Dropping out of school was the solution and getting away from home the remedy for a restless, ambitious teenager. In those days it was regarded as downright scandalous for a young girl to leave home. In my parents' estimation it was simply "not nice," and in their circle it was a certain indication that I was "going to the dogs." Against all protestations, and from my birthplace of Sheffield, it was to London I fled.

Within two days of leaving home and with but five pounds in my pocket (this princely sum represented a married man's weekly wage then), I had found myself a job with the J. Arthur Rank Organization a few miles from Uxbridge. My "digs" consisted of a room in the two-bedroom government-subsidized home of Joe and Sylvia Grubb of No. 3 Denham Close, within walking distance of Denham Film Studios. My career was launched. My salary was two pounds and ten shillings a week. My job was assistant to the director of location. In actual fact, I was little more than an errand girl, but I was thrilled to the core and could not have cared less about the title or the menial duties I was sometimes called upon to perform.

The film being made was *Caesar and Cleopatra,* and I was thrust into a milieu that was exciting, novel, and filled with glamor. To be called upon to hand the exquisite Vivien Leigh a glass of water between takes, or to be asked by Stewart (Jimmy) Granger, "Where the hell's Pinky, girl?" (Pinky Green was the producer), was enough to set my girlish heart aflutter.

No wonder I was stagestruck from that day on. With memory sharpened for detail I graduated to continuity girl, assistant to casting director, and eventually landed in the office of the director himself, the temperamental Hungarian Gabriel Pascal. Meeting

George Bernard Shaw was but one of the highlights of that all too short-lived career.

The "doodle bugs" (rocket bombs) flooded the skies of the southern English counties. With flames spurting from the rear, they lumbered across the inky heavens like giant firecrackers maimed in flight. When the fearful noise and the fire fizzled out, they dropped to earth to explode and kill.

These, at least, one could see. It was the unnerving experience of the German V-2 rockets that began to undermine one's courage. With no more warning than the piercing shriek of its descending whistle, this fiendish instrument of destruction hurtled through space to find its victim. The final "crump" of the explosion was the only reassurance one had to be still alive.

Death rained from the skies and sent me scuttling back to my middle-class Yorkshire background, where everyone seemed so narrow-minded and provincial in outlook. The people of Sheffield were, nevertheless, as brave and as strong as the tempered steel for which the city was famous. Home of the great factories that produced the machines of war, it received violent punishment from the mighty Luftwaffe. Few of England's principal cities escaped the intense nightly bombing raids. Few, indeed, were those who knew what it was to sleep in their own beds and not in the tin shelters erected in all of England's backyards and into which we crept with blankets, flashlights, and water, from dusk to daybreak seven nights a week.

Thankfully, I was able to return to London at war's end. The great city had spoiled me for life anywhere else. I had tasted adventure, independence, and moderate success in all that I had attempted. Now I looked for further challenges. To be young, single, and away from the strictly conventional background of my upbringing and in the capital of the world (to me) was glorious. England was joyously throwing off the cares and tightly reined emotions of a wartime nation under fire. There were opportunities galore as she struggled to get back on her feet again.

In battle-scarred Europe, work of a different nature cried out for help. As the evidence of Hitler's horrendous actions was revealed, relief workers were desperately sought to carry out rehabilitation programs in the concentration camps. It was to one such organization that I volunteered my services. Life was suddenly stripped of glamor. More urgent needs stirred my conscience. The call I answered then left an echo within me for the rest of my life.

I turned around. The sound of the lilting accent of the West Indies broke into my reveries. Sure enough, several brown-skinned, white-smiled Jamaicans were conversing away a few seats back. Ah, yes, one of my sisters had written to say how changed England was these days. Jamaicans, Indians, Pakistanis, and scores of Arabs all making quite an impact, and not without a little friction, upon the hitherto stereotyped and insular way of life of the British people.

Well, the houses haven't changed at any rate. Gray stone-slab terrace-type dwellings stretched the entire length of street after street. All with prim little front gardens and neatly clipped hedges. Low iron gates protected each property and reminded the passerby that behind it and up the short flagstone path each home was quite private. Despite a communal appearance, this was the Englishman's home and castle, of which he was king . . . and don't you dare forget it.

The conductor tapped me on the arm. "If you'll change at the next stop, you can get a number fourteen that will take you directly to Euston Station."

"Oh, fine, thank you." Alighting from the bus, I savored with increasing pleasure the sight of Londoners going about their business, the great stores open since nine-thirty, alive with shoppers entering and exiting.

What on earth are all those people sitting in the street for? I walked toward the bus stop, located at the entrance of one of London's largest department stores. At pavement's edge squatted a dozen black-robed women. They were chattering away excitedly and waving their arms about in great animation. Surrounding them on all sides were cartons, boxes, and paper shopping bags. Arabic assailed my ears.

"*Kulshi maboul.*" ("Everything is lovely.")

"*Aiwah, queyess keteer.*" ("Yes, very nice.")

"*Bookrah kamaan?*" ("We come again tomorrow?")

"*Insha Allah.*" ("God willing.")

I understood their remarks; it was clear they had been on a shopping spree. Until I had met Marco, Arabs and the Arabic tongue were things that had existed only in movies. The kind where Sydney Greenstreet and Peter Lorre moved among flowing-robed Arabs in full headdress with daggers at waist. Camels and desert shots portrayed Hollywood's version and my total concept of Middle Eastern countries.

Marco's parents were of those parts. They had come to England as youngsters, but their native language had been Arabic, and between themselves and their tight ghettolike circle it was spoken exclusively. Marco had received written and spoken Arabic lessons from a tutor as a boy, and over the years I had picked up a few words and phrases from him.

Meeting him at a benefit in London, I had known nothing of his background. I was too impressed with his tanned good looks, his perfectly even, dazzling white teeth, and his towering height, resplendent in tuxedo and black tie as he smiled his own introduction to me: "I'm from Manchester and my name is Marco Shalom."

My thoughts were interrupted as two Rolls-Royce limousines glided to a stop. Uniformed chauffeurs sprang out to open the doors and the trunk. With parcels interred, the sedate vehicles scooped up the women and purred smoothly away. I smiled at the comic scene. From *souks* (the Eastern marketplace) to Selfridges was a far cry.

The London scene was vastly changed as much by its inhabitants as by the many modern buildings newly erected over once bombed-out crater sites that had scarred a fondly remembered street.

Diddle-de-da, diddle-de-da, the wheels of the train had not changed their tune. Heavens, could it be twenty-eight years since I had taken that first train ride from London to Manchester to meet, at Marco's early insistence, his entire family? He was one of nine children and had thirteen cousins living next door. After that first acquaintance, there had been but three dates before he had proposed to me and promised "no ordeal, just a very quiet family meeting." I was looked over by no less than twenty-six "just family" members. It was very much an ordeal.

My brother, married by then and himself living in Manchester, had, with all good intentions, made a few inquiries about this "Marco Shalom fellow you seem to be so keen on. They are

Sephardic people, you know, and a very clannish lot. Like to marry among themselves. Decent family but no money. Most of them are in the rag trade. They believe in business more than the professions. Wouldn't have thought you'd like 'em, and actually they don't welcome outsiders either. You'll see what I mean."

I couldn't have seen a thing even had I wanted to, and I didn't. Love was truly blind. I had an absorbing career, earning a salary a married man with a family living in the provinces might well have envied. Public relations, speaking tours, setting up committees to carry out the programs for the relief and rehabilitation organization for which I worked, and all an extension of that which had occupied me abroad after the war.

The stimulation of cultural activities was not to be found anywhere outside London in those days. I was constantly meeting all kinds of interesting personalities. My friends were a glorious hodgepodge of wild bohemians or much-traveled, cultivated people of means. It was the perfect life any bachelor girl could dream of, but I was suddenly no longer asleep. I had fallen madly in love with this tall, handsome young textile exporter from Manchester.

With my brother's warning in mind, the only thing I did think to say at the time Marco asked me to marry him, and this after only three dates, was, "Perhaps you should ask your mother's permission first." I was not being facetious. These people liked to marry among their own kind, and I always felt it the greatest mistake that he told his parents he was going to marry me rather than ask for their opinion first. I had never felt wholeheartedly welcomed into the family from the beginning. Now, speeding northward, I found myself very nervous about the duty call I would have to make upon my mother-in-law.

Grimy, gray, rainy Manchester. What a scruffy-looking railway station it was.

I called my brother's home, only to be informed by a maid that neither he nor my sister-in-law were in but that they were expected back shortly. "May I tell madam who called, please?"

"Certainly. Mr. Preston's sister. Please tell him that I called from the station and that I expect to be at the house in about thirty-five minutes."

I decided to take a taxi. It would give me the opportunity of passing by the places I'd like to see again. I intended to be in England only a few days. If not for my affection for my brother and two sisters (a third one lived in Malta), I would not have been in the country at all. With beloved parents gone and family ties apart, England now held only sad memories for me.

"Driver, will you please go along Barlow Moor Road and pass the crematorium." How friends had made fun of Marco and me when we bought our first home in that section. Defensively I used to say, when giving directions how to find us, "We're right near the dead center of Manchester," and, "Oh, well, at least we've no noisy neighbors." (Ah, the snobbery of those early married days.)

"Tha means Chorlton-cum-Hardy then, eh?" The taxi man's flat Lancashire accent was as unattractive now as then. "Ay it be raht bah park then?"

"Yes, it's just by the park where the number eighty bus used to terminate. Hardy Lane, I think it was called."

"Oh, ay, ah knows juss where tha means. It's raht bah park."

The park was those few green acres where the retired folk donned soft shoes of an afternoon to play bowls across a velvet carpet of grass. The little park where, when Marco lost his business during England's bad recession in the early fifties and couldn't get a job, I surprised him one night by announcing, "I've been granted the concession for the kiosk in Chorlton Park. For the summer season I'll sell ice cream, candies, and soft drinks. It will make a few pounds to help us out."

"What about the children?" We had two by then—Anthony, two and a half years old, and Michael, scarcely twelve months and still in a baby carriage.

"I'll take them with me, what else? I can't go out to work while they are so small. I wouldn't trust anyone to look after them, and in any case, it would hardly be worthwhile if I had to pay someone to do so. Don't worry, I'll manage."

And manage I did. At twelve-thirty, after the children had been fed, I walked across to the park, Tony on his little three-wheel scooter and Michael in his carriage. The little kiosk attracted all the schoolchildren returning to classes from lunch at home. Their pennies bought bulls' eyes, jelly babies, and licorice whirls. At five o'clock the old folks finished their game of bowls and came over for soft drinks and ice cream. Those threepenny bits and sixpenny pieces went a long way toward paying the bills of that difficult fifth year of our marriage.

Marco was pleased but disturbed. No middle-class wife *ever* worked. His family and relatives were dismayed to such an extent that they would not even refer to it, let alone patronize it. What a disgrace, a daughter-in-law selling candy in a park. Clang! Another black mark against me.

"People will talk, you know. My wife running a kiosk in a park."

"Do people pay our bills?"

"You know what I mean."

I knew only too well what he meant. *Tacleefe*, an arabic word much used in his circles. Then, as now, it implied a ritual of unnecessary formalities and flowery insincerities. Lots of fuss and ceremony, and all of it meaningless (and hypocritical) baloney. A spade was (is) never called a spade. The tongue was (is) always in the cheek.

Those first years of married life in Manchester obliged me to swallow enough *tacleefe* to last me a lifetime.

Financially, things went from bad to worse, and we decided to emigrate. Canada awaited us eagerly. No affidavits, visas, or job offers were necessary. One just filled out a form and virtually stepped onto the ship. It was as simple as that. Marco went first to find a job and a home to which he could bring us. I stayed behind to sell the house and contents, the income from which I eked out for the children and me to live on.

"Crematorium's on tha left, juss up road." The taxi man's words pulled me from the past. There on the right was our house. What a sorry sight it looked now. Flaking, bilious green paint, a scraggly hedge, and an unkempt-looking front garden. Too many memories came unbidden to mind; I was sorry I had decided to come this way. The car quickly passed through this section of town, and soon we left the city suburbs behind.

Now we entered Hale, an area in which some of the most prestigious homes in the county of Cheshire are to be found. The taxi bowled along past stately oak, elm, and silver birch trees and turned into a sweeping driveway. Crocuses and daffodils graced the borders of the lawns. A large greenhouse was visible between the rhododendron bushes. Tennis courts with dismantled nets were partially shielded from inquisitive eyes by tall and imperious fir trees. The copper beech was about to burst into bud. The sycamore remained gaunt and barren. The grass was lush, the driveway immaculately pebbled. A Rolls-Royce and a Jaguar were parked near the massive front portico.

Cab dismissed and pack hoisted, I walked up to the front door. My brother, Archie, had certainly done well for himself. A brilliant mind and a head for business opportunities had enabled him at twenty-two, with a degree in civil engineering, to start to spin the wheel of fortune. Circumstances and acumen had stood him in good stead. He had been a wealthy man for some years now.

Feeling like the poor relation, I rang the bell. It seemed no one was going to answer the door. I looked at the house; it was of Tudor style. Massive oak beams rafted the doorway and surrounded the large mullion-paned windows. The door was studded with great iron nails and bore a heavy brass knocker. Perhaps the bell was out of order. I picked up the knocker to rap on the door just as it opened. It almost threw me off balance, my agitation further compounded by the sight of a uniformed manservant.

Good Lord! I didn't know Archie had a butler! He was tall and lean of build. His black frock coat made him appear even more angular. His face was sparse of flesh and his nose aquiline. I disliked him instantly and felt at once that he was looking down that beaky nose with utter disdain at my dumpy, backpacked figure. Before he got the chance to tell me that I had come to the wrong house, I quickly said, "Good afternoon. I am Mr. Preston's. sister. My brother and Mrs. Preston are expecting me. I called from the railway station a little while ago."

His mouth opened to reveal an ill-fitting set of dentures, or perhaps it was the shock of my appearance that caused them to slip. In any case, his lips snapped shut and his Adam's apple slid up and down as he gulped. "Yes, modom. Ahem, er, what is the name, modom?"

"Mrs. Shalom. I'm from the United States."

"Er, yes, Mrs. Sonnon. Just one moment, Mrs. Sonnon. I'll inform modom you are here. Mr. Preston is not at home. Excuse me, please."

He left me standing at the door, which while talking he had discreetly tried to close. It was now barely ajar, and I felt quite stupid just standing there. (The heck with it; push it open and go inside, you fool. You are not a traveling salesperson. It's your brother's home.)

57

My diminutive sister-in-law appeared, a petite Scottish lass. "For goodness' sake, come in, pet, come in will you now." Her Scottish burr was just as pronounced as ever and quite pleasant to hear. "What on earth is that?" She looked at my pack now resting on the ground as she leaned forward to plant a chaste kiss into the air. I was glad she hadn't smudged her lipstick. She was, as always, groomed to perfection. I felt, as always, like a towering bulky frump, even though I am only five feet one inch tall.

"Archie will be here any moment. He just called from the golf club, and a friend is dropping him off. What a surprise. We weren't at all sure when to expect you. Will you be staying long then?"

I quickly put her mind at ease. "No, not more than a couple of days."

"Oh, Archie will be disappointed."

I preferred to ignore the implication that his might be the only regret at the brevity of my stay and watched with ill-concealed amusement at the butler's attempt to carry my pack with the kind of dignity doubtless reserved for more conventional and costly luggage.

The room we entered was elegantly furnished and formal enough to be called anything but a sitting room. Ensconced in the downy softness of a custom-made sofa, I was invited to kick off my shoes and make myself at home. "Nothing to spoil here. I'm just about ready to throw all this stuff out and redo the whole place." (Wish it could be thrown across the Atlantic to my apartment.)

My brother's arrival spared me from commiserating with my sister-in-law's problems about the difficulties of finding good servants. With a butler, parlormaid, housekeeper, and gardener to maintain harmoniously, I didn't doubt the trials to be endured.

My pleasure at seeing my brother was somewhat diminished on hearing that my youngest sister Audrey, was visiting our oldest sister, Theba, in Malta and that my younger sister, Nettie, had at the last minute decided to join her doctor-husband at a medical convention in Sweden. As for Marco's mother: "Well, you're out of luck, my dear. She's in Israel visiting her daughter."

I breathed a guilty sigh of relief. "In that case, my stay will be even shorter. England at this time of year is not for me. I'll be off in twenty-four hours, since I have to be in Paris by the weekend anyway. I could not have been so near and not come to see you."

Fortunately, my brother and I have a great understanding between us. Straight talk only strengthens the love we have for each other. A mutual respect for the other's differences, a tolerance for our individual idiosyncracies, and an admiration for each other's qualities bind us close for all the distance of ocean and hours that separate us.

We talked the night away, and I slept for the remainder of my stay.

"Your attention, please. Will all passengers on flight BE 55 to Paris please proceed to the departure gate." It seemed as if my visit had been for no more than a change of planes.

"That's me, Arch. Good-bye, darling. Thanks for seeing me off. Take care."

"Good-bye love, and you take care too. Shame you couldn't stay longer."

"Next time. Maybe. Why don't you come and see us in Miami?"

A nod. A hug. A kiss . . . and then a sad ache. That lost and empty feeling that gnaws at the stomach when memories flood the senses with painful sweetness.

England's verdant pastures dropped beneath me. The swirling clouds caught up my thoughts, now plunged back in time to years gone by. I wanted to cry my heart out. I wanted to cling to all that was left of my childhood, down there, down there. I blinked hard and pushed aside the nostalgic tug of yesterday.

Plus ça change, plus c'est la même chose. Well, perhaps here and there Paris had changed, but in the quarter I visited, everything looked exactly as it had on my last visit ten years ago, and heavens, even on my first one twenty years before that! Just after the war, in fact.

Paris this time for me was only for a brief stay with an old friend, one of the very few with whom I had kept in touch for over thirty years and possibly the only one now who linked me to the past, a reminder of my single days.

The name of Rothschild has connoted considerable wealth and power for over a century. It is much less known for the example this family has set as great philanthropists, humanitarians, benefactors, and leaders in the community. Always ready to answer a call if a deserving cause needed their support. Always willing to perform a duty and often a chore, if lending their illustrious name or presence assured a more generous response. Setting an example in leadership was regarded by the Rothschilds as a moral obligation, and it was one that was never shirked.

It was Naomi, the daughter of the late Baron and Baroness Lionel de Rothschild, whom I was now visiting in Paris. I had not seen her for some years, though we exchanged letters regularly.

We had met while we were both engaged in social welfare work in London and had liked each other on first sight. Naomi, with her slender willowy figure, serious dark eyes, and expressive fluttering hands, had a smile that enveloped the world with kindness, warmth, and sincerity. I think it was my high spirits, lack of inhibition, and total disregard for convention that might have appealed to her.

Her mother, Lady Lionel, was the honorary chairman of the committee on which I served. She preferred to be addressed as Mrs. de Rothschild. She cared little for titles and more about people, especially those in less fortunate circumstances. She was a great lady in the finest tradition.

Naomi had inherited her gentle mother's true breeding and noble character. She gave of herself unstintingly if her services could in any way—through her affiliation with an organization or involvement in a cause—help alleviate the sufferings of others.

It was with great joy that I had accepted her invitation to stay with her for my few days in Paris.

On my arrival at Le Bourget Airport, I parked my duffle bag in the checkroom and with my small nylon bag, my capacious shoulder bag, a few hastily changed dollars, and a profusion of incorrectly spoken French, I strode out into the crisp Parisian air.

The strangest feeling came over me as I boarded the bus that was to take me to Les Invalides Terminal. It was as if I had suddenly stepped back in time. I was that eager young woman who held the world in her hands.

Like the butterfly emerging from its chrysalis, I felt I was flying free of all encumbrances. No longer was I a married woman. I was Sabina Celia Evie Prepsler. Mrs. Marco Shalom was some other person, a stranger who existed in an unreal world far removed from the present time.

There was no one of whom to ask permission. There was no one to censure, disapprove, criticize, or say, "It's not nice; what will people say?"

I was me, that somewhat giddy young girl who in her day had defied convention and the restrictions of class and upbringing. I really *could* do as I wished, go where I wanted, say, act, and think just as I damn well pleased. And the feeling was glorious.

I was in Paris on my very own and loving it, and the city was as beautiful as only Paris can be in the spring.

The area where Naomi lived, the sixteenth *arrondissement,* is one of the most gracious parts of residential Paris, and was especially lovely now with its broad treelined avenues and its little squares, with shrubs bursting into bloom, seats for the elderly, the tired, the bird feeders or the young mothers watching their little ones play in the sandboxes, and spiked railings all around to fend off the dangers of the busy street beyond.

I loved the grand old homes with their facades so French that in no way could they be mistaken for anything else; the monuments, scattered so liberally that one could never forget France's glorious heroes, whether of battle, philosophy, or the arts, or men of peace.

Since my arrival I had been straining hard to attune my ear to the sound of the language. French, as spoken by Parisians, had not changed one bit. It was still a gobble, gobble, down in the throat, and I was hard put to understand what was being said all around me.

There was all too little time for practicing my French, for I stayed indoors to chatter Naomi's head off (in English) about the past and where our lives had taken us during those earlier days.

At the end of the war in Europe, I joined a volunteer organization under the auspices of the United Nations Relief and Rehabilitation Administration (UNRRA) and in conjunction with the American Joint Distribution Committee. Its function was to train volunteers to work in the field.

Those fields were the concentration camps. The tragedies of war-torn Europe and some of the horrors I was made aware of during those years had an effect upon me that not only changed my life but will remain with me to the end of it.

Naomi's work had concentrated upon the children who had earlier been cared for by various subsidiary relief organizations.

These were the youngsters who had been sheltered and hidden when their parents were taken away by the Nazis, children who had managed to survive internment camps or young people who had escaped and had been found wandering, starving, and half-demented.

At one point I had worked for a year in the homes that were established in various châteaux in France, many of them around Paris. Les Maisons des Enfants des Deportées were the centers where adult camp survivors joined forces with volunteer workers to rehabilitate themselves and the children in their care. I was sent wherever the need was greatest, willingly accepting whatever assignment was given to me. I felt completely fulfilled in this work. I could not accompany the children when they boarded the illegal ships that were to take them to Palestine, but their hopes, prayers, and songs I shared and sang. To this day I weep uncontrollably at any reminder of that period of anguish for those homeless, stateless, suffering refugees.

Talking with Naomi took up almost all the time I spent in Paris. I ventured out only once. Wrapped in Naomi's furs (she insisted I would turn to ice in my poplin raincoat), I attended for the very first time an elegant reception of French *haute couture*.

The salon was a mass of flowers. The red carpets, huge, ornate crystal chandeliers, and gilded velvet-upholstered chairs were most impressive. I tried to adopt a nonchalant air as I glanced around at the motley guests assembled there by invitation only. Surely some were celebrities and film stars, hiding behind those big dark glasses.

The famed Parisian designer's collection was far from spectacular. I was most disappointed, but the mannequins' masklike faces and mincing walks were sheer fascination. It was an outing of the greatest fun, enhanced by all the fuss and fawning. I loved it all —especially wearing Naomi's furs.

While out, I took advantage to make inquiries about flights to Tehran. There were no problems; it was just as Dick had said, en route all the way. It seemed such a simple matter to make the necessary adjustment to my ticket that I decided on impulse to go, resolving to call the Ellinsons that same evening and advise them of my plans.

I had no luck in communicating with them and so resorted to sending a telegram care of the American Embassy, which I felt would reach them with more certainty than the sketchy-looking address that Dick had hastily scribbled down.

My friends in Paris commented that poor communications were not the only problems that troubled Iran. It was a country undergoing many changes. Recent reports of unpleasant incidents, which in themselves were not uncommon or dissimilar to those in other Middle Eastern countries, might have more significance in Iran owing to the prolonged absence of the shah, ostensibly on an extended vacation. That he and his family should be away for so long had caused speculation about the nation's internal politics, which had evidently been in disarray for some time.

I paid scant attention to this commentary, for I was raptly engrossed in looking at the pictured splendors of a civilization whose infancy dates back more than 7,000 years. The magnificent descriptions of ancient Persia, together with my friends' account of a personal visit and their fascination with the country, had enraptured me. To encounter people and to visit places far removed from anything I had ever known were surely the reasons I was making this journey in the first place. Yes, it was an opportunity not to be missed, and after all, I did have friends there.

I avoided mentioning this, however, when I received a call from Marco telling me that confirmation of my hotel in Delhi had just arrived and that I must be sure to keep to it, as accommodations would be hard to find and "I know best." Everything else was fine, and Michael had greatly impressed Marco with his culinary skills. "Who knows, I may yet become a vegetarian, except that I'm not too keen on some of this paper, string, and sawdust stuff that Mike calls seaweed, bamboo shoots, and alfalfa."

I felt a few pangs of homesickness not untinged with guilt. Even being in Paris was full of nostalgia. I had come only to see a dear friend, but time had slipped back thirty years. Now it must move on. This all-too-brief sojourn was but a whisper of an echo, not the hollow return, of voices from the past. It was the gentle murmur of a life so removed from my present style that the sight of Naomi's priceless paintings and *objets d'art* moved me near to tears.

Exquisitely prepared meals were discreetly served by proud family retainers in heirloom silver and on the finest porcelain. Superb wines from the family's vineyards gave luster to the sparkle of magnificent crystal goblets as we dined on furniture mellow from centuries of love and inherited tradition.

It was an atmosphere of calm acceptance that culture is attainable by all but understood by few. It breathed so gently there in that peaceful home that it was not hard to give myself up to its rarefied embrace.

It was a world so different from my Formica, stainless steel, and drip-dry existence in Miami Beach.

4

Iran

I had been mistaken in thinking that the fear of flying had something to do with a feminist book. It had nothing to do with printed matter and everything to do with the flight I was now making on Iran Air to Tehran. Generally, it is the weather that determines a smooth or troublesome voyage; on this particular occasion it was the passengers who created the condition.

From a few moments after takeoff, pandemonium reigned. At first I thought I was about to witness a hijacking operation. The man in the seat behind me began to leap up and down and to shout, in a language I did not understand, to someone farther down the plane, each time clutching the back of my seat with such violence as to cause minor injuries to my entire nervous system.

Evidently the response to his calls was unsatisfactory, as he decided to make a personal investigation and lumbered into the aisle. His appearance heralded an outburst of great hilarity. The former steady buzz of conversation now erupted into a roar of excited greetings. What on earth was going on? I wondered. Not being able to understand a word of the strange sounds that assailed my ears, I cautiously got to my feet to see what was taking place. Whether by design or chance, the few female passengers on board were grouped way up front. The rest of the passengers seemed to be dark-skinned, swarthy-complexioned men, in conventional attire for the most part. Two, seated together, wore skullcaps and loose robes. Those wearing Western dress had removed their jackets and were now loosening their ties, some their shoes. All wore an air of complete relaxation. A few sat perched on the arms of the aisle seats; others stood hanging over the heads of seated passengers. An atmosphere of high spirits had invaded the plane.

The burly bouncer of the seat behind me had now advanced a few steps down the aisle. His hand was being grasped by all who could reach him; some embraced him warmly. One offered him a bottle, which was received with a full-throated roar of hilarity.

That did it. Laughter and shrieks of merriment pealed out. Corks popped and more bottles appeared. Those who were already standing now started swaying and cavorting. The noise was deafening. A high-pitched trill pierced the air. It sent a chill through my body. It was the nearest thing to what I believed from movies to be an Apache Indian's war cry. It came from the shrouded black-robed women. An ululation of the tongue produced this high shrill note that was maintained continuously, and which others took up. I noted that the tongue appeared to move rapidly up and down in the mouth; it was a strange sight, the significance of which puzzled me. Perhaps a wedding had taken place earlier. Surely they couldn't all be relatives. They certainly seemed to be one big happy family intent on having a jolly time. I was quite bewildered and looked around for a stewardess of whom I could ask a question.

Two of them were at the back of the plane trying to launch a cart of drinks, which, when perceived, was hailed by cries of approval. One passenger swooped down upon the women, grasped the cart, and attempted to assist in the dispensation of drinks.

An announcement was made in English, and in a language I presumed to be Farsi, requesting that everyone be seated. Since this was completely ignored, I began to wonder if my earlier impression that these were Iranians returning home was incorrect.

As the cart approached me, I raised my hand to ask, "Please, what on earth is going on?" The stewardess, black hair swept up, kohl-ringed dark eyes dominating a face that reminded me of Empress Farah, shrugged her shoulders, registered pain, and said nothing. The second stewardess, rosy-cheeked, with blue eyes and short curly blond hair, smiled cheerily at me and in a pronounced British accent said, "Real loony bin, isn't it? Don't worry. They don't usually carry on this way. It's the Iranian New Year, you see. Imagine, I've got to make this flight twice more yet. It's ghastly, isn't it?"

"Hardly conducive to sleep," I replied.

She laughed, shaking her curls. "I wish we'd never started the drinks; we'll never get to the meal now. They're impossible—and wait, it gets worse. See you later." She and her companion managed to push and pull their way a few yards along and I was left to ruminate over my Pepsi-Cola, experiencing a sensation of misgivings. My uneasiness was further increased by a feeling of nausea. The acrid smell of strong tobacco and the odor of human bodies were beginning to have an effect upon me. Earlier hopes of napping had long since been abandoned; now I merely wished to survive. The smoke was drying my throat, and my eyes smarted to the point of watering.

Toilet doors were being pounded upon by the stewardesses, who had noticed passengers entering while smoking. No one sat down when requested. There was not the slightest vestige of order anywhere, yet everyone smiled profusely and an air of genial conviviality prevailed.

The British stewardess appeared at my elbow. "How are you doing?"

"Breathing, just about," I answered jokingly.

"My name is Susan. Are you going to Tehran?" She perched herself on the arm of my seat. She had evidently resigned herself to the situation with good grace.

"Yes," I replied, and seized the opportunity to voice my surfaced misgivings. "In the event that I am not met, could you tell me what part of the city this address is in and how much a taxi fare might be?" I fished out my address book and pointed to the carefully printed copy of Dick Ellinson's scribbled note.

Susan looked at it in bewilderment. "This isn't an address. It just says second floor."

"What do you mean, second floor?"

"I'm telling you, dear, *tabageh bawlaw* in Farsi just means 'second floor.' Where's the rest of the address?"

"This is *all* of it. Look, isn't this the number and the name of the street, 27535 *Tabageh Bawlaw?* What else could it mean? It has to be right, surely?"

"Well, it's not, and you're in a mess unless you have a telephone number. Is this the telephone number here?" She pointed to the next line.

"Yes, I tried that number from Paris, but I couldn't get

through. It seemed to be out of order or changed or something."

"Oh, that's not at all surprising. Numbers are always being changed, and even when they are the right ones, they're more often than not out of order. What do your friends do? Are they Iranian or British?"

"Neither," I replied. "The husband is an American married to an Iranian girl. He is serving with the American Embassy, and thank goodness I thought of sending a telegram to him there, so I expect everything will be all right. If not, could you give me the names of a couple of hotels, and I'll simply take a cab and try and contact them through the embassy the next day?"

"Oh, you poor dear." Susan seemed genuinely concerned. "You'll have a hard time getting a cab and even worse, a hotel. You couldn't have arrived at a worse time than the Iranian New Year. At *Nowrouz*, just about everyone comes home. You can see from this planeload how festivities commence even in the air. If you thought this was bad, wait until we land. I do hope your friends meet you."

She went on to tell me that she was engaged to an Iranian boy but had grave doubts about the marriage. Parents traditionally choose the wives of their sons, and foreign girls are not favored at all. A woman's place altogether was held in inferior regard, yet, ironically, there was less objection, and often rejoicing, when their girls married men from other countries. Susan got up abruptly. "I'll be back. Try and get some rest. You'll be glad of it later."

Her words had a disconcerting effect upon me. I opened my little notebook and stared in disbelief at my "second floor" address. How could it be possible? Dick Ellinson was certainly the absent-minded professor type, but this was absurd. Even allowing for his haste to catch his plane, he couldn't have been so careless.

Being of a nature that never accepts disappointments the first time around, I timidly broached the young man who sat next to me. Unlike the rest of the passengers, he had not joined in the merrymaking. Other than an occasional remark to the young lad in the seat in front of him, his attention had been riveted to a paperback book that I now saw was written in English. Perhaps he wasn't an Iranian. I ventured, "Do you speak English? I see you are reading it. Are you an Iranian, by the way? I hope you don't mind my asking?"

"Yes, I speak English, I am an Iranian, and I don't mind at all."

"Would you be kind enough to tell me what this means?" I offered him my notebook and pointed to the "address." Perhaps Susan's knowledge of Farsi was faulty and she had been mistaken.

"The number is probably a telephone one, and the *tabageh bawlaw* just means 'second floor.' It is probably an apartment building." He smiled at me and went on, "I couldn't help over-hearing your conversation with the stewardess and I do hope your friends meet you, because at *Nowrouz* you really will have a problem. Tehran just goes wild. My brother and I are returning home from school in Geneva for the holidays. It is a time for great family celebrations."

"Well," I said, adopting a bright note, "I sent my friends a telegram at the American Embassy, so I expect everything will be all right."

The young man flashed me a less-than-optimistic smile. "The airport will be very crowded. It may not be easy for you to see your friends. If you should miss them, I will help you get a taxi, though I don't know which hotel to suggest because at this time of the year they are always quite full." He leaned forward to speak to his brother, who nodded in apparent agreement. Not having understood what he said, I was thankful if it had been on my account. The idea of going from one hotel to another was less than appealing, and what was even worse, how on earth was I going to make myself understood in this absolutely gibberish language? Let it be a lesson, I cautioned myself. In the future, when you know you'll be arriving in a strange country late at night and possibly be unable to make yourself understood, make a hotel reservation in advance. Meanwhile, don't let these two young men out of your sight once we have landed.

The lineup for immigration was horrendous. Hundreds of pass-engers, evidently from previous flights, jammed all exit lanes. My stomach, queasy as it had been before, now took a sickening lurch for the worse. The two young men were ahead of me, and I called out to them, less to make conversation than to remind them of my presence and their promise. "Pretty crowded, isn't it?"

The young man raised a palm and rolled his eyes heavenward in a mute appeal to Allah. "Wait," he answered, "wait until we get out. I think we may have difficulty in getting a taxi."

No distinction was made between foreigners and nationals, so I was able to stick close to the two men with leechlike tenacity.

I felt a tug on my sleeve, which scared the life out of me. It was Susan, who with her little flight bag in hand was, with the other crew members, heading for a separate exit unavailable to the passengers. "Good-bye. Hope you're met. My God, look at these lines. You poor thing. You'll be here for hours. I can't wait, as the crew is allowed straight through and there's special transport for us. You'll be all right, I'm sure. Cheerio." She walked on a few paces, paused, turned around, and came back to my side. Fishing in her purse, she found an envelope, on which she scribbled something down and handed it to me. She then fumbled in her change purse and pressed a couple of coins into my hand. "I feel terrible leaving you like this, but I'm going straight to my boyfriend's place. Here is a number to call if you have problems. I sometimes stay here with a stewardess friend of mine. I don't know her schedule, so she may not be there, but if you reach her, tell her I told you to call. I must go now. Good-bye, good luck."

The concern she showed in turning back served to increase my apprehension, not lessen it. I wanted to ask her a dozen things, express my gratitude, throw my arms around her, but my little angel of mercy had already passed out of my life, her jaunty cap quickly lost among all the bobbing heads around me. I felt an overwhelming sense of loss. I could not hear a word of English, not even French; surely I could not be the only European among all these travelers. People, people everywhere, yet never had I felt more isolated and alone.

Recognizing and collecting my pack was easy—it had the abandoned look I felt was on my face, and must have been sitting there forlornly for an hour and a half at least. No one at customs evinced the slightest interest in its contents. Thankfully I seized it, keeping a watchful eye on the two brothers, now claiming a suitcase apiece and starting toward the exit. They were only two or three heads in front of me, and I was reassured by a smile and a wave as we proceeded forward.

If the lines at immigration had seemed horrendous, they were nothing compared to the sea of faces waiting in the main arrivals hall. My mouth dropped open and I gasped in dismay. It was a human carpet from the very exit of the customs area to the black night beyond the portals, several hundred feet ahead.

The men seemed darker-skinned and swarthier than any on the plane. Many wore skullcaps and robes. Others wore berets and dark-colored high-necked sweaters from which rose faces without necks, the dominant feature of which were the black flashing eyes. It was a mass of black-shrouded shapes and black shining eyes. No necks anywhere. Incongruous. Frightening. I was appalled. Hope abandoned me as nausea took over with such intensity that my legs were reduced to jelly. There was no earthly chance that I could possibly see the Ellinsons if they had come to meet me, or that they could ever see me either. I looked for the two young men. They had disappeared.

In the grip of sheer panic, I was being pressed forward by the crowd. Someone tripped against my pack and made angry noises at me. Automatically I responded in English, "I'm sorry." Then in French, "*Je m'excuse, pardon, excusez-moi.*" I was wasting my breath with apologies, but my voice reached the young men I could not see, and an arm shot up over some heads. "English lady, English lady, over here!"

I moved at a snail's pace toward the arm, now the face, oh, thank God, now the man. "I'm here. Yes, I'm fine." What lies. Fine? I felt as sick as a dog.

"Have you seen your friends?" he shouted above the noise.

I gave a slightly hysterical giggle at the absurdity of his question. "No, I don't seem to see them." I couldn't see the shoes on my feet; what a lunatic reply. What an idiotic question. Be thankful he was there.

My pack was taken over, and I held on to one of the straps as we inched slowly forward.

"Stay beside me; stay with me," was all he said. Nothing in this world at that moment would have induced me to leave him. I clung on in sheer desperation. The smell was overpowering. I was hot and perspiring, my clothes damp and sticking to my skin. I felt wretched and angry with myself. Fool, fool, all that talk about wanting to feel free. (Now you know how it feels to be free *and stranded* at two o'clock in the morning in a foreign country.)

After a slow and painful advance we found ourselves outside, though only discernible by the confusion of vehicles. Here the cars merged with the crowds, and it seemed impossible for either pedestrians or vehicular traffic to move without overrunning each other. My young companion suddenly let out a cry and waved his hand. Within seconds his brother was at our side accompanied by another young man. The crowd eddied around us as the men

71

embraced. After several seconds of hugging and looking, joyous greetings and fervent embraces were repeated until I must have come into focus, for the stranger stopped, looked, and asked in Farsi who I was. I smiled and waited for an introduction to be made as all three got into a fast-paced conversation, during which the newcomer looked repeatedly at me and shook his head from time to time. I heard the word *taxi* and got the impression that they had given up hope of securing one. No wonder, I thought as I looked around. Cars of all shapes, sizes, and vintages abounded, but not one bore a Taxi sign.

Feeling that I had better get into the act somehow or other before I was thrown out of it altogether, I asked the only man I had so far spoken to, "What is your name? Mine is Sabina Shalom."

"My name is Armin. This is my brother Kamah and our friend Isaal."

I summoned what I hoped was a dazzling smile. I had to make them my friends. If they just left me standing there, what could I do? I couldn't face struggling through those crowds back into the terminal; the very thought made me feel faint. Yet I had to relieve them of the responsibility of my welfare. Halfheartedly I asked, "Is there a chance of finding a telephone somewhere?"

Armin shook his head.

"Well, if there are no taxis, perhaps I should go back inside and wait on a seat till daybreak. I really cannot trouble you and your friend anymore." My heart sank as I said the words.

"No, you cannot stay at the airport all night. Not alone. It wouldn't be wise. Not at *Nowrouz.*"

Was this holiday an ominous or joyous event? I cursed myself for arriving on such an ill-timed date. A few further words among the trio apparently resolved the situation, for Armin took my arm, Isaal my pack, and I was gently prodded into movement.

Laboriously we picked our way between cars, carts, porters with baggage piled high on shoulder, head, and arms, and black-robed figures with covered heads and veils drawn across their faces, and suddenly lots of children. They must have come with their parents to meet friends and relatives coming home for *Nowrouz.*

Nowrouz. Nowrouz. The word danced crazily in my head. Of

all times of the year I could have chosen to come, it had to be *Nowrouz*.

We walked for ten minutes before I could make out streets and buildings that were not part of the airport complex. Another five minutes found us in a small side street heavily lined with parked cars. We halted at a Volkswagen Beetle. The pack and the suitcases seemed to diminish the car's minute size; however, there was room for the luggage and the four of us. Armin opened the door and beckoned me, "Please to come in. There is no need to be afraid."

Until that moment I had been afraid only of being left by the young men at the airport. I had flinched at the thought of struggling amid those ghastly crowds to try and find a telephone, with no certainty of getting an answer. I had been apprehensive of changing money, dreaded the ordeal of getting a taxi, and been dismayed by the prospect of full hotels, all on the assumption of making myself understood in English.

Now, all of a sudden, I became paralyzed with a new fear, the instant I was told not to be afraid. What on earth could I be thinking of? It was three o'clock in the morning and I was about to get into a car with three complete strangers, all men. It was an insane thing to do, but what was my option? Brave the dark streets alone and try to find my way back to the airport? Never. Yet if I did summon up enough courage to do this, it would mean sitting up all night on a bench with drunks, thieves, and beggars for company. Hardly an appealing alternative either. Again, if I hesitated now and betrayed my misgivings, it could give rise to speculations not even contemplated by the men. Oh, God! This was terrible. Who knew where they might take me and to what? (Well, you can't stand in the street all night either, so get in, get in, they're beginning to look puzzled. They are probably being kind and have taken pity on you.) Hell, what could happen to me anyway? Only my head, my life, my money, my jewelry. (What the devil did I bring it for? Idiot, you could have managed fine without it, even at Naomi's lovely dinner party.)

The decision was traumatic. It wasn't even a decision. As all the fearful possibilities flashed through my mind, no matter what action I contemplated, I found myself, like an automaton, entering the car. I hunched myself up small by the window and stared hard into the inky blackness. Was I really doing this mad thing? (Well, Marco, what else could I have done, damn it?)

The men got in, Armin, alas, sitting up front with Isaal, Kamah in the back with me but already leaning forward and engaged in conversation. I felt completely cut off from all communication with them.

The neon lighting gave an eerie appearance to the surroundings. Signs written in Arabic flashed into view here and there on the buildings we were now quickly leaving behind.

We picked up speed and were soon whizzing through an open area with not even a tree in sight. It looked like a multilaned divided highway and was quite deserted. As we passed through open country, great dark masses hemmed us in. These must be the Elburz Mountains, I thought. Did these people live in the interior of the country, or what? We must have been traveling for forty minutes or thereabouts. I couldn't see my watch in the darkness, but it seemed an endless journey considering the high speed at which Isaal was driving.

The three spoke rapidly and with great animation. The language was totally incomprehensible; I couldn't catch a single word that meant anything to me at all. I decided to speak and perhaps allay my growing consternation at the length of the journey. I leaned forward. "Whereabouts are we, Armin? Is it much farther? You seem to live a long way from the city."

"No one lives in the city. It takes hours to go from one end of Tehran to the other. We go to friends. We shall soon be there."

"Will I be able to make a telephone call from your friends'? Is there a telephone?" I hoped my voice did not sound too anxious.

"Yes, everything will be all right. We shall soon be there."

It was not the first time in my life that my idea of time did not coincide with that of others. After a further fifteen minutes of driving, during which we passed into and out of several small villages, and my hopes of arriving were summoned and dismissed with similar velocity, I began to think that they must be heading for the very borders of the country, never mind the city.

A few straggly buildings came into view, the streets narrowing and branching off into side streets, down one of which we now proceeded. We came to an abrupt halt before a large stone wall and a small metal door. They all jumped out. Armin came around to my side and opened the door, saying, "Please."

I stepped out of the car. The driver was already rapping on the door, which was quickly flung open by a young man with a beard. At the sight of Armin and Kamah, he threw himself upon them, and the ritual of kisses, gazes, and embraces was repeated several times until, with arms around each other's shoulders, they preceded me down a short path, through an open door and the entrance to a house. I stood for a second but was gently pushed forward by Isaal, who led me in the wake of the others ahead.

A pale yellowish light illuminated the rather drab interior. The room, whose walls and floor were of stone, was furnished with a couch, a long low table, and many cushions. A profusion of plastic flowers adorned the table and hung from wall sconces. A large carpet hung on one of the walls, which gave way to a narrow dark corridor. Two curtained recesses led from the room, apparently the principal one of the house.

The bearded young man smiled at me and motioned me to sit down, speaking all the while to his friends. No one attempted to introduce me, so I smiled back and sat down, glad to ease myself against the cushions. Fatigue swept over me, almost excluding the initial alarm I experienced when no female figures appeared.

The four men conversed nonstop. I was totally ignored. My eyes began to close. It was a tremendous effort to pull my eyelids open. I looked at my watch; it was four-thirty in the morning. The pungent smell of smoke made me splutter into a more awakened state and I realized I was being offered a dark brown paper-wrapped cigarette. I declined, whereupon I was offered a small glass of some amber-colored liquid. This I also refused, feeling nervous lest I appear ungracious.

I took advantage of my presence being thus acknowledged to ask Armin if I could now make a telephone call. He readily agreed, saying that he would do this for me, because whoever answered would probably do so in Farsi.

I gave Armin the number I had called from Paris and the name of my friends. He fared badly. Not only did the number appear to be incorrect, but the person he woke up evidently expressed his annoyance in less-than-friendly words. Armin pulled a face and shrugged his shoulders as he replaced the instrument. I suggested he then try the American Embassy and could he please get the number from their information service. This he did and wrote it down on a pad by the phone. He dialed the number and handed me the phone.

What relief! A masculine voice answered in English, "Marine Guard Davis speaking."

"Oh, thank goodness. Please can you give me the telephone number of Dick Ellinson? He is embassy personnel. I am a friend, just arrived in Tehran, and I'm stranded."

"No, I'm sorry ma'am, we're not allowed to give out numbers."

"Oh, well, I have the number they gave me, but it must have been changed, because he wasn't known by the people who answered. Would you tell me then if the number I have is incorrect?"

"No, ma'am, I'm afraid I can't."

"Look, Marine Guard Davis, I'm only asking to verify my number with yours. It may be wrong by just one digit or something. Surely you can refer to your directory and tell me that much, can't you?"

"I'm sorry, ma'am, we are not allowed to give out any information. Security, you see, ma'am."

"No, I don't see. When someone is stranded in a foreign country and is a friend, there should be a little flexibility. If you would just take the trouble to check your directory, you would see that I do have his number. It may now be the old number if he's changed it, but it was his number. He gave it to me. They are expecting me, and I have to get in touch with them. If you can't help me, then who can?"

"I'm afraid no one can. I'm the only one on duty, and I cannot help you. I am sorry, ma'am, but it's regulations. Security regulations. I'm sorry."

"But Guard Davis," I stuttered on desperately (mustn't let him hang up whatever happens), "I understand your position. Please, can't you see mine? I simply do not know how to get in touch with these friends of mine, and I am in a mess. Can't you suggest something? Anything?"

"Ma'am, I really am sorry, but like I say, it's a security measure." (Oh, if he says that again I shall scream.) "I am not allowed to divulge any information whatsoever. There is nothing I can do, ma'am."

"Very well. What time does the embassy staff come to work?"

"No one will be coming to work today, ma'am. The embassy

is closed. There's another two days of holiday. It's the Iranian New Year."

God! As if I didn't already know all about this damn New Year. I thought fast and hard.

"I see. Well, when is your superior officer on duty, please?"

"That would be the military, ma'am. You're speaking now to the embassy."

"Oh, well, military then." (I could kill you, Guard Davis, you obstinate, wretched man.) "I'd like to speak to someone in military who can give me some advice, which evidently you are not in a position to do. What number shall I call please?" I struggled to sound polite.

"Ma'am, I cannot give you that number either."

Things were going from bad to worse. It seemed unbelievable.

The hopelessness of this interminable conversation, exasperation, and utter weariness swept over me. I could have wept hot, salty tears right into Guard Davis's ear. With a concentrated effort at sweet reasonability, I summoned strength for a last appeal. "I understand your position, Guard Davis. Let me give you the number here. It is the private home of people I do not know but who were kind enough to let me make this call. I can't explain too much, and I cannot stay here indefinitely. If you would just call your superior, explain my position, and ask if he would contact Mr. Ellinson, he will quickly verify that all this is true and that I am his friend, and then Dick can call me back here directly himself. Do you follow me? Do you see what I mean?"

"Yes, ma'am, I follow you."

Praise the Lord. Hallelujah. He had followed me. But would he do it? There were tears trembling in my voice as I asked, "Could you do that for me then, Guard Davis . . . please?"

"Yes, ma'am, I can do that for you. What is the number you are speaking from?"

I looked at the phone; there was no number on it. I called out to Armin and asked him what it was. He in turn asked his friend, nodded his head, and translated the number back to me in English. I gave it to Guard Davis and added, "You won't let me down, will you? I mean, I know you wouldn't intend to, but if anything goes wrong or your superior officer isn't available or Mr. Ellinson isn't contacted, you will let me know, won't you?"

The thought of hanging up the phone was almost unbearable.

Once done, it was the end. "Please, you won't leave me wondering and waiting, not knowing what has happened, will you, Guard Davis?" Only a monster could have ignored such desperate repetition.

"All right, ma'am, I'll do that. I'll let you know. Good-bye, ma'am."

I replaced the instrument feeling drained and exhausted. I had been shrieking into the telephone for some of the time, I was sure. The line had been faint, and I was anxious to make myself clearly understood. It was evident that I had made myself distinctly so to the young men, for they were eyeing me curiously and speaking rapidly among themselves. When Armin spoke to me, I had the uneasy feeling that something was amiss.

"Please, you rest now? Why don't you come in here and rest for some time?" His words seemed strange, his smile less than sincere. He pushed aside the curtain of one of the recesses, and the light from the naked bulb in the main room revealed a large mattress lying on the floor. The other boys nodded and smiled in general assent.

My heart turned over. I knew it instantly. From the moment I entered the house and realized there were no females around, I had felt uneasy. They had plotted this from the start. I was kidnapped. That was it. Armin had known about my friends in the embassy on the plane, aware that I would have difficulties contacting them. Now, from the conversation he'd overheard with the guard, he could see little help, if any, coming from that direction. He had probably given the wrong number, too. All part of the plan the four of them had cooked up together. It was commonplace these days. Anyone connected with the diplomatic service was fair game. They were constantly in jeopardy all over the world. It didn't matter who I was—I had a connection with the embassy and that was enough to hold me hostage. They had hatched a perfect scheme. My God! Bad enough to think I was kidnapped, what if they had worse things in mind? Now they want me to lie down—but no, that's preposterous. They were only youngsters. The oldest couldn't be more than twenty-five; I was old enough to be their mother. What young man wants to seduce a mother figure? That was a speculation I didn't much care for either. My spotty psychological reading did not rule out such possibilities. It is the experience rather than the charms of older women that is thought to attract young men. Anyway, I'll not lie down. That's the last thing I'll do. They'll not get me into that room and onto any mattress. My back was breaking, my head throbbing with fatigue. It was nearly five o'clock in the morning; no wonder I was exhausted. I would have given anything to have rested under other circumstances, but I struggled with a faint smile and said, "Thank you, I'm not really tired."

Armin shrugged as Isaal came forward with a long drink I could have badly used. But no, it could be drugged. I said I wasn't at all thirsty. I tried to sound alert and at ease. It was a wonder I made any sounds at all. My tongue clung to the roof of my mouth with dryness. At ease? What a joke. Try to be casual. Ask a few questions. Do they live here alone? How is it they are not with their families at New Year? Are any of them working, studying, something? (Other than kidnapping and contemplating rape? —the last came unbidden to my mind.) No. No. Don't ask anything. You'll only sound anxious. They'll see you are afraid. Smile. Look relaxed.

The young man whose house we were in and whose name I never did discover appeared with a tray of fruit. They intend to lull me into a pleasant and unsuspecting frame of mind, no doubt. I had heard that Eastern custom was one that always plied visitors with food and drink. They'd probably coated it with some concoction, having had no success getting me to drink. In these parts anything was possible. The state I was now in, everything was possible.

I decided to take an orange and avoid causing offense by constantly refusing hospitality. Surely the thick skin had protected the flesh of the fruit from contamination. I peeled the skin carefully and slowly so as to delay eating it and was saved from further dilemma by the ringing of the telephone.

Armin took it and handed the instrument to me. All was well. He hadn't lied about the number after all. I wasn't kidnapped. Rape and robbery had not been planned.

But all was *not* well. Far from it.

"Marine Guard Davis, ma'am. I have spoken to the sergeant on duty and he says there is no one called Richard Ellinson in the embassy directory. You must be mistaken."

"No, no, don't go. Wait a minute. I sent a telegram to the embassy, so it must have been received."

"Ma'am, the embassy has been closed since Wednesday. Embassy personnel in Tehran generally work on Saturdays and Sundays, but this being New Year and all, the staff would have finished this week on Tuesday night. It's a five-day national holiday and a lot of folks go away. There would have been no one to receive your telegram even if Mr. Ellison did work here, which it doesn't look like he does."

I could tell he had done his duty and wanted to be done with me too. Weakly I said, "Well, thank you for all the trouble you've gone to. I'm sorry to have bothered you. I guess nothing more can be done, then?"

Although it was a question, I did not expect an answer. I was not disappointed. He gave none. "That's right, ma'am. Sorry. Good-bye."

I did not have to explain anything to Armin. He guessed the outcome by the expression on my face. I looked in my purse for the number Susan the stewardess had given me. It was a last resort now that all other hopes had been dashed. The number rang and rang; there was no one there to answer. I hung up. Fighting back the rise of helplessness that now threatened to overcome me, I walked back to the couch, sat down, and leaned my head back against the cushions. I felt drained physically and emotionally, and it was all I could do to hold back the tears. I closed my eyes tightly for a moment so that no one would notice. Isaal had fallen asleep in his chair. Kamah was showing photographs to the young man of the house. Armin had been watching me and showed signs of restlessness. With a slight edge to his voice he said, "We can try the embassy later on, but you really should rest now."

I must have fallen asleep as he was talking. I awoke to see that my watch said eight o'clock. It may have been later, for I had not adjusted it to the local time. I looked around. There was no one in sight. The dish of fruit remained exactly as it had been; the bottle, glasses, and dirty ashtrays littered the table. There was neither sight nor sound of a living thing. Stiff and aching in every limb, I got to my feet, slipped out of my shoes, and tiptoed across the floor to the bedroom, fully expecting to see someone sleeping there. It was empty, as was the other room. I walked along the stone-floored corridor toward the kitchen. Not a soul stirred there either.

The dark room boasted a low shallow stone sink served by a single faucet. A wooden draining board was supported by legs but no cupboards underneath. There were two pails on the floor nearby and a roughly hewn wooden table on which lay an assortment of dishes. A few utensils hung on the walls, against one of which was a coal-burning black cast-iron stove. Was I alone in the place?

The back door opened to my touch and led into a small garden in which grew a variety of vegetables. It was surrounded by a very high wall. I hastily went inside and to the front door. It was locked and there was no key. I shook and turned the handle. It did not give. I wrenched and pulled, but to no avail. I was locked in the house. I was a prisoner. I had been kidnapped after all.

I visualized the headlines: ENGLISHWOMAN MYSTERIOUSLY DISAPPEARS IN TEHRAN. I thought of Marco and the boys. He had been so right with his words of warning. I had been so headstrong and obstinate when he had said it just wasn't right for me to go off alone and without reservations at proper hotels.

I'll call him. Yes, that's what I'll do. I'll somehow manage to make the operator understand and put a call in at once. It would be, what, four o'clock, five o'clock in the morning? Never mind the scare of being awakened at that time; what about the scare he would have when I told him of my plight? No, that's no good. What could he do? He'd try to contact someone in Washington perhaps. He wouldn't know what to do. I wasn't too optimistic about getting help this way; still, I had to try something.

Perhaps I could call the embassy here again. There would be a different guard on duty. With no one in the house I could explain now that I had been kidnapped. No, Armin would not have left the telephone number around. Anyway, they've probably cut the phone wires. I walked over to find out.

The door rattled. A key turned in the lock. In walked Armin, Isaal, and the young man of the house. Kamah was not with them. My heart beat wildly. I stood paralyzed. Trapped.

Armin came over to me with outstretched hand, all smiles. "Good morning, how do you do?" I knew he meant "How are you?" but I was too afraid to smile at his comic greeting. He did not wait for my reply and went on, "We went over to Isaal's house, as he had not been there all night. We left you sleeping and

81

thought it best to lock the door, as you were alone. We thought we would be back before you awakened again. We shall have some good tea now, yes? Then we shall see what we can do."

Tears began to stream down my face. There was no way I could stop them. Relief and exhaustion at last found an outlet. Armin was quite bewildered. "What is wrong? Are you ill?"

I heard myself confessing my fears. "No, I was afraid when I found myself alone, and being so weary and unable to reach my friends, I began to think stupid things." I gulped and sniffed and said no more.

"We try the telephone again and then I call my father if we have not the luck. He knows many important people. He will know what to do, though he is in Shiraz. I go there this afternoon. It is my home."

Everything fell magically into place. What dreadful tricks an overtired body and brain can play with one's imagination. Reason and common sense had deserted me on the purely superficial aspects of unusual circumstances. I looked at the note pad beside the telephone. There were the two numbers written down: the embassy's and Susan's. I smiled a heartfelt, grateful smile. "Thank you, Armin. I really don't know what to say. I've given you so much trouble. I'm a complete stranger to you, after all."

"In our country there are no strangers. Only our guests. You are an honored guest. It is our pleasure to help you." Armin turned to Isaal and continued speaking in Farsi. Isaal went in the direction of the kitchen, soon to return with glasses of hot fresh tea, which I now sipped appreciatively. Fresh tears started to well up. If only Armin had uttered those beautiful words earlier, my fears would have fled. I got up and made my way to the bathroom. A few moments later, as I was combing my hair, Armin called out, "Missis, Missis! Please to come here!" I hastened back and was handed the telephone.

"Hello, to whom am I speaking?" my voice quavered. Could it possibly be Dick Ellinson?

"Sabina, is that you? This is Susan Pearson—the stewardess, Susan."

"Oh, Susan, God bless you for being there. Where are you? How did you know to call this number?"

"I didn't call you. The man who's with you called the number I gave you. I'm at the flat. My boyfriend went to visit his mother and dropped me off here for a few hours. I needed a few things and wanted to see if my girl friend was coming in. What's the matter? Why are you so upset? Are you all right? What happened? Isn't the man your friend?"

As quickly as I could I told Susan what had happened, omitting all that my lurid imagination had supplied. I explained that I had tried her number with no luck, and repeated what had happened at the embassy. She cut in with a moan of sympathy. "Oh, you poor dear, what a time you've had. Well, look, get yourself over here and we'll sort something out together. You can always stay here for a while. You won't be stranded anymore. Let me speak to the young man."

Armin took over, nodding and murmuring. "Yes, yes, I know where, just a minute, I take pen. I write down. I ask my friend." Isaal was consulted, notes were taken, and the phone was handed back to me. "Everything's settled, Sabina. Your friend is going to bring you over right away. It will take about an hour and a quarter if they don't get lost. See you soon. Good-bye."

I collected my things and moved about briskly. I felt wide awake and marveled at how the mind can reactivate a weary body when it has suddenly been lightened of preoccupation. Armin noticed my hasty actions and smiled. "No hurry. Isaal went to fetch my brother Kamah. He likes Isaal's sister and stayed to see her, as we have to leave for Shiraz this afternoon."

"Oh, will taking me to Susan's inconvenience you? Perhaps I could get a taxi? In the daytime it must be easier to find one."

"No, we are too far away. No need to worry. It is quite good. We go to the airport in any case by eleven-thirty. You see, it is quite good."

Good? Yes, it *was* good. It had been a frightening experience. I had been alone, afraid, and helpless, but I had got through it without going to pieces or instinctively turning to someone else to bale me out. I hadn't called Marco. Thank God for that—he would have immediately told me to come home for sure. It *was* good, because in no way had the experience affected my feelings about continuing with the rest of my journey. It had only cautioned me to try and plan more carefully whenever I could.

It had been a good lesson, and I now felt more confident about coping with further unforeseen difficulties that might well lie ahead of me. I knew somehow or other I would manage on my own.

"Can you drink tea without milk?" Susan had prepared a little tray. "There's not much in the house, except these few biscuits, and I don't use the local milk in any case."

It was an hour and a half later, and I was stretched out on a cloth-covered couch in Susan's friend's apartment. The bright sunshine lit up a modern, newly constructed one-bedroom dwelling. The kitchen area was part of the living room, and Susan was now pouring hot water into a real English-style tea pot. This she covered with a knitted woolen bonnet, a tea cosy. I hadn't seen one in many years. I smiled gratefully. "Anything, just anything is fine with me, Susan." I was in a daze. I had slept all the way over here, and my eyes felt hot and swollen. My head seemed to be floating about on a stick, but my heart was light. It was daytime and I hadn't been kidnapped or harmed and I had a friend of whom I could ask questions. Susan would tell me where to exchange some money and would help me call a few hotels. Once I had secured accommodations I could think over my plans, and in a few days, when the embassy reopened, there would be time enough to ask about Dick Ellinson. Putting my thoughts aside, I asked Susan if everything was all right with her boyfriend. I sensed that she was a little upset.

She was anxious to unburden her problems. It seemed that her fiancé's mother had refused to allow her son to bring her to their home, and so he had gone alone.

"Although he is so Western in many ways, he still defers to some of the customs of his family. His mother intends to pick out the girl he marries and has made it clear it should be one of their own kind. I am a complete outsider. In faith, nationality, everything. She simply will not receive me. Can you believe that in this day and age there should be a situation like this?"

"As a matter of fact, Susan, I am not at all surprised. You see, my husband's family came from the Levant. They had exactly the same ideas and to some degree still do. At first I never felt I had been totally approved of either, as Marco disregarded their preference that he choose a wife from their own circle. Would you believe that to this day, when I am introduced as 'Marco's wife,' he is invariably asked, 'Is she one of us?' "

"It's different with their daughters, though, isn't it?" Susan was bitter. "They're only too glad to marry them off to the first suitor, whatever nationality."

"Yes, that's the irony of it. I often tease my husband that being a capable wife counted for nothing with his family when I first met them all."

"Capable?" Susan fumed. "Why, do you know his sisters never step into the kitchen, let alone put their dainty hands into dishwater. They are waited on hand and foot by servants—whom they treat like dirt, by the way—and they spend their time in the beauty parlor, dressing up for teas, cards, and gossip. Empty-headed spendthrifts—they make me sick."

"Ah, Susan," I said gently. "I know only too well what you mean. Had I been like that, but one of their own kind, everyone would have found me the perfect wife. Now I've been married for almost thirty years, so I don't feel as strongly about all that anymore. You see, dear, one dare not be different. It is neither understood nor liked. You must fit the mold and then it's all right. Unfortunately, a little bit of you gets crushed each day until the original you is lost. This, maybe, is one of the reasons I wanted to get away. To try and find something of the old me. The spirit I used to have as a single girl, before I was made to feel I had to tow the line once married."

"I know in my heart you are right, Sabina. We talk of marriage, but I just know that when it comes down to it, he'll not oppose his parents, otherwise we wouldn't have such arguments about the role of women in today's world. I keep telling myself to finish with him, and in any case living here among his family I would always feel as if I were on trial."

"Unless you like the idea of walking four paces behind your husband and concealing your natural talents and abilities, Susan, I honestly think you might be happier marrying one of your own kind. Someone who will value you, be proud of you, and appreciate your true worth. Believe me, I speak from my own experiences."

"As a matter of fact, there are too many strange things going on here to encourage me not to stay, never mind marry." Susan shook her head, lifted a finger, and looked earnestly at me as she spoke. "You were very lucky things turned out the way they did last night. No one knew of your whereabouts, and if these people hadn't been so decent, it might have been a very different situation."

"What do you mean?" I asked.

"Well, there's so much rumor, it's hard to know what to believe, but I think this country is headed for big trouble, but *big trouble,* now that the shah has left."

I told her about my abortive attempts to obtain information from the American Embassy. "The thing that puzzles me most is that they said there was no Ellinson on the staff."

"You don't have to worry, Sabina. You are welcome to stay here. I expect some word from my girl friend today. If she doesn't come in, you might be lonely, though. It is quite a long way out of the city, and I go back to London tomorrow."

"No, thank you, Susan. You have been more than kind. I would like to have one more try at the embassy, though, because the guards will have changed duty and I'll put my questions in a different way. I know the ropes better now."

This time I asked if a message could be passed on to the officer in charge of the military.

"Yes, ma'am. Certainly, ma'am."

"Would you please have him call me at this number as soon as possible. The matter is extremely urgent." I left my name and Susan's number with the guard.

Within minutes a Captain Williams called me back and sympathetically listened to my tale of woe. I explained that I had sent a telegram to the embassy but the guard had told me not only was it closed for several days and that the person to whom it was addressed would not have received it, but that there was no such name among embassy personnel. Was it possible, I asked, that Dick Ellinson was military?

Captain Williams asked me to hold on for a few moments. He then cheerfully informed me that in the military they had a noncommissioned officer by the name of Douglas R. Ellinson. Could this be the same person?

I said it had to be, but I could not understand why he was now a military person when he had definitely been an embassy staff member before his transfer to Iran. At all events, I was happy to take a chance on Douglas R. Ellinson if Captain Williams would be good enough to do likewise.

We compared telephone numbers and they differed. Captain Williams apologized for not being able to divulge the number he had. "Security reasons, you know." (Oh, yes, I knew all about that!) He offered to make the call himself, and whatever the outcome, he would let me know. With hope renewed I awaited his call, only to be told that there had been no reply or that the phone could also be out of order. "We have a terrible time here with the telephones. Of course, there is just the possibility that the family could have gone away for a few days, because" (I knew, I knew!) "it is the Iranian New Year, you see. I'll tell you what I'll do. I'll send a driver round to the house, just in case the phone is out of order and they may not have gone away."

When next the telephone rang, it was no less than Douglas R. Ellinson. Richard, Dick, our friend from New York, later Bogotá, now in Tehran and with the military.

"Well, Sabina, how about that. When did you show up? We weren't expecting you yet. You said you'd let us know in advance."

I explained that I had tried, and wearily went through the whole story of the telephone attempts, the telegram sent to the embassy, and, with some asperity in my voice, the incomplete "second floor" address.

"Oh, yes, the telephone numbers are always getting screwed up. As for the telegram, it will probably reach me Monday, or maybe Tuesday. Don't worry, I'll get it. It will reach me all right, I'm sure."

Don't worry, he says. It will be all right. Oh, yes, quite all right if I had been abducted, raped, kidnapped, whatever, and he not even *known* at the embassy. Yes, what about that?

"How come when I asked for you at the embassy no one knew your name?"

"Yes, well, that's a long story. Let's not talk more on the phone. I'll be right over to fetch you. Whereabouts is it?"

I put Susan on the phone to give instructions again.

The mystery was over. He came. With fervent thanks and an exchange of addresses and embraces, I left Susan to reflect upon her love life in peace.

In Dick's station wagon, with my own inner peace restored, I looked about me. The sleeping city of last night's prowling ghosts had shed the murky shapes that stalked the darkened hours of stillness, imagination's prey. Now fully awake in the day's bright light, Tehran extended a sparkling invitation to all.

The ride seemed partly repetitious of the previous night's experience. Clusters of simple dwellings that fringed the outskirts of the city slowly dwindled away on straggly streets. With little warning we were suddenly hurtled onto triple-laned highways and wide-open spaces to be thrust some thirty minutes later into all the bustle of the town's center.

Here, rising 148 feet into the air, the Shahyad Tower sifts through its great archway a continuous stream of all conceivable modes of transportation, many of which seemed bent on destruction or at least partial demolition. Stalled traffic, irate drivers, damaged vehicles, helpless-looking police officers, and animated bystanders all joined in the fray, expressing irreconcilable opinions.

It is said that 1 out of every 10 Iranians chooses to live in Tehran and that the city's population of some 4 million residents increases at the rate of 200,000 each year—and proportionately the traffic, no doubt.

Contrasts were quite phenomenal. As we proceeded toward the residential area in which the Ellinsons lived, dirt streets, thick with ridges, took over from the wide highways. The farther out from the city one reached, the worse the roads became. Potholes, broken cement walls, cracked and crumbling sidewalk slabs, were in evidence everywhere.

A chauffeured Mercedes-Benz streaked past us, scattering gravel against a baggy-breeched, beret-capped man leading a laden donkey. Seconds later a single motor scooter chugged along, ridden by a black shape with robes flapping away from high-heeled shoes confidently placed on the footpedals. Now, smoother paved roads boasted several grand homes, all surrounded by high cement walls and barred by great iron gates, in front of which uniformed guards patrolled. Adjacent to these formidable establishments, a group of flat-roofed shacks, each with but a single window and a flimsy door, nestled as if for protection from their impregnable neighbors. A half-dozen dirty gray sheep huddled together in the rubble of a demolished nearby shack. Common to all the streets were the open drainage ditches carrying sewage. They ran parallel to the sidewalks along the sides of the roads. The channels were no more than three feet wide, but a poor jumper trying to cross to the other side of the street got wet feet from water that was anything but aromatic.

"You'll see many anomalies in Tehran," said Dick as he skillfully swerved to avoid a donkey and cart coming out of a side street. "We live in one of the nicest parts of the town, but it is an awfully long way to the city center." He pulled up at the front of a large house surrounded by a low iron railing, giving several short blasts of the car's horn.

Nan came running out of the house before I had gotten out of the car, and embraced me warmly. Her name was really Naheet, but Nan was far more in keeping with the American ways and outlook that she had happily adopted many years ago. Married for eight years, this was her first long visit home, and she loved being back among her family. She told me how much they were all looking forward to meeting her friend from America. "Sabina, you couldn't have come at a better time than *Nowrouz.*"

Well, that was a change. Up to now nothing could have been worse. It was a time for attending family parties, visiting relatives, exchanging gifts, a time for much celebration. Tonight was a huge gathering of family and friends at her Uncle Nessim's house, and she couldn't wait to introduce me to everyone who would be assembled there.

The Ellinsons lived in a spacious eight-room apartment on the now-infamous "second floor" of a converted house, the lower part of which was occupied by the landlord and owner. Nan had acquired the excellent daily services of an elderly woman, who cleaned, cooked, and cared for the new infant when Nan had to go out. Their little boy of four and his six-year-old sister attended a private American school a short distance away. It was a well-ordered household into which they invited me to stay. Nan silenced my protests. "We had in mind a nice little nontouristy hotel for you, knowing you would feel this way, but frankly the distance we would have to cover there and back every time we wanted to see you makes your staying with us easier and safer. It really is far more practical, besides which, there's plenty of room, I've got help, and we'd love to have you. So no more arguments, please." I did not need much persuasion, for I had already witnessed the vast distances into and out of the city, and the inconvenience it would have caused that very same evening as we set out for Uncle Nessim's house.

Leaving behind winding, uneven dirt lanes, we drove unexpectedly into the broad cypress-lined Pahlavi Avenue which stretched for miles and rivaled any of the famed Parisian boulevards. Gaily flagged poles and multicolored lights strung between the trees imparted a festive air, and the whole section was brightly illuminated by the tall arc-shaped neon streetlamps.

The houses were most impressive, protected by high walls or tall sculptured hedges. Barrier poles or gates across the entrance ensured privacy, further implemented from little sentry boxes, where a uniformed watchman controlled access to and from the grounds. We now entered such a gateway. The guard touched his peaked cap as we approached and murmured a greeting. The gate swung open, and we proceeded up a curved driveway flanked by lawns and flowering shrubs to a house so grand it could have been featured in the pages of *Architectural Digest*. I drew a gasp of amazement. Surely this could not be the home of an ordinary citizen? Cypress trees surrounded the two-storied white pavilion. Latticed arches rose from the balconies, and the soft glow of lamps behind fretted window shutters, together with the light from lamps scattered throughout the gardens, gave a fairy tale appearance to the setting. I would not have been at all surprised had a peacock strutted across the path.

An attendant relieved us of the car, and before entering the house, I paused for a moment to breathe in the fragrance of the garden. Orange blossom and attar of roses.

Blue-green mosaic tiles were set into the risers of the entrance steps and led to handsome, wide, and welcomingly open double doors, at the sides of which two uniformed maids were stationed.

A wide marble staircase ascended from the semicircular entrance area, the floor of which was tiled in marble with an inlaid design in the center. Gracing the walls on either side were gilt-edged chairs and side tables, the latter supporting massive floral decorations, the perfume from which hung heavily in the air.

Our host and hostess came forward to greet us—Uncle Nessim, tall, silver-haired, and looking far younger than his seventy years, and Aunt Farida, short, plump, brown-haired, with smiling dark eyes, simply dressed in navy blue silk relieved by an elaborate gold and diamond brooch. I was thankful to have packed my black-print silk-jersey dress, my black high-heeled sandals, and my modest three-strand pearl necklace and my diamond stud and pearl earrings. (I remembered my son's words, "You won't need stuff like that.")

Introduced as "my friend from America," I was much fussed over, and as everyone spoke English or French, I quickly felt at ease, albeit amused at the profusion of kisses and hugs that were bestowed upon me by complete strangers. There must have been fifty guests, and with few exceptions, all were family members. Nan's mother, a sweet, quiet, rather sad lady, having lost her husband eighteen months before, was one of five sisters and seven brothers. As all of them were married, with children and grand-children, this was not an unusual number when all of them assembled.

Uncle Nessim had amassed his wealth establishing a chain of supermarkets many years ago. He was well known and well liked, playing a leading role in the community, and respected as much for his participation in communal affairs as for his generous donations to charitable causes. His home reflected taste, a love of art, and the means to indulge in its acquisition.

As we walked through the main reception area I noticed the marble-skirting tiles. Predominantly pale blue in tone, they were traced by a delicate tree pattern, intertwined with leaves in green, stronger blues, and touched here and there with yellow and red. It was a rich contrast to the creamy marble-tiled floors that now led us toward the principal salon.

Here, gilt-edged mirrors enlarged the room, the furniture of which was ornately carved, heavy, and upholstered in deep-mulberry-colored velvet. The windows were encased with fringed and bobbled satin brocade of a similar shade. Crystal chandeliers were suspended from intricately decorated ceilings. Crystal and gilt wall sconces sparkled with electrically illuminated candle-shaped bulbs. The only adornment of the one large wall was a magnificent carpet that shone with the luster of pure silk and was woven in shades of apple-green, emerald-green, rose, and varying tones of scarlet. Nan, seeing my admiring glance, whispered, "It's a priceless example of the best Persian silk carpet to be found today. The art is fast disappearing."

The celebration of *Nowrouz* heralded the spring. The array of the fashionably attired ladies marked, with color and elegance, the change of the seasons. There was no sign here of the shrouded black *chador* worn by the women in the streets. Nor did there seem to be any evidence of male dominance over the women, although the men had shown preference for company of their own sex by gathering in groups away from the ladies. These were soon dispersed when the double doors at the end of the room were opened to reveal a twenty-foot-long table draped with a hand-embroidered cloth and bearing a variety of beautifully presented foods on heavy silver platters. Two uniformed, white-gloved male servants were in attendance.

The table setting reflected a special Persian custom at *Nowrouz*. Nan explained that there had to be seven items of food, all of which began with the letter *s*. This was called the *haft-sin*, and included *samanoo* (stems of wheat cooked in a special way), *sabzeh* (a sprouted grain), sumac, hyacinth, garlic, vinegar, and apples (these last four all begin with the letter *s* in Farsi). A bowl of goldfish completed the requirements. Symbolically, even in the poorest home, the food should basically consist of bread, olives, fish, cheese, yogurt, eggs, sour cream, and salt. An additional sweet is made from sesame flour and sugar, and all are associated with the celebration of *Nowrouz*. Of course, these are not the only foods served when fifty people gather together for a festive dinner party.

The table looked so sumptuous that I asked if I might take a photograph. My hosts were quite amused and pleased that I wanted to record "the humble offerings of our home."

Rice, of course, was the mainstay, and it was offered in a variety of colors. *Chelo-kabab* was rice and grilled lamb, spiced with unusual seasonings, and to which raw egg yolk had been added. *Pillar* (pilaf) was rice decorated with pine nuts, slightly green from minced pistachio and fragrant with lemon. *Sabzi pallav* was another meat-and-rice dish. *Kukuye sabzi* was a casserole of baked vegetables and chopped nuts. Duck, cooked to perfection with walnuts and the juice of pomegranate, was called *fesenjon*. Apricots adorned steaming platters of chicken, surrounded by tiny meat-filled eggplants, topped with prunes. *Esfenaj-va-mast* was a spinach-and-yogurt combination. There were baby squashes filled with a spicy ground-meat mixture in a mint-and-lemon sauce, and a porcelain tureen of clear broth in which floated small nut-filled meatballs. Bowls of salad greens and dishes of olives, pickled turnips, pureed eggplant, braised celery, artichokes, and roasted spiced peppers completed the banquet. Tales from the *Arabian Nights* had surely been inspired by tables such as these.

Food was continually served from then until well after midnight, when we left. Glasses of hot tea were ritually handed around at intervals of fifteen minutes, and, in between, selections of little cakes, sherbet, glazed fruits, nuts, chocolates, and flat round mints. All notions of sticking to a spartan diet had been discarded the moment I set eyes on the table. The sweets and candies I bravely resisted, however, and was quite relieved that no pressure was brought to bear upon me to sample them.

Nan confessed on the way home that since her return to Tehran she had put on weight, largely because of the family dinners and teas she was constantly attending. I thought of Susan's comments in this respect and asked Nan if there were many job opportunities for women to follow. I learned that until recently, unless one was a student at the university, it had generally been frowned upon for an upper-or middle-class woman to work. Female employees were generally to be found in domestic service, in agriculture, or in laundry and restaurant-kitchen work, though educated women were now entering business and the professions in ever-increasing numbers.

"There have been many changes in recent years, yet the old and the new are in constant conflict," Dick said, and went on to explain that with the increased use of Western technology, giant strides had been made—land reform, industrialization, improved incomes, even moderate attempts to emancipate women. "Religious factions complicate the role of women in society, and you have already seen examples of those who embrace Western dress and those who choose, or are obligated, to wear the veil, which was officially discarded several years ago. You will see what I mean when Nan takes you into town. The robes and veils are an indication of outlook."

The attitude of the men was clearly evident when we visited the bazaars. Women, shrouded but for the eyes, scurried about, anxious to be done with their marketing. Others hovered over braziers, pots, and pans at the back of the little stalls and stores. Rarely did they appear to engage the interest of a customer. They were pushed into the background, clearly treated as inferiors, regarded as servants. No liberated women here, I thought.

The great arcades, comprising miles of intricate passageways, were lit with naked electric bulbs suspended high between the stores. This was the heart of an Eastern marketplace. The wares were a fascination of crafts, bric-a-brac, spices, leather goods, and freshly made breads and sweet cakes.

Hand-embroidered fabrics lay alongside those of nylon and polyester. Inlaid silver trays and brass and copper trinkets vied in competition with cheap tin pots and pans. Filigree jewelry of traditional Persian design was outflanked by Western brand-name wristwatches. Traditional hand-stitched slippers and sandals lay incongruously displayed beside gaudy plastic thongs. The variety was endless, but I did not stop to buy, for I wanted to move on to the carpet section. Were not Persian carpets the legends upon which rescued princesses were flown?

The carpet merchants hold a special place in the bazaar. This area is much less crowded, and the stores led into warehouses with several times more space to display their wares. The dealers were older men who looked one over with dark hooded eyes, their expressions betraying nothing, their hands fingering their beads hanging from neck to waist. Wise and knowing, they sense who is there to buy and who is merely passing the time of day.

Luckily, the young son of one of the proprietors waited on me. He was anxious to practice his English and answered my questions readily. Had he not been so attentive, I doubt I would have seen some of the exquisite Kashans, Kilims, or the darker-colored Baluchistans. Some are made of the finest silk thread; others, of cotton and wool. Some glow with the soft sheen of velvet, while others change their color and character according to the way the light strikes the soft pile. The art of carpet-weaving is slowly dying. Once, a single man or his wife and family would pool their skills and create a masterpiece of history, pride, and tradition. Now the demand is for the factory-made carpet, chemically colored by dyes, rather than for carpets woven into patterns by hand. "Our people cannot afford them nowadays, and skilled hands would rather turn to the modern factories, where they get better pay."

I asked for prices but got so confused with the currency that I wished I hadn't. So many *toman*s to the dollar and one hundred *dinar*s made a *rial* and how many *rial*s did he say made a *toman*? Anyway, I wasn't buying, and the young man knew it.

I left the bazaar and thought to buy some cheese from a street vendor. It was goat cheese, wrapped in large flat leaves protected from flies by clear plastic sheets. I wasn't sure I would eat it, but I wanted a photograph of the veiled women making their purchases and I patiently awaited my turn.

A few men had gathered around, curious perhaps about the European-dressed woman in their midst. I smiled at the cheese vendor, pointing to the cheese and displaying a bill in my hand indicating at the same time my camera. The man thought he was making a sale, and neither of us felt a photograph was injurious to the transaction between us. The men thought otherwise. First one man cursed and raised his hand as if to destroy my camera. Another shouted at the vendor and began to push him about. The women scurried away, and I hastily followed suit, thrusting my camera underneath my jacket. I couldn't understand the nasty scene now fully raging. Like Lot's wife, curiosity got the better of me and I turned around. No longer within range of repercussion, I whipped out my camera and clicked away, then walked on, victorious and cheeseless.

Ahmad Emami, a cousin of Nan's who was studying history at Tehran's university, had passed by the house to pick up some books on loan from Dick. He had visited Nan in the States some years before, and it was an excellent opportunity for me to ask how he felt about the differences in life-styles and the changes that were taking place in his country.

"We are in the process of a revolution," he said, much to Nan's alarm and my surprise. "The changes are so dynamic that many of our people cannot comprehend what the future can hold for them in the way of progress."

He went on to speak of the recently decreed free education and medical care for all Iranians. Women were slowly beginning to shake off the age-old tyranny of Islamic tradition. Land reforms broke up the ancient feudal holdings and distributed smaller tracts to individual farmers. "Once, a single landlord owned as many as a hundred villages; he not only owned the land but controlled the lives of the villagers as well. It was tantamount to slavery. All that has changed."

I had the opportunity to see village life for myself. The thirteenth day of the New Year is the day of the picnic, and all Iranians celebrate a family gathering out of doors. Before the New

Year commences, a "cake" of wheat called *sabzeh* is prepared. Sometimes lentil or barley is used. This is dampened and covered with a wet cloth and left to sprout. By the thirteenth day the shoots are green and several inches high, and the "cake" is taken by the family on the picnic. It is thrown into the fields or a river, and with it goes all ill feelings, quarrels, or any bad luck that may have befallen one throughout the year. The unmarried girls make a wish for a husband, while the young married women wish for a pregnancy or the birth of a healthy child if not already blessed by this event.

As we traveled through the countryside, it was clear that Iran was a country on the move and hard at it. Communications networks spread their tentacles all along the highways. Factories, housing projects, schools, and clinics often seemed to be plunked down in the most desolate urban parts, the highways and mountains their only neighbors until such time as growth and population distinguished them as towns.

A two-hour drive out of the city and one is in a different world, where the villagers cultivate their land with methods and tools that are antiquated beyond belief. Their weather-beaten faces, roughened hands, and bent frames reap poor rewards from the incessant toil.

Their sun-dried mud-brick homes invariably cluster around the local bathhouse and the mosque. Here, five times a day, devout Moslems prostrate themselves in prayer. I later learned that prayer is an expression of the total acceptance of a way of life, not the simple observance of a ritual. Religion was not a *part* of life, it was *all* of it. To my Western concepts, it was beyond comprehension that a people could be governed politically, emotionally, and spiritually by purely religious beliefs. Even more disturbing were the words of the Prophet, "*Al-Kufru millatun wahida*"—"All who do not subscribe to Islam are infidels, unbelievers without religion, without souls." The words of Kipling sprang to mind: "Oh, East is East, and West is West, and never the twain shall meet." The desert was too vast to cross these differences.

Some differences were highly amusing, especially with regard to the cleaning and sale of carpets.

In the town of Rey, dunking them in a natural spring-water well and then spreading them out on the stony hillsides to dry out constitutes the only acceptable method of cleaning.

Conversely, in the towns, carpets are deliberately rolled out in the streets for traffic to pass over them. This is thought to enhance the aged appearance of the carpet and increase its value.

From the poverty of the country folk and the sight of men and women astride donkeys I returned to Tehran and the double-decker buses and the incredible wealth of the priceless treasures at the Markazi Bank. It is here that the crown jewels are displayed, the greatest single collection of precious gems in the world.

Armed guards carefully check handbags and pockets. Cameras are strictly forbidden. All who come to view the collection are under constant surveillance, and no wonder.

The very walls of the chamber seem aflame with iridescence. Display case upon display case fill the aisles and line the walls, all protected by strong steel railings three feet away from the glass-enclosed jewels. At first, the impact of such dazzling splendor hurts the eye. The senses can hardly take in the enormity and brilliance of the precious stones.

There are platters bearing whole grams of gems not less than ten carats each. Diamonds and emeralds as large as a woman's fist dwarf hundreds that are the size of a half-dollar and thousands that are the size of a quarter. Any plateful would seem to be sufficient to buy a small emerging nation.

Many of the large stones are set into crowns, diadems, and tiaras. There are bejeweled cuffs, scabbards, epaulets, belts, and buckles. Pearls, rubies, sapphires, and diamonds are set in designs of consummate skill to adorn garments used for state occasions. Necklaces, rings, pendants, brooches, earrings, bracelets—all are fashioned in diamonds, emeralds, and a multitude of precious stones.

One of the oldest gems in the world is the incalculably precious Daria-i-Nur diamond. It is there. The modern Pahlavi crown is there. The fabulous Globe of Jewels, set with more than fifty-five precious stones, is there.

The cumulative effect of such beauty and the wealth it represents was quite overpowering. Stunned, I walked unsteadily outside to see a skullcapped man in loose flapping robes struggle with his donkey and the sacks and crates the poor beast dragged along.

The old and the new are out of step. Industrialization is on the march, but the pace is too fast, and many lag behind. Tehran, with all its haste to don new and stylish clothes, was a city of motley contrasts and confusion.

Wherever one travels, one never loses sight of the mountains. Unchanging and constant, they affirm the existence of a country that, for an archaeologist, is paradise. A civilization that goes back more than 7,000 years and even as the reborn Persian Empire is still 2,500 years old.

Shiraz, Persepolis, and Isfahan were excursions into such ancient history that years of study and volumes of words could not do justice to the eons of a developing civilization. The ancient sites, tombs, mosques, palaces, sculptures, and excavations required the professionally trained guide whose life had been spent in research in this field.

I thought of these magnificent monuments of centuries past, the domes and cupolas that glistened in the crisp clear light, the walls completely covered with multicolored tiles and intricate and beautiful Arabic script. And again the mountains, the splendid towering mountains.

The rugged Elburz, snowcapped and separating the Elbura with fertile valleys on one side and the Caspian Sea on the other. The old trade routes, still followed by the nomads of many different tribes, that skirt the mighty Zagros Mountains. And the Makran coastal region, which rises up like a fractured wall.

A country that 2,500 years ago was the kingdom of Darius, who said, "This my kingdom, the land of brave men and handsome horses. May Ahura Mazda keep it under his protection for evermore. O Thou, who rulest after me as king of this land, if thou wishes to keep it lasting and prosperous, avoid falsehood and mete out punishment to the liar. Be benevolent, forebearing, and just."

I was at loss to understand the shaken head, the whispered dissent, the reluctance to speak of government administration and the deeper implications of the changing social fabric. The veil had been banished, but one of a different kind seemed to lie across the nation's countenance.

My hosts spoke of the magnificently endowed units in modern hospitals, equipped with the latest medical and scientific technology. "They are proudly shown off to visitors, and closed up when they've left. There are no skilled technicians and doctors to staff them, you see." The same was said of impressive machines of computer wizardry—easily attainable, as were the simpler instruments, for all who could afford to simply consign them to idleness when they broke down.

The Literacy Corps, established some years back, goes into the country to teach and disseminate birth-control information. Foundations and scholarships offer students every opportunity to increase their knowledge of the Western world. Experts brought in from other countries have implemented training programs and self-maintenance systems. Surely this meant fewer hungry mouths, less unemployment, deeper understanding with other countries, greater prosperity?

I hesitantly raised these questions on my last evening in Tehran at a farewell dinner party in my honor. The meal was over. The men were enjoying their cigarettes and liqueurs; the ladies were relaxed and gossiping. Perhaps I should not have been surprised that my remarks seemed to have been misunderstood, or were they being intentionally ignored?

One of the ladies did respond. She smiled benignly at all around her. "My dears, can you believe that my chauffeur has just purchased on the credit system a television set that cost seven hundred U.S. dollars and my maid of fifteen years has given *me* notice." She turned courteously to me. "You see, it is getting quite impossible to find good servants these days, now that factory conditions have been so improved. Really, I just don't know what this country is coming to."

5
India

My last few days in Tehran had been hectic: sending flowers to those who had shown me so much kindness, checking on my flights, and saying good-byes. Attempts to put my future travel plans in order had been abortive, with one exception. I had confirmed my hotel accommodations in Delhi. I had learned my lesson. I would not arrive anywhere late at night without knowing where I was going to sleep.

With great excitement I looked forward to this next stage of my journey. I had always been fascinated by India. From everything I had ever read or seen, the country was one of enormous complexity. For centuries, warriors, spiritual leaders, politicians, economists, and scholars have attempted to wrestle with the imponderables that are India. Now I was about to discover this phenomenon for myself.

Aboard an Air India plane, I sought the assistance of the gentle, dark-eyed, sari-robed stewardess. Soft-spoken and solicitous of my needs, she quickly supplied me with a blanket and agreed not to disturb me, even for food or other refreshment, if I should doze off. Wrapped up and belted in, I inflated the little plastic cushion brought from home, slipped on my own pillowcase, snuggled my face into it, and slept.

My need to eat was often ignored, but sleeping whenever I could had become vital. It was especially desirable on this leg of my journey, as I had made a prior decision to change planes in Delhi and fly straight to Agra to see one of the famed wonders of the world, the Taj Mahal. We would be arriving at the crack of dawn in Delhi, and the first plane to Agra was at 6 A.M. If I took advantage of being at the airport to check my pack, I would be unhampered and could catch that early plane. The only other flight of the day was in the afternoon, and I knew I would not want to hang around the airport for ten hours. This plan made good sense, providing I could remain vertical!

The thud and rumble of wheels on the tarmac awakened me from a deep sleep that felt like four minutes rather than four hours. I barely had time to shake myself out of my torpor, let alone swing into top gear for swift action. I breezed through immigration and customs in a flash. I was amazed and delighted. Everything seemed so efficient and contrary to what I had expected—chaos! The white-uniformed official barely glanced at my British passport. Perhaps the emblem on the cover had stirred a familiar indifference, or was it the effect of the words the insignia bore: *"Honi soit qui mal y pense"* ("Evil to him who evil thinks"). Good or bad, the effects were speedy, and I encountered no language problems to inhibit my inquiries. I was informed that all local flights were from another terminal, and I was willingly escorted there by the white-clad agent of Indian Airlines.

I hurried along at his side. Time was short for my next departure. Concentrating on his figure, I was only vaguely aware of the blur of dark-skinned faces milling around. Later; you'll look later. Hurry now, check the pack, get your seat, move it. Watch it, you nearly knocked down a pair of enormous black eyes in a wasted frame wrapped in rags. I was momentarily stunned by the shock of this encounter, but so intent was I on securing a seat on what I was told would be a crowded plane that the full impact did not fully register. Once I was checked in at the counter, I relaxed and started to take stock of my surroundings. The plane was delayed. We would not be leaving for twenty minutes.

The pearly haze of dawn's early light had long since surrendered to the crystal-clear illumination of day, now fully broken. The brilliance of color that met my eye wherever I looked seemed a dazzling kaleidoscope. The blues, greens, reds, yellows, and purples of the women's saris struck me as jewels glinting in the morning sun. In movement they flashed as emeralds, topazes, sapphires, and amethysts against the darkness of skin, the blackness of hair, long and braided, the whiteness of teeth, and the vibrant circle of color the women place above the brow, center forehead.

The area in which I stood was densely packed. It appeared to serve as an entrance hall, check-in counter, and arrival and departure lounge all rolled into one. I wound my way through the throng to get outside. The smell of perspiration and perfume inside had cloyed at my senses. My empty stomach had delivered warning signals to my head, and I needed a good whiff of fresh air.

The only thing fresh about the air outside was the recent animal droppings. I felt quite nauseated. The sights of dogs, carts, horses, oxen, and donkeys blending with vendors, beggars, children, baggy pants, turbaned heads, bearded faces, and white-robed men everywhere defied description. Everything seemed white, white, white. The men were in nothing but white. Calf-length frock coats, high of neck, long of sleeve. Buttoned to the hip or flaring out to reveal straight narrow-legged trousers or loose, flapping, balloonlike pants. All white, all white.

There were mothers with babes swaddled against their hips and toddlers clutching at their skirts, and there were young girls, some in uniform, all with hair long, smooth, and straight, as black as coal and twice as shiny. There were old women whose lined faces were as etched as the intricate carving of the ivory trinkets they offered for sale; men on crutches, hobbling, peddling. All were silent, though; no wheedling or whining. Young boys pulled, darted, carried, dragged, munched—but all white, white.

Ah, the taxi men. In their colored trousers and multitoned nylon shirts they looked quite out of place. I was besieged at once. "Lady, lady, I take you in my taxi. I give you best price and noble service." I smiled and walked on to be greeted by a vendor of drinks, his cart gaily decorated with the brightest of painted flowers and designs. A large cauldron rested amid ships, and a big ladle hung on a hook from one of the two side poles that sported a rope strung across and from which fluttered many colored flags and pennants. Freshly squeezed gastroenteritis was not for me, thirst notwithstanding. Better go inside and look for a *bureau de change*, and with local currency buy something bottled. No, better get back to the departure lounge. Thirst, stomach, money, will have to wait until Agra. It is only a thirty-minute flight.

Our small craft winged aloft. I could not remember being in so small a plane. How odd, I mused; back home I never gave airplanes so much as a thought. They were just all big. Big and comfortable. Big and noisy. Big and smoky, but always big. I didn't even know what kind of plane this was. It held about forty passengers, all Indians, I judged by their dark skin and dress. A cold drink was offered, but I declined. Stay firm of resolve and strong of will. Do you want to get dysentery your first day in India? When you get to Agra you'll have breakfast at the airport restaurant.

Kheria, the airport for Agra, had no restaurant, not even a snack bar, but I was able to exchange some money. I bought a bottle of soda from a man standing behind a frail wooden counter that threatened to collapse any moment from the weight of the bottles it bravely supported. My first purchase in India caused great offense when I produced from my shoulder bag my tin mug, into which I transferred the contents of the bottle, declining the ice cubes and the glass, freshly rinsed out in a pail of water, that had been handed to me.

With thirst unquenched, I hastened outside the group of sheds that constituted the terminal to find several taxis lined up. I asked one of the drivers if there were any local buses and at what time they might be due. It seemed that none were expected to appear at all, and I was courteously offered a free ride to the main hotel, where I could get information about transportation or avail myself of a choice of excursions.

Having little to lose, I accepted the offer even though I was dubious about the ride being free of charge. The distance was very short and along a road pleasantly relieved by cool green fields and foliage. Within minutes we arrived at a splendid-looking hotel— the famed Clarks Shiraz, where an impressive red-turbaned, white-uniformed doorman sprang to open the taxi door. I snapped him with my Polaroid instant camera and presented him with the results. He was delighted. My taxi driver's expression alternated between envy and anticipation, so that I felt obliged to treat him similarly. His beaming smile and childlike glee were a pleasure to witness, and true to his word, he did not charge me for the ride. It was part of the tourist service offered by his company. Leaving his parked taxi, he accompanied me inside the hotel to meet his employer and discuss how I might best reach the Taj Mahal, several miles away.

I decided to hire the same taxi and driver by the hour rather than take an excursion tour or pursue inquiries about local transport. Both alternatives meant an indefinite wait, one subject to there being enough people, the other depending upon an erratic schedule. With the matter settled, I repaired to the cool, spacious, Victorian-styled dining room for breakfast.

My waiter, soft-spoken and amenable to my every wish, listened patiently as I insisted upon only boiling water for my tea. I ordered two lightly boiled eggs, toast, and marmalade and said I would be back in five minutes, enough time to visit a spotlessly clean ladies' room with a solicitous white-sari-clad motherly soul in attendance.

I had never tasted tea more delicious. What impertinence, I chided myself, telling an Indian how to make tea! The toast was not soggy, and the eggs were just right. It was a fantastic meal. Of course, not having eaten anything for fifteen hours may have contributed largely to the enjoyment. It was not yet eight o'clock in the morning.

Refreshed and fortified, I settled myself comfortably in the taxi with a luxurious feeling of well-being and anticipation. I was in India! It was my very first day and I was off to Agra to see the Taj Mahal.

The car bumped along the uneven road, banked on either side by red sandy earth. Dust billowed a fine spray across the windows, obliging the driver to make an occasional stop to clean them. Each time he got out, he entered into a smiling conversation in Hindustani with whoever passed by.

At no time was the roadway empty of people. Children, some in school uniform, carrying their satchels of books, on the way to class, turned to stare. Women walked sedately by, their baskets and urns perched securely on their heads steady as a rock, bodies erect and proud of carriage. It was fascinating to watch. The men, for the most part, wore *dhoti*s (long loincloths), as many turbaned as not. All who wore turbans also wore beards. They would be Sikhs, and beneath the turban their hair would be waist length, never having been cut.

As we entered a village I saw a large placard bearing the words Family Planning Centre. I asked the driver to stop; I wanted to investigate. In less than twenty minutes of driving through the countryside the sights of poverty and backward conditions had assaulted my consciousness. From my years of social work I was well acquainted with the dire consequences of overpopulation. Forgotten for the moment were the tourist attractions. Remembered were my reasons for making this journey in the first place. I wanted to "get with the people of the world," as well as see it. Ah, but would they want to get with me?

The village consisted of a cluster of mud huts and a few red-sandstone-brick stores. Of ramshackle appearance, they bore an air of dilapidation. Some were no more than wooden structures with slats of tin roofing. The little stores opened onto the street and possessed no visible doors or shutters as protection against inclement weather or pilferage.

I asked the driver to stop at one such store and, from the money I had exchanged at the airport, thrust a note into his hand and suggested he buy some refreshment and wait for me there; I would be back in a little while. He seemed quite nonplussed and shook his head from side to side. "Oh, no, madam, I will be taking you wherever you wish to be taken." Only when I explained that I wanted to visit the Family Planning Centre did he cease to remonstrate. With some embarrassment, he quickly agreed not to accompany me.

I retraced my steps to where I had seen the notice and turned into a narrow dirt alley. The earth was very red and dry except for a thin, muddy ribbon of sludge on one side. An acrid smell assailed my nostrils and momentarily filled me with revulsion. It was the wetness of urine and human feces. I walked on, exciting the interest of several ragged-looking children and a few native women, who turned or stopped to stare at me as I smiled a greeting. "Good morning. I am a visitor. I would like to see the Family Planning Centre. Could you please show me where it is?"

"Yes, I'll show you, just now I am going." The voice came from a young woman who carried not only a child in her arms but one in her belly. A little late for family planning, I thought. I thanked her and followed her for a few minutes until, with an indication of her hand, she beckoned me to precede her into a one-room shack.

Like others we had passed, the walls were made of mud and dung, baked dry and hard in the sun. It did not boast a complete roof. Several bamboo poles supported a partial covering of thatch and rusted tin. A piece of cloth hung on a wire, stretched between two hooks in the wall, served as a curtain to provide privacy for the corner of the room that held a *charpoy*—this could hardly be called a bed; rather, it consisted of a flimsy wooden frame strung with ropes and covered with a dingy piece of material.

A wooden table and several straight-backed chairs against one of the walls completed the furnishings. There were two posters affixed to the walls. One was a large diagram of the female pelvis; the other, a printed notice that, upon entering, I couldn't distinguish clearly enough to read.

Seated at the table, straightening out some leaflets and arranging a display of various contraceptive devices, was a middle-aged woman dressed in a white cotton sari. My pregnant companion and I were the only other occupants of the Family Planning Centre.

I introduced myself as a social worker and said that I was interested in finding out what success the clinic was having in the village. I explained that I had seen the notice while driving through and hoped she did not mind.

The woman at the table smiled a warm greeting and assured me I was most welcome. It seemed Dr. Bhandari had studied in England and was widely traveled. She was a woman with a cause and passionately devoted to helping her fellow countrywomen educate themselves in matters of birth control and general hygiene.

"The main trouble in all the villages," she was happy to expound, "is that the women are ignorant and fearful. Anything contrary to nature and religion is looked upon with suspicion. Often the women are so undernourished and anemic that some of the devices cause bleeding, and other methods are not always used correctly. Because of this, most of the methods are unsatisfactory and unreliable solutions to the problems of birth control. The only way is vasectomy. The men, of course, fear it will make them impotent. Furthermore, they often forbid their wives to come here at all. So, you see, our job is not an easy one."

As she spoke, I was now able to read the notice. It bore the words of Indira Gandhi: "We must act decisively and bring down the birth rate speedily to prevent the doubling of our population in a mere twenty years. We should not hesitate to take steps which might be described as drastic. Some personal rights have to be kept in abeyance for the human right of the nation. The right to live, the right to progress."

Dr. Bhandari noticed my glance. It was clear that she was a fervent admirer of Mrs. Gandhi, and she interpreted my question before I asked it.

"Yes, there were measures during the emergency that many of our people and Westerners thought harsh. Taking the men from the fields to undergo an operation may seem drastic, but when one is right in the middle of dire poverty and sheer starvation, when mothers and babies are dying of malnutrition, only the strongest of actions, no matter what is said, can help our country. Mrs. Gandhi is right, and I doubt that there are many women who would disagree."

I left sadder and wiser, knowing full well that her temporary stay in the village would do little to achieve effective results. She had told me that there were far too few women doctors to serve a nation of 600 million, 80 percent of whom lived in villages and small towns. The Indian women did not favor male gynecologists. The Indian men did not like vasectomy. It was a dismal outlook.

My wanderings around the streets gave me an even more depressing view. I chanced upon what seemed the village square. At least, it was the center of much activity, its popularity as a gathering place doubtless owing to the only water faucet the village possessed and from which everyone drew their supply. Women and children filled their urns and pitchers; others filled pails and squatted nearby to wash clothes. Mothers washed their infants.

There appeared to be a drainage ditch running alongside a mud wall, where dogs raised a leg and men and children relieved themselves quite openly. The women were more discreet. Their robes always managed to conceal their bodies. It was the squatting position they adopted that indicated what they were about. I was shocked but fascinated. I wanted to take a good look but didn't dare. No one at home will believe me, I thought, but it would have been an outrage of decency to have tried to take photographs. I felt I was spying upon aspects of human behavior that were private despite the open exposure.

I hoped my stares had not been noticed, and I walked to where I could take photographs of some of the children who had been following me and who now gathered quickly around me as I produced my camera.

Big eyes, dark eyes, hungry, curious, suspicious eyes—I wanted to capture those soul-searing expressions on film. My heart ached for these ragged little mites, many of whom were naked. I steeled myself against giving them a few coins, for I knew it would create pandemonium. I would never get away, and time was going by.

A woman came toward me, an infant in her arms, a child at her side, and her swollen belly evidence of yet another child. The baby's limbs were matchstick thin. The face was all eyes and vacant. The head rested listlessly against its mother's shoulder. The skin bore a transparent, almost bluish pallor. It had the look of death.

In shock I made a hasty turn and all but fell over a moving object at my feet. It was half of a man. He was strapped onto a little platform with wheels. He had lost both legs. He used his hands to propel himself along; they were wrapped in filthy bandages. His face was covered in sores. The features had lost definition. My God, was he a leper?

No, no, I didn't want to know. I didn't want to see. I did not want to look around me anymore. All that my eyes had taken in, my senses were rejecting.

The wretchedness of the dwellings, the hunger and misery of the daily struggle to exist, brought an unbidden flood of memories to my mind. The haggard faces and skeletonlike bodies of concentration camp survivors swam momentarily before my eyes.

What difference does history make? What difference is the geographic location? Human suffering the world over is the same. Appalling. Terrifying. And why? Why?

Had I come to India to see things that would revive old wounds? No, no. I'd come to Agra to see the beautiful Taj Mahal. What was I doing here, lingering amid all this ugliness? Where was my driver? "Yes, we'll go on now. Straight to the Taj Mahal. Right away, please."

I closed my eyes to blot out any further distressing sights. It didn't work. I could not obliterate all that I had seen. I took out my diary and started to add up all the expenses of the day. I'm a duffer at figures; addition and subtraction never fail to send me into a tizzy. Now, though, it was a welcome distraction, and indeed I soon began to look around me again.

Straggly dwellings heralded the approach to a larger village and an obvious indication that here, commerce and enterprise existed and were vigorously pursued. The car braked suddenly and I was thrown forward. A cow had nonchalantly ambled directly into our path. Poor beast—its wretched bones almost pierced the sagging skin that covered its scraggy frame. This sacred animal must never be harmed. It looked as if it had never been fed. It was allowed to wander at will into a store, into a temple, into a house. How much better off it would have been tethered in a stall and fed than wandering homeless, free, and hungry.

Bicycles by the dozen went by. I photographed one with a woman being carried across the handlebars and a man sitting behind the rider. What a feat of balance. Indeed, some of the scenes before my eyes would have made great acts for any circus.

Water buffalo, goats, donkeys, sheep, and oxen passed by. Carts on rickety wheels were pulled by emaciated horses. Now a camel; no, two; no, three. A rope connected each one as they bore their heavy load. With lumpy gait and leery eye, they seemed to look down from their great height with an air of disdain on their animal friends of a much lower order. There was not one, other than a dog perhaps, that was not engaged in dragging, bearing, moving, or pushing every conceivable item.

Nor were the men and women spared such toil. Figures in saris carried water jars, sometimes two- and three-tiered, held high aloft on shoulder or head. They contrasted sharply with the men, whose bent frames bore heavy sacks of grain or bales of cotton. Without exception, the men were clad in *lungis* (wraparound skirts) or *dhotis*, both made from coarse homespun fabric that had probably been white in its natural state but that now was gray and grimy, the familiar color of relentless, unremitting labor.

We crossed the Jumna River, on the banks of which scores of women were washing clothes—if one could call beating, flailing, banging with sticks, stones, and any other implement that could guarantee the murder of the fabric, washing. Where did they find the strength to sustain such wrestling matches with their laundry?

The streets were thick with people. Could it be market day? No, my driver informed me, no day was market day. "Everyone works hard, madam. All busy people. Just same busy like me."

Ahead, a group of six young men, three on either side, carried on their shoulders a flat board strewn with flowers. As we neared them, I heard them singing. It was a strange plaintive chant, which, as we drew nearer, I realized was a dirge. They were young boys bearing the remains of a loved one. The body must have been that of a child. If not, it was of a very wasted creature.

The flower-covered cloth had barely shape or form. It seemed gossamer-light to carry.

I asked the driver where it was being taken, thinking of the funeral pyres about which I had read. He told me the river. Many believe that if the dead are cast into the river, the spirit is borne along with the current to another life. The general custom is cremation at the waters' edge, whereupon the ashes are cast into the river, but in the case of children, especially in the villages, different customs are sometimes observed. I recalled Marco's descriptions of the practices he had heard about when he was in India. In Bombay, he had said, the Parsis believed that the earth, air, fire, and water were sacred. God is in everything. They leave their dead in designated places, called towers of silence. Here, the naked bodies are left exposed to the elements. It is not a lengthy process, for the vultures quickly do their work. Only these birds of prey are thus, of all God's creatures, defiled.

Another is the belief in the holiness of the rivers. For some, there exists the conviction that the blessed waters of the great Ganges would heal them of all their ills. Little regard is given to the fact that animals defecate, clothes are laundered, and elephants wash in the river's murky depths. Many make pilgrimages for days and weeks in order to immerse themselves as part of a holy ritual. So convinced are they of its curative powers that they drink freely of the polluted waters. Urns, jars, phials, and all manner of containers are used to fill up and carry away the precious liquid for those who are too old or too sick to make the journey, so that they too might be helped and made well again. I wondered how many have died from cholera, malaria, typhoid, and all the other diseases that spring from such beliefs in this plagued and troubled country.

No matter where I looked I was in for a shock. I laughed with relief to see a boy of no more than seven years push and pull, beat and tug his donkey to move. As if to show the world who was boss, the sly-faced animal peremptorily sat down in the middle of the road, causing all the traffic to veer around or screech to a stop.

I marveled at the way a woman squatted in the roadway to breast-feed her infant without exposing one inch of bare flesh. Squatting seemed a common practice. At most street corners I saw little groups of men and women carrying on conversations or perhaps transacting business in a squatting position. It always seemed to be accomplished with grace.

"I take madam to see the Fort first?"

"No, thank you. The Taj Mahal first, please." I wanted to lose myself in its legendary beauty. I was anxious for a quick escape from much that I had seen to that which, from picture postcards, travel brochures, and films, embodied the very essence of romanticisim and architectural perfection.

"Madam knows the story of Taj Mahal?"

I knew a little, but always anxious to learn more, I assured my driver that I would be delighted to hear whatever he could tell me.

"Ah, madam, it is a beautiful love story. It was built by Shah Jahan in memory of his favorite wife, the lovely Arjumand. He called her Mumtaz Mahal, the 'Pearl of his palace.' They were lovely family. Fourteen children. Fine family, yes. Great ruler, Shah Jahan. He loved Mumtaz so much that when she died, his heart was broken. Quite broken, madam. For nearly twenty years many people built Taj. Maybe twenty thousand people. Yes, many people worked to build Taj. You will see, madam, finest marble, precious stones, and jewels. Shah Jahan wanted greatest monument in the world for his beautiful wife. He was a noble warrior. Many wars. He lived as an emperor with fine clothes. The finest. They say his robes were made of gold and he wore diamonds, pearls, and rubies in his turbans. He lost his greatest jewel when the lovely Mumtaz died. She was the song of his soul. Now from all over the world they come to see Taj Mahal. We are very proud of it. Yes, madam, from all over the world they come."

As he spoke, I busied myself loading my camera for slides and my Polaroid for instant pictures. Never having owned a camera in my life, I was still clumsy with the 35-millimeter one. Despite the practice of having used six rolls of film already, loading still gave me problems. The Polaroid was excellent, as I saw my mistakes straightaway and could make adjustments to rectify them. Had I not been thus occupied, I might well have spotted the dome and towers of the famed building from many a curve in the road. Only when the car came to an abrupt halt did I realize we had arrived.

We had stopped at the side of a massive red sandstone gateway. I could only glimpse the dark recess of the entrance. There were very few people about—a few Indian couples and a handful of children. I heard German spoken and saw two flaxen-haired young men in very brief shorts, loaded down with superior-look-

111

ing photographic equipment. Professionals on an assignment, I thought. I was the only single, white-skinned woman there, my skirt and blouse a clear indication that I was a Westerner and an invitation for the children to cluster around me.

I dispensed a few coins and left them to argue the toss. With feelings of mounting excitement, I made my way toward the colossal archway. The huge metal doors were studded with brass knobs. Festooning the curve of the great doorway in graceful Arabic script were the words *Al fajr* ("the dawn").

In a delirium of anticipation I hastened to pay for admission to see one of the reputed seven wonders of the world. A secret dream of mine come true.

India's architectural homage to one of the greatest love stories of all times.

I stepped through the darkened archway into the brilliant sunshine and was momentarily stunned by the incredible glistening magnificence ahead. Spread before me were two avenues of trees and flowerless beds, laid out with great precision. Each flanked a series of marble pools and fountains.

The eye was compelled to travel along this verdant approach as if by design, so as to accustom one's sight to the revelation of dazzling splendor that arose at the verge of the horizon. There, like a massive jeweled crown, resting on velvet tiers of marble and reposing in perfect harmony with nature, was the famed mausoleum.

A brilliant blue backdrop, the sky itself yielded to the sublime domination of the great milky white dome reigning in supreme majesty, casting its hypnotic spell on all who gazed upon it. The four spiraling minarets, one at each corner but quite separate from the principal sanctuary, thrust upward into the heavens as if to stand guard and protect its charge against the elements. The creamy richness of their smooth, phallic symmetry shocks the senses. They are of geometric perfection.

I stood quite still. The assault of such physical beauty was quite sensual in its effect upon me. The swelling breast of the dome, the slender nave of glistening water, the upright, pulsing minarets, made me reel. I felt heady. Dizzy. Soaring. It was a glorious moment, more like ten, during which I remained motionless, fumbling at last for a handkerchief. My face was wet with tears.

I used up a complete roll of 35-millimeter film and a full pack of Polaroid film. I did not realize at the time how lucky I was to have been among so few visitors. I asked one of the German boys to try and get a picture of me alone in front of the building. He did. Many of the instant photographs came out beautifully, showing a rare sight of a deserted Taj Mahal. I was quite thrilled.

Of all the millions of people who come from all over the world to visit this shrine, I had the greatest good fortune to have experienced this unforgettable sight in almost virtual solitude.

It was not yet nine o'clock on a cool hushed morning of an early April day.

I came away saddened by so much beauty. I felt drained in the way I am affected when I listen to great music. Feelings of elation experienced earlier now gave way to an infinite longing to have the world made more beautiful. Within those gardens such serenity and timelessness reposed. Without, such misery and suffering dwelt. The gross injustices of this world, the struggle to exist, the cruelties of man upon the innocent.

I paid scant heed on leaving the grounds to an air-conditioned bus that had just arrived and was about to disgorge its passengers. I noticed, however, the sign it bore: We March Now to Progress.

I decided to catch the early afternoon plane back to Delhi. It had been enough for one day, and I suddenly felt very tired. Was it only travel fatigue that now accounted for my heavy heart and sinking feelings? Marco had cautioned me to be prepared for grim sights and shocks. If village life was primitive, what would the overcrowded slums of Delhi be like? I had the feeling that nothing I had read or heard about India could really convey the stark realities of life as I would see it. The best thing I could do for myself in preparation for what might lie ahead would be a good night's rest. I was thankful I had reserved accommodations awaiting me.

The sudden stop of the car awoke me from a brief nap. The driver, all smiles, opened the door and beckoned me to enter an artifacts store.

"This is an ivory and marble factory. You will get excellent prices here, isn't it?"

"I am sorry, but I'm not interested in buying anything, thank you."

My refusal did not trouble him in the least, and he persisted, "Just to see, madam. Perhaps you may change your mind instantly."

I obliged out of sheer courtesy, but both he and the proprietor were visibly perplexed and offended that I refused wares that were in fact ridiculously cheap and superb in craftmanship. My trip was not to be one of gift buying. The taxi had been my indulgence. Presents for myself or others had no place in my strict budget. I left with no souvenirs and no regrets.

There was a slightly uncomfortable silence as we drove on. I broke it with a request. "I would like to stop at the post office, please." I wanted to buy a set of stamps for Marco. This was the one exception to the no-presents rule. I had made a point of this in every country I visited, and the stamps were the only gift I would give him. The time and trouble this often involved were far exceeded by the pleasure I knew this would bring him. The difficulties of just finding a post office or trying to make myself understood were offset by knowing exactly what to get and of course the satisfaction that the price was always right!

From bitter experience in Tehran's city post office I knew that the village one here would be far less an ordeal than waiting until I got to Delhi. It was not busy, and I was sure I would be out within five minutes. I had not banked on waiting fifteen minutes for a cow to amble in, stand around, and then slowly stalk out. No one said a word; no one shooed a sound; no one seemed to mind in the slightest.

I behaved in a like manner, having no other option. At last I approached the counter.

"I would like a complete set of your current stamps, please."

"Ah! You send letters to England, yes?"

"No. I just want one of every kind you have, please."

A puzzled look, a polite smile, a tilt of the head, and a long hesitation greeted my request.

"Ah, madam, that would be quite impossible."

"Why is it impossible?"

"I do not have them all."

"Very well. Then give me all you do have, please."

"Maybe it is too expensive?"

"No, it will be quite all right. May I have them now, please?"

A drawer was opened. He fumbled inside and carefully produced a selection of stamps, which he laid out one by one for my inspection. I never thought to give him the courtesy of examining them. He had laid them out with such precision, and here I was grabbing them up and hastily sticking them on a plain envelope I had with me for this very purpose. The clerk's puzzled look increased visibly. Nothing was said as he laboriously started to add up what I owed him. The transaction completed, I paid him, and as he gave me my change he informed me, "Maybe you see the man over there. He has more stamps than I do. Maybe complete set. Maybe different series."

Was I mad! Patience, for now came the tricky part. "Thank you, this is all right. Would you please cancel them?" I pushed the envelope, now completely covered with stamps, toward him across the open counter.

Dismay, calamity, and shock all registered upon his face. "Oh, no, I cannot do that."

"Why not?"

"It is not permitted."

"Then will you let me do it?"

"Oh, no. That would be quite against the regulations."

I could not possibly imagine what regulations prohibited someone from canceling their own stamps. Surely such a regulation could never have been invented?

It was evident that the poor man suspected a catch in all this that might somehow lead to his discredit. He shrank back as if to detach himself from all further involvment with me. With a jerk of his chin he indicated the clerk at another window a few feet away. "Ask him. He can give permission. Maybe he can do it." He clearly wanted to be rid of me.

I stepped across to "him" and with a slight economy of the truth I brightly said, "The man over there said you could cancel my stamps for me, please?"

"Which man? What stamps? Those stamps? No, I can't, but *he* can."

I shuttled back to the first man, determined to have done with this nonsense once and for all. I reached inside the window and grabbed the rubber stamp. Smiling broadly and working at lightning speed, I canceled every stamp myself, saying as I did so, "He says it's all right for me to cancel them here. There, it's done. Thank you very much."

Before the stunned fellow had time to collect his wits and tell me I couldn't do it, I had done it. With a cheerful "good day" tossed into the air, I exited with as much rapid grace as I could muster. I got back into the car and was quickly on my way to the airport and all that awaited me in Delhi.

At three o'clock in the afternoon, the sun was high and merciless at Palam Airport. I stepped out into the blazing heat and surveyed the scene, wondering what form of transport to take. The feverish activity I had noticed in the early hours of the morning seemed to have lessened in intensity, but the choices of locomotion had doubled. A whole fleet of buses awaited my patronage. So far, no language problems had inhibited my inquiries, so there was no good reason why I should not take a bus. On second thought, arriving at the Oberoi Intercontinental Hotel by bus and walking in with a backpack might not encourage an approving reception or honoring my reservation if I was regarded as a "freaky" lady. Perhaps, in this case, a taxi might be best.

The driver, all smiles, put my pack in the trunk, opened the door with a flourish, and invited me to step inside and be seated on the cloth-covered seat that barely hid the torn plastic upholstery. Bobbles, fringes, and all manner of adornments decorated the front and back windows.

With great bravado, he turned on the ignition key. He then turned a reassuring smile toward me when a rasping wheeze issued a stubborn denial to burst into life. With great concentration, a sideways tilt of the head, and a gesture I was fast becoming familiar with, he smiled again when a death rattlelike shudder passed through the vehicle at his second abortive attempt. We were certainly making progress.

At last, with the persistence of a bronchial coughing spasm, the vehicle's bowels seemed to be on the move, and with a great spurt forward, we set off.

The sudden jerk not only sent me pitching forward, but caused moderate pandemonium among the assortment of animals I had noticed on my earlier morning inspection of the airport vicinity. Cows, dogs, horses, goats, and donkeys scattered with confusion and squeals as we swerved in their midst, narrowly missing people and other forms of transport. My driver further alarmed me by taking his eyes off the scene to turn around, smile at me, and wave his hand in a gesture of great friendliness to indicate that all was perfectly fine. We ultimately settled down to a steady chug and soon the sights of New Delhi began to unfold before my devouring eyes.

Wide-open, broad streets, stately avenues, great lawns, and parks were all but deserted now in the hot afternoon sun. We drove down Kitchener Road and onto a gracious curving crescent, then turned onto Raj Path (King's Road) and drove toward a splendid arch, reminiscent of the Arc de Triomphe in Paris. My driver confirmed that this was the famous India Gate, and I envisioned those grand parades of former days, when elephants bearing princes in costly robes, would ride in pomp and splendor beneath elaborate canopies, and thousands of colorfully dressed, flag-waving citizens would cheer the spectacle, unmindful of the significance of the occasion.

I thought of the days of the famous British generals, the mighty monarchs whose very title, Defender of the Faith, Emperor of India, sounded all-powerful; and the viceroys, those governors, who administered, interpreted, and imperialistically laid down the law. Many of the streets bore English names, and the Victorian architecture of numerous fine buildings we passed amply attested to a long and industrious British rule. I basked in blissful ignorance and delight at my first glimpses of New Delhi.

We turned onto a broad avenue possessing the intriguing name Dr. Zakir Hussain, and arrived in grand style at the flag-bedecked entrance of the hotel. I settled the taxi fare and left the driver to yield the secrets of his trunk to the eager hands of porters anxious to assist guests with their luggage.

The lobby, with its cool marble, thick carpets, and glittering chandeliers, was as luxurious as I could have wished had I not vowed to be flexible in my standards when the occasion required. I glanced around; the usual little boutiques clustered around the entrance had attracted a sprinkling of tourists, judging by their Western dress and pale complexions.

My room was comfortable, clean, but not as luxurious as I had anticipated. The well-appointed marble bathroom, with its huge inviting tub, was, by contrast, sumptuous and promised joyous relief to my now-weary body aching with tiredness and longing to submit to a protracted warm soak.

My first night's sleep in India commenced at five o'clock on a sunny afternoon and on an empty stomach. I was far too tired to eat. I awoke some fifteen hours later. It had been a sleep a newborn baby might well have envied.

The notice stating accommodation rates affixed to the door reminded me the next morning that I should give some thought to the financial aspect of staying on here. I would rest up in a little luxury first, and meanwhile make inquiries as to what might be my less expensive alternatives. Now what to do about some breakfast?

I saw that my heating gadget would not work on the voltage. That ruled out making a hot drink of tea. Before leaving Tehran, I had stocked up on several little cartons of pasteurized cheese (the individual foil-wrapped kind) and some flat crisp breads. I had my Sego Bars and my packets of tea and instant dried milk, but how could I make tea? Simple.

From room service I ordered two hard-boiled eggs, an apple, an orange, and two pitchers of hot water. "Yes, that's right, two large pots of boiling—must be boiling—water, please."

This was the kind of breakfast I ordered in my room every time I stayed in a "proper" hotel or a place where my heating unit would not work. Two eggs, my crisp bread, and sometimes cheese made a protein-rich and quite satisfying meal that sustained me well into the day. My own tea bags popped into pitchers of hot water provided me with something to drink. (I was sure that with an order of other things, there would be no charge for the hot water.) The thought that fresh milk might not be pasteurized, made the use of my dried milk all the more desirable, and my fruit was thoroughly washed against any possible contamination under the special faucet in the bathroom labeled "for drinking only." The surplus hot water gave me extra tea that, when cooled, went into my flat-sided camper's canteen and provided me with a drink on a hot, thirst-provoking day. The fruit and a Sego Bar offered an admirable lunch, and best of all, I was spared the dilemma of choosing where to eat. No trudging around looking and wondering if an expensive restaurant might be a "safer" one, or having to opt for a simpler establishment where the standard of cleanliness would be dubious but the economy certain. No getting hungrier, hotter, and crankier by the minute; only a glorious sense of freedom from the usual concept of meals when traveling. I could stop to eat whenever and wherever it suited me. There was also the added attraction that I was losing weight in following such a diet.

In my room, it was simple to assemble my day's "meals." Later, I carefully concealed all evidence of my preparations. My tin mug, the packets of food, and all my little utensils were wrapped in a towel and put in my drawer, where I hoped no chambermaid's wondering eyes would see them. After all, wasn't I staying at the poshest hotel in town?

While waiting for room service to bring up my "banquet," I consulted the New Delhi telephone directory. I noted down the telephone numbers of the Visitors' Information Bureau and the American Express office. In a casual, almost negative way I also looked for the name of someone I had met in the United States three years before.

Komal Singh was her name, and she was as lovely to look at as she was charming to know. She was an Indian girl, and had told me that her family and her home were in New Delhi. Our acquaintance had been brief, but had blossomed in a short time as to have become meaningful.

We had met on a Greyhound bus during a trip I was making to visit my sons, at that time students in college.

We were both traveling to the West Coast and had decided we would make a side trip to see the Grand Canyon. We had been the only two passengers to abandon the bus at the point at which the decision to make the detour was possible. We enjoyed each other's company as much for being two alien souls as for the variety of interests we had in common. Komal's modesty, the refinements of her speech, and the simple sincerity of her outlook were so refreshing in one so young that she quite captivated me from the first. She was young enough to be my daughter but wise enough to be my teacher. She had been dressed in jeans and a T-shirt, and until she told me that she had studied in England, I had assumed she was a college student in the States. She had just visited her sister in Washington, D. C., and was now on her way to stay with friends in California.

On parting, we had exchanged addresses and later occasional greetings. As is wont to happen when vast distances rule out all hope of meeting again, the correspondence, if such it could be called, died a natural death.

I did not hold out much hope of finding her in the telephone book. She might no longer be living in Delhi. She might not be living any longer in India, for that matter.

The telephone book revealed page after page of "Singh." It was like a "Smith" or a "Brown." I had just about given up when I spotted the address I had kept all these years. With excitement I called the number. A voice in dialect answered. It was not Komal. A pause ensued and then in precise English I found myself talking to Mrs. Singh, Komal's mother, who quickly put her daughter on the phone. She eagerly bombarded me with questions and reminiscences. After a few moments of lively talk, she said, "Look, I'm not working today and can use my father's car. I will be right over to fetch you." What a lovely welcome. I felt most fortunate that our slight friendship had been renewed with such warmth.

There was no awkwardness in our reunion. I was joyously embraced. With her arm about my shoulder she led me toward a little British Morris Minor car that belied its name and gave us major Morris service. Komal whizzed me around the sights of New Delhi well into the afternoon. Apart from a brief pause for a cold drink (bottled and no ice for me), our excursion was non-stop.

First, the Diplomatic Enclave, as it is called, which houses all the government offices. Then the Secretariat, the Stadium, Parliament House, and the Presidential Palace, all very fine and impressive buildings set in beautifully laid-out gardens. We passed many shaded lawns, parks, and treelined courtyards; wide, wide avenues but very few people. Those I saw walked sedately under the shade of large black umbrellas.

Komal explained, "You will not see many people walking about in this part of the city. The distances are too great and the heat is too much for them. Most, of course, are at lunch right now. In other parts of the city you will see a lot more activity. There is an excellent government-sponsored tour you must take whenever you are ready to sightsee on your own. Now let us go home —my mother is expecting us for tea."

It was all very pleasant indeed and not at all as I had imagined. Of course, I told myself, things must be vastly changed since the days when Marco was here. Obviously over the years progress and improvements must have taken place. He was outdated; conditions were much better today.

We turned off the main road and came to a halt in front of a neat row of Victorian terrace houses. Much of all I had seen reminded me of the days of British rule. I felt now that I could have been standing in a London mews, everything seemed so familiar. Komal preceded me up a flight of stone steps. The door was painted a bright blue and bore a heavy brass knocker, with which Komal rapped smartly against the wood. It was opened by an elderly woman wearing a white cotton sari. Her gray hair was smooth and braided and hung halfway down her back. It was Komal's *ayah* (nurse) from infancy. Komal spoke to her in dialect, to which the woman nodded and disappeared as we entered.

The open door led straight into the living room. The wooden floor was covered by a large Indian carpet in muted shades that blended unobtrusively with the different styles of furniture that stood upon it. It was an odd assemblage. Some pieces looked as if they had been inherited antiques. Others were modern in style. Common to all were the unifying cushions that were scattered about in an attempt to harmoniously combine the total effect.

Several cloth hangings and oil paintings graced the walls, which were distempered in a soft grayish green shade. Other than a portrait of a young girl in Eastern dress, the paintings were of country or mountain scenes, which imparted a feeling of peace and tranquillity to the room.

An archway led to a narrow corridor, of which little was visible, because of the draped curtains stretched across. Komal pointed to a fabric-upholstered sofa and motioned me to sit down, crossing as she did so to switch on two lamps that rested on tables at either side of the couch.

Although it was only four o'clock in the afternoon, the room was quite dark due to the heavy curtains that partially shielded the two windows along the street side of the house.

Mrs. Singh entered the room. She was a charming, cultured woman of serene composure and refined features. She smiled warmly as she extended a cool limp hand in greeting.

Almost immediately a bearer appeared with a tray of tea and an assortment of little sweetmeats. Some were made from finely ground rice and covered with a gooey syrup. Others looked like coconut macaroons. There were fried crispy puffs, rather hot and

121

peppery and tasting of nutmeg. All were scrumptious confections, and with several cups of tea to wash them down, I felt replete and several thousand calories fatter.

We exchanged polite talk at first. Mrs. Singh wanted to know all about my husband and sons. I felt it prudent not to dwell on the "liberated" aspect of my absence from home. I had read of the deferential role of women in marriages that were often arranged matches, and I had no desire at this point to get into a discussion of cultural or traditional differences in outlook.

Komal spoke rapidly to her mother in dialect, doubtless Punjabi, as the name Singh implied and from the way Komal was dressed. Whereas Mrs. Singh wore a lemon-colored sari, Komal's tunic and loose pajamalike trousers were in the traditional Punjabi style.

That the conversation concerned me was obvious. After a few seconds of discussion I became enlightened. It seemed that Komal had mentioned my remark about finding less expensive accommodations. They had a friend whose daughter was currently away in Chandigarh, and they felt sure I would be welcome to stay there. Anxious not to abuse this extraordinary piece of luck, I quickly asked that I be regarded as a paying guest. They assured me this would be arranged.

Moving to the residence of Mr. Surgit Singh (no relation to Komal and her mother) was quite a change from the chandeliered, marble luxury of the hotel. An old stone house, much like an English country home, it was large, airy, and had plenty of bathrooms—doubtless one reason I saw so remarkably little of those who lived there. Though Mr. Singh was not a relative, my welcome was as one of the family.

The nicest aspect of all was being among Indians in their own home. On the few occasions when I was able to be present at a family gathering, I witnessed the extraordinary phenomenon of parental authority that ruled in this household and that perhaps was common to most families.

Mr. Singh's thirty-year-old son deferred to his father in every matter. It might have been a small expenditure of a personal nature or one affecting the administration of the family business. On these occasions Mr. Singh junior paid no attention whatsoever to his wife, nor did he caress or play with his children in his father's presence. His father made all the decisions concerning the running of the house, and even as to where his grandchildren would attend school.

There seemed to be no resentment whatsoever. On the contrary, an atmosphere of calm acceptance pervaded the house. Everyone went quietly about his or her occupation. All seemed to have their own specific duties.

There were evenings, however, when a mood of conviviality encouraged the liveliest of conversations. These were the times when I was drawn into the discussions, and a great hunger for knowledge of the ways of the Western world was displayed.

Food, religion, and politics were always favorite topics. Religion especially was one subject that illustrated the Indians' enormous capacity for respect and tolerance.

Eating, fasting, and dieting were regarded as the personal observance of one's belief and quite the normal way to live. No one thought anything strange at all about my daily food preparations. I maintained my hard-boiled eggs and tea practice each morning, and it was accepted without curiosity or even much interest. I learned that in some religions the carrying of one's own utensils is a common habit, and only those of the same religion are permitted to touch the food or prepare the meals. This was very comforting when I set off for the day with my camper's spoon, knife, fork, and provisions. That I took with me my own food, canteen, and mug seemed to incur great respect. Perhaps they assumed that I too was observing some personal religious adherence to diet. I did not feel it necessary to enlighten anyone that this was in the interests of economy and weight loss. No one asked; no one wanted to know. I felt most comfortable and happy to be in so tolerant an atmosphere.

It was here that I became aware of the overwhelming complexities of this multireligious, multicaste, multilingual nation. The confusion of conflicting social customs, mores, and superstitions and the complicated characteristics of the Indian outlook were a way of life that surely bore no comparison to any other nation on this earth. The concept of *dharma* (duty) was predominant. It was unchangeable. It was unchallengeable. It influenced one's entire attitude and the acceptance of one's station in life.

I awoke that first morning to find an envelope slipped beneath my door. It was from Komal and contained a hand-drawn map of the main streets of the city center and a note telling me that she had arranged to have a ticket waiting for me at the Government of India Tourist Office. The tour would commence at 1:30 P.M. and I was warned that I must *only* take a taxi there or I would get hopelessly lost. With four hours to find my way, I disregarded her advice. I relished the idea of walking until fatigue set in and then taking a bus. Lack of stamina eventually prompted me to look for a bus stop. A group of people standing and squatting suggested they were also waiting for such transport.

I made my way toward them, conscious of the difference in dress and hoping someone would speak English.

All of them spoke English. At least it *seemed* that all of them spoke English, for a chorus of voices assured me that this was the right stop for the right bus. I don't know how on earth I ever managed to get on it, but I credited it to being white-skinned, Western-dressed, and rather good at mountaineering!

It was an experience not to be missed if not to be repeated. People hung onto the steps, hung onto the uprights of the windows (there were no window panes), hung onto the straps, and hung onto each other. Small children and parcels, as if no distinction existed between them, were passed unceremoniously in and out of the windows. Willing hands assisted in these operations, as if all were members of one family. No one turned a hair.

I asked for Connaught Place and everyone assented. It seemed that all buses went there. The Valhalla and Mecca of New Delhi transport. It had to be the *in* place. The noise of the passengers, together with the groaning and straining of a bus in childbirth every time the gears were changed, all but drowned the valiant attempts of the conductor to enlighten us as to the various stops. I hadn't the remotest idea of the direction in which we were traveling, for all I could see were stomachs, shoulders, or heads that pressed in upon me on all sides. I was jammed as tight as a sardine in a can, and the odor was not altogether as savory.

I began to itch, but I couldn't scratch. I was aware only of a forward or backward movement as I swayed with a mass of shapes. No one seemed to give way an inch until, miraculously, the rocking stopped with a sudden jerk as the bus ground to a halt and belched out the passengers. I found myself standing in Connaught Place with my fare still clutched in my hand.

The area was huge, with a parklike center in its midst. Unlike the deserted air of the parts of New Delhi I had previously seen, here it teemed and throbbed with the feverish pulse of commerce and life of the street.

Small stores, banks, American Express, and other international offices. Insurance companies, restaurants, hotels, snack bars, and dozens of carts on huge wheels, selling an infinite variety of things to eat and drink for the brave of heart and strong of stomach.

Other than a conglomeration of buses, hundreds of bicycles dominated the scene. I had never seen so many. A close runner-up were the scooters. These were "naturally air-conditioned" three-wheel motorcycles, and they bore the exalted rank of "taxi." They were very popular and a great choice of locomotion if one was impervious to dust in one's hair, eyes, and clothes. Additional choices were the horse-drawn carriages or the carriages harnessed to bicycles. These sported collapsible hoods. Looking at the emaciated horses and the wobbly wheels, I wondered which would collapse first. I was not inspired with confidence in the reliability of any of these forms of transport, and hoped I would not have to entrust my safe passage to them.

Oversized red letter boxes struck a familiar note, just like the English ones, with their wide black mouths and large round bodies, ready and waiting to receive the constant stream of mail that poured in unremittingly.

There was nothing familiar or nostalgic about the young boys who squatted against the red betel-stained walls, offering for sale packets of nuts or bundles of scrubbed vegetables.

I picked my way gingerly over broken concrete slabs and refuse-piled gutters to pause and watch a shoemaker sitting on his little stool, patching and hammering footware. His tools on the ground beside him, his hand darted back and forth to extract from his mouth a nail or two as often as was needed.

A woman lay full-length on the sidewalk against the wall of an archway. Was she sleeping? Was she dying? Marco had told me, "They just lie down in the streets and die like flies." Why didn't someone go to her and see? Why didn't someone ask? Help? Should I do something? What?

I walked on. Beggars and cripples seemed to be everywhere. Their expressions were awful. The eyes held despair, or was it madness? I shuddered. I didn't want to know.

A bundle of dirty rags crawled by. I couldn't distinguish any limbs in it at all. I hurried my pace and forced myself to look across at the park. The green foliage offered a temporary escape from my chaotic thoughts. Get with the people, I had said to myself. I didn't think it could be like this. Lice is probably all you'll get, my girl; lice or disease. You'd just better snap out of it and get to that tourist office. Go on your sightseeing trip and leave it at that.

In my distress, I had walked quite some distance and felt sure I must have passed the place, so I turned and walked back. I still couldn't find it, and time was speeding by. I walked in the opposite direction again. I had no number to go by, and Connaught Place was a huge area. I asked for help and could not believe that no one seemed to know where their own Government Tourist Office was. Everyone disagreed. One told me this way, another said that way, and I soon had a crowd of well-meaning people around me, all giving opinions on everything except how to find where I wanted to go.

"You are from London, yes?" "You like Delhi?" "I have a cousin in Notting Hill. You maybe know him—his name is Ramjan?"

I simply raced off in the middle of their remarks. It was nearly time for the tour to start, and Komal's prophetic words had come true. I was lost. Hot, perspiring, and in a shattered state of nerves, I spotted a few people entering a bus that looked less dilapidated than most. That must be it. I flew in front of it and asked the driver if this was the tour bus and where the tour office was. He said it was and pointed behind him to a shop that bore no name on its window. I must have passed the place twice. I sped inside, gasped out my name, and asked if there was a ticket awaiting me and how much I owed.

"Yes, here is your ticket. Everything is in order; there is nothing to pay. All is settled. If you will please be getting seated, the bus is going on the instant."

I flopped down into a window seat. The bus was half empty and, as best I could judge, occupied only by Indians. The different dialects and their way of dress seemed to indicate that they had come from different regions of the country. One young Indian girl, in her teens I imagined, was actually wearing blue jeans with the incongruous combination of the traditional sari's miniblouse.

I mopped my wet forehead and crimson face, took a long drink of tea from my canteen, and closed my eyes in momentary relief. Now I could relax and enjoy the anticipation of a pleasant afternoon of sightseeing in Old Delhi. It was a part of the city some distance from here and much removed perhaps from some of the upsetting things I had just seen.

The progress of traffic was sheer fascination. How anyone got anywhere was a mystery that only a lengthy passage of time might unravel! Buses were no match for the odd cow that strayed across its path. The bullock-drawn carts piled high with sacks encouraged the taxis to weave in and out like the shuttle of a loom. Everywhere I looked, people were carrying something. Hand-pulled carts were laden with crates, boxes, furniture, vegetables, even a piano. Perched on heads were pots, baskets, and, heavens, even a bed. Everything was carried on the head. Some feats. Some heads.

Most of the stops we made revealed many splendid sights: the Red Fort, with its great walls and historic associations; temples, tombs, domes, minarets, spires, and the tranquil Raj Ghat gardens, where Mahatma Gandhi had been cremated.

We now approached the ancient Kashmir Gate and came to a stop at Jama Masjid, the largest mosque in India.

If earlier I had thought Connaught Place had worn an impoverished air, it was prosperous and flourishing by comparison to the section we were now in. If I had thought I had seen crowds of people before, they were casual throngs compared to the seething mass I now looked at from the window of the bus.

Everyone alighted, and I followed to climb the innumerable steps. This was the highlight of the tour. To see the great mosque was an attraction for those who lived in different parts of the country as well as for those who were visiting it. There must have been a hundred steps; I was only conscious of the massive structure above and had lost count. For no accountable reason, I stopped in my ascent, turned around, and looked down. As far as my eye could see and from a vantage point of some forty or so feet high, I encountered a sight that filled me with incredulity.

A great human tide had flooded the section. A lavalike living flow, slowly, inexorably, ponderously crawling along in its precarious pursuit of life.

An unrecognizable urge swept over me, and I found myself descending the steps, all sightseeing forgotten. There was something here I had to know. I wanted to know. A masochistic impulse to mingle with the crowds might provide me with answers to the unformed questions and to the vague uneasy feelings with which I had been troubled all day.

They flocked the sidewalks; they lined the gutters; they lay prone in the square and all over the great steps of the mosque. It was as if they had been scattered like rice from a burst sack. Why were they all concentrated here? Was it the dominating presence of the mosque? Was it the center of this section? Or was the whole area, all of the section? I felt I was standing in the very heart of India.

This was what Marco must have meant when he said "They just lie down in the streets and die like flies." *This* was the grim and sordid reality of this country. This was Old Delhi. It was a living death.

The profusion of beggars. The deformed bodies. A stump of an arm, or a leg wrapped in or exposed from filthy bandages. Some with limbs covered with weeping sores. Some with features swollen and purple and faces mottled from disease.

The emaciated animals. The rabid-looking dogs. The becrutched cripples. The young girls, their gray skin and hollow cheeks those of old women. And the old women, indifferent now to modesty, their bodies broken from childbearing, their loose scraggy breasts swaying from careless folds of dirty, rotted rags. The *sadhu* (holy man), stark naked, with eyes all but covered by the mop of hair falling around the face, in clumps and knots.

The stench of urine, which received constant renewal. The litter, the foul decay of garbage. The piles of refuse to which children added their fecal contributions. Oh, the children. Worst of all, the children.

Tumbling, streaming from every doorway, on every step, in every alley, their matchstick-thin limbs supporting great distended bellies. The eight- or nine-year-old, carrying on its hip a one-year-old, one arm around the infant, the other permanently outstretched. The hopeful, waiting, cupped palm for the carelessly tossed coin. The tangled hair, the torn rags, the bare, scabby feet, the sore-ringed mouth. The nose, from which the running snot escapes the darting tongue and sniffled gulp. And the great, black, kohl-ringed eyes.

Oh, India. India. What is to become of you? Who is there to help you? Who is there who knows? Who is there who cares?

My God, my God. India does not need nuclear weapons.

She needs food.
India's enemy is no one foe.
It is famine.
I felt sick with anger. An overwhelming rage took hold of me. I wanted to scream and shout and shake all the fat and rich, the well-fed, the overfed. The powers, presidents, premiers, and principals. I wanted—I wanted—I did not know *what* I wanted, except relief from my feelings of helplessness and inadequacy in the face of this vile degradation of the human body. And what of the spirit?

Here there was no spirit. Here there was no soul. Here were just the dregs of humanity, huddled together, waiting to die. There was a terrible passivity about it. They were resigned. They had accepted their fate. It was their destiny.

I knew now why I had been compelled to walk among them. I had not wanted to believe such wretchedness existed. I had to come to terms with my own revulsion, which had been growing inside me and which I had tried to push away. At a distance, or behind glass walls, the senses remain inviolate, detached. But here on the streets, among these pitiful remnants of humanity, I could not escape the loathsome reality. Nor did I wish to.

When in a lifetime is one *forced* to think about and see, but *really see,* how the "other half lives"? I was sick at heart, for I knew that only death could be their hope in life. Death would be a blessed relief from an existence that had been of no meaning. Death was welcomed, for it promised another life in which pain and suffering had no part.

Is this how you meant it to be, God?
I turned back to the waiting coach. A pregnant woman, her baby swaddled on her back and a toddler at her skirt, was poking through a pile of refuse upon which a dog had urinated. She offered the older child some vile scrap she had unearthed. I thought I would vomit.

A beggar stopped a few paces in front of me to scratch his genitals; then, with a rasping gurgle, he expectorated a volume of sputum right across my path. I flinched and frantically turned in another direction.

Oh, horror. Horror. No more now, no more. Get back to the bus. Why are you torturing yourself? It is too vast for you to comprehend. You can do nothing. Nothing.

I hastened my pace and got out my camera. Who will believe me? I must take a few photographs. I have to make people care. It was not a wise decision. Children swarmed around me. I walked on. They followed. I felt like the Pied Piper of Hamelin. If only I could lead them through some magic door to Utopia, where they would never go hungry again. Inspiration flashed upon me. Never mind my 35-millimeter camera. If I used the Polaroid I could give them instant photographs; they would surely like that. I whipped out my SX-70 Land camera and began to shoot away.

Eyes widened with suspicion at first. Curiosity followed, and then utter joy. As the pictures took shape and color, they jumped and squealed with pleasure, then began fighting, snatching, and arguing as to who should have what. Several more children, with lightning speed, came from nowhere and joined an ever-widening circle. I had used two packs of film already. With only ten to a pack and Polaroid film madly expensive when bought abroad, I hesitated to use more. How could I have done? With so many anxious eyes upon me and wasted little fingers tugging at me, I tossed prudence aside and took a picture of each and every one of them.

What price a child's happiness? Joy at a dollar apiece? Humility engulfed me. I felt ashamed of my earlier hesitation to bring a speck of pleasure into their impoverished world.

The hot plastic seat of the bus was welcome. The heat out there had been trying, the smells nauseating. All that I had seen had a cumulative effect that was now making me feel quite physically ill. There was a sick, tight knot in the pit of my stomach. My head ached; my throat felt dry. The intensity of my feelings had exhausted me, as if I had run a mile. I took a drink from my canteen. The tepid, now-flat tea tasted of the plastic casing, but it was welcome. I leaned my head against the side of the window, thought of lice, and straightened myself up again, but closed my eyes.

As soon as the bus left Old Delhi behind, I began to feel better. Out of sight, out of mind? Hardly. What I had seen had been overwhelming in its social implication, but the way I had reacted to it was of a deeply personal nature. The whole was now taking shape in my mind as an irreconcilable and irrevocable fact. It was there. It existed. It could not be blotted out. It had to be accepted, but an attempt had to be made to put everything into proper perspective.

How, I thought, does one put cancer into perspective?

My eyes remained closed for the whole of the return journey. My feelings of anger gradually dissipated. I reflected quietly and, I hoped, more rationally. It was no good ranting and raving. What could be done? Even the surgeon's knife cannot always cut out the disease. The country's ailments were of such complexity, how could I possibly hope to understand? Religion and superstition played as great a part as illiteracy and poverty. And what of the entire caste system? As for help from outside? When had *I* ever been confronted with the needs of India?

Why were such things so rarely, if ever, seen on our television at home? Must we always be fed entertainment? Are we meant to go through life ignorant of—and indifferent to—the sufferings of others? Is the pursuit of pleasure the only relief from boredom we care to know? What an impoverished world we inhabit if financial gain is the only reward we seek for the application of our efforts.

Is there no social conscience? If we do not know, who then shoulders the responsibility of enlightening us? The media?

Could not our newspapers and magazines print a little less scandal and a lot more humanity? If ratings were less important than reason, might not idealism transcend avarice? Seeing the world's pain might help lessen it.

Is it not even worth a try?

Is it such a huge sacrifice for each one of us to assume the tiniest fraction of responsibility for one of God's creatures? To give a dollar, one can of food, one pair of shoes? A skirt, a shirt, a care. Would there not be a mighty collection of cans and shoes and cares with which to touch another's life? The possibilities are without limit. It is the desire that is lacking.

And in the final analysis, when words are but dreams (and, yes, I dream), if nothing solved, and nothing helped, and it did not even comfort—

We tried. At least we tried.

Dark clouds of gloom rolled over me. What was the use? What did it all mean? Where was the sense in it? What was the answer? *Where was God?*

I went straight back to my room and lay down on the bed. I

felt utterly depressed and had no heart for anything. An infinite sadness possessed me, and I stared with vacant eyes at the ceiling till darkness crept over the windowsill. My thoughts, like falling leaves caught in a gale, twirled in dervishlike frenzy to rob me of sleep.

The village doctor had said that Mrs. Gandhi's way was the only way, that she was right in advocating obligatory vasectomy, which some called inhuman. With a yearly increase of 13 million mouths to feed, who is qualified to judge? The victims or the victimized?

Ah, Mrs. Gandhi. If only I could meet her and ask her some of my questions. One who influenced the lives of 600 million people must surely have some of the answers?

Perhaps I could meet her. How? When? Why not?

Mrs. Singh invited me to dinner. It was a Saturday evening, and there were to be other guests. It may have been a dinner party planned long before I arrived, but the interest shown by Komal as to what I was going to wear made me wonder if I was the guest of honor. I was not to know and did not ask. I was most flattered to have been invited.

Glad to have brought several stateside gifts with me, I chose for Komal and Mrs. Singh pantyhose, some nylon lingerie, and a few cosmetics. For Mr. Singh, whom I had not yet met, I had a Parker pen-and-pencil set. I also purchased a bouquet of fresh tightly curled deep-red roses for Mrs. Singh.

I arrived a little early and was introduced to the only person in the room, retired Air Marshal Singh, Komal's father (good heavens, why hadn't she told me?). He was tall, handsome, very distinguished-looking, and every inch a military man. He was a Sikh—a race famed as warriors. His proud and dignified bearing was enhanced by a fine moustache and a silky gray beard, the length of which was rolled around a fine elastic band that appeared to vanish into his turban. This was a lovely shade of turquoise blue and wrapped with such precision around his head that it looked as if it had been molded from one piece. His voice was soft and mellifluous, and his eyes held a twinkle. He was utterly charming. I was totally smitten.

Other guests arrived: Mr. Rajiv Gulati, an economist, and his wife, Alka, a doctor in hospital service; Mr. Hari Khanna, a contributing editor at the daily newspaper, and his lovely young wife, Uma; a former minister of agriculture and his wife, the founder and principal of a women's college; Mr. Ramesh Kapoor, a university professor, sad, scholarly, and widowered. Not for long, I thought, as I was introduced finally to Mrs. Tamri Mehta, so young and also bereaved.

The conversation was informative, touching upon India's economic prospects, but serious issues were soon forgotten and much laughter ensued when we spoke about the universal problems of tourists away from home.

I desperately wanted to comment on some of the sights I had seen, but felt that my intense feelings might betray me and cause possible offense. I decided, however, to ask what my chances might be of meeting Mrs. Gandhi. There was a sudden stop in the conversation, and I felt I had made a serious *faux pas*. I could have died.

One pair of raised male eyebrows indicated that the request was a little unusual. One guest carefully expressed misgivings that I would be successful.

Mr. Khanna launched into a lengthy speech about freedom of the press that seemed totally irrelevant, and Mr. Kapoor thought it was a highly dubious, if not quite forlorn, hope. None of the women spoke except Mrs. Mehta. Her late husband had been employed in government service, and she was a staunch admirer of Mrs. Gandhi. She had no hesitation in encouraging me. "If Mrs. Gandhi is at her residence, she could be receiving tomorrow."

No further information was proferred, and I decided against asking for more advice. I knew I could easily ask anyone the address of Mrs. Gandhi's residence; the rest would be up to me, and I would have to think it over.

The announcement that dinner was to be served made a timely break in all further speculations and restored the conversation to its former convivial nature. With alacrity the guests made their way to the buffet table. My mouth was already collecting saliva in anticipation. I had not had a decent hot meal for weeks.

What a gastronomical experience awaited me. Hitherto, all I had ever known about Indian food had been a not very hot or authentic curry, cautiously sampled in some London restaurant on a date with a young man when I was still in my teens.

Spread before me was an array of such tempting-looking dishes that any ladylike reserve was cast to the winds, and I helped myself liberally. I took a mouthful of curry. The very flames of hell could not have seared my mouth more. *It was hot.* I tried bravely to hide my violent reaction, but only those deprived of sight could have failed to witness my distress.

My eyes watered, my nose dripped, my head steamed!

I gurgled; I coughed; I gasped; I damn near choked. I blindly reached out for something, anything, to drink. Gone were my resolutions not to touch ice or drink water. Diarrhea, typhoid, and malaria were not given as much as a fleeting thought. I accepted whatever was put into my hand and swallowed it blindly. I couldn't see; my eyes were streaming. The drink was sickly sweet and bore no resemblance to the fruit when I was offered a second orange Fanta soda to drink. It didn't matter; I downed another one.

When I had recovered, to the amusement of everyone, myself included, I approached the other dishes with much more respect, omitting the curried ones altogether.

I carefully sampled the chicken *tandoori.* This was a Punjabi favorite, baked in a clay oven and covered with a rich sauce. It was delicious. *Keema nan* was a crusty bread stuffed with ground lamb and chopped onions. *Pilau,* rice colored with saffron and to which peas had been added, joined forces on my plate with an assortment of cooked vegetables. And, of course, *chapati,* a flat unleavened bread with which I scooped up *dhal,* a dish made from lentils and split peas.

Desserts were a dream for a skinny person, a nightmare of indecision for an overweight one. I looked and asked and contented myself with just a tiny nibble of everything.

*Jalebi*s were pretzel-like sweetmeats soaked in a gooey syrup. There were little rice puddings, quite transformed with raisins, almonds, and pistachio. *Gulab jaman* was the doughnut I had tasted when I came for tea, but this time it was flavored with rose water and quite different. And then—ah!—*burfi,* a chewy fudge-like concoction, over which I weakened and had seconds.

If any still felt hungry, though it must surely be to refresh the palate rather than to satisfy the appetite, a huge platter of fresh fruit was brought to the table—mangos, pears, oranges, guavas, bananas, and pomegranates. It was a splendid and sumptuous meal.

Tea and conversation followed with no less distinction; even my Polaroid enjoyed a modest success. I took, and gave, photographs to all the guests, saving only one or two for myself.

The evening terminated promptly at ten-thirty. It almost seemed as if it had been predetermined, for everyone rose as if by one accord.

The day starts early for most Indian families. Working hours can be as many as fourteen a day, seven days a week.

I was glad to get to bed, for I had made up my mind that I would be up at the crack of dawn to find my way to the residence of Mrs. Gandhi.

Would she see me? Was it possible? I could only try.

Indira Gandhi was a powerful figure. She was a woman I desperately wanted to meet. I cautioned myself not to expect too much. Not to hope too strongly. Not to be too optimistic. I wanted to prepare myself for a refusal.

After all, I thought, you've got some cool nerve. What makes you think that the prime minister of India, the leader of 600 million people and a world figure, is just going to receive you, Sabina Shalom, a housewife from Miami Beach?

Walking down Safdar Jang Road at six-thirty on Sunday morning, I could feel the special stillness of the hour. I heard the birds celebrate a new day in the jacaranda trees and listened attentively to their song.

The foliage was cool and moist and fresh. The fragrance of jasmine pervaded my senses and heightened my nervous anticipation. The excitement I felt was tinged with apprehension.

Several people approached a wide-open gateway. A guard standing on duty confirmed my impression that this must be Mrs. Gandhi's house. I hastened my pace to join those who were entering the grounds. The guard made no attempt to stop or question anyone. I passed through and freely mingled with the rest as they made their way toward the house.

The garden was large and neat, but I imagined a greater expanse behind the low-lying construction in white stucco that faced me as I walked up the gravel drive. The front porch was supported by four columns and graced by flowering potted shrubs on either side of the main entrance. Architecturally, the residence had no special features and was less impressive than I had imagined it would be.

I followed those preceding me toward a large tent erected on the right-hand side of the lawn and facing the front of the house. Only three sides were enclosed so as to permit an L-shaped arrangement of chairs, of which there were about eighty. Less than half were occupied, and all by Indians.

I sat down on the first chair I came to, feeling very self-conscious. All the women wore saris, part of which (the *paloo*) covered their heads as a mark of respect for the woman they were about to see. Robed as they were from head to toe, I looked all the more conspicuous with my knees sticking out from the hem of my skirt, and my long-sleeved blouse a clear indication of my European background.

There were more men than women, and none of them wore ties or jackets, dressed for the most part in *kurtas* (rajah jackets, high at the throat and tunic-length), worn over tight trousers—jodhpurs. The rest wore simple shirts and slacks. Such informality surprised me, as I presumed their presence was one of a formal mission.

I spoke to no one, and indeed there was little conversation among those about me. Perhaps they, like me, were rehearsing in their minds the requests, petitions, or grievances that had brought them here.

I had neither a request nor a petition, just an overwhelming desire to meet one of the great women of this world. India's evolution had always held a tremendous interest for me. It had gained its independence from Great Britain soon after the war, at the time when I was deeply involved with refugees flocking to the newly born state of Israel. Both countries were trying to free themselves from the stranglehold of British imperialism.

My scant knowledge had been improved by the stories Marco had recounted of the days when, as an army major, he had served in India at that very time. The mob riots, the looting, and the bloody massacre between Muslim and Hindu were the tragic events that precipitated the transfer of power from British to Indian hands.

Indira Gandhi had witnessed the unfolding of her country's destiny at the side of her illustrious father, Jawaharlal Nehru, the prime minister of the new nation. Indira Priyadarshini ("Dear to

Behold") had been born and nurtured in a political milieu. From the earliest days of her childhood it was clear that she was destined for high office.

In the palatial home of her grandfather Motilal Nehru, all of India's powerful figures gathered. Mahatma Gandhi, although not related, was like an uncle to her. He, together with Indira's father and grandfather, formed the foundation of the noncooperation movement. Peaceful resistance. In her grandfather's home, the Constitution of India was drawn up. The Nehru report was drafted and presented to the British government demanding an end to British rule and the granting of dominion status to India.

From Mahatma Gandhi, Indira learned of the ease with which one can dispense with luxury and accept a simple and austere life. As a child, sitting in the lap of her grandfather, she listened to the words of Einstein, Romain Rolland, Ernst Toller, and the wise Sir Rabindranath Tagore, poet, playwright, and winner of the Nobel Prize for literature.

If, as a child, she did not comprehend the nature of their contribution to world thought, she sensed the true importance of their philosophies. The little girl became committed to the service of her country; her thirteenth birthday was marked by a card from her father, then in a British jail for the fifth time, that said, "Fear is a bad thing and unworthy of you. Be brave and all the rest will follow. May you grow up to be a courageous soldier in India's service."

Her father, a distinguished Cambridge scholar, influenced her persuasions. Indira, studying at Oxford, cemented her own political thought that prepared her for the ultimate role she would later fill as India began to make its historical impact upon the world.

Indira was drawn into the maelstrom of political life by the need to serve at her father's side upon the death of his wife. She filled the role of hostess and became her father's closest aide, filial love strengthened by his dependence upon her. Even her husband, Feroze Gandhi (unrelated to Mahatma), whom she married in 1942 and who died in 1960, took second place to her father, for she was imbued with a sense of belonging to India and India's people. Hers was a duty, a commitment, and a dedication to the country she loved and only wanted to serve.

All this went through my mind as I sat still and stiff on my hard chair, my eyes glued to the central portion of the house and the darkened doorway from which I expected Mrs. Gandhi to appear.

What was I going to say? Why had I come? Would I now be so overcome with nerves as to become tongue-tied and simply gape at this world figure? I felt hot and cold at the thought. It was agonizing.

At precisely eight o'clock Mrs. Gandhi appeared, accompanied by two male attendants. She wore a short-sleeved, round-necked white blouse, a *choli*. A maroon paisley sari of fine cotton was draped around her waist and drawn over her left shoulder to hang loosely at her side. No midriff was exposed, nor did she bear the slightest hint of makeup. A long necklace of large amber beads and a simple watch were her only adornments.

Four or five paces away from the entrance to the tent and the chair upon which I sat she paused to place her palms together in the customary gesture of *namaste*—a beautiful symbol of prayer and peace.

My God! I was standing in front of Indira Gandhi, prime minister of India. The woman who controls the destiny of 600 million people. A woman whom I admired as the very embodiment of statesmanship and synonymous with woman's achievement in today's society, and here I was—Sabina Shalom, the little housewife from Miami Beach—struck dumb!

My adrenaline flowed. My pulse beat frantically. My throat was dry and tight. Come on, pluck up your courage and speak, damn it. In a second she will have passed by and you will have lost an opportunity that will never come again in your lifetime.

The words came out by themselves as some inner force propelled me to take a step toward her. I heard another person utter my thoughts.

"Madam Gandhi, forgive me for addressing you. I am a social worker and have traveled halfway around the world to tell you how much I admire you and ask if you would honor me with a few moments of your time when convenient."

There, it was said. It was over. Would she pass by, deigning to look at me? Would she wither me with an icy look of contempt? My knees felt very unsteady.

"What is your name?"

Her voice was quiet and cultured, her manner grave but kind. Her eyes were dark and sad. She stood in front of me unsmiling. Regal.

"Sabina Shalom. In Hebrew my name means 'peace and greeting.' "

"Yes, I know." Turning to one of her aides, she said, "You may take this lady into the house. I will see her later."

I was escorted to the front porch and walked as one in a dream. Mrs. Gandhi had consented to see me privately. I couldn't quite believe it had happened.

The aide led the way into the cool recesses of the house.

The entrance was square, its red tiles smooth and shiny. The facing wall gave way to a narrow hall on the left and one on the right. A visitor could see nothing of the house unless he traversed these corridors.

The aide took the right wing and almost immediately opened the door of a small room into which he gestured me to enter. It was sparsley furnished with a muted rose-colored *dhurrie* rug partially covering the inlaid wooden floor. In one corner an upholstered chair was drawn up next to a small oval table, on which rested a bowl of fresh, sweet-smelling white blossoms. A fabric-covered couch stood against one wall, opposite several upright chairs. The walls were painted in a pale apricot shade, and all the woodwork, a sparkling white. The brightness of the day filtered through the flimsy, long beige curtains of the two casement windows. It was obviously a small reception room, inexpensively furnished and of the utmost simplicity.

I thought of the walls and floors of inlaid marble, the gilded tiles, and mosaics of the palaces and temples I had seen. I remembered the exquisitely carved ivory screens, the cabinets, and the *objets d'art,* encrusted with semiprecious stones and decorated with delicate gold leaf. Why, some of the furniture in the hotel had been more impressive than the spartan chair I now sat upon, alone in this room. Austerity and economy were certainly practiced and not just preached here.

I tried to think of appropriate questions to ask, but my mind was a complete blank. I recalled Dr. Bhandari's words, "They are not in the middle of it. Mrs. Gandhi is right, there is no other way." I remembered the notice on the wall: "We should not hesitate to take steps which might be described as drastic . . ."

I thought of the slums of Old Delhi.

The questions I wanted to ask were in my heart, not on my tongue.

A full three quarters of an hour went by before Mrs. Gandhi appeared. Her entrance startled me—she seemed to have glided into the chamber. I stood up immediately. She was quite alone. We shook hands, and she motioned me to sit down. I sat on the couch, while Mrs. Gandhi took the upholstered chair.

Her presence radiated a vibrant inner force. There was a magnetism about her that made me feel drawn to her. She did not smile or make any attempt to put me at ease. Her face was composed and serious. She was direct in her choice of words. I need not have worried as to what I should say, for she at once took control. Arranging the folds of her sari, she said, "And what are you doing in our country, Mrs. Shalom? You say you are a social worker. Are you alone or are you with some agency?"

I replied that I was quite alone and anxious to understand cultures and conditions of some of the less privileged countries of the world. She glanced at my wedding ring.

"Do you have a husband?"

"Yes, of almost thirty years, and from whom I have taken a leave of absence—with his approval, of course." Her look of amusement encouraged me to add, "Being free in this way, I can meet and stay, when possible, with people who befriend me. I seek such experiences to learn their ways of life, for otherwise travel, to me, would be a meaningless excursion."

Her expression changed from a wry smile to one of mild approval. "Do you regard yourself as a liberated woman?"

"I prefer to say I am of liberal views. A liberated woman suggests one formerly enslaved and this I have never felt. Of course, the concept of marriage in my day was very different from that of today."

"With a leave of absence, as you call it, it would seem that your views have changed somewhat?" Her eyes smiled directly at me.

"Not so much my views, Madam Prime Minister, as my advancing years. My sons are grown, my responsibilities have lessened, and I am fortunate in having an understanding, if not always a comprehending, husband."

"I have read a great deal about the controversy of the Equal Rights Amendment. The feminist movement has gained great momentum over the past few years, has it not?" Her face was quite animated. At the mention of women's rights her eyes shone with enthusiasm. There was no doubt where her sentiments lay. "I presume you support their goals?"

"Yes, I believe it to be a sound educational process if it gains society's approval. This, for the majority of women, is a necessary justification for them to feel free to make their considered choices and in which they should, of course, have equal rights."

Mrs. Gandhi appeared reflective. "Yes, indeed, though I sometimes wonder if the greater freedom women are enjoying in many parts of the world has contributed to, or detracted from, the success of today's marriages. The divorce rate in the States is very high, I understand. Marriage seems a mere formality. Quite unfashionable, in fact."

Our conversation proceeded to the socially disruptive effects of unstable or unwedded relationships on children. I mentioned my visit with Dr. Bhandari at the clinic. Mrs. Gandhi spoke of the difficulties she encountered in the implementation of many of her health measures.

"Generally speaking, India's birthrate has dropped remarkably. Of course, you must understand that family planning has long been a vigorously pursued program of my government's administration. There will always be opposition in some sections. We have so much prejudice—even to our anticholera immunization plan to protect those exposed to contaminated water after floods. Many rejected this measure out of ignorance and fear of injections. Elsewhere, parents rushed to take their children out of school, convinced that they were to be sterilized."

As she spoke, I thought of the tragedy that the children of India are born into. A retinal image of all that I had seen in Old Delhi swam before my eyes as if a painting hung before me, spilling across the canvas all the wretchedness of the human condition. I knew I had to speak of that which throbbed so sorely in my heart.

Mrs. Gandhi's next remark prompted me to do so. "Have you seen much that has interested you in my country?"

"I have seen many lovely things, Mrs. Gandhi, but nothing has affected me as deeply as the suffering of your people that I saw in Old Delhi. The children especially distressed me. What is to become of them?" My voice was unsteady, and there was an unexpected stinging at the back of my eyes. A long moment of silence made me wonder if I had caused offense. As if Mrs. Gandhi did not know the full extent of those festering sores in her own backyard.

A great sadness swept over her. She lowered her eyes and bowed her head. She took a deep breath and seemed to have withdrawn into herself as if shrouded by a cloak of grief. The continued silence made me go on nervously, "Forgive me, Madam Prime Minister. I would not have spoken so indelicately had I not worked among concentration camp victims after the war. To see human suffering destroys me completely, and I just wanted to tell you that I feel India's pain deeply. I saw beyond what was visible, for this, I realize, does not even skim the surface. What can be done?" My voice trembled. I was shocked to have become so emotional, and also at my own temerity. Who was I to speak so brashly?

Her reaction was unexpected from one who held such power.

She raised her head and looked at me, neither offended by my words nor dismayed by my distress. If my eyes were blurred, hers were full of compassion. The sad smile that hovered about her mouth and the gentle expression of her eyes enveloped me with infinite kindness.

"I am not displeased with your words; on the contrary, I am greatly moved by your concern," she spoke softly. "I understand the intensity of your feelings because I am an intense person myself. We are all part of the same world, and I have grave misgivings as to the way it is going. The world has eyes, but it does not see. Those who speak of the infringement of liberties do not find the answers to the desperation of our people. As I have said so many times, the only liberty the poor have is the liberty to starve. I try to do what has to be done. It is easy to criticize. It is difficult to care. It is quite apparent that you do, and I am most touched."

With this she got up and abruptly changed the conversation. In a brighter tone she asked, "And where are your travels going to take you, Mrs. Shalom?"

I mentioned that I was en route to Australia and then across the South Pacific ultimately to Easter Island, but the stop that held the greatest interest for me was Papua New Guinea. I explained that it was especially exciting to me because of its recent emergence as a new and more enlightened nation from a hitherto almost primitive age.

"Yes, there are many nations struggling for a more democratic way of government. The problems of democracy, of course, are when they fail to solve all of our ills, but then, no system can do that."

She held out her hand to me, and as I grasped it I asked if I might take a photograph.

"Certainly," she agreed instantly. "It is not bright enough in here. Let us go outside."

Several photographs were taken with my 35-millimeter and my Polaroid. I was especially grateful that she permitted an aide to take one of us standing together beneath the portico of the house.

We shook hands again. Her clasp was cool and firm.

"Good-bye, Sabina Shalom, and good luck to you."

"Good-bye, Mrs. Gandhi, and thank you so much. It has been a privilege I shall remember all my life."

My words did not seem to displease her. She stood there, the epitome of graciousness. With a slight inclination of her gray-streaked head, she smiled, turned away, and walked inside the house.

Good-bye, great stateswoman. I stood there for a moment staring into the darkened entrance. I had met the woman who controls the destinies of a people, a woman who defied world opinion and sometimes alienated those to whom she turned for friendship by dint of straight talk, free of guile. Her only interest was in the well-being of her country. Popularity was of lesser concern. She attempted to govern an ungovernable nation. In a country like India, with its multiracial, multilingual, multicaste multimillions, who is to say what the right way is, or if there is a way at all?

Whatever the newspapers and magazines said of her in less-than-flattering terms, I didn't care. Some called her ruthless, imperialistic, determined to have her own way. Could it be, perhaps, that her way is the only way?

It is strange, I thought; whenever Indira Gandhi is spoken of, it always seems to be the men who criticize her the most severely.

Woman to woman we had met, and I admired her as such.

To have undertaken the task of governing a country like India is a burden that any mortal, regardless of sex, would surely stumble in shouldering.

I walked slowly out of the grounds and back along Safdar Jang Road. The sun, filtering through the foliage, shed its dappled light across the broad treelined avenue. I felt inspired, yet strangely sad. A line from Tagore's *Stray Birds* came to mind: "Who drives me forward like fate? The myself, striding on my back."

I felt an ache deep in my chest. Feelings long since buried now swept over me with such intensity that I felt weak inside. I knew it was an overemotional reaction, but I didn't care. I surrendered myself completely to the illumination of my kaleidoscopic thoughts. I longed with every fiber of my being to be a young, single woman again, free of all ties, obligations, and duties, even free of love for those to whom I was bound. I wanted to experience once more the joy and satisfaction of working among those who had nothing left to give when I had so much. This was what had been lacking these past few years. The giving of my very self in the service of a cause.

I thought of my life with Marco, the boys, and all that I had left behind. It seemed unreal, like life on another planet. One where an automobile and a television set were regarded as paramount to one's participation in the daily struggle to survive. That fiercely competitive "free" world in which man is enslaved solely for failure to recognize the necessity of freedom from vanity and greed. Free to admit to the needs of others and free to embrace service in their cause. From a life of futility and the constant question, "What is it all for?" to a life of fulfillment and unlimited satisfaction. And at the end of the road, ah, to look back and feel free to claim the supreme peace of the answer: "My life had meaning. I did something worthwhile."

Oh, Marco, Marco, I know you would understand. How often have you wished you could gather up all your aggravations, all those impossible, demanding, selfish clients, and open up your office window and throw the lot out? How often have I begged you to do just that? They don't deserve you and, my darling, you'd live a damn sight longer without them. Be a free, unfettered soul; come out here and join me. Who needs a car, a mortgage, and the patronage and approval of those to whom we are indebted for the trappings of the Western world?

We need only a cause to make life really worth living, and if we had each other to serve it, how glorious a life it could be. Our needs would be taken care of. We'd work a year or two or three, maybe, and then we'd do what ever we damn well pleased. Why

144

not? What are we in this world for at all, if we have to sublimate forever every dream and hope and all our wishful thinking?

As I neared Lodi Road, I came back to earth. The impact of all I had experienced greatly affected me. It was no use dreaming like this. Such fantasies were those of a very little child, and I recognized that sometimes I was just that.

I was no longer the social worker of earlier days. I could not hope to shake off all my ties and commitments. I had allowed myself the luxury of indulgence in impossible dreams, conjuring up all kinds of impractical situations, from which normalcy now rescued me.

I hailed the driver of a horse-drawn carriage and asked him to take me to the Oberoi Hotel. Perhaps there would be a letter from Marco to pull me back into the reality of my life.

One had been awaiting me for three days:

"I am busier than ever, there are simply not enough hours in the day. Michael is great fun and a terrific cook, though sometimes these vegetarian meals seem to be all paper, grass, and string. He says it's good macrobiotic food, whatever that means. The place is a mess, but who cares? I realize your outlook is far healthier. To be constantly cleaning and tidying would make me quite sick if I did it all the time. . . ."

I smiled as I tucked the letter into my purse. How could I possibly expect him to understand what had taken posession of me with so sad and persistent an ache? How could I explain these feelings? I could only feel them, that was all.

There was no way, *no way*, to reconcile the shock of India's reality within the framework of my own responsibilities at home. I would have to distance myself completely to see the total picture in proper perspective. I knew I couldn't stay in India forever. Reason prevailed over an emotional surrender to sentiments that had been spawned in younger years. Perhaps it would be best for my peace of mind to leave the country at once. . . .

As soon as the aircraft lifted its wings, I felt I had made a great mistake. I found myself longing to go back, for I knew I would never have the chance again.

I wanted another chance to know the country's people. I wanted to understand, not question, the implacable calm of those kind and gentle souls who, like children, were so anxious to please.

I wanted to see the beauty of Kashmir, so that I might better bear the pain of Calcutta and Bombay.

I wanted to be a part of their feasts and their festivals. To hear Indian music in the villages and see the young girls dance.

I wanted to share the happiness and laughter at their weddings and understand the acceptance of grief for their dead.

I wanted to talk with the students and the wise old men, and I wanted their patience and love and brotherhood to be my own.

I wanted to learn, and I wanted India to teach me. To teach me about living, for I knew nothing.

I wanted to find my own *dharma*—there, among those simple folk, so hardworking, so full of their bittersweet philosophy of life.

I knew I would never again be quite the same person, for India had touched me in a way that would indelibly remain.

I knew it would take a lifetime to learn and see all that this great country was.

And I knew the searing pain of rejection for a Westerner could never be a part of it all.

I had fallen in love with India, and as I left her, I cried.

Going my way?

Long-haired, barefoot Michael looks more like the backpacker *I* should be seeing off.

Of the millions who visit the Taj Mahal daily, I had the good fortune to be there virtually alone.

Vice Air Marshal and Mrs. Singh, and Komal.

Saying good-bye to Indira Gandhi.

The Lord Mayor and Lady Mayoress
Alderman Leo Port, M.B.E., and Mrs. Port
request the pleasure of the company of
Sabina Shalom
at a Reception at the Town Hall,
5.30 p.m., Thursday, 12th May, 1977
To honour Mr. HARRY SEIDLER
on his award of The Gold Medal of
The Royal Australian Institute of Architects 1976

R.S.V.P.
LORD-MAYOR'S SECRETARY
TOWN HALL, SYDNEY, 2000
TEL. 2 0263 EXT. 9593

PLEASE PRESENT THIS CARD

My friend
the Lord Mayor
of Sydney.

The King of Tonga
and I.

The many-tonned monolith, hollow eyes staring out beyond time itself, and I, a refugee from the twentieth century.

Not a tree, nor a leaf, nor a bird or a human being. I set my camera on a rock to capture this special moment on Easter Island.

6

Papua New Guinea

Somewhere I had read that half the fun of a journey was in getting there. I was enroute now to Australia, the halfway point in my travels, with stops in Bangkok, Hong Kong, Manila, and Papua New Guinea. From the time I left India, fun was hardly a word I would have used to describe my reactions to Bangkok.

Stifling humidity had reduced my energies to near-zero level. Inhibited as I was by the language barrier, my few Thai phrases and the addresses I had written down and waved about proved less than effective. People were kind and patient, but alas generally unfamiliar with the location of the places I wanted to visit.

Getting around on public transportation was an exercise in dogged determination to overcome the inability to communicate. My spirits flagged as my feet swelled. Thrilled as I was to see the incredibly ornate architecture of Thai temples, palaces, shrines, gardens, and galleries, the overwhelming fatigue I experienced quickly diminished a waning enthusiasm to make trips into the countryside. An outing by boat along the canals revealed a fascinating glimpse of the floating markets. Here, the vividly colored fresh fruits and vegetables were dazzlingly displayed and sold from boats skillfully manned by dark-skinned, smiling faces. Most were young girls and boys, attractive and Asian of feature but without an Oriental appearance. Renewed were the sights of poverty in the pole-supported shacks that rose from the river and in which crowded families lived. In its flowing waters, bodies were bathed, clothes were washed, and refuse and sewage were discarded. My depression at the increasingly familiar aspects of human deprivation was somewhat alleviated by an invitation to join a group of French tourists I met on this outing to see a little nightlife. It was ill-advised to go about alone at night, and I was glad of this opportunity to be among others.

Broad-minded in sexual matters as I regarded myself to be, I was shocked, fascinated, and nauseated, in that order, to witness on stage in a nightclub a live performance of copulation and other extraordinary feats of sexual exhibitionism. It was my last night in Bangkok and full of surprises, which, to be honest, I had later to admit to myself I was glad, albeit embarrassed, to have experienced.

Arriving in Hong Kong was a sheer delight. The weather alone, with the temperature at a heavenly seventy degrees, was enough to restore my usual buoyant spirits and thrilling anticipation of a new country. These first few moments of fresh sights and sounds were the times when I missed Marco the most. In India he had been greatly in my thoughts, but it was only here, in this unique spot where East meets West head on, that I suddenly found myself longing to share this experience with him with an intensity stronger than in any other place thus far.

The initial impact of yellow skins, slanted eyes, masklike faces, and impenetrable expressions quite stunned me. I walked around streets with English names and Chinese lettering, in a daze. A profusion of banners in every conceivable color and with vertical Chinese print adorned buildings, stores, smaller shops, and restaurants on main thoroughfares and the winding narrower back streets. Other than the white-uniformed, helmeted police perched imperiously on their little boxes to direct traffic, everyone seemed to be dressed alike in loose-trousered, tunic-bloused black garments. Most wore wide-brimmed straw cone-shaped hats. An exception was occasionally noted among the young boys, who, in their short black kimonos, pulled passenger-bearing rickshaws. Older faces, often synonymous with bent backs, bore pole-supported baskets on their shoulders.

The yellow faces that thronged the streets, the singsong language so strange to my ears, and the smell of garlic, ginger, coriander, dried fish, and the sweat of human bodies engaged in relentless toil made a powerful impression upon me, and all this before I reached the waterfront.

*   *   *

Ah! The glorious sight of the harbor. A forest of masts and funnels clad the water between the Kowloon peninsula and the mainland, across which the ferries ceaselessly plowed with raucous intermittent honking. Bat-sailed junks, in unending procession, wended between sleek white luxury liners, commercial steamers, and rusty scarred freighters, the combined sirens of which pierced the air like the discordant notes of an atonal symphony. Sampans, motorboats, and low-lying flat canoes contributed to this canvas of riotous color and motion. I felt like pinching myself to be sure it was true. Yes, I was really here in the Orient, and I was enthralled.

To add to my delight and amusement, I was able to secure a room at the YMCA, which was situated on the waterfront next to the famed Peninsula Hotel, one of the most prestigious luxury hotels in the city. My room was carpeted, simply but comfortably furnished, with a bath *en suite* and a spectacular view of the harbor —a room that, had I been staying at the Peninsula, would have cost five times as much.

I settled in happily for a three- or four-day stay, during which I intended to make a few business inquiries for Marco and leisurely sightsee in this little British Crown Colony jewel where I had already discovered enough English was spoken so as to permit me to get around with ease on public transportation. From here, too, I would check on my flight to Manila and my connection from there to Papua New Guinea, with time enough to advise my hosts in Australia that I was well on my way.

Those had been my plans, but they did not work out quite that way. Seated in a comfortable armchair in the commercial section of the American Embassy library, I was making notes from a trade journal of business contacts when, without warning, the room spun around and blackness engulfed me.

A middle-aged woman and a young man had their arms around me. "Are you ill? Do you think you can walk? Let us take you to the infirmary."

Now a white-uniformed figure and a warm Scottish voice embraced me, and I became vaguely aware of being placed on a couch.

"There me lass, just lie down here will you now and dinna fret yourself. I'll be getting you a nice cup of tea."

A blur of voices reached me from the door. "Nurse McKenzie,

we've got to get her out of here. She's not personnel, and we cannot accept the responsibility."

"Ay, lad, you're right. But you canna put the wee soul into the street, can you now? She'll be fine after a good cup of tea. Dinna fret, I'll take care of everything. Leave it to me."

Nurse McKenzie was back in no time with a steaming mug of hot sweet tea and biscuits. It revived me instantly, and I attempted to put my feet on the floor. "I'm sorry to have put you on the spot; I couldn't help overhearing the remarks, and I quite understand your position. I do feel much better now. I cannot imagine what happened. I expect I must have fainted."

"Dinna fret yerself now. I want to take your blood pressure, and you are not going anywhere for a few minutes, not until I know something about you and I'm satisfied you are fit to walk. Have you eaten anything recently? Where have you come from? Are you with friends? At a hotel?"

I answered hesitantly that my diet had been skimpy and limited, and told her of the great distance I had already traveled. I had no friends in Hong Kong, I was en route to Australia via Manila and Papua New Guinea, and I was entirely on my own.

"Sounds like travel fatigue to me, lass. That and not eating right. Your pressure is way down. I'm going to put you in a taxi and send you to bed to rest for at least two days and to eat proper meals. Do you hear me?"

I followed Nurse McKenzie's advice to the letter.

That was ten days ago, and now I was nervously awaiting a scheduled early-morning flight from Manila to Port Moresby. At first the announcement had been a "short delay." One hour later, passengers were told that technical difficulties had been encountered and a further two-hour wait could be expected. Sixty minutes beyond that time all passengers were advised to leave the departure lounge, as the problem could not be solved, spare parts were being flown in, and there would be an indefinite delay.

I had made no hotel reservation in Port Moresby. The midmorning arrival would have given me plenty of time to look around and see what kind of accommodations might be available. Surely there would not be that many people visiting a country like Papua New Guinea? Whatever kind of hotels there were, what kinds of visitors would fill them? Anthropologists? No, they live among the natives in tents or huts. Government officials? Businessmen? Yes, perhaps, but certainly not many tourists. No, I hadn't thought it necessary to inquire about hotels when I felt I would be arriving at a time of the day to find out for myself.

The contemplation now of a late-evening arrival tended to lessen the excitement I had felt when first proceeding to the departure gate. All that I knew about the country had been gleaned from a short documentary feature on television or some lurid accounts written by intrepid explorers. I had entertained grand illusions of myself as a daring female adventurer while poring over the map at home. Indeed, the very idea of visiting a country whose people lived primitively spelled for me the ultimate escape to a world far removed from anything I had ever known.

Compared with the generally accepted social structures of today's civilized countries, Papua New Guinea might well be regarded as still emerging from the Stone Age. Of the isolated tribes of thousands of years ago, a kaleidoscope of distinct cultures exists today. Almost 700 groups retain their separate languages and traditions. They are unique and united by a strong pride in their fiercely democratic country while clinging passionately to the beliefs and customs handed down by their tribal forefathers.

Thinking it best not to have taken off and have something drop off the plane, I philosophically considered what my options might be on arrival now that the seven-hour flight was under way. Turning to the gentleman beside me, who had been awakened by the meal the stewardess had placed before him, I said, "Excuse me, are you a visitor or a resident of Papua?"

Before answering me he looked at his tray, waved to the attendant to remove it, and asked her to bring him some champagne. He spoke with a heavy German accent. "Never eat on planes in dis part of de vorld, but de champagne ees gut. *Ja*, ees gut. You haff some, *ja?*" He lowered his bottle to my glass.

"No, thank you, I never drink on planes. You live in Port Moresby perhaps?"

"Me, ach no, I liff in Madang. I teach there. I loff it. Ees a beautiful spot unt von you must visit. You are a tourist, *ja?*" He downed his second glass.

"Yes." I replied, anxious to elicit more information before he became too inebriated to answer coherently. He was steadily refilling his third glass.

"It looks like a very late arrival now," I went on. "Will I be able to exchange some money? Will there be taxis? Could you recommend a hotel?"

"Notting vill be open. Mebee no taxis. You vant a tip from me?"

"Yes, please." I felt quite humble.

"Der ees only von 'otel in town unt usually der bus mits der passengers. Everyvon takes it, as der are never any taxis around ven von needs von. Doze mitout reservations find der 'otel full unt haff to sit up all night in der loppy. I stay at a small 'otel near der airport only a few yards avay. You can valk. No taxi, no bus, no expense, and alvays a bed. You take my tip, *ja?*"

I assented and hastened to ask about the advisability of making trips into the interior, mentioning that I planned to make Goroka my base. I had heard that the Highlands provinces were quite beautiful, but was it correct that local transport was available? Was it safe for women to go about alone?

Karl was most informative. Far from becoming drunk, he seemed to become more alert. I was disappointed when his loquacity was cut short by the announcement to fasten seat belts.

"I go to Madang tomorrow. I liff my baggage at de airport. You say you go to Goroka, *ja?* Zo, you liff your baggage alzo, *nein?*"

"An excellent idea if there is a luggage place open."

"Ach, *nein.* Notting ees oppen. I know der pipple on duty. Dey put it in der office unt lock it up. No guarantee against steal, of course, but von takes shances in dis contry."

I wondered what chances I might be taking as I silently followed Karl from the airport into the night. He had been right in his predictions. There had not been a taxi in sight, and the few passengers who had not been met by private cars crowded into the hotel minibus, which quickly disappeared into the inky blackness.

Karl and I set off quite alone. There was an air of complete desolation about us, which was in no way dispelled by the jerk of Karl's head and his words, "Der 'otel ees over der. Vee soon arrive."

We walked along a narrow paved road, starkly but only briefly illuminated by the spotlights of the airport building. The grass verges on either side seemed quite flat, as if we were in a clearing or a park. I saw there were trees, not tall and few in number, and as the lighting receded, we walked on for yards at a time in pitch blackness. An occasional streetlamp every 100 yards or so cast hazy pools of visibility, which when come upon felt to me like the great gulps of air one takes into the lungs to sustain one for a further spurt of underwater swimming. I chattered furiously, feeling the need for distraction, as I could not see anything at all "over there."

I was beginning to think I should have stayed with that busload of people. Safety in numbers, as they say, and what if I had stayed up all night in a lobby armchair? I wouldn't be prey to the unpleasant thoughts now crawling all over me.

"Why would the downtown hotel have been so full?" I asked. "There couldn't have been more than a dozen passengers, and they didn't look especially like tourists needing accommodations."

My companion mumbled into the darkness. His speech was indistinct, or perhaps it was that I lagged a pace or two behind him.

"De 'otel ees alvays full because vee haff a lot of visiting officials since vee haff independence. De Australian administration ees now much more busy mit government visdrawal. Surely you know dees tings?"

I stuttered shamefacedly, "Just a little; that is, not very much, actually." If heard, my reply was ignored. His tone of condescension implied that little else could be expected from a tourist, a *hausfrau*.

A hazy glow ahead gave way to steadily increasing bright lights. Flowering bushes came into view. The prickling anxiety I had felt left me instantly as we approached a building of respectable size and construction.

It was a proper hotel, with a foyer and a carpeted lobby, no less. A few potted shrubs added a little grace to the shabby armchairs scattered about in groups of three on a carpet that, on second inspection, had seen better days. We advanced toward the reception desk, where a solitary young man in a short-sleeved shirt was busily consulting his papers.

He looked up as Karl approached. "Ah, good evening, Herr Fischer. You had a rotten trip, I expect?" His voice had an Australian twang.

"*Ja*, problems, alvays problems. You haff my room?"

"Of course, Herr Fischer. And the lady?" I was by this time

standing beside Karl, but on reference to the "lady" as the young man's outstretched hand reached toward the board of keys, I inched away from Karl's side. It occurred to me that perhaps I was considered part of the baggage that would be sent along to Karl's room. I spoke up quickly.

"Good evening. I also require a room, please. Herr Fischer recommended your charming hotel to me." It was not idle flattery, for I was most thankful to find myself in such a civilized-looking establishment. My present concern, however, was to establish quite clearly that I had no connection with Herr Fischer other than as an independent fellow traveler.

A look passed between them that I didn't care to interpret. I stood there and smiled. Inwardly I panicked. What if the clerk said there were no rooms left? What if the exchanged glance meant, "I'll go along with whatever you want, Herr Fischer"? What if Karl now turned with a patronizing (God, lecherous!) smile and said, "Dat ees allright. I vill take care of der lady. She can share my room." What if the German professor often brought ladies to the hotel to take care of? Was this the reason he had suggested the hotel in the first place?

The clerk confirmed my suspicions as he began slowly to shake his head. Oh, my God, I'll bet Fischer bribes him with a handsome tip for this little act. The place can't be full; there isn't a soul in the lobby.

"Well, the only room I can give you, madam, is rather small and has no air conditioning. We're having a lot of trouble getting repairs done." He pursed his lips together and addressed Karl. "Davara sent us a lot of guests earlier in the evening, as they had too many confirmed reservations for tonight."

I didn't know who or what Davara was, and I didn't care. He had a room. Small, without air conditioning, but he had a room. Great, fine, I'll take it—I would have bought it! "That's all right, it will do just fine," I said.

Karl turned and proferred a very correct handshake. "*Guten nacht.* I hope you vill manage to slip. Ees not gut mitout air conditioning."

I stretched my hand out, grateful at the outcome and anxious to thank him. He raised it to his bearded and moustached face and scratched it with a kiss.

The clerk showed me the way to my room. The door was opened, the key handed to me, the light switched on. I entered, locked the door, and stepped back. It certainly was a small room. My God! It was an oven. The bedding was clean, the furnishings were modern and pleasing, the floor was carpeted, and there was a small and spotless bathroom—but the entire room was a *furnace*.

I gasped for air and went straight to the window, which was tightly closed. Flinging it open brought some relief. The night air was warm, there was a slight breeze, but there were no screens across the window and already I was feeling the sting of a mosquito bite.

Well, that had to be my choice. Either I was going to suffocate to death or get bitten to it. I settled on the mosquitoes. If I covered myself from head to toe with the sheet, leaving just a tiny air hole for breathing, maybe it wouldn't be too bad, especially since I felt tired enough to sleep through anything.

The mosquitoes fed upon a banquet, through which I evidently did sleep. The next morning I was covered with red, angry-looking swollen lumps, the pricklings of which refused to yield to the long tepid shower I took. The daytime clerk looked pityingly at me as I checked out.

"My, those do look nasty. Shouldn't have left your windows open. Of course, you've taken antimalaria precautions, haven't you?"

"Antimalaria?" I looked at him in horror. "No, I didn't know I was supposed to." I shriveled with shame at my ignorance. After all, I had mentioned my itinerary to the doctor. I had updated my smallpox vaccination, received a booster for typhoid-paratyphoid-tetanus, and what about my sore arm and temperature from those two cholera shots? Well, what about them? No one said anything about antimalaria shots, and that's what matters now.

Weakly I asked, "Is there anything I can do about it?"

"I doubt it. Probably too late. Should have been done six weeks ago." He dismissed me with a curt shrug of the shoulders and turned away. I scratched myself all the way back to the airport to take a nine o'clock morning flight to Goroka, in the Highlands provinces.

Antimalaria protection was not my only concern as I prepared to board the aircraft. It was a tiny Fokker propeller plane carrying

160

just three other passengers. I had never seen so small a plane, and I was scared to death. Climbing the rickety steps, I repeated to myself, Right foot, right foot. Be sure to step on with the right foot and everything will be all right. It was a silly childish notion I had clung to throughout the years, like the one about stepping onto flagstone sidewalks. "Squares, squares, no lions, no bears." How the echo of distant times float into one's consciousness at the most unexpected moments.

The pilot, a handsome, curly-blond-haired youngster of about twenty-six years of age, was standing in the cockpit. He was chatting away to a middle-aged man, a fellow countryman judging from their Australian accents. The two remaining passengers were already seated—one a pale-complexioned young man absorbed in the contents of his briefcase; the other, I assumed from the clothing he wore, a native Papua New Guinean. I stared at him in utter fascination, hardly able to tear my eyes away to attend to seat-belt regulations. Now, buckled in, I looked again, hoping my scrutiny would not be too obvious. He sat as still as a statue, looking straight ahead and seemingly impervious to the bumpy flight now in progress.

His face was so black as to be almost blue. His profile possessed a high shiny forehead framed by close-cropped, tight, fuzzy yet glossy hair. The skin stretched smoothly over prominent cheekbones and led to a finely etched mouth with full mauve-shaded lips. The nose had an aquiline bridge, the nostrils wide and flaring. His jawline was sharp and interesting, and a slender supple neck sloped hairlessly to the shoulders. He seemed totally unaware of my concentrated gaze and continued to stare calmly ahead. I was struck by his balance, by the long eyelashes thickly fringing the deep-set black eyes, the oddly hairless eyebrows, and, strangest of all, the absence of any whiskers or facial hair. Back to the sloping shoulders, the tranquillity, the silent poise . . . Of course! I was staring at a strongly featured Papua New Guinean woman!

She was wearing a short, shapeless, smocklike garment made of a brightly colored cotton fabric with a design of red and green hibiscus flowers. The square neckline and tiny puffed sleeves were bordered with yellow rickrack braid. The dress hung loosely on her slender frame, following the contours of her body only where she sat. She wore a finely braided yellow-and-brown straw armband. Protruding from underneath the seat was an extraordinarily

161

large-splayed pair of feet, encased in bright-green rubber thongs. A woven gaily patterned string shoulder bag rested in her lap.

My attention was abruptly distracted by the sudden swerve of the plane, followed by a steep dive. To my horror I saw high mountains rising sharply on either side, which seemed to clear the wing tips of the craft by no more than a few yards. Nature had carved an opening through which we were now weaving. The scenery was quite spectacular.

The jagged peaks that had so terrified me moments ago had surrendered to less threatening undulations. Myriad refractions of sun and light winked, glittered, and dappled the hollows and crevices with subtle diffusions of amber and slate.

Now, in an ever-widening pathway, descending ridges covered the slopes with tea and coffee plantations. Terraced by nature, they appeared to be moist with running water. Here and there a small village clung precariously to the mountainsides, showing us its garden petticoats, verdant and shining. Patches of dense forest stained the hillside inclines with every imaginable shade of green.

Afraid though I was, I could not help marveling at God's handiwork.

As the plane dipped and lurched, giant pandans reached up toward us, their roots sprouting high out of the ground like bundles of bound sausages. Tall, feathery grasses bent and waved as if in sad lamentation when caught in the airflow of our passing plane. I felt our noisy flying machine had violated earth's children.

My stomach had begun to make strong objections, and since no paper bags were evident, I groped for a plastic one and a handkerchief from the depths of my trusty shoulder bag. The other passengers seemed totally unperturbed. The young man was writing; the older one was sleeping, his head rolling about like an orange. My native lady was as still and as calm as ever. The pilot's back looked totally relaxed. Apparently this bumpy flight was quite normal, but I longed for its speedy termination, especially since we were now flying through thick mist. Each pocket of turbulent air tossed the craft up and down. I visualized the ease with which it could be dashed against the mountainside, thankful in a way that the clouds prevented me from seeing the lurking death that I was convinced awaited us all. It was a terrifying experience to be in so small a plane, yet I realized that a large one could not have navigated so dangerous a route.

"Here we go." The sudden exclamation from the pilot scared me even more. I thought the end had come. He directed a reassuring smile at me. "Had you worried back there, eh? Well, it's all right now. Hang on, we'll have Nellie down any moment." For the life of me I couldn't see where he proposed to land this "Nellie," and I didn't care for the word *down* either.

The swirling clouds gave way to patches of bright blue. The mountains had blended smoothly into the sky. We had emerged onto a wide and welcome green plateau, on which an elevation of ground looked like an inverted, oblong cake pan. A thin, flat, ribbonlike landing strip became visible. From the air it looked as if a workman had rolled out his tape measure. As we approached the tarmac, it seemed hardly broad or long enough to accommodate even our small craft, which bounced up and down like a ball as it touched down. I gripped my seat hard, my feet pressing desperately against the floor as if such exertions affected the brakes. The plane slid to a smooth stop with only a few yards to spare at the end of the runway. The pilot had earned his wings but seemed to think nothing of it as he nonchalantly swung himself aground and extended a helping hand to assist me as I tottered off the plane.

Shaken, I made my way to the small waiting room. My legs felt like Jell-O, and my face must have looked as white as a sheet, for a plump and pretty woman came up to me and asked, "Are you all right? You look proper poorly." It was an expression I hadn't heard in years, and I immediately took her to be an Englishwoman.

"Well, I do feel a bit groggy. I've never flown in so small a plane before, and it was a bit rough, though none of the others seemed to mind." I looked around to see how they were faring, but all had disappeared.

"Just let me collect my package, luv. I'll be back in a jiffy. Why don't you sit down?"

There was no taxi in sight, and only two airport staff members were visible. I decided sitting down for a jiffy was an excellent idea. What a friendly woman to have shown concern for me. She was back carrying a large parcel. "Are you feeling a bit better now? Are you a visitor then? What brought you to the Highlands? Can I give you a lift? I've got me 'ubby's jeep outside. Where'll you be staying, then?"

"Thank you, I'm fine now. Yes, I am a visitor. I came to the Highlands because I had heard of the lovely excursions one can make from Goroka and I wanted to see the interior parts of the country, not just the main towns. I don't have a hotel; perhaps you can suggest a place that's modest but decent. There is a town, isn't there?"

"Oh, yes, we're a town. Well, a village really. You're in the Highlands now, you know. Let me see now—I expect the Bird of Paradise would be best for you." Seeing my puzzled expression, she added, "It's a hotel. Nice and clean and quite proper." I wondered if other places were regarded as improper, but thanked her for the suggestion and for the ride as we climbed into her jeep.

We lurched and bumped along; she handled the vehicle like a toy. It appeared that her husband was on a two-year contract with the Australian government. Their three children were at boarding school in Brisbane.

"That's the worst part about coming up here." She waved her hand toward a row of prefabricated houses on stilts. "We all live in houses like that, but farther into the interior some of the conditions are so backward that most of us Ockies prefer to leave the kids at home."

"Ockies?"

"Aussies. All the same. For Australians, you know. There's quite a few of us out here, though there were more before independence."

The ride was quite short and gave me little time to see more than the dirt road with wide culverts on either side. The billowing dust obliterated almost all but the foliage. We ground to an abrupt halt in front of the wide hotel steps, my thanks cut short by a sudden revving up of the engine, a wave of her hand, and a cheery, "Ta, ra, then. Good luck."

I was disappointed at being deprived of the opportunity to invite her in to have a cup of tea with me. I entered the lobby. This, the reception area, and the lounge were all lumped together. Two young men were sprawled in armchairs. The middle-aged woman behind the desk sounded Australian. Where were all the natives in grass and feathers that the postcards had promised me? A black face appeared at my side. Silently he placed my pack on his shoulders. I looked at him incredulously, for a bone was pierced through his septum. He padded noiselessly in front of me, barefoot, clad in a calf-length white wraparound skirt, and a bright green T-shirt emblazoned with a multicolored bird— the bird of paradise, the country's national emblem.

I had been told it was the custom not to tip, but I felt a little uncomfortable about not doing so. A flashing smile that revealed a few missing teeth reassured me that no tip had been expected as the door of my room closed behind me. It was large, bright, and clean, with white walls, a red-painted stone floor, a double bed, and a vivid turquoise upholstered chair. A small shelf in the adjacent bathroom held an electrically heated jug, two cups and saucers, spoons, tea and coffee bags, and little packets of dehydrated milk. How like an American motel. My wide picture window opened onto a well-kept lawn with a view of Mount Michael, just as the room clerk had promised me.

I made myself a hot drink of coffee, had a Sego Bar, and felt refreshed and ready for action.

As soon as I had left the hotel steps, I felt that *action* was the right word. It was as if I had wandered onto a movie set and the director had ordered, "Camera, lights, action!" Everywhere there was activity and color.

I had arrived in Goroka on market day, and all about me were dark skins in shades varying from light coffee to copper, bronze, mud-brown, soot-brown, and ebony-black. The street corner I turned brought me to a thoroughfare that led me past small government offices flying the national flag to the marketplace, where all the outlying villagers converged to sell their wares. Dressed in their Sunday best, they had come to buy or be seen, chat and visit, barter and participate in this important outing. I stood stock-still to stare at sights my eyes could not at first take in or my senses absorb. I felt I would have to pinch myself to see if this was really true and I was indeed in the town of Goroka, Papua New Guinea. Me, here, actually witnessing this incredible, glorious promenade?

If I had thought the woman on the plane was strangely dressed, her outfit was dull and unimaginative compared to the mode of dress I now saw.

There were long skirts, short skirts, grass skirts, no skirts. Sweater tops, T-shirts, blouses, halter tops, bikini tops, topless tops. My God, the women are bare-breasted! And that one—what on earth is she wearing across her chest? A tall woman had crossed my path. Around her neck she wore something furry. It looked

165

like a small animal about the size of a rat. Surely not? Yes, that was exactly what it was. A dead rat, ugh! Around her abdomen hung a straw skirt that reached midcalf, the sides quite open as she walked to reveal her full, smooth, naked thighs and calfs. Into her short curly black hair she had stuck just one feather. Both wrists and ankles were embraced by wide woven grass bands. She walked erect, oblivious to my stares. Her skin had a polished red cast, and she was quite beautiful.

Many wore a variety of feathered headdresses. Even those who sported more conventional clothing, garments that covered most parts of the body, were robed in the brightest of colors. Some men wore khaki shorts (I later learned these were greatly coveted items); others, men included, wore dresses, full-length smocks, shifts, or long wraparound skirts. I did not see one unadorned chest. Those who were not decked out with rows of beads or shells wore garlands of flowers or feathers. One man I passed wore a long string of large yellow teeth as a necklace, which clonked and clinked as he went by. No, I dismissed the thought. They were too large to be human teeth. Here was a man with an old sailor's cap on his head. He looked quite incongruous in a short-sleeved, knee-length dress. Great hooped earrings hung from his ears, and he carried a gnarled wooden stick that he occasionally brandished in the air as a trophy.

For heaven's sake, what have those two women done to their faces? Scored across both cheeks and down the center of the nose were blue tattoo marks, stenciled in several straight lines.

Now I saw a woman who wore across her forehead a wide string band that descended down across her shoulders and widened out into a large woven sack from which an infant peered out sucking on a length of fresh-cut sugarcane.

Here was a fine couple. They looked as if they were about to go into battle. Their headdresses were incredibly high-mounted crowns of bird-of-paradise feathers, beetle backs, and shells. These were attached to woven string bands that encircled their foreheads and kept the headpieces firmly in place. Their faces were striped with red and yellow paint, and blue and white dots were daubed all around the eyes.

The man was bare-chested but for several rows of colored shells that he wore around his neck. His pelvis was scantily covered by a brief loincloth that was suspended from numerous bands of painted beads and plaited straw loosely tied low around his belly. Similar bands of straw and shells encased his upper arms.

His wife, if such she was, made an equally impressive sight. She wore three or four fur pieces threaded on a leather string around her neck, above which a curved, shiny metal band encircled her throat. The elongated nipples that slid into view beneath the furs had bright yellow adornments attached to them. The rest of her torso was skimpily covered with palm fronds, mounted around the lower abdomen on a belt of plaited straw interspersed with chicken feathers to soften the abrasion against her skin. Around her wrists and ankles were gaily painted wide woven straw bands.

Both had bonelike skewers pierced through their nostrils. Their earlobes were greatly misshapen from the weight of the numerous and heavy disks that hung from them.

Their bodies glistened from liberally applied grease or oil, which gave off a most repugnant odor as they passed by. I later discovered that pig fat is a favorite emollient, which even when rancid, is generously applied.

I was stunned by all that met my eye. To be seeing in the flesh, the naked abundance of which was not lacking, that which hitherto had been conveyed only by magazine photographs or a documentary I had seen many years back, was an experience that almost felt unreal. Praying that my camera would not let me down, I used up several rolls of film trying to capture this exotic parade.

There were several small stores along the street, including a pharmacy, to which I now hastened. I would buy more film and also ask about malaria protection. The Australian pharmacist confirmed the earlier advice I had been given. "Yes, you should have taken tablets six weeks prior to arriving in the country. No harm in starting them now. At least if you do come down with malaria, it might lessen the severity of the attack." He allowed me to purchase Camoquin without a prescription and suggested I take one a day for six weeks even if I left the country before then. It was here that I saw that the money I had exchanged was not going to go very far, and I made my way into the bank adjacent to the drugstore. The *kina* was equivalent to $1.25, and little could be bought for a *kina*, a large, heavy, and silver-looking coin made from a variety of alloys. The *toea* was the equivalent of a cent, and the currency system differed little from our own, so calculations were easy.

After exchanging some traveler's checks, I made my way to the post office. This was housed in a corrugated tin building and staffed by English-speaking civil servants, natives of Goroka. I purchased for Marco a fine set of commemorative stamps marking the independence of Papua New Guinea, the eventful ceremonies of which were enthusiastically recounted by the postal clerks as they handed the stamps to me.

"It was very fine, missis. We are humbly proud to be new nation now. We must all work harder even if it gets very hot sometimes."

"Yes, we must work harder with all nations," his colleague chimed in. "The Australian government has been good to us. They are our friends, and Great Britain too. I myself is glad. I myself is grateful. I myself say Europeans and Australians stay here and work with us now, not go away."

The resolve to work harder terminated abruptly, as it was three o'clock and time for the post office to close. I spent the next two hours walking around the streets and the marketplace, which seemed to trade exclusively in fruits and vegetables—melons, beans, corn, yams, taros, sweet potatoes, coconuts—although I encountered an occasional pig roasting over an open charcoal pit. Many nude figures of both sexes squatted here and there on the ground. The men whittled away at pieces of tree bark; the women wove net bags and plaited long strings and bands.

I saw a stationary bus and went toward it, hoping the driver could speak some English so that I could ask about trips to the outlying areas.

"Apinoon, missis."

I smiled a greeting. What had he meant? Of course, "good afternoon." Well, that was an easy one. "Apinoon, sir," I said.

He rewarded me with a dazzling grin and a spate of Pidgin English too fast to comprehend a word. My puzzled look elicited a simpler phrase.

"Missis, yu no savvy Pidgin?"

I nodded my head. "Yes, right. Missis no savvy Pidgin." I pointed to my watch and asked, "Bus for Mount Hagen—what time leave?" It seemed it left each day at noon, for he pointed to the midday numeral on my watch.

"Mi laikum yu, missis." He bared his discolored teeth, and a gnarled hand touched my arm. Really? Well, that will do for one day, I decided, and slowly made my way back to the hotel.

The lobby was full of people. Where had they all come from? I had hardly seen one European-dressed person on the streets, and now, in the bar area, white-skinned young and old men congregated everywhere. One of the women who worked in the hotel was chatting to a uniformed young man. She smiled at me and beckoned me to join them. I was glad of the opportunity to verify bus schedules and ask whether Western women could go about unaccompanied and why so few of them were in evidence.

I was informed that the Australian government sent out teams of technical men to work on vast construction projects that were often located in parts of the country where the lack of suitable accommodations precluded wives and children from being with them. Other visitors were mainly Australian businessmen engaged in negotiations that ranged from involvements with tea, coffee, sugar, or tobacco plantations to the importation of various consumer goods and plastic sundries. The Asian Development Bank, the Papua New Guinea Bank, and the Australian government, together with overseas conglomerates, largely influenced the rapid development of the country. Both the industrial growth and the agricultural growth were astounding, yet tribal superstitions and customs were still an integral part of the culture.

I learned that there were hundreds of missionaries of all faiths, although Christianity had been introduced in the late nineteenth century. All religions were accommodated. In the health and educational spheres, teams of Australian Volunteers Abroad (similar in concept to the American Peace Corps) worked closely with government administrative personnel. In the outlying areas a district officer and his trained native patrol officer tried to encourage a healthy respect for law and order, a somewhat difficult task. Settling tribal disputes was neither easy nor enviable. The officers were regarded as "outside" men, and in the distant areas their visits were rare enough in any case.

It seemed naïve, in view of the widespread civilizing influences, to bring up the subject of cannibalism. I braved ridicule to ask whether any recent incidents had been reported.

A shaken head, several amused smiles, and one specifically jesting voice, while assuring me that the government had banned such practices, confided that constant surveillance was impossible to maintain in the remote villages. A shrug of the shoulders lent emphasis to the implication that nobody else confirmed or refuted. That night, in contemplating the trip I intended to make the very next day, a nagging doubt floated around in my head. How could offenders be brought to trial? Without a body there would be no proof of a crime committed. If the evidence had been eaten! I shuddered at the thought and slept badly.

The clouds hung heavy and low the following morning. There was more than a suggestion of rain in the air. Undeterred, I set off to catch the midday bus to Mount Hagen, a journey of three to four hours. I had been warned that it could take much longer owing to poor road conditions as a result of recent heavy rains. The consequent erosions in the mountain passes had caused landslides, obstructing various sections of the road and causing delays. However, repairs were underway, and all buses were operating. I was unconcerned, for I had all the time in the world and was well prepared with my usual provisions. My folded raincoat lay inside my shoulder bag and covered my canteen of tea, some fruit, and the Sego Bars. I had thrown in a sweater, toothbrush, toothpaste, and a few sundry items. One never knew, and like a good scout, I wanted to be prepared for any eventuality.

I arrived well in advance of the bus departure time to find three-quarter-full occupancy. Despite being the only white-skinned, Western-dressed woman on board, I encountered no curious glances. It was almost disconcerting to be of such scant interest. My stares were obvious to the point of rudeness, but no one seemed to notice.

A young man in khaki trousers and a multicolored shirt entered the bus. He was light-brown-skinned and looked about twenty-six years of age. Immediately behind him followed two American-looking young fellows of similar age. Their fresh smiling faces and buoyant spirits attracted me instantly, and as soon as I heard them speaking English, I left my seat and went up to the front of the bus where they had seated themselves. I made no apology for bursting into their conversation. "Someone from home? Please can I join you?" I was made welcome, and as seats near the driver did not seem to be popular, there was thankfully plenty of room for me beside them.

The single man was a teacher from Port Moresby, native-born and educated locally. He was traveling to the Chimbu Province. The Americans were missionaries on their way to Mount Hagen. I had a host of questions to ask them. They were no less interested in me. We got on famously.

The bus left on time—that is to say, only twenty minutes late. The countryside was quite beautiful, with rolling hills rising almost directly from the shrub-lined highway, although the view was often obscured by the swirling dust that frothed redly around the bus windows. The promised rain had not fallen.

The grating screech of a constantly engaging gearbox as we labored up the winding road drowned out our attempts at conversation. I quickly gave up and closed my eyes. The dust had begun to sting them despite my having worn sunglasses. The chugging and groaning, the lurching and bumping, along the rough roads and around blind corners suddenly ceased, and the bus slid to an unceremonious halt. It had suffered a massive cardiac arrest.

Hood up, parts out, tools strewn about, advice given—all to no avail. Gas pedal depressed, various sections pushed, banged, and kicked, and still not the slightest flicker of life. The key continued to yield a dull click when turned in the ignition. Many of the passengers were already fading into the bush, chanting a solemn requiem for the soul of the departed vehicle.

The two missionaries, Jim Tasker and Jim Mitchell (who called himself James to avoid confusion), accepted the calamity quite philosophically. The young teacher's acceptance was also reassuring. I had been introduced to him, but his name eluded me, as it sounded so strange. He had spent several minutes discussing the mishap with the bus driver. They had spoken in Hiri Motu, and he now informed us that the fellow was setting off for Goroka to obtain spare parts or a tow.

"It will take him a good three hours unless he is lucky enough to get a ride. There isn't much traffic this side of Goroka because the Daulo is always going out."

I learned that the Daulo was the mountain pass between Goroka and Mount Hagen. Heavy rains sometimes washed away the bridge or caused heavy mud slides, preventing the heavy, produce-carrying trucks from getting through.

Our choices were simple. We could sit on the bus and wait, or we could sit on the road and wait. We could also set off walking, as many of the passengers had already done.

"Well, Yabwinaje," said Jim, turning to the teacher with the difficult name (What was it he said? Jabajeena? Yapaneeja?), "what do you think we should do?"

"The missis here said she'd like to see a village. There is a compound quite near here I can take her to, and if we all walk in that direction, we might be lucky and get a ride along the way."

The two missionaries looked at each other dubiously. James had mentioned that he had spent some months training in Mexico and spoke Spanish, so I hastily whispered to him in that language.

"Look, I don't want either of you to feel obliged to agree for my sake. I would love to see a village, but do you think it will be all right for me to go with him alone?"

James smiled and replied in English. "Well, Jim and I have seen many villages, but we are always glad to talk with the people. I think you would be just fine with Yabwinaje if Jim prefers to wait it out here, or we can also walk along."

With a generous smile Jim butted in, "Sure thing, fine with me, always glad to see the villagers. We've nothing to lose and might as well begin walking in any case."

"Thank you. It is good of you." I turned to the teacher, intent on having a stab at his name. "How far away is the village?" The name wouldn't come out.

"The turnoff is about a mile or so down the road, if I remember correctly. After that it's only a short way. Very nearby."

It seemed much farther than a mile before we left the main road and turned onto a well-trodden path. Not one vehicle had passed us during this time in either direction, and James commented that the rumor of mudslides blocking the Daulo Pass might well be true. We all felt pleased with the decision to walk rather than wait, and the men calculated we could visit the village and be back long before the driver could return. I plunged into the foliage after Yabwinaje, ahead of the men, feeling quite excited at this turn of events.

I was wearing my cotton skirt and T-shirt underneath my cotton safari-type jacket, which I was glad to have, as the tempera-

172

ture was several degrees cooler due to the tall trees. The brush beneath my feet scratched my ankles and tore my stockings, and my sneakers were wet from muddy patches here and there. I was far too excited to mind especially, when a strong white glare appeared through the foliage that had darkened the day around us, heralding the approach of the village.

Yabwinaje gave a whoop of delight. "I haven't been here since I was a *monki.*" Seeing my puzzled look, he said, "A little boy is a *monki.*"

The compound was actually a clearing at the end of a mountain promontory. I saw the gradual dropping away of the ground that gave way to gently sloping ridges. Yabwinaje explained that settlements were traditionally placed in this fashion for safety against marauders or attacking hostile tribes. The deserted appearance was due to the men working on the plantations and the women attending the vegetable gardens lower down the slopes.

Suddenly several children, completely naked and ranging in age from three to six years, raced toward us, squealing excited greetings at the unexpected arrival of visitors. Yabwinaje broke into a run and sprinted off to meet them, temporarily disappearing behind one of the huts. These ringed the perimeter and were made of timber slabs stacked in an upright circle beneath a conical grass thatched roof.

A woman emerged from one of them, stooping as she came through the doorway. She was quite tall as she straightened up and was covered from chest to midcalf in a brightly colored cotton saronglike garment. Her shoulders were bare. She wore no ornaments, but seemed to be pressing a small wad of cloth to her body. Behind her appeared a strange apparition. At first I could not distinguish whether it was male or female.

As the form moved behind the woman now advancing toward us, two dried leather pouches attached to the upper part of the body were set into motion. I realized that the loose flapping pieces of crinkled skin were the flat pendulous breasts of a very worn old woman. Other than a few strands of plaited grass hanging from a string around her waist, she was totally nude. Her hair was a frizzy black cap, razor-trimmed so close to the scalp as to be almost indistinguishable from it. Her skin was a dry bark, the lips differing so little in color that only when the mouth opened did the black cavity delineate its outline. The limbs were skinny to the point of emaciation, and now two matchstick-thin arms stretched out toward the tall woman. The wad of material changed hands. I realized now that it was a small infant.

Jim and James showed no surprise at the scene. I presumed they might have seen many such sights. I was enthralled and asked, "Do either of you understand what the women are saying to each other?"

"No, but they seem quite pleased to see us. Ah, here comes Yabwinaje."

He was accompanied by an elderly man. The stooped figure wore only a codpiece, the string of which passed between the buttocks and was tied around the waist. Other than this, he was quite naked and unadorned. He and the old woman joined Yabwinaje and walked toward us. The woman holding the baby was seated in front of one of the huts, rocking herself back and forth and singing in a high-pitched tone. It was a primitive sound, quite monotonous and, after awhile, jarring to the ear.

"Apinoon," James said. "Apinoon, master," Jim said. I decided to have a crack. "Apinoon, masta and missis." I knew I could hardly go wrong wishing them a good afternoon. They all laughed, and Yabwinaje spoke rapidly in dialect to the man.

I asked James if he was the village chief. "Something like that," he replied. He and Jim had haltingly entered into the conversation, which was now in Pidgin and during which English-sounding words were often discernible. I was most impressed that they could converse, and wished I, too, could communicate as the woman tugged at my arm and said words I could not comprehend.

"She wants to show you the baby," Yabwinaje explained. "Let us see the child, and then I'll take you around the compound." We went over to the squatting figure. A gnarled hand with five dirty broken nails pulled the cover back to reveal an infant of just a few days old. To my utter astonishment (though I do not know what else I expected), a perfectly normal, sweet-featured, wrinkle-faced baby peered out. It looked like any other newborn child in the world. Adorable. I asked if I could take a photograph, and thankfully no objections were raised, other than the mother's insistence on holding the baby herself.

As we went around the compound I asked Yabwinaje how and where the women gave birth. Was there any medical assistance available if things went wrong? What sort of hygiene existed? Was

174

there a high incidence of bacterial infection or infant mortality? He could not answer all my questions, but told me it was common practice for the women to go down to the river's edge to give birth. Here, in the most primitive way, the umbilical cord is cut with knives washed in the stream. The mother and new baby are immersed in the water as a cleansing, not superstitious, ritual and then helped back to the village. After a few days' rest (and, one presumes, survival from pneumonia), the mother returns to the vegetable garden and an older woman, too feeble to work, takes care of the infant.

Yabwinaje was much more at home commenting upon the political and sociological aspects of his country.

"That's our prime minister, Michael Somare." He pointed to a photographic print on the wall of the hut we had entered. "He led us forward into independence. Now we fly our own flag and belong to the family of nations. We still have a long way to go before tribal payback fighting ceases. Some of our traditional customs will always survive, but through our system of local government councils, our people are becoming more involved with economic development. Private enterprise is encouraged, and we have made a lot of progress. We still need help from our friends in Australia, but self-government is working very well."

I was most impressed by his fervor. "You sound like a politician."

"Well, any man can stand up and say what he thinks. This is a democracy. There was a time, once, when only a great warrior could become a tribal chief. Now a good speaker can become a powerful 'bigman' and leader in our councils and government. Everyone over eighteen can vote, and even those who cannot read or write can indicate their choice of candidate in the elections through our photoballot system. They can point to their choice, and it will be recorded for them. One man, one vote. Very proper."

It was a fine speech, and his enthusiasm could well qualify him for a life in politics. Papua New Guinea, willingly or otherwise, had weathered Dutch, German, British, Australian, and, for a fierce and terrible time, Japanese occupation. Now a member of the United Nations, it could well use the intelligent ambitions of its native sons. The 1,500-mile-long dragon-shaped island of Papua New Guinea shares a common border with West Irian. It is a rich and verdant land. Its vast rugged mountain ranges, swampy plains, and 700 different languages hampered but did not prohibit many areas from dealing commercially with one another. Moreover, in thirty years the island had become a firm trading partner of various Asian countries. Universities were producing capable teachers, doctors, engineers, and lawyers. Young men and women were entering all the professions, and for those of more technical leaning, the technical university trained skilled workers and agricultural experts. Yabwinaje was most proud of his country's achievements. I was no less impressed, yet as we entered the smoky, dark interior of one of the huts, I couldn't help feeling that the compound and the way of life here were a million years away from the civilization of which he spoke.

Bare of furniture, the earthen floors were dotted with straw mats. "These are *tasol*s and used for sleeping on," Yabwinaje said. "Now we must get back to the others and return to the bus."

I looked at my watch. We had left the road at about two-fifteen in the afternoon; it was now nearly four o'clock. The driver was calculated to get back to his vehicle around five-thirty, and we had a walk of approximately an hour or so ahead of us. The old chief was not at all happy when we left the village for the road.

"We were expected to stay for the evening meal, when the rest of the villagers would be back. He was upset that his hospitality was refused."

We had set a vigorous pace, but now, as the road came into view, James said we could slow down. The warm sun had dropped low in the sky, and a slight mist brought a chill to the air. I was looking forward to the moderate warmth of the bus, which I expected we would see any moment the next curve was rounded.

We seemed to be walking on and on, and still no bus in sight. Yabwinaje suddenly stopped dead and announced with certainty in his voice, "The bus is not here anymore. It has gone."

"Must be farther along, Yabwinaje," Jim said.

"No. Look at the tree over there." He pointed to a clump of granite and bushes against the hillside, where a partially uprooted tree lay diagonally against the road. "We left the bus here. Exactly here."

I said nothing. I was in shock. I was also suddenly feeling very tired.

"The driver must have been lucky. He managed to fix the bus

and move it back to Goroka or on toward Chimbu. We are nearer to Sinasina than Goroka, so I think we would be better off walking in that direction." Yabwinaje looked dubiously at me and continued, "There might be some new posts along the way, but not for the missis."

The thought of stumbling along the rocky dirt road in the fast-approaching night for an indefinite number of miles appalled me. I also felt I was a burden to the men, who could march at a more vigorous pace and perhaps reach a place that appeared to be taboo for women. I felt a helpless sick knot in my stomach at the alternative—sitting out the night on the road alone. No, they wouldn't leave me alone, surely?

A happy thought erased the doubtful face of Yabwinaje. "Of course, we could go back to the compound and spend the night there."

Without stopping to appreciate the possibilities of this additional choice, I blurted out, "Would it be safe? I mean they are primitive people and . . ." My voice trailed off lamely.

"As safe there as you would be in the dark on the road," Jim said in an approving way.

"Yes, in such circumstances you must have faith and trust in the Lord, Sabina." James smiled an assurance at me.

"Well, I do have faith, and I do trust the Lord, but . . ." I bit my lip. "I'm not sure we should trust the natives. After all, look what happened to Michael Rockefeller." I felt a little stupid coming out with that, but never mind, facts were facts. Lord or no Lord, there had never been any satisfactory explanations of his mysterious disappearance. I turned to James for corroboration. "Don't you remember? No body was ever found, and that could mean—well, it could mean cannabalism, couldn't it?"

Yabwinaje burst out laughing. It was all very well for him to be amused. He had been born in this country. He spoke the language, but even he might not be fully acquainted with the ways of a tribespeople in a village he had not visited since boyhood. Doubtless he could defend himself and the two men also. The natives were used to missionaries. But women? White ones? *Plump* ones?

"No, missis, no need to worry. The villagers are friendly people. They will not harm us. Sometimes, yes, there have been fights between warriors of different villages with old scores to settle.

They've made raids in the night and have killed each other. Infighting among the villagers, however, is rare and usually only when bargaining for wives if they feel they have been cheated."

"Just the same, Yabwinaje," James spoke slowly and carefully, "I do know that cases of murder come constantly to trial. The administration is plagued with the heated and complicated disagreements it has to try and resolve. Often these are never settled satisfactorily."

"Yes, this is a fact." Yabwinaje nodded his head. A slow grin spread across his face as he went on. "It is a long time since I have heard of anyone eating their victims. It is forbidden, and the custom is dying out except perhaps on Saturday nights." His whole body shook with laughter, and I knew he was deliberately teasing me.

Had the matter been less macabre, I might have appreciated the humor. James's remark hardly reassured me either. "Don't be scared, Sabina. You are not meant for roasting. Not in this world anyway. The Lord has other plans for you."

I smiled weakly. The alternatives were grim; I must hope for the best.

"Though Reverend Chalmers lost his head," Jim piped in. "Of course, it was on his second visit. Missionaries were not always popular."

"Now stop scaring Sabina," James responded. "Besides, that was way back in 1865 or thereabouts."

Yabwinaje thumped Jim's back, and Jim whooped with laughter and thumped him back. I remained silent. Doubtful. Apprehensive and helpless, for I had no choice if I wished to stay with the men. We had arrived at the cutoff in the road. Within the hour it would be dusk and quite cold. The temperature had dropped considerably, and in the mountainous parts of the Highlands the nights are known to be chilly. Walking indefinitely along the road in the dark and cold was no more inviting than resting at the compound, where we would be surrounded by primitive people and subject to primitive customs. Both held potential risks as far as I was concerned.

Yabwinaje had been treated as a friend by the villagers, and they had seemed very pleasant. Jim and James were God-fearing men of His calling. I was not alone. Yes, I must have faith. With this determination I plunged into the brush with them, the path much gloomier now than before.

Dusk was falling as we emerged into the clearing, now alive with activity. Children came running from all directions with screams of excitement. The babble of voices was pierced by ululations. It was the shrill wailing of the womenfolk and quite unnerving, as was the sight of so many near-naked men and women.

They clustered around us, including the mother I had met earlier. She must have explained our previous visit, for the women near me nodded their heads, and some touched me in gestures of friendliness, I hoped. The men, too, were eyeing me up and down. It was a welcome interest, for Jim and James were smiling and conversing just a few yards away. Their gestures indicated less fluency than I had given them credit for. Perhaps I could have a try, in that case.

"Mi laikum yu. Mi laikum village." I pointed my finger at myself first, then at those around me and, with a sweeping motion of my hand, took in the thatched huts. Now the coup de grâce. "Mi laikum being here."

Whoops and shrill laughter broke out on all sides. The women patted my hands and stroked my arms. Quite sisterly, I thought, and felt relieved and thankful.

The commotion brought Jim and James over; they looked pleased with me. "You see, they like you already. You have nothing to worry about. The lady is not for burning."

I wished he hadn't said that. Doubtless he had intended to reassure me with a jocular remark. It had the reverse effect. What if they liked me enough to fancy a taste of me? I edged my way to Jim and James, who were now heading toward the main hut. I resolved to make no further attempts at Pidgin. I would just smile, listen attentively to try and catch what was said, and say nothing. *Nothing*, remember.

Despite my uneasiness I could not help being enthralled by the scene before me. Darting flames from the recently kindled fires cast shadows that leaped about dervishlike in abandon. It was hard to distinguish which were the dark-skinned naked bodies and which the illusions of the fires. The women's anklets and bracelets clinked, the bones worn through the nostrils gleamed, and the necklaces of dog's teeth made faint thumping sounds against the chests of those who passed about me.

Yabwinaje came to tell us to join a group of squatting tribespeople for the meal. We sat among them on the bare ground in a semicircle around the fire. Something on large flat leaves was offered to us to eat. I could not make out what it was and hesitated to bring it to my mouth. Having gone without anything to eat since ten o'clock that morning, I was no longer hungry. The longer I wait to eat, the less hungry I get. I found this a source of great convenience on many an occasion on my trip. The men, however, were famished and showed surprise at my reluctance. They were tucking away the food and urged me to do likewise.

"It's a kind of a stew with vegetables and all kinds of things thrown in," Yabwinaje advised me.

I recalled the conversation in the hotel lobby the previous evening and shuddered at what might now be offered to me. The natives, I had been told, were extremely partial to rat. I had certainly seen a fondness for wearing it. Readily available, it might well be a favorite dish. My stomach heaved at the thought. "No, thank you. I'm not at all hungry. I couldn't eat a thing. Really, nothing, thank you."

Jim and James paused to look at me, astonished. Yabwinaje leaned forward insistently. "You must eat. You will offend them. Eat just a little. It's mostly taro and yam."

James now attempted to persuade me. "He's right. Eating with them has important tribal significance; you must try. A little nibble here and there will go a long way toward avoiding insult. It's really quite good."

"Oh, James," I was almost hysterical. I swallowed hard, fighting down the sensation to vomit. Saliva had welled up inside my mouth and the urge to do so was strong. I felt panic-stricken. "I can't, James, I feel sick."

At that moment inspiration struck me like a bolt of lightning. My hand darted into my shoulder bag placed between my crossed legs. Out came my raincoat. I thrust it behind me. Out came my canteen. I placed it beside me. Out came one, two, three Sego Bars, a hard-boiled egg, and an apple. "Look, you can tell them I have a very strict religion of my own that forbids me to eat anything except my own food." I brandished a Sego Bar in the air. "You see, I carry these things about with me wherever I go." I picked up the canteen and swished the cold tea around. "Even what I drink. Tell them, go on, tell them. You can say the spirits will punish me otherwise."

Jim and James looked at me incredulously, their faces registering shock. Had the situation not been so desperate for me, my earnestness would have been hysterically funny. The comic aspects were not lost upon me even as I spoke. "Look, these people believe in spirits and strange gods, don't they? It's better than causing offense, isn't it? No one thought it odd when I produced my own food in India. Surely it's worth a try?"

Of course, I knew it was ridiculous to speak of India. Here there was no comparison. The whole act was absurd, but desperate situations called for desperate measures, I reasoned. Anything was better than nothing. Anything was better than rat!

The crisis passed, if indeed it had arisen. Everyone went on eating, and I doubted that anyone had ever stopped. The three men were so concerned with conforming to tribal ways that I began to wonder if their earlier assurances had been ill-founded. Maybe the villagers did not behave in the way the men had previously assumed.

Darkness had deepened. The fires gradually subsided, and many people had gone into their huts. Yabwinaje informed us that the two men would join one family in one hut and that I was to go with him and join another family in a different hut.

When I asked to remain with the men, Yabwinaje said coldly, "It has all been settled, missis. You will be better off with me."

I did not like his words or the tone of his voice. Family or no family, I was not going with him into a hut alone, without the others. Yabwinaje was educated and spoke the language, but he was still a native-born Papua New Guinean. He might still hold with many of his countrymen's beliefs and customs. He spoke Hiri Motu and I could not even speak Pidgin. How would I know what might be discussed, privately entertained, or actively encouraged if I were to be alone with him and the villagers in a hut some distance away from Jim and James?

Did not the Eskimos loan out their wives for the pleasure of their visitors? What if the custom here was to loan out the visitors? Who knew what strange practices could be observed in a tribal society like this? Why should I allow myself to be in this position? Foolish or not, I wasn't going to, and that was that.

I spoke up in Spanish to James. "I'm sorry to be a nuisance, but how do I know I can trust him? I wouldn't know what was being said, and I would be quite helpless if he involved me in a situation I couldn't handle. I know it sounds silly, but I don't care. I want to be with you and Jim. Please." I felt fragile, stupid, and childish. My voice whined, and I felt ashamed.

James put a protective arm around my shoulder. (God bless him, he had understood.) "I think she should be with us, Yabwinaje, and you too. We should all be together. Won't you try and arrange something?" His voice was kind but authoritative. Perhaps he, too, harbored misgivings. At any rate, he had appreciated the possibilities, remote or otherwise, of my being alone and unable to communicate.

It was finally sorted out, and all four of us now approached the doorway of a hut barely outlined in the intermittent flickering of a dying fire. The men had to bend over almost double to enter. I stooped with head and shoulders lowered to follow. Had I not done so, the smell alone would have felled me instantly to the ground. It was vile. I took a step inside and reached for Jim's hand but caught his shirt by mistake.

"Sorry," I gasped, unable to finish my words, for the rank odor caught the intake of my breath and all but choked me.

"S'all right. Where's your hand?" Jim grabbed it as we shuffled with hesitant steps into the darkness. James's voice rang out above the din, "Feel your way along by the back of the hut, where there is room to move along and you won't fall over anyone."

I put my other hand out behind me to reach for the wall. This, made from planks of tree bark, was lined with split cane. I was careful to pat the wall rather than run my hand along it and possibly encounter splinters. I remembered from the earlier inspection I had made with Yabwinaje that each hut had a sunken hollow in the ground that contained a pile of hot stones to provide warmth. As my eyes became accustomed to the darkness, I was able to make out various shapes huddled around the pit. The place seemed crammed with bodies.

I could not tell which voice came from which body. There were several children judging from the timbre and excitable speech pattern. Yabwinaje divined my thoughts. "The father and two of his sons left to make room for us, but there is still the old man, his wife, their daughter-in-law, and her daughter. Also two pickaninnies and one eighteen-month-old baby. With us that makes eleven. I said we would not be very comfortable if we all stayed together. You will not be able to lie down, but if you sit like me—can you see me? This is the best position, with your back against the wall."

"Back against the wall" were hardly the most comforting of words—they had a somewhat final ring to them. I sensed, rather than saw, Jim squatting down, and I followed suit, gingerly shuffling back on my haunches until I felt the hard wooden planks against my back. Everything had taken place within moments of entering the hut. The noise, the smell, the darkness; it had been quite bewildering. I was glad I was next to Jim. James's voice came from across the hut. "Everything all right there?"

"Just fine" from Jim, and "Yes, fine" from me. What else could I say? I thought. Yabwinaje had divined my feelings, for he said, "Well, we could have still been walking along the road." He was right, of course, and I felt resigned, with a more positive outlook.

Two figures around the entrance pulled into place an obstruction to secure the doorway against intruders. Total blackness now engulfed us, and the two men laughed as they stumbled over recumbent bodies. "Sori try, masta," and "Sori tumas, missis." Jim said it was a courteous apology for stepping over us, not a reference to the possibility of night visitors. Great, I thought, just my luck to be the one nearest the doorway.

My eyes began to ache from staring into the darkness. The smoke made them water and sting, yet I could not bring myself to keep them closed. It was quite stupid, for I could not see a thing, yet I felt somehow more vulnerable when I closed them for a few minutes at a time. The smoke from the fire pit clung along the thatch of the roof and mingled with the smell of urine and pig fat. I had stopped being grateful for a warm place in which to spend the night.

My head felt hot and thick from the putrid air, such as there was. I groped around inside my shoulder bag, which I had placed between my outstretched legs. Out came my raincoat, which I wrapped around my legs. I slipped into my sweater and wrapped my scarf triangular-fashion across my nose and mouth in the hope that it would filter out some of the smell.

Jim, aware of my shufflings to get comfortable, offered to share his blanket with me. It wasn't a proper blanket as much as a piece of rough-textured material that smelled of skunk when first passed around. I had refused it, not only because I was put off by the smell but because I did have my sweater and raincoat, and Jim and James had nothing more than their khaki jacket-type shirts.

I declined it now as then, but was glad to have the chance of a few words with Jim. The darkness and the feeling of people around me whom I could not see were quite disturbing.

My legs felt stiff and my spine seemed to be permanently curved. I moved my shoulder bag against the wall and wriggled the small of my back into it. I tucked my raincoat tighter around my legs, for the straw beneath me was scratchy, and I felt a chill rising from the floor.

The chatter of high-pitched voices began to diminish, and a variety of snorts, belches, and coughs ensued. These, the customary preliminaries to sleep, gradually subsided, and the conversation seemed to be limited to short phrases, as if questions had been asked and answered.

Silence seeped softly into the darkness like a fog that rolls in from the sea—stealthily, menacingly, and all-enveloping.

I must have dozed off for a short time. Suddenly I awoke in full possession of my senses and alert to danger. It was only the whimpering of a small child, but trying to recapture that blissful state of sleep now eluded me completely. My legs felt cramped, and my neck ached all the way down into my spine. I cautiously tried to bend my knees, anxious not to disturb Jim. He stirred and his thigh pressed against mine. I was glad of the warmth this contact brought. It was somehow reassuring, for when patting the ground on the other side of me, I realized there was no one immediately there, and I wished I had placed myself between Jim and James.

A faint haze pierced the chinks around the doorway. At first I panicked, thinking a night prowler was out there. It was the steady light from a fully risen moon, just enough light to perceive shapeless forms of sleeping bodies and, to my left, the vague lumpiness of Jim's boots. I felt much comforted, for Jim had large feet and he was a big man. If he had to kick someone with those big shoes of his, he would surely inflict some damage. Good!

My thoughts turned to Marco and the boys. What would he have said had he seen me now? He had never liked the idea of my

184

being in these parts in the first place, despite my promises to take the greatest care and exercise common sense at all times.

Heavens, I had set out this morning with sensible enough plans. Ending it in a native hut could not possibly have been foreseen. Perhaps I had not been adult enough or realistic in imagining that I could go traipsing off alone by public transport, which I had been warned might be unreliable, into parts of the country I knew little about and where I would certainly encounter few who could speak English.

Meeting Jim and James had been most fortunate. They had spoken enthusiastically about their work and their experiences with the people. The Seventh Day Adventist missionaries had established many excellent educational facilities, from which trained young people eagerly sought channels into which their skills could be turned to profit-making ventures. Teaching was an especially honored profession. Having Yabwinaje with us had made me feel quite confident when we had set off walking to visit the compound for the first time.

James had spoken of the greater cooperation between the small villages in combined group development. It all helped to lessen rivalry and enmity.

"Of course, we have a long way to go before Christianity is fully accepted by the natives. I sometimes feel that religion is regarded as a trade-off. If things go well for them, the teachings of the Lord are fine. If they suffer reverses—well, it's a different story."

I remembered his words as I leaned my head back against the matting of the wall. Perhaps it would be wiser if I sought advice about places I could visit from the volunteer social agencies in Mount Hagen. Those who worked "in the field" would provide far better advice than the odd bits of information I picked up here and there.

Failing that, I might be better off making inquiries about an organized outing—the one thing I had so far avoided and frankly disliked. They always whizzed one around the free sights. Stops at the places where one wanted to linger were always cut short in order to leave far too much time for shopping. Nevertheless, the wilds of the Highlands provinces could not be compared to the more civilized cities, and perhaps now this was the time to take a conducted tour. After all, here I was in the mountainous regions of a country barely on the threshold of maturity. It still clung to a way of life beyond belief of the average Westerner. Here I was, itchy, uncomfortable, afraid of bodily harm. The same me who at home complained when the air-conditioner didn't cool enough, or the television went on the blink, and "Why can't we have a dishwasher? Everyone I know has one."

It all seemed incongruous. Was it all true? Am I really here, or am I dreaming? Dreaming? . . .

A blood-curdling scream woke me. Terror coursed through my veins. Jim was shaking me violently. Pandemonium had broken out. James was bellowing in Pidgin; Yabwinaje, in Hiri Motu. It was the most awful din.

The door was being pounded upon and was now wrenched open. Jim and James were patting me on the shoulder. "There, you are all right." I realized that the scream had been mine. The scratchy blanket had grazed my ankles through Jim's movement in his sleep and I had imagined it was a rat. Perhaps it was my earlier horror of rat being offered at the evening meal that had surfaced from my subconscious. I felt terrible at having woken the entire village. The hullabaloo had brought a crowd of figures hovering around the doorway and clearly outlined in the moon-light. How could I begin to apologize?

My attempts were subdued. Jim and James were so kind. Not a hint of reproof or criticism. Tears welled up in my eyes as Jim, with his arm about my shoulder, said, "Don't worry. Yabwinaje is explaining everything. Here, rest your head against my shoulder and try to relax now."

The noise gradually subsided. The men outside went away. The family in our hut slowly ceased to mutter. The children went back to sleep. Peace and quiet reigned once more—except in my heart.

Oh, Mongi, Mongi, where are you? What am I doing here? What kind of a fool am I? A silly, ignorant, foolish one. That is what I am.

Back on the main road we had walked for a good half-hour. It was only six o'clock, and the morning air was crisp and cool. I had decided that no matter which direction the transport might come from, I would take it. I would walk along with the men until either a bus or hitch presented itself. Surely before the midday heat some vehicle would pass us.

A bus came along soon after, with Goroka as its destination. I said a grateful good-bye and clambered into it. The thought of a warm shower and a change of clothes more than compensated for not sticking to my original plan of going to Mount Hagen. I would try again another day, when road conditions might be more assured. The Bird of Paradise awaited me with all the modest comforts that I, the spoiled Westerner that I was, now fully appreciated.

Within twenty-four hours I had contracted malaria. I was convinced it could be nothing else. My head ached intolerably. My throat was parched and felt like raw meat; every swallow was agonizingly painful. My arms, legs, back, and even fingertips ached, but worse was the fever. One minute I was throwing the covers off, streaming with perspiration, and the next minute I was shaking and shivering with a chill that no amount of covers, even the rug from the floor piled on top of the blankets, could assuage. It was malaria for sure. What was I to do?

The hotel administrator suggested the local doctor, but why not first "give it a day or two with aspirin and hot drinks. We get little incidence of malaria in the Highlands—it is so cool here. Sounds more like flu to me."

The sweet girl at the reception desk, and whose voice I was most frequently in touch with, said otherwise. "You should get yourself to Port Moresby if you possibly can. There is much better medical treatment available there than here. That is where you probably picked up the germ, I expect."

Weak though I felt, I took her advice, especially as she called ahead to reserve me a room in the Davara Hotel. This was the one the hotel clerk had referred to on my first night in Port Moresby.

Once on the way, I began to feel much better. Perhaps it was only a touch of flu after all. Ensconced in my bed at the Davara Hotel, I soon changed my mind as the chills and the fever started all over again. This was a fine mess. How could I stay crocked up in a hotel bedroom to be cared (or uncared) for by hotel staff and at the mercy of a doctor whose training and prescriptions I might hesitate to accept? Far better to get myself to Melbourne, where Elizabeth and Harry would be able to recommend an English-speaking doctor schooled and experienced in ways that were more familiar to my Western concepts of medicine.

I immediately contacted the airlines. Qantas spoke of an impending air strike, unsure that their twice weekly service would be in operation. I explained that I was ill and that in order to be met by my friends, any telegram I sent should indicate a definite flight and date. Did they think it best I change my ticket and fly by Air Niugini, the national airlines of Papua New Guinea?

"Send your telegram, luv. One way or another we'll get you there. The strike won't happen before the week is out. We'll reserve you a seat on our flight three days from now. If anything happens between now and then, we'll get you on Air Niugini. Not to worry. Feel better. We'll be calling you."

With such friendly and helpful advice I did not hesitate to send a telegram advising Elizabeth and Harry of the details of my flight. I suggested they check with both airlines in the event of any possible changes between now and the date of my arrival.

This dispatched, I staggered back to my hotel bedroom determined to stay in bed and overcome whatever it was that made me feel so ill. It seemed to be the general custom in these parts to provide hotel guests with an electrically heated water pitcher, crockery, and tea or coffee bags in their rooms. I was able to make myself hot drinks and awaited the arrival of the doctor whom the hotel clerk had suggested and whom he had arranged for me to see.

"Better you see doctor sooner than later, missis. If nothing wrong, nothing lost. If something wrong, you sooner put right." It was sound advice.

A brisk and efficient Papua New Guinean doctor attended me in the most professional way I could have wished. His doctorate in medicine had been earned in one of Australia's finest university hospitals, followed by a two-year internship there. He had returned to his own country to practice tropical medicine. I couldn't have been in better hands, I felt sure.

"You do not have malaria. Not even a trace of it. It takes about two weeks or more before you would have come down with it. You may have a viral infection. Change of climate. Touch of flu perhaps. Hard to say. Are you eating properly? Travel fatigue? Sleeping all right? Blood pressure on the low side. Are you under any particular tension?"

188

I smiled and nodded vaguely. There seemed little point in relating how I had been living and what I had been doing these past few months. I didn't have malaria, and that was all that mattered. A good rest, more aspirins, a few balanced meals, and a lot less moving around for the time being were his suggestions. I knew I could follow his advice far more effectively as a house-guest in Melbourne than as a hotel guest in Port Moresby. I was so relieved not to have anything seriously wrong with me that even with his advice in mind, I had begun to contemplate staying where I was and, when rested, returning to the Highlands again.

I knew this was ill-advised, besides which, how could I possibly send another telegram to the Hemsworths telling them I've changed my mind? Not only would it confuse Elizabeth and Harry and perhaps disrupt their plans, it was also uncomplimentary to hasten to them when feeling ill, but calmly stay on here when feeling better just to suit myself.

The more recovered I felt, the sadder I became with my decision to leave. English was widely spoken in Port Moresby, and the Melanesian Pidgin here contained more English words. I was able to converse quite well with the local townspeople and listened raptly to the tales of the old women as they sat weaving their mats from the long sago fronds. Their remedies for sick pickaninnies and those for preventing or aiding conception were of a sorcery to make the hair curl.

The fishermen were no less steeped in superstition as they blamed the white man's trickery on a poor day's catch. Like the women in the street, they were friendly enough to laugh if they couldn't understand me, and glad to stop and talk to me when they could.

Traders of artifacts were suspicious at first, yet courted the foreigner's patronage with tales of magic and promises of good luck to anyone who bought their wares. No use trying to bargain. The price was fixed, and they firmly said why.

"Yu pela got moni. Yu pela got altogeda sumtin. Mi pela got nutting." Yes, the Westerners had money and, to his way of life, had just about everything anyone could ever want. The life of his countrymen was still in a world of rites, superstitions, and strange gods. But did we differ so vastly when it came to greed, warring, and killing?

A visit to the National Museum and Art Gallery on Touraguba

Hill greatly illuminated the country's historical past, but a visit to the House of Assembly, Papua New Guinea's parliament, only obscured my understanding of the nation's future. Here the elected representatives of the people have donned the robes of statehood. They have joined the family of man and are now represented in the United Nations Assembly.

In the streets, however, my questions on politics were of little interest to storekeepers and the vendors of fruits and vegetables. "Mi no savvy dispela sumting. Im sumting belong white man's tasol." ("I don't understand all that. It is white man's business.")

I wondered how long it would be before these simple people became immersed in the mainstream of the modern world into which this transition now plunged them? Would self-government bring peace and prosperity, or would the lack of education, struggling to keep apace with progress, only lead to an even greater return to primitive passions and breed more hatred, jealousy, and tribal conflict? How long would it take for world influences to taint these unsophisticated, almost childlike people once they had joined the brotherhood of nations?

Progress meant, to their innocent minds, the means with which to emulate the white man, especially his possessions. Tractors, trucks, and the transistor radio.

The white man's knowledge was the more desired for the belief that it had been deliberately withheld. Much of it was magic. The clouds hid the magic from them. The white man's worldly goods were jealously coveted. These, the tangibles, were the only things that counted. "America goes to moon. More powerful than Australia. White man camp on our lands. Cut our trees, dig holes, spoil hunting. Make money. Our people get nothing."

Study and application had little meaning except to the few select student bodies. To the townsfolk and even to the most primitive villager, commerce was universally understood and embraced. Buying and selling had overcome all language barriers for generations of traders. With statehood conferred, increased opportunities to exchange goods with the Western world were opening up.

This unspoiled nation had joined the race to discard its precious heritage for the visions of riches believed to exist in the white man's world. Ancient carvings and religious artifacts that were once thought to ward off sickness and evil spirits now willingly exchanged ownership for an outboard motor for the fisherman's boat.

Culture was the trade-off, commercialism the exchange. Papua New Guinea was coming of age.

In nine days I could not have hoped to understand the full implications of independence. I could only recall the simplicity of life in the spectacular beauty of the mountainous regions. There I had glimpsed a way of life beyond anything I could ever have remotely envisioned. It had been a unique and thrilling experience. There, the spirit of *wantok* (friendship) flourished and, I prayed, would remain.

"Bipo mipela no bin savi long taim yu kam niupela. Tasol bai yu go nau, olsem wantok bilong mi."

"It was a long time before you came to us, a stranger. Now you go, leaving us as a friend."

7

My Friend the Lord Mayor

Tullamarine Airport in Melbourne is a splendid construction, the least like an airport I had ever seen. The spacious entrance hall and great lofty part-glass roof gave me the feeling of being in an ultramodern convention hall. It would have been admirably suited for an exhibition of industrial machinery or the display of the aircraft its function served.

Plants and shrubs grew in huge urns and concrete boxes; polished terrazzo flagstone floors shone like burnished copper pans; and sculptured benches accommodated those awaiting arrivals or departures. It was on such a seat that I now waited for my host and hostess, Harry and Elizabeth Hemsworth.

I was more nervous than excited. Elizabeth was completely unknown to me, and my acquaintance with Harry was founded only upon his brief visit to us when we had lived in Detroit. Marco's friendship had been formed and nurtured through school days; mine now had to stand the test of the intimacy and closeness that inevitably results when one is a houseguest.

How long would they expect me to stay? I had in mind only a week or so at most. Would this cause offense? Were they expecting me to stay two, three, four weeks? I had a lot of traveling ahead of me. I wanted to see other parts of Australia, then move on to New Zealand, Tonga, Fiji, Tahiti, and Easter Island. I would have to play it by ear and see how things went. I was here now and resolved to be an excellent guest. Make my bed and keep my room tidy, of course. Leave the bathroom spotless, help with the dishes, and eat whatever was put before me without breathing a word about dieting. Perhaps I'll say from the outset that I thought of only a week's visit. That might settle it. A wise guest never overstays a welcome, and they, too, might be relieved to know they weren't going to be stuck with me for an indefinite period of time.

I expected they would think my backpack eccentric, but there was nothing freaky about my clothes. I had enough clever accessories to ring the changes so that Elizabeth, at any rate, need not fear embarrassment when going out with me or introducing me to friends, should the occasion arise.

My thoughts had kept me occupied for more than half an hour. After another ten minutes had gone by, I began to feel the vague uneasiness that assails one when elements of doubt begin to surface as distinct possibilities. Had they met with an accident? A flat tire on the road? Could it be that my telegram had not arrived? In a place like Port Moresby, who knew what manner of efficiency, or lack of it, existed? Perhaps it would be as well to inquire at the check-in counter to see if there was a message for me.

I made my way to the Qantas desk. In the air and on the ground they had all been such a friendly, helpful, smiling crew. Maybe they could assist me with a telephone call if there was no message.

The female staff member was chatting with an older woman who had come up to the desk. There were just the two of them. No passengers seemed to be expected, and all the arriving ones had already left. I awaited my turn to speak; they terminated their conversation, and the Qantas girl turned to me with a cheery smile. "Can I help you?"

"Yes, please. I wondered whether there might be a message for me. My name is Sabina Shalom and—" I could not finish my sentence, for the woman standing nearby seized my arm and with great excitement said, "Hang on, hang on." I couldn't imagine what on earth she was so agitated about, and looked nervously around.

She continued with increased excitement and velocity, "Oh, I am glad I found you, I was getting fair worried I was." Good gracious, can this be Elizabeth Hemsworth? I wondered. Had Harry married an older woman? A widow, lonely but wealthy perhaps? Well, it often happens that way, and what of it if she makes him happy.

"I'm Ethel Baker, Lizzie's next-door neighbor. She had to go to England. Her brother called to say her father was dying—" My interruption of "Oh, no!" went by unnoticed. "Yes, seems as if he was taken poorly all of a sudden. Looks like he's on his deathbed, poor soul. They left the day before yesterday."

"You mean they have both gone?"

"Oh, yes, they left together. Harry wouldn't let her go alone. She was that upset, poor lamb."

"Yes, of course." I stood there dumbfounded. "Poor Elizabeth," was about all I could manage to say. The irony of the situation came home to me with a shock. Here I had traveled to the end of the world only to find that the very couple at whose instigation this trip had been made possible was not now in town. It was comical in a rather paralyzing kind of way. Marco would never have let me make the trip in the first place had he not felt that their invitation assured me of a home and a welcome by friends in so distant a land.

My face must have registered dismay, for Mrs. Baker went on hastily, "Don't worry. Lizzie told me all about you. For the last two weeks I've heard nothing else, she was that excited about you coming, more than Harry even." She paused to take off her glasses and wipe her brow. "Well, here you are, and I'm real pleased to see you. I was getting fair worried I was."

What seemed "fair" to Mrs. Baker appeared quite gloomy to me. "Did they get my telegram from Port Moresby before they left?"

"Oh, yes. That's why I'm here to meet you. Poor soul, she was that upset. Did you like Port Moresby, then? I didn't think much of it me self. Went there with me late 'usband once. Thought it was right broken down lookin'." She stopped as if to recall some ancient incident worthy of recounting. I hastily seized the opportunity to break in. I had to know the worst.

"Did they say they preferred me to stay in a hotel, or am I able to stay at their house?" Halfheartedly I added, "I can hardly turn around and go back home after coming all this way, can I, Mrs. Baker?"

"Ethel, call me Ethel, and can I call you Sabina? It's a pretty name, isn't it? Yes, you 'ave come a long way, 'aven't you? The United States, Lizzie said. I'd like to go there me self one day." My question remained unanswered. I tried to get Ethel Baker back on the track again. "Did they leave instructions with you, then?"

"Oh, yes. I was just coming to that. Lizzie gave me the keys to the house. She always does when they go away. I water her plants and take in the mail, and she does the same for me. It's so important to get on well with your neighbor, isn't it?"

I made no comment, still awaiting my fate.

"Yes, I 'ave the keys and you can stay in the house. The only thing is . . ." Her voice trailed off as I began to fiddle with my backpack, anxious to inaugurate some movement in any direction. "Well, I'll explain everything on the way. I 'ave me own car." The maneuver had been effective. Ethel moved forward. "Here, let me take your hand grip. Fancy using one of those 'aversacks. Good idea, really."

I hoisted my pack and was glad of Ethel's help with my hand luggage. It was quite heavy with the weight of the beautiful hand-macramed fringed shawl I had brought as a gift for Elizabeth. I had dragged it halfway across the world, its weight and bulk a burden I had cursed on many an occasion. Parking it in a checkroom whenever I could had not been without worries of pilferage either. Now it had come home, and with it a large bottle of cologne, two ties, and a belt for Harry. After all their traveling, the intended gifts were now not going to find their recipients.

"Poor Elizabeth, what a shock for her," I murmured as we comfortably bowled along wide-open country roads in an ancient but well-preserved Rover car. "She must have got my telegram about the same time she heard the news of her father."

"Actually, no. Yours came the very morning they were leaving and put her into a fair dither it did, an' all. She'd received your card from Hong Kong saying you were going to be delayed, and what with you going on to Papua an' all that, she hadn't thought to see you for another two or three weeks or more."

I decided not to explain any of my reasons lest it provoke a lengthy tale. She was a pleasant and kindly soul, and I was most grateful that she had come to the airport. After all, she could have left a message for me to take a taxi. I would just have to exercise a little tact to keep her to the point, which right now was to ascertain what was the best and most correct thing for me to do.

"Well, Ethel, if I may?" She nodded her head vigorously and gave me an encouraging smile. Her face changed totally. She seemed suddenly years younger. Relaxed and happily driving along, she seemed to be loving the role of hostess she had been called upon to play. Perhaps she was a lonely widow indeed, and my coming and Elizabeth's going had brought an element of excitement into an otherwise dull life. "Did they seem comfortable about letting me stay in their house? You see, I've never met Elizabeth and I would quite understand how she'd feel about a strange woman in her home."

"Well, I was just coming to that." It seemed as if Ethel was always going somewhere but never quite got there. "It's quite all right your staying in the house. Lizzie said to tell you to make yourself right at 'ome. I was thinking, though, that you might like to stay with me till they get back. I'm on me own, being widowed, you see. Except for Whiskey, that is. Whiskey's me dog. Big feller. There's quite a bit of crime going on in these parts. I wouldn't be without me Whiskey." She chuckled at the intended joke. "I don't drink me self, that's why I fancied calling 'im Whiskey. It's rather amusing, isn't it?"

"Oh, yes, it's hilarious." I hoped my words hadn't sounded sarcastic. It wasn't that the dog's name was unamusing, nor in truth that Ethel herself was unfunny. She was quite funny, in fact. What had struck me as hilarious, in a comic-tragic fashion, was the whole situation. I felt in limbo somehow. Flat, let down, and yet almost not caring. Relieved even. Perhaps it was the unfulfillment of expectation. Everywhere else I had relied on my own initiative, had been left to my own resources. Here I had prepared myself to acquiesce to whatever would be expected of me and to some extent relax and let someone take care of me for a brief while. Although the invitation to Australia had not been the focal point of my plans, not in the way Marco had viewed it, nevertheless my present position was something of an anticlimax.

Ethel broke into my thoughts. "So I really do think you'd be better off staying with me, if you'd like to, that is." I murmured something about not wishing to impose, but, "Yes, thank you so much, maybe just a few days," thinking as I spoke that changes in my future travel plans might now be expedient.

Ethel's house was welcoming in its untidiness, and I felt quite at home. Whiskey, whose German Shepherd size and ferocious bark filled me with terror on first sight, turned out to be a gentle dog, delighted with the extra attention he received from me. Ethel was the soul of kindness, fussing and clucking over me, thrilled to have someone to whom she could show her lifetime of photographs.

Elizabeth had left me a little note and some telephone numbers of her friends to call. I felt uncomfortable about that and didn't do so. One, however, did call me—Nina Brach, a tall, willowy blonde, attractive, cultured, and anxious to show me around Melbourne. The houses, streets, stores, and people were of so strong a British flavor, I felt I might as well have been in England. Of particular charm were the "lacy" grillwork facades of the carefully preserved Victorian buildings, mainly private dwellings. In the city, tram cars, each with its own driver and conductor, clanged the bells and grunted along the wide streets that boasted stores of a vaguely old-fashioned design, with window displays to match.

I made several excursions out of Melbourne on my own. The surrounding countryside was quite lovely out in the Blue Mountains region. I visited the unique Botanical Gardens, the specimens of which are said to be unequaled in the world. A five-hour bus ride through the natural setting of the kangaroo and koala bear took me to tiny Phillip Island. Here, at precisely the same hour every day, when dusk is just about turning to night, hundreds of fat, bursting-bellied penguins come waddling out of the sea together. They stagger across the sand dunes, where their young lay awaiting their return. The penguins regurgitate all the fish they had eaten during the day, which their young now feed upon. It was a fascinating sight, clearly illuminated by huge floodlights and an abundance of severe warnings that flash photographs were forbidden.

I was fortunate to have been invited to a private luncheon honoring the Australian prime minister, who was the guest speaker. It was an enlightening experience and one that clearly demonstrated the fervor of pro-British feeling. Australia, now one of the Commonwealth nations, had for some time enjoyed full autonomous rule. It was no less surprising to hear such expressions of loyalty to the Crown and the ardent wish to further strengthen the ties with Mother England. That same day, an air-controllers' strike was declared. It had been fermenting for some time, and now it swiftly paralyzed the country.

"It's them there communists," Ethel said. She was thrilled that I had conversed with the prime minister and gazed sadly at the Polaroid photograph of the two of us standing chatting. "Poor feller, them commies are trying to get 'im out, you know. They want the conservatives out so as they can get in. They're very

197

strong 'ere, you know." She sighed and went on, "If it's not one thing, it's another. Next'll be a postal strike, you'll see. Them commies are at the bottom of all these 'ere strikes. Wot's worse is that they're getting stronger all the time. They'll be in power one of these days. Mark my words."

Her ominous warning and the havoc caused by the standstill of all air transport prompted me to talk of leaving by bus or train. I quickly realized that these forms of transportation were also vulnerable and might join in the strike as a sign of support.

Television reported the chaos caused by visitors who couldn't get out of the country and nationals who couldn't get in; about hotels that were swamped by tourists who hadn't planned on staying; and about the additional schedules to augment train and bus service, already sold out for days in advance.

Ethel was most understanding when I confided that I might have to leave without seeing Elizabeth and Harry. I was beginning to feel uneasy about overstaying my welcome, though I had tried to show my appreciation by taking Ethel out to dinner and giving her a bottle of perfume intended for Elizabeth.

There had been no word from the Hemsworths about their own situation, but whatever the outcome, they, like everyone else, would not be able to return to the country until the strike was over. I confided my dilemma to Nina. "If I wait until they come back, I could hardly leave within a day or two. The strike can also go on another week, according to the news reports, and I can't stay at Ethel's much longer either."

"She loves having you, you silly girl. She told me it was a tonic to have you around. You can come and stay with me if that's all you're worried about." Nine put her arm around me in a welcoming gesture.

"No, thank you, Nina. It's very sweet of you, but there's more to it than that. Even if the Hemsworths get back soon, Elizabeth may be in no mood to entertain a woman she's never met. She'll be in mourning, I expect—Ethel says she adored her father."

A telegram arrived the next morning. It said that Elizabeth's father had died, the funeral was over, and they hoped to be back within the week, strike permitting.

Nina was most supportive of my decision to leave before the Hemsworths returned. "Elizabeth will be feeling very depressed and low. It won't be a comfortable situation for either of you. I guess you are right, Sabina." When I outlined my plans to visit New Zealand, she looked aghast at my polyester skirt. "I hope you've got warmer clothes than that?"

I felt utterly stupid in confessing that I had sent all my warmer garments back home from Hong Kong, thinking that the farther south I went, the warmer it would become. I had completely overlooked the reverse of the seasons in this hemisphere. Autumn had tapped with chilly fingers at night and early morning against my bedroom window, but the sunny days in Melbourne had been pleasant and mild. Now I began to express my doubts as to how much of New Zealand I would see if the cold weather was about to set in.

"Oh, you must go," Nina encouraged me. "It would be a great pity to be in this part of the world and not visit the South Island especially, but, oh, dear, those clothes of yours—wait, I have an idea." She took me home and produced from her wardrobe several items of woolen clothing. "These are all too short for me. Please take them; they'll just be right for your height." I accepted with gratitude a warm turtleneck sweater, a woolen knit skirt with matching cardigan, and a pair of flannel slacks. I felt all set for the South Pole, let alone the South Island. All that was missing was my transport to Sydney.

At eight o'clock the following morning I said a tentative good-bye to Ethel as she deposited me at the railway station. I left my pack, the now-empty nylon bag rolled up and tied to the straps, at the checkroom, and joined the long line waiting for the ticket office to open. I hoped to get one of the few seats that had recently been made available on a first come, first served basis. Alas, nothing was left for that day. By the time my turn came, I accepted a sleeping berth for a date five days ahead. I wondered how on earth I could walk out just as the Hemsworths might be walking in. "If I try my luck again tomorrow for a nonallocated seat, will I be able to return the one I have just purchased?" I attempted an appealing look at the clerk behind the grid.

"Yes, that will be all right." He lowered his voice and said, "If you can get back here at four o'clock and go to advance ticket returns, you might be lucky enough to get a cancellation on one of tonight's trains. That's the time when we know for sure, as departures are at six P.M. and six-thirty P.M. Otherwise try your luck again tomorrow."

I thanked him for his tip, and bless his heart, it was a winner. At precisely four o'clock I handed in my sleeper reservation in exchange for a canceled coach seat on the 6 o'clock evening train for Sydney. Sitting up all night for a fourteen-hour journey was a happier prospect than facing a bereaved hostess and feeling uncomfortable about a stay that was now against my true inclinations.

My dilemma had been resolved. My fears were now dispelled. My visit to the Hemsworths was simply not meant to be.

Sydney, Sydney. It was great to be free of obligations. To be able to please myself again and do, go, wherever I wished. Not to worry about causing offense or doing the wrong thing. I'm just not good at being a visitor. I'm best as a paying guest. The kind that appears for breakfast and creeps in to sleep at night and that other times is not seen at all. Well, no more worries on that score, but where was I going to sleep tonight?

First things first: park the pack. I went to the checkroom, thinking I would extract a few items now to avoid returning later in the day if I secured accommodations a long way from the station. "Do you mind if I just take a few things out right here?" I asked the man behind the counter.

"That's all right with me, miss. Just move it along a bit. You'll be fine right there."

I undid the top flap and groped around in the upper pocket. No nightgown there. I was sure I had put it in together with the underwear and stockings. Well, then, try the side pockets. Out came the sneakers, the sewing kit, and the plastic bag with my little bottles of aspirin, sore throat tablets, cough medicine, and liquid detergent. The nylon string with four clothespins dangling followed; then the canteen and my knife, fork, spoon, and tin mug. But nothing soft and squelchy remained inside. Oh, hell, it looks as if I shall have to get everything out of the top part. I wish the man would stop looking at me. I began to feel hot, sweaty, and very angry with myself.

Oh, no! A brassiere fell on the floor. I scooped it up but not soon enough. "You're getting yourself into a right pickle, aren't you?" A young man was standing beside me and seemed vastly entertained. I could hardly blame him. Everything under the sun was falling out or dropping from rolled up garments now disheveled from prodding fingers.

"Do you always travel like that?" he asked.

Crimson-faced, I answered, "Never."

He smiled. "Hang on, you'll be all right." "Hang on" seemed to be a universal expression in Australia. It meant wait a minute, take your time, or calm down, depending on the nature of the circumstances. It seemed especially appropriate at the moment, for everything I possessed was hanging.

Having located the things I needed at last, I stuffed the rest back any old way. It was a mess, but I didn't care. I only wanted to have done with it. "Damn thing's all right on my back. I'm just not a very good packer, that's all," I mumbled defensively.

"I think you are a great packer." A pair of gray eyes twinkled in his fresh face. He was fair-haired and about twenty-three years of age. "I'd love to see my mum do what you're doing. You sound English and a long way from home."

"Yes, I am a long way from home, which is the United States for me." I was pleased with his words of praise, ill-deserved though they were. What he didn't seem to appreciate was that middle-aged "mums" had different requirements from younger backpackers. Those braless, girdleless, blue-jeaned, barefoot nymphs seemed to need next to nothing to roam around the world, whereas I would have felt stark naked without those items that had so incriminatingly fallen out of my pack a few moments ago.

"Are you arriving or leaving?"

"Arriving," I replied.

"Good luck to you," he said. "If you haven't got somewhere to stay, you'll need it. This place is jammed."

I looked around for a phone booth, thinking I had better start making a few calls and locate the Visitors' Information Center. No point in trying the YMCA; that was sure to be full. Why not call the Polaroid Corporation first? My camera had let me down when I had wanted extra pictures of the prime minister in Melbourne, and I had been told to say hello by the Polaroid people in Cambridge, Massachusetts. While my camera is being fixed, they might be able to advise me about lesser-known hotels, as the principal ones were sure to be full. At least I could go there, since they knew

201

about me, perhaps expected me, and I would be able to sit more comfortably there to search through the phone book than in a booth.

The reception to my phone call was overwhelming. Jean Blackwell, the public relations woman, knew all about me. "Yes, we were told you'd be calling us. Welcome to Australia. We are all waiting to meet you. We are right near the station at Smail Street. Take a cab and come over right away."

I was royally received. My camera was whisked off to be checked over, and I was whisked into the inner sanctum of the managing director's office to be regaled with coffee and biscuits and many questions. One of the first was about where I was staying in Sydney. I said nowhere so far. I then asked if I could use their telephone directory and phone to see what I could come up with, and if the situation was really as bad as I'd heard.

"Indeed it is," Mr. Laker informed me. "So bad that the lord mayor made a public appeal to all the citizens of Sydney to open their doors to stranded tourists. You see, many are running low on funds, not just to pay for accommodations but also to pay for three meals a day, and some are traveling with families. It's quite a serious situation."

I was escorted to a little office and told to make myself comfortable, since the man to whom it belonged was away on vacation. Mr. Laker came by a little later to ask if I had been lucky in securing a hotel, and when I reported that so far I had not, he seemed strangely pleased.

"Would you care to accept the hospitality of my home? I have felt very guilty about not responding to the lord mayor's appeal. My wife keeps telling me we should, but"—he hesitated a little uncomfortably—"well, one never knows the kind of person we might end up with. I hardly think you'd make off with the silver, and my wife would be very happy to know we've done our little bit for the stranded tourists."

I accepted with one proviso. "Do let me continue looking for something for tomorrow night. But for this evening, thank you very much, it's very kind of you." This was agreed upon and I persisted with my inquiries, deciding on impulse to call the town hall to ask about the public's response to the lord mayor's appeal.

I spoke to the lord mayor's secretary, saying that I was a visitor and a journalist and that I would like to know whether the lord mayor's request had met with success. Was she able to give me any details, since I felt it would make a very appealing human interest story. Perhaps the lord mayor himself might care to make a personal comment if he could find time for me. I left my name and telephone number as requested and mentioned that I would be here for only about another hour. I then continued my search for a room but drew a blank with all the hotels centrally located in the town. I decided to have a try at the ones the women in the office had suggested, for they were well outside the city center.

The telephone rang, and I answered with a simple "Hello," thinking it was intended for the rightful owner of the office in which I sat. A male voice responded.

"Leo Port here."

"Who?"

"Leo Port, lord mayor of Sydney."

"Oh. Er . . ." Heavens, what do I call him? In the States it's "Mr. President" or "Mr. Mayor." In England it's "Your Worship." What on earth do they say in Australia? I gulped. "Oh, Lord Mayor," was all I managed to stutter out. The male voice went on, "I would like to speak to Sabina Shalom, please."

"Yes, sir" (can't go wrong with that), "you are."

"Ah. Well, how do you do, Sabina Shalom. Is it Miss or Mrs.?"

"Mrs."

"Well, Mrs. Shalom, I understand you spoke to my secretary about my appeal. By the way, is your name really Shalom, as in 'peace,' 'welcome,' or 'hello'?"

"Yes, sir. You pronounce it perfectly, and it is spelled exactly like it sounds—Shalom, as in 'peace.' "

"That is just the most beautiful name."

"And I'm quite nice too, actually," I found myself quipping.

"I'm sure you are. Look here, with a name like that I simply have to meet you. Are you in the city? Could you get over here within fifteen minutes? I have a meeting in an hour's time, but we could have a cup of tea together and a few minutes' chat if you can make it?"

"How kind of you, sir." My head was spinning. "I'll be right over." I flew into Jean's office in an absolute dither. "Guess what, the lord mayor just called me and asked me over for a cup of tea at the town hall. Can I get there within fifteen minutes?"

"What are you talking about, Sabina? My God, you've just

arrived in Sydney barely an hour ago, and you're off to have tea with the lord mayor already. How did it happen? Let me call you a cab. It'll only take you ten minutes. How super. Wait till I tell the girls."

I followed the uniformed attendant down the long, red-carpeted town hall corridors. Everything was very hushed, as if people crept about and lowered their voices to no more than a whisper. Innumerable turns eventually brought us to the office of the lord mayor's secretary, who smiled a welcome and gestured me to be seated. "The lord mayor will see you in a moment."

"Please, would you tell me how I address the lord mayor in conversation?" I asked her.

"Just 'My Lord Mayor' will be fine, Mrs. Shalom." She picked up her telephone to answer a buzz. "Yes, sir." She stood up and said, "Would you come this way, Mrs. Shalom. The lord mayor will see you now."

I got up feeling quite excited. My goodness, I hope he's as nice as his voice sounded. Wish I had been able to have my hair done. What am I going to say? I smoothed down my skirt, which, thanks to some polyester fiber, was almost wrinkle-free. I wore a long-sleeved blouse and looked quite neat.

The door opened and then closed behind me as I stepped into the room. The figure seated at the huge desk rose at my entrance. The Right Honorable Leo Port, lord mayor of Sydney, came forward to greet me.

He was about five feet ten inches tall, topped with crisp, curly graying hair. His complexion was fresh and smooth, and his cheeks glowed with a healthy pink bloom. He looked about forty-three but could have been much older. He was dressed in a navy blue blazer and what seemed to be a club or fraternity tie. He was well groomed but with a casual air. His teeth were white and even, his smile warm and friendly, transforming pleasant but ordinary features into quite good looks. He made his way around the great desk and advanced to meet me. I took a few hesitant steps into the spacious room and found my hand grasped firmly. My murmur of "How do you do" was lost in the animation of his greeting.

"Shalom, Sabina Shalom. It really is the most beautiful name and you do it justice. Please sit here." He walked back to his desk and sat down. I took the proferred chair, a richly upholstered Chippendale one, and preened inside like a peacock.

"Welcome to Sydney, Mrs. Shalom. May I call you Sabina?" He did not wait to see if he had been granted permission. I was in such a daze I would have granted him anything. He was utterly charming. I was quite captivated.

"How long have you been in Sydney, Sabina? What are you doing in our fair city and where have you come from? London I suppose?"

"No, My Lord Mayor." (That sounds great, considering I've had no practice.) "I am from the United States and I arrived in Sydney at eight o'clock this morning."

"Really? Then welcome indeed to Sydney. How did you get here and where from? Are you vacationing? Are you traveling alone? Tell me all about yourself and let us have a cup of tea. I'm sure you must be ready for one."

He stretched his hand out to press a bell. Within seconds the door opened and a liveried footman appeared with a great silver tray and tea service, which was placed on a side table along one wall.

It was a large room, carpeted in a thick plush pile. The French windows were floor-to-ceiling and opened onto a small balcony outside. A large gilt-framed portrait of Her Majesty, Queen Elizabeth II, adorned one wall. A ceiling-height rich mahogany bookcase lined with books covered the wall opposite the lord mayor's desk. This was in the Chippendale style, with elaborately carved cabriole legs and the pie-crust carved edge.

I sipped my tea appreciatively from a fine white gold-rimmed china cup embossed with the lord mayor's crest. A small silver dish of biscuits was placed in front of me, and the footman then retired from the room.

The lord mayor sat back in his great armchair, serenely looking at me as I prattled away about my "leave of absence with pay" and the countries I had visited and hoped still to see. I came to a sudden stop, feeling very self-conscious at his quiet scrutiny. God, I must look awful after that night's journey sitting upright on the train. I had freshened myself up and changed my blouse in the travelers' aid office at the station; still, sitting on my elaborate chair in the lord mayor's parlor, with those gray-blue humorous eyes upon me, I could not help feeling less than groomed.

"Sabina Shalom, eh?" was all he murmured as I resorted to sipping more tea. "So you have taken a marriage sabbatical, have you? I must tell my wife about this. She'll get a great kick out of it and maybe a few ideas herself. By the way, where are you staying?"

"Nowhere yet. I was calling hotels when you telephoned me at the Polaroid offices. I hadn't had any luck so far, but this evening—"

He interrupted me. "Well, you need not make any more calls because your problem is solved. You will be my guest. A guest of Sydney. A good friend of mine has placed a hotel suite at my disposal should the need arise. It is yours. You may move in at once. You will be very comfortable. It is a lovely hotel that my friend owns."

"Thank you, My Lord Mayor. I really don't know what to say. You are most kind. There is just one thing. I mentioned Mr. Laker's offer for that night and said it would be ungracious now to turn it down. Could I move into the hotel tomorrow? You do understand, sir?"

"Of course. I think that is very correct of you, Sabina, and please, no more, sir, and this lord mayor stuff. My name is Leo. I am sure you are sensible enough to know when to be more formal. Between the two of us it's Leo, all right?"

"Yes, Leo." My God, he is an absolute charmer.

"Is that your Polaroid camera?"

"No, mine is being checked over. They lent me this in the meantime."

"Good enough. Let's have some photographs then." He stretched out his hand to the bell again. The secretary appeared at the door. "Have Mr. Carter come in, will you please?" He turned to me. "Mr. Carter is the town clerk. I'd like you to meet him, and he can take some pictures of us as well."

We sat in silence for a few moments. I had the feeling that he didn't quite know what else to say to me. He just sat there smiling, and I just sat there and smiled back. There seemed to be an invisible bond of warmth and friendship between us. I felt he was attracted to me, and I certainly felt attracted to him. We looked at each other in mutual admiration. It was delicious.

Any questions I might have entertained about his appeal had completely fled from my mind. Nothing could have been farther

206

from my thoughts. I could not have cared a hoot. All I was aware of was Leo Port's charm and the heady effect it was having upon me.

Mr. Carter entered the room with a discreet knock.

"Oh, I want you to meet an absolutely delightful lady. This is Mrs. Shalom. Isn't that just the most lovely name, eh? Sabina, this is Leon Carter, our town clerk."

Somberly dressed in a dark suit and tie, a tall gray-haired man, lean of build and long of nose, exchanged handshakes and "how do you dos" with me.

"I'm putting Mrs. Shalom up at the Boulevard Hotel. She only arrived this morning and has no accommodations. I would like you to make some arrangements for her to have the use of a car and a chauffeur. See what is available, and er—"

"Yes, My Lord Mayor?"

"Have an invitation made out for Mrs. Shalom to attend my private reception tomorrow evening, will you please. You can bring that to us right away. When is my meeting? There's time, isn't there?"

"Yes, sir. Certainly, plenty of time. You have about fifteen minutes yet."

"Excellent. Very good. You'll attend to the car arrangements?"

"Yes, sir. Right away."

"Good. Well, Sabina, I think you are going to enjoy your stay with us. I think Mrs. Shalom will find Sydney quite hospitable, wouldn't you say so, Leon? Now, how about some photographs?"

These were taken in front of the portrait of the queen. Mr. Carter then left, reappearing a short while later with a gilt-edged invitation for the reception the following evening. The lord mayor got up to leave for his meeting and, taking my hand in his, said, "Leon will take care of you now. Anything you need or want to know, just ask him. I will see you at my reception tomorrow, of course, but give me a call about this time tomorrow, and if I am free, perhaps we can have lunch together. In any event, call me so that I can arrange to have you comfortably installed in the hotel. I'll speak to my friend later on. Now do call me, all right?" He looked deeply into my eyes. I felt weak inside. "Yes, I'll call you."

"Good. Well, good-bye for now, Sabina Shalom." He strode purposefully from the room. I stood by my chair, my head in a whirl. There was no doubt that Leo Port certainly loved my name. He had used it over and over again.

I asked Mr. Carter if I might telephone the Polaroid people. I had promised to advise them of my movements so as to coordinate my return there with Mr. Laker's journey home.

"So glad you called. We were thinking of trying to reach you," Jean said. "Mr. Laker wants you to meet us for lunch at the Yacht Club around one o'clock if you are free."

The club was in the loveliest of settings. Our table overlooked well-trimmed but modest lawns that sloped down to the waterfront and all the magnificence of Sydney's vast harbor. The sweeping vista, perfectly crescent-shaped, stretched on and on. Green-shrubbed hillocks dipped into the sea at some points; houses with gaily colored roofs clung to other, smoother, verdant slopes in a profusion of tumbled disorder. The sun, high in the midday sky, reflected the satin-silk sheen of the waters, and all that met the eye was ablaze and shining like a blade of stainless steel. The crisp fresh wind rocked hundreds of boats at anchor. The hoisted sails were puffed and billowed out like laundered sheets hung out to dry. It was a splendid sight.

Keith Laker and his two top executive women were delightful company. They not only were attractive and chic but discreetly efficient as well. Keith, a handsome, soft-spoken man in his forties, was shyly charming. No big boss talk here. The entire company had struck me from the first as a happy and harmonious family of workers with an affectionate respect for the firm yet quiet dignity of their boss. They were grand people to be with. They made their office my headquarters if needed. They took care of all my rolls of film, my camera, and provided a fresh, generous supply of film for further use.

Mr. and Mrs. Laker and their guitar-playing son were no-less-delightful hosts in their charming house, which was one of those that I had seen clinging to the hillside. My first twenty-four hours in Sydney could not have been called anything less than eventful. I fell blissfully asleep wondering if I had not been dreaming the whole day long.

The next morning I went to the Polaroid offices to call the town hall. The secretary expressed the lord mayor's apologies at being unable to lunch with me, but he would see me that evening

208

at his reception. Meanwhile, I was expected at the Boulevard Hotel, and he hoped I would be very comfortable.

Flowers and a huge basket of fresh fruit awaited me in my suite. I felt like Cinderella and, yes, there was even a ball. Well, a reception in the town hall was close enough. I was glad of the afternoon to myself, having declined the use of the lord mayor's chauffeured car for today in preference for the following day. I had things to do. Borrowing an iron, for one, to touch up my black-print silk-jersey dress. Mr. Carter had been thoughtful enough to mention that the affair was a "dark-suit occasion. The ladies will dress up a bit, of course, but not long gowns. Silky things, you know."

Out came the black high-heeled sandals; out came the black clutch purse. My jewelry was rescued from the brown manila envelope pushed inside my sneakers. How many times had my stomach turned over when I had failed to locate its hiding place. My three-strand pearl necklace, my diamond stud and pearl earrings, modest in size but perfect in quality, now came into their own. With my diamond ring on my finger and seven very thin imitation-gold bangles (that were always thought to be real) on my wrist, I felt quite confident that I would look as well turned out as any other female guest.

The reception was a glittering affair indeed, my Lord Mayor in his official robes, a heavy gold chain and medallion hanging around his neck. His face shone not only with pleasure at being among his personal friends but also with fine beads of perspiration caused by the cumbersome long gown and the chains. He looked quite splendid, as indeed did the town clerk, duly robed and wigged for the occasion as well. I took many photographs until Mrs. Port, to whom I was introduced, said, "Come along, Sabina Shalom. I've heard all about you, and there are several people I want to present you to, but no more photographs or else I shall introduce you as the Florida Flasher." She was a charming lady. Petite, plump, brunette, and very vivacious. They were a lovely family, the Leo Ports. I met two of their three sons and one daughter.

Rappaport was the original family name. Leo's parents had fled to Australia from Nazi Germany in the earlier days of Hitler's persecution of the Jews. Young Leopold, attending public (that is, private) school, had battled with anti-Semitism even on the rugby field. His excellence in sports gradually gained him acceptance among his peers, for academically he had quickly distinguished himself as their equal. Graduating with a degree in electrical and mechanical engineering, he eventually founded his own consulting company and soon after began to revitalizing civic affairs. The poor refugee boy, uprooted from his native country, coming to a new country and a foreign language, had grown into a young man who won the confidence and approval of civic leaders. As he matured in years and experience, he undertook daring and imaginative reconstruction projects of Sydney's city center. His innovations and far-reaching plans made him much sought-after, especially when his monthly television appearances on his own *Inventors* show familiarized and endeared to him to the public at large. His natural charm swept aside the barriers of protocol and formality, and established him as Sydney's most popular lord mayor.

Leo Port never forgot his background and nobly represented his Jewish heritage. The reception I attended that night was unique to me and, I would not doubt, unique in the annals of lord mayors' receptions as well. Every morsel of food that was offered was of the Jewish cuisine.

Fish balls, chopped liver puffs, miniature potato pancakes, herring tidbits in wine or cream, gefilte fish slices speared on toothpicks and capped with carrot slices, kosher cocktail frankfurters, chopped and fried fish patties, delicate smoked salmon with cream cheese, knishes, chopped egg and onion on tiny rounds of rye bread, chopped herring on toasted squares, and cheese blintzes, hot and melting in the mouth. What an ethnic banquet.

I was introduced to Professor and Mrs. Cowan, originally from England. "And where were you born, Mrs. Shalom? Such a lovely name, isn't it?"

I was beginning to feel like a name and not a person anymore. "I was born in Sheffield."

"Fancy that. We came from Sheffield, too. After we left Germany of course."

We soon discovered mutual interests when party talk turned to the area of social work, in which Renata Cowan was engaged. "I am deeply involved in the work of the Spastics Center here. I would love to take you there and show you what we have accomplished. Our Center is quite unique. There is not another like it anywhere."

We exchanged telephone numbers and agreed to call each other to arrange a mutually convenient time for a visit to the Center. This put me in mind to give Marco a call, too. I was simply bursting to tell him of all that had been happening to me.

I returned to my hotel and struggled to keep my eyes open until one o'clock in the morning, which I knew would be ten o'clock in Miami, by which time Marco should have reached his office. I made the call, collect.

"Darling, is anything the matter?" Marco sounded anxious.

"No, everything is fine, wonderful in fact. Why?"

"Your voice. It sounds so weak and tired. Are you all right?"

"I'm marvelous. It's just that it is one o'clock in the morning here, so maybe that's why my voice sounds tired. Besides, I've been living it up a bit."

"What do you mean, living it up? As long as you are still *living*, it's okay with me. It's ages since I've heard from you."

"I have written constantly, but there's a slow-down in mail service and a postal strike is imminent. That, together with other strikes going on here, may account for the delay of my letters. Are you and Michael all right?"

"Sure, fine. Tony's back now, and living with us, and we're all getting along marvelously. So what have you been up to?"

"Oh, Marco, I wish you were here, though of course it wouldn't have happened if you had been. Everything is like a fairy tale. I'll write you all the details, since I can't tell you everything now. This must be costing you a fortune."

I started to recount some of the recent events, but there was too much to catch up on, and we cut the conversation short, content to know that the other was well. I fell asleep quickly in the warmth and comfort of hearing Marco's voice.

The air was fresh and crisp. A pale, watery sun streaked through wisps of trailing clouds as Renata Cowan drove me along suburban roads to the open country and the Spastics Center of New South Wales.

"The entire concept was the brainchild of Mr. and Mrs. Neil McLeod about thirty years ago, when doctors told them their child could not be helped." Renata unfolded a most inspiring story. "They formed a group of parents with afflicted children and decided to do something themselves. Arthur Sullivan lent them a big old house and one organization lent them two old cars. Volunteer help, appeals for money, and donations of building materials enabled hundreds of men, parents, their friends, and people from all walks of life to actually build stone by stone one of the largest single cerebral palsy units in existence at that time."

Renata explained that a unique experiment was conceived and succeeded. "Every parent whose child is treated here is expected and obligated to give a specific amount of volunteer time. Fathers are required to work one day a month, generally on weekends. It is wonderful to see what many unskilled hands have accomplished."

"I suppose a parent's involvement in this way also accomplishes an even more valuable psychological benefit?" It was beyond me to imagine the heartache a parent must suffer.

"Oh, yes indeed." Renata was now piloting me across the stony parking lot toward the main Center building, one of several low-lying concrete structures. "Parents of a cerebral palsy infant or child have a desperate need to adjust to this problem. They cannot discuss it with friends or anyone who has no knowledge of such personal distress. To be able to talk over their child's and their own difficulties with other parents often provides the framework of group therapy. This is all the more effective for being unstaged and a natural outcome of common interests.

"The Center assesses the strengths of the handicapped, not their weaknesses. They are taught to utilize whatever skills can be harnessed to productivity. Some will succeed academically, while others benefit more from manual training, enabling them to join the work force."

I was amazed to see a young girl in a wheelchair typing away by means of a device strapped around her forehead. A young man, seated at a table, applied nimble fingers from a deformed wrist, pressing out small plastic circles from a machine.

"The finished product is the work of many handicapped people," the director now explained to me as we walked from section to section in the training workshop. "They are paid by piecework, and the completed unit is eventually submitted alongside that of any other competing company bidding for a contract. You see, the pay packet is the ultimate incentive, while at the same time providing a sense of dignity and worth. The worker knows he can contribute to the labor market, and socially of course, the contact with others similarly afflicted encourages him to go on to greater skills with increased confidence of finding work elsewhere in industry."

Compassion stirred within me. Why shouldn't these young and older people take their place alongside able-bodied folk? Why should they be wheeled in front of a television set and left to watch "a lovely program, dear, while Mother's busy"? Here at the Center, a preschool clinic, a physiotherapy department, and speech and occupational therapy were but a few of the services provided and to which dental, orthopedic, psychological, and medical care were contributed by professional men and women without the payment of fees.

"You are very quiet, Sabina," Renata commented as we drove back to Sydney. "It is very impressive, isn't it?" I knew she was referring to the Center, and indeed I had been both impressed and moved by all I had seen.

"It's just the realization of how easily one takes for granted the ability to run and shout and play, and even to do the things we don't want to do."

"Well, don't be depressed. We are all very encouraged and enthusiastic at the Center. We just need a lot more money." Brightly she changed the conversation. "How are you enjoying your stay in Sydney, Sabina? You were lucky to have met Leo Port. He is the kindest and friendliest person; he and his wife, Edith, are much loved in this community."

Lucky I was indeed. While the air-controllers' strike continued and talk of a postal strike gained momentum, I remained oblivious to these threats to undermine poor Australia's economic stability. For my part, it enabled me to enjoy the luxuries of living in style. Sleeping in style would be a more accurate description, for I never once charged a meal to the account. I felt this would be an abuse of the kindness shown to me. The huge basket of fruit that had greeted me upon arrival was nowhere near depleted and amply augmented my usual diet of Sego Bars, eggs, cheese, and the occasional packet of instant soup. A refrigerator in my suite held my supplies, and an electrically heated water pitcher gave me the means with which to make my hot drinks. It really did not seem necessary to charge meals. It was more than enough to be ensconced in the luxury of a penthouse suite in a first-class hotel absolutely gratis when, but so short a while back, I had been sleeping on the earthen floor of a native hut in Papua New Guinea.

From cannibal country and stewed rat for dinner to caviar and champagne with the lord mayor of Sydney was no minor metamorphosis. No, the air-controllers' strike had been most fortunate as far as I was concerned.

The hotel management had placed a typewriter at my disposal. With the postal strike a distinct possibility, I decided I had better dash off a letter to Tonga, which after New Zealand was to be my next stop. I was looking forward to going there, as I was determined to meet the king of that tiny island. This desire was not born from caprice or sudden whim, but whenever the urge to "run away from it all" came upon me, it was to the island of Tonga that my imagination whisked me. Now that I was in this part of the world, I would see for myself the haven that so far had only existed in my fantasies. Meeting its titular head simply seemed a matter of course.

Here in Sydney I was told by one who had attended the same private school as the king that it might not be as easy as I seemed to think. I decided therefore to write a letter in advance of my arrival requesting the honor of an audience with His Majesty. My typed letter was accompanied by a brief biographical note about myself, which indicated I was a journalist. This small stretch of the imagination (though not altogether unfounded) might gain my request some advantage. At least it was better than no reason at all for asking to meet with King Tauf'ahau Tupou IV.

My days were eventfully filled. When I was not being chauffeured in a mayoral limousine, kind friends I had made invited me to sightsee, attend a dinner party, or visit the spectacular Opera House. It was not the season for opera, but the music of the symphony orchestra in that great concert hall was no less thrilling an experience.

I shivered in my silk-jersey dress as the winds whipped across the waters of the bay. Ladies clutched their skirts and tried to shield their freshly waved hair from destruction as they mounted the entrance steps. Once inside the incredible stone edifice from which the walls emerged like a configuration of nature, the poignancy of Mahler burned through me. Cold was but a color. White

214

and pure, to be washed away by hazy hues of lavender and taupe or ripped asunder by the blaze of crimson passion, that is Mahler. The music affected me deeply. Tears escaped from my tightly closed eyes, and a longing for Marco swept over me with such intensity that I felt quite faint.

"Sabina, I really think you will have to forego New Zealand. It's only autumn here and you are shivering away. In the fjords of the South Island it is already winter and you will turn to ice, I'm convinced."

This was a piece of good advice I could not afford to ignore. When a resolution to end the air-controllers' strike was unexpectedly announced, it also heralded the end of my stay in Sydney. As a stranded visitor, the hospitality I had enjoyed had been generously extended to me. Now I had no good reason to prolong my visit, and I hastened to the airlines to make changes to my ticket. It was not surprising to find all flights out of Sydney heavily booked, and I found myself obliged to take one to New Zealand after all—to Christchurch, not Auckland, from where I would later make the connection for Tongatapu. The strike had caused a backlog of all the schedules, and I took what was soonest available.

Notes of thanks and flowers were hastily dispatched to those whose kindness to me I could never hope to repay. With sad brevity and a hurried embrace of a very dear lord mayor, I expressed my gratitude and affection on parting. The time had come to move on.

I called Ethel Baker to say good-bye. She informed me that Liz and Harry would not be back for three or four days. They were stuck in Hong Kong, making the best of an enforced stay while waiting for the first available seats. All flights were booked solid, and everyone was clamoring for space.

How ironic, I mused. I had come and gone without even seeing them, yet they had been instrumental in making my journey possible from the very first.

8

The King and I

How right my friends had been. New Zealand was preparing for winter, and Christchurch felt like the South Pole. Indeed, an icy blast swept over the South Island. It was an advance warning of the weather to come, for which I was ill-prepared.

Thankful for the warm garments Nina had pressed upon me in Melbourne, I was still without any serviceable topcoat. The penetrating cold pierced my thin poplin raincoat, which was as useless as if it had been made out of paper.

I shivered. I shook. I chattered, trembled, and quaked with cold. A grip of ice seized my body, and I quivered as one in a spasm of palsy. Making my way around the streets to find accommodations for the night, I cursed my thin cotton panties and held my nylon hose in contempt. Long-legged thermal underwear would have been the thing to wear.

There was no visitors' bureau and no help from the tourist information office. "I'm sorry, but we are closed now." The young woman mouthed the words behind the glass door, impervious to my pleading look. She pointed to her right and said, "Hotel," and I turned away and went in search of her recommendation. It was no time to think of economies. At five o'clock, the evening was drawing in and I intended to take whatever came along at whatever price. It was a fruitless search, or perhaps I had taken the wrong direction, but all I came across was a scruffy-looking establishment called a "Guest House." With a sinking feeling of resignation, I went inside. The entrance hall was so drab and oppressive, it did little to decrease my gloomy prognoses. I took a room rather than run the risk of not finding a better alternative by braving the streets again. The room was spartan, clean but cheerless. The bathroom had a huge casement window and an ancient enameled tub, the pristine whiteness of which was scarred by a brownish yellow streak of rust beneath the faucet. It looked as cold and as inviting as a grave.

It was not yet dark, barely six o'clock, but I felt desperately tired, chilled, and dispirited. This was such a dreadful anticlimax to all the days preceding my departure from Sydney. I had noticed a fish-and-chips shop a few doors away from the hotel, and the smell had whetted my appetite. Now, despite my fatigue, I decided to venture out, since it was so close, and give myself a fish-and-chips treat. It would be something hot for a change.

The owners, to my surprise, were Greek, not English as I had expected. I had finished my chips before the fish was ready. They were heavenly. A dirty-aproned, dark-haired motherly soul plunked another scoopful of chips alongside the fish as she handed me the hot paper-wrapped food.

"Is good? Is all right? Where you from?" She flashed a beaming smile at me, revealing two glistening, gold-capped teeth.

It was moist, warm, and cheerful inside that shabby little store. A makeshift counter ran along one wall for the convenience of those patrons who wanted to "eat in"; the piled-high stack of cut-up newspapers was available for those who wanted to "eat out."

"What is like America? I go there someday." The Greek lady nodded her head in vigorous affirmation of her intent. I offered my grease-tipped hand in a gesture of appreciation and friendship. She had not charged me for the extra chips. I felt a little like Liberty extending a welcome on behalf of all those "tired and huddled masses" who had come to the United States and had made good. This Greek lady, with her kindness and vigor, was the stuff from which nations flourish—hard-working, alive with interest and industry and that warm human appeal to which one cannot help but respond.

As I left the shop the smell of oil and fish was quickly obliterated from my clothes. The chill wind had gathered strength. In great wet gusts it tore through me. Gales of rain blew hard at my legs and plastered the thin poplin coat to my side, soaking through my clothes, now sopping wet. With one hand I

217

clutched my rain hat; with the other I tried to hold down the open flapping part of my coat. It was only a few yards back to the hotel, but far enough to arrive drenched to the skin. I could not wait to leave New Zealand.

I hurried into a hot bath, the effects of which rapidly evaporated as the wind howled through the gaps of the window frame while I dried myself. There was no central heating, just a single-bar electric radiator set into the wall. It was as good as useless. What little warmth I retained from my long hot soak now drained from me completely as I gingerly sidled into the cold white sheets of an enormous double bed. It could have accommodated four persons. It felt to me as if it encompassed the vast wastelands of the entire South Pole.

I wrenched the sheet and blankets from imprisonment around the mattress and wrapped myself up into them cocoonlike. It was no use. My feet were frozen; my body had turned into ice. I lay in utter congealed wretchedness.

The neon lighting from the streetlamps outside filtered in through the thin curtains. It imparted an eery look to the room; the purplish rays, reflected through the mirror, lay across the bed. I felt as cold and as rigid as a corpse.

It was the first and only time in my life that I had ever lain in bed with a carpet and the cushions of an easy chair piled on top of the bedcovers.

Mercifully, when sleep came, it was deep and satisfying, punctuated by a single but altogether pleasant dream that the King of Tonga had invited me to stay at his palace.

Tonga, also known as the Friendly Islands, rests securely on the International Dateline, the first country in the world to greet each new day. It lies southeast of Fiji and southwest of Samoa. Over 150 gems of this once Crown jewel lie scattered in the sparkling waters of the South Pacific. They have a total land area of 269 square miles, and only 45 of the 150 islands are inhabited. Just 3 of them carry the bulk of the population, which numbers about 90,000 in all.

Once a part of the British Empire, Tonga now enjoys full independence while remaining a loyal member of the British Commonwealth. My first knowledge of this tiny kingdom came about on the occasion of the coronation of Her Majesty, Queen

Elizabeth II, to which were invited all the crowned heads of the world and representatives of most of its countries.

Despite the glittering radiance of the queen of England's jewels, and the splendor of the golden state carriage and the richness of the ermine-trimmed and pearl-encrusted state robes that befitted the occasion, it was Queen Salote of Tonga who stole the show. Watching the ceremony on television left me with an impression I never forgot. Tonga from that day on spelled for me the ultimate escape to a fantasy island that did indeed exist.

Queen Salote not only stole—she also won. She won the hearts of the cool reserved English, already warming up from the excitement generated on an occasion of pomp and tradition in the grandest manner.

The queen of Tonga dwarfed the staid pallor of all Europe's royalty. She was huge. She was black. She was handsome. She was a magnificent monument. Her statuesque figure was heightened by her winning charm. Her smile and dazzling white teeth were captivating. When, on television, she extended the warmest of welcomes to anyone who cared to visit her in Tonga, I felt the invitation was personally meant for me. One day, I vowed, I would go, and now here I was, on my way. Queen Salote had dropped in on England; I was returning the visit. Alas, she died in 1965, and I was a little late to take up the invitation. I felt sure, however, that her son, King Tauf'ahau Tupou, who now reigned over this island kingdom, would be no less gracious in his welcome than his mother had been, so many years before.

Friends in Melbourne had encouraged me to believe I would have no problem in meeting the king. Some had actually gone to school with him and said he was referred to simply as "George." "Nice feller," one had said. "You'll like him. Succeeded to the throne in sixty-seven, you know. Friendly sort of bloke, takes after his mother."

In Sydney it had been just the reverse. "What on earth do you want to go to Tonga for? A real dump of a place. As for meeting the king, not so easy, not like his mother. He's quite snobbish about whom he mixes with." I mentioned the encouragement from a Melbourne school chum of the king. "Don't believe a word of it. Chances are he never even spoke to Tupou."

I sat now on the plane, glad that I had written a letter requesting an audience with His Majesty before I left Australia. It would have arrived a week or so ago, I guessed. Long enough for the biographical sketch I had enclosed with my letter to be digested and considered.

After all, I reasoned, Indira Gandhi had received me. The prime minister of Australia had given me a little interview, and if my reception by the lord mayor of Sydney was anything to go by, hospitality and a welcome seemed assured in these parts. The Friendly Islands were not so called for nothing. I was sure they would live up to their name. I started to scribble a little note to Marco: "I'm now off to Tonga to meet the king . . ."

Our two-engine B-11 aircraft whirred to a stop, sending up clouds of dust in a miniature sandstorm. I couldn't see what Nuku'alofa Airport looked like. As we had come in to land I hadn't seen anything that even resembled an airport. It looked as if the plane was to be put down in the middle of a field. Now, with so much dust billowing around, perhaps we had landed in some flats in the sand. Until I stepped down from the plane I did not know what to expect.

A large signpost cleared up any misgivings. It read: WELCOME TO THE KINGDOM OF TONGA. I took a photograph of it just to assure myself that this really was the place, for the two or three low-lying buildings could have been plunked down anywhere that banana and palm trees grow. It was extremely quiet all around, with none of the activity one normally associates with airports, even those in the middle of fields.

A few of the passengers on the plane were well ahead of me as I walked down the pebble path laid between banana fronds and small flowering bushes. Some had already entered one of the buildings, which I saw was little more than a shed, open in the back. None of them looked as I expected Tongans to look, though I was not too sure how they would look. Some of the passengers were Samoan, as I had overheard their comments about connecting flights home, and two had been Englishmen judging by their British accent. I hadn't paid much attention to anyone else, since I had been busy writing my letter to Marco.

As I entered the shed, the two Englishmen were jumping into a waiting jeep. They either had no baggage or were so well known to the officials that their departure was not impeded by customs inspection.

Authority was represented by extremely tall—at least six feet four or five inches—light-brown-skinned men. All were dressed in a white short-sleeved, open-necked, military-type shirt and a calf-length, heavy black cotton wraparound skirt. One of the officials wore a black brimmed hat similar to those worn by the Royal Canadian Mounted Police, and all wore open-toed, ankle-strapped leather sandals upon bare feet. All four men were exceptionally handsome.

It never occurred to me that their language could be anything but English. Now I heard the strangest of sounds—clipped vowels and dipthongs set to some primitive, atonal music.

One of the officials flashed me a welcoming smile and beckoned me toward a wooden table, saying, "Madam, if you will please step this way." His English was perfect. I was much relieved.

My first remark caused something of a flurry. "May I please make a telephone call to the palace?"

The poor fellow, intent upon stamping my passport, appeared quite bemused. He paused and looked at me with grave concern, his expression clearly indicating doubts as to whether to stamp me in or out. Evidently he came to the conclusion that I seemed harmless enough, and while stamping me in with his right hand he waved his left in the direction behind his shoulder, saying, "Oh, you'll have to go over there. We have no telephones here."

I thanked him, pocketed my passport, and walked out of the shed in the "over there" direction. I spotted my backpack lying on the floor awaiting collection, but as long as it had come off the plane, there was no urgency to claim it then and there. It could wait until I had called the palace. I wanted to find out straight away if my letter had been received and if an appointment had been set up. I felt sure I would get through to a secretary who could apprise me of the situation, and then I would know where I stood with respect to the number of days I might stay in Tonga.

All I could see "over there" was a thatch-roofed, pole-supported hut, open on all sides, and not a sign of a telephone anywhere. The only, and indeed most visible, sight was the most enormous man I had ever seen.

He was dressed exactly like the officials in the arrival shed. Standing at attention, straight and stiff, he must have been quite seven feet tall. An ancient large black Cadillac was parked beside him. I felt like an ant as I approached him. With my head raised at an angle of forty-five degrees, I said, "Excuse me, sir." I strained my voice to travel the distance of his height. "I was told there was a telephone over here. I wish to call the palace, but I don't see any telephone at all."

He looked down upon my five feet one inch. "No, madam, there is no telephone, but I am here to take you to the palace. Where is your luggage, madam?"

What's this? The palace had sent a car for me? How could that be? How could they have known when I was arriving? True, I had given an approximate date, and there was only one direct flight a week, but still! . . . "Well, my luggage is over there." (Everything in this place is "over there.") I pointed to the shed I had just left. "It's an orange backpack." I shriveled at the thought of the king's chauffeur seeing my pack, and worse, the thought of transporting it to—where? The palace? Cannot be. "Excuse me, but have I understood you correctly? You mean you are especially here to meet me and take me to the palace?"

"Yes, indeed I am, madam. I meet all the king's guests. I recently drove His Royal Highness Prince Charles all around the island. Now, if you would care to step into the car, madam, I will collect your bag and we will go at once."

I stood in absolute astonishment. I could not believe my ears. What a fantastic reception! The palace had actually sent a car for me. Well, no good looking like a country bumpkin, girl. Get in, get in, and behave as if you are perfectly accustomed to such attention. If my face had betrayed my shocked pleasure and disbelief, it would not have been visible to the chauffeur. All he could see of me when I looked straight in front was the top of my head.

My flaming-orange pack was carried like a small paper bag and duly deposited in the trunk of the car. The back-seat door was closed behind me with a ceremonial flourish, and the chauffeur, with a couple of short, cheery honks of the horn, set off on the road.

I sat back, indulging in the most improbable conjectures. For a car to have been sent for me surely implied that someone at the palace intended to receive me. That someone could only be the king. Who else? Well now, to be welcomed like this, perhaps I was going to be invited to stay at the palace? I remembered my dream, which was all my imagination needed to fire it to the wildest of heights. Tonga was a tiny country. They were all doubtless friendly, simple people who knew little about, and perhaps cared even less for, protocol, formalities, and all the trappings one normally associates with royalty. The king was a royal personage in his own country, but perhaps through schooling abroad and mixing with a cross section of the middle class he had been less subjected to the generally accepted notions of royal behavior. My flights of fantasy knew no bounds, and I began to formulate in my mind the correct expressions of gratitude and thanks for the honor that was about to come my way.

The road was dusty, sparsely inhabited by human beings, and edged with coconut palms and an occasional banana plantation. I thought it would not ill-befit a guest of His Majesty to make some pleasant remark to his chauffeur.

"I would like to be able to greet the king with some appropriate words in Tongan. How would I say, for example, 'It is most gracious of Your Royal Majesty to receive me'?"

"You would have to write it down, madam. You see, there are several different forms of address, depending upon the occasion. Excuse me, madam, but at which hotel are you staying?"

"Hotel? Well, I don't really know yet. We shall see what transpires after my audience with the king, which I expect will take place very shortly."

"An audience with His Majesty?" The chauffeur took his eyes off the road ahead to swing around and look at me.

"Why, yes," I replied. "You said you met all the king's guests and that you were taking me to the palace, did you not?"

"Indeed I am taking you to the palace, madam. In fact, here we are. These are the grounds, there is the gate, and here are the guards. But now, which hotel shall I take you to?"

I looked at him with dismay and growing consternation. "It seems that there has been some misunderstanding. I was under the impression that you were taking me to the palace as one of the king's guests. I gathered you had been sent to take me there...." My voice trailed off weakly. Feeling confused and a little stupid, and with a growing sense of anger, I stumbled on, "Look, are you the king's chauffeur, or aren't you?"

"Yes, madam. I am indeed the king's chauffeur, and furthermore I am the retired chief head of police. My name is Mr. Lee, and I drive all the guests of His Majesty. I have shown you the palace, madam, and now please allow me to take you to your hotel."

"Shown me the palace?" I repeated blankly. "You mean you only intended to show me the palace, not take me to the king?"

Mr. Lee was silent. He looked at me strangely. I felt embarrassed and not a little foolish. Trying to recover my composure, I forced myself to continue. "Mr. Lee, I came to Tonga with the express purpose of meeting the king. When, at the airport, you said you were taking me to the palace, I naturally assumed it was for this very reason. Evidently there has been a mistake. Now, what can I do to correct matters?"

"I am most sorry, madam. I have brought you to the palace and I can do no more. Perhaps in the morning you can see the king's private secretary, and he will be able to make the necessary arrangements for you. May we now proceed to your hotel?" It was clear that as far as he was concerned this was the end of the matter. For me it was not.

Undaunted, hope rising anew, I smiled expansively. "Let us go straight away then to see the king's private secretary. My time is very limited here in Tonga, and I haven't a moment to lose."

"Madam, it is too late now. Mr. Maketti will have left his office and gone home."

"Then," I persisted, "let us go to Mr. Maketti's house. Please, Mr. Lee, I would be most appreciative if we could do that."

I realized that without his cooperation I would lose ground and would have to go through all kinds of fuss and possible red tape on the following day. I still clung to the childish belief that all obstacles could be swept aside, and it was with great relief that I noted the resigned acquiescence on Mr. Lee's face as he started up the car.

As we drove toward the home of the private secretary, I wondered at my own naïveté as to have really believed that the king had sent a car for me. How *could* I have thought that he planned to grant me an audience and might even have invited me to stay as his guest? Just the same, I told myself by way of excuse, Mrs. Gandhi had invited me into *her* house. The lord mayor of Sydney had made me as *his* guest; it wasn't as if the most unexpected things had not happened to me recently.

"There he is, madam, just getting out of his car." Mr. Lee

pointed a finger at the windshield. I didn't wait for him to open the door. Fearful that Mr. Maketti would turn into the gateway of his house, I leaped out of the car and hastened toward a man of average height, dressed in the seemingly typical black wraparound skirt. He wore a white open-necked shirt and an unusual kind of sash around his waist.

I must have looked a strange sight running toward him, waving my hand and calling out, "Mr. Maketti, Mr. Maketti, just a moment, please."

He paused just as he was about to open the gate. I addressed him with deference. "As the king's private secretary, I understand, Mr. Maketti, that you would be able to make the necessary arrangements for me to have an audience with His Majesty?" I gave him my name and added that I had written a formal request to this effect not long ago, when in Australia.

While I had not expected Mr. Maketti to fall over himself with delight at meeting me, I was ill-prepared for the look of shock that now registered across his face.

"Madam," he said, "I know nothing about your letter, nor am I familiar with your name. No one is granted an audience with His Majesty just on request. If you would care to present yourself at my office in the morning, I will give the matter my careful consideration." My hopes sank as he went on to explain that in any case it was very doubtful he could do anything for me tomorrow, since there was a special privy council meeting at ten o'clock and in all probability the king would go off fishing in the afternoon. No, there would be no point in me holding out any hopes of an audience for that day. It might be possible after the weekend, perhaps Monday or Tuesday of the following week. His subdued tone of voice implied that he didn't really think much of my hopes at any time, but he might as well be polite about it.

Mr. Maketti seemed a gentle person. Neither his size nor his manner had been too intimidating. The moment had come when I thought a little playacting might be in order, and I decided to try a bluff. I drew myself up as tall as I could and, with as much confidence as I could muster, said, "Mr. Maketti, you say there is a special meeting at ten o'clock and that His Majesty may go off fishing in the afternoon. I leave the following day, so the only time left would be after the meeting and before His Majesty adjourns for the rest of the day. Now, if you feel you are not in a position to expedite matters, would you care to give me the name of the American or British ambassador here, so that I may consult with him and see if his recommendations could be made directly to His Majesty and thus spare you further inconvenience?"

The words sounded asinine to my ears. I knew I presented a crumpled and disheveled appearance. I felt I had nothing to lose by this gambit, and I prepared myself for the disappointment that was to come. Mr. Maketti quite surprised me. With a cordiality totally unexpected, he responded, "There is no American ambassador, madam, but Mr. Lee knows the house of the British high commissioner and can take you to see him if you so wish."

He must be glad to be getting rid of me, I thought, or as Tonga was a proud member of the Commonwealth, perhaps my strong British accent and my weak bit of bluff had done the trick.

It was neither. Mr. Maketti must have regretted mentioning His Majesty's schedule, for he went on in a tone of voice just the slightest bit ingratiating. "I would appreciate it, madam, if you would refrain from mentioning the events I referred to. It would not be at all correct. Not in my position, you understand?"

Perhaps my bit of theater and the confidence with which I had spoken had also made him wonder who I might be and if I might relate something to his discredit.

"Rest assured, sir." I spoke confidentially. "I will mention nothing that could possibly cause you any embarrassment. You have been most helpful, and I will be at your office at nine o'clock. Perhaps when you have seen my credentials"—what credentials?—"and with a word from the commissioner, you may find it possible to arrange an appointment before His Majesty concludes his affairs for the day."

Mr. Maketti bowed slightly, escorted me back to the car and deferentially opened the door. Mr. Lee, who had maintained a stony silence throughout, drove me now, with dusk fast approaching, to the residence of the British high commissioner.

Tall trees, high bushes, and the dust of the road obscured from view any houses there might have been in the section through which we passed. A break in the foliage revealed a white-painted fence that encircled large grounds and a substantial-looking white wood-frame house. As we turned into the driveway, Mr. Lee mumbled, "I would be glad, madam, if you would overlook anything I have said about Mr. Maketti and His Majesty when you speak with the commissioner."

I assured him I would respect his wish and wondered whether the man I was now calling on was someone to be afraid of. I also began to have doubts about the wisdom of insisting upon this visit for the sake of impressing Mr. Maketti. I would have to go through with it now. I could hardly tell Mr. Lee to turn around. Both had been so concerned about their implication in all this, and all a result of my ridiculous display of histrionics. Poor fellows. Poor me. What on earth was I doing, mounting the broad steps of this imposing residence of the British high commissioner to Tonga?

I cast about in my mind as to what I could say. I could think of nothing except express the infantile wish, it now seemed to me, to meet the king. All I could hear in my head were Marco's admonitions. "Why do you do these things—why?" My reply was always the same. "I don't know, Mong, I get obsessed by a challenge. The harder something is, the more I want to tackle it." He'd shrug and say, "You know you are a nut sometimes, don't you?"

He's right. I am, I am. It was no good saying, "I'm sorry, Mong, please bail me out." No, the show must go on. Some show, I thought. Me with my rumpled skirt, flustered and untidy from my journey; oh yes, it was some show. I straightened my shoulders, smoothed over my hair, and braved myself to face the music.

A white-uniformed houseboy stood at the top of the broad steps. The sound and lights of the car had probably prompted him to take his position to welcome guests. Without asking a single question, my name, or whom I wished to see, he led me forward onto a wide veranda. It was bamboo-furnished and screened from the road by lush foliage and multicolored flora.

A newspaper was lowered. A pair of cool blue eyes swept over me from top to toe. Sir Humphrey Augustine Arthington-Davy rose to greet me. He was as urbane and as English in manner and formality as if he had been dressed in morning coat and striped trousers instead of a pair of white shorts and a gaily printed short-sleeved shirt.

Having decided to see this charade through, I threw myself into the role with abandon. The whole thing had assumed comic proportions, really. I decided at that instant I might just as well play it to the hilt and have a good time. Here I was, with night fast approaching, no place as yet to stay, and calling upon the British high commissioner. Either he would treat me with crusty British disdain (if he heard me out, that is) or, worse, he would pierce me with a look and have me shown out. With a "may as well hang for a sheep as for a lamb" feeling, I thrust out my hand as I walked toward him. "Please forgive me for calling on you like this. My name is Sabina Shalom. How do you do?" My hand was taken, but without waiting for a response I went on hastily, "I have only just arrived in Tonga with hopes of meeting the king. Mr. Lee, whom you doubtless know, and who is waiting outside, led me to believe, innocently I am sure, that it was but a matter of driving me to the palace. I completely misunderstood his intentions and alas was naïve enough to think that meeting His Majesty was a simple affair. Mr. Maketti, whom I have just seen, thought a visit to you, sir, might help straighten things out. . . ." My voice trailed off. It had not come out quite as I had hoped, and I lamely added, "I'm not sure now that I should have imposed upon you. It's all my own silly fault, of course. Er, well, I hope you don't mind?"

Not a muscle in Sir Humphrey's face had moved. I could not fathom the expression in his eyes. His gaze had been steady and intent upon me as I spoke. This was no doomed diplomat sent out to graze in Tonga. Not this one, my girl. I suppose all diplomats bear the same characteristics. The skilled ones, that is. One can never figure out what they are thinking.

His voice was well modulated, his accent cultured. He was about sixty years old, and when he spoke, it was in a tone that put me immediately at ease.

Gesturing toward a comfortably upholstered bamboo armchair, he said, "Won't you sit down. Can I get you something to drink?" I felt enormous relief and gratefully complied. I asked for a Pepsi-Cola, which was served within moments in an exquisite crystal glass on a handsome silver tray. As Sir Humphrey murmured a few words to the houseboy, I took stock of him. He was a tall man of over six feet, with straight, smoothed-back hair that was quite thick and white. He was tanned and had a fresh complexion. If not for the scar on his cheek, which looked like the result of a burn or an accident, and which plastic surgery had attempted to mini-mize, he would have been exceedingly handsome. The scar had caused some distortion on the right side of the face, which was turned in my direction. I tried hard not to think about it so as to be able to concentrate on the further words of explanation that I felt were now awaited.

I eased myself thankfully against the soft cushions. I sipped my drink slowly and tried to adopt a nonchalant air. At my host's invitation I began to recount the whole sorry tale. I introduced a humorous twist and poked occasional fun at myself, hoping to convey that I regarded the episode as a lark and perhaps appear less of a foolish woman.

I detected a twinkle in Sir Humphrey's eye, so I spiced things up a bit to take full advantage of his evident amusement, trying all the while to extricate my stupidity with as much aplomb as I could gracefully lay claim to. I could see now that he was vastly diverted. As a matter of fact, I had rather begun to enjoy myself too.

"My dear lady," he said, chortling, at the conclusion of the story, "haven't been as entertained as this for years. No, by George. It's a positive howl. I say, won't you have something else to drink?"

I demurred, relief far outweighing thirst. "You're most kind, but no, thank you. Besides, Mr. Lee is waiting outside. You do know him, don't you? He says he is the king's chauffeur?"

"Oh, yes, he is, but more in the capacity of chauffeur for the king's guests than as His Majesty's personal driver. He is also the retired chief head of police and takes advantage of the now fewer calls upon his time to use the car occasionally as a taxi."

"Ah! That explains everything," I said. "Still, he did mislead me by the way he put things. Of course, I should not have been so naïve either."

"You will find, dear lady," Sir Humphrey rumbled on, "that here in Tonga your interpretation of what is said is not quite what was meant. Our people are like happy children. Simple and well-meaning, but they draw their conclusions from feelings, not from facts. It can be quite confusing sometimes. They have quaint notions, and one has to get used to the complications of speech and viewpoint to understand the nature of the Tongans."

Sir Humphrey went on to explain some of the interesting customs of Tongan culture. I learned that there is a very strong class system that dictates a certain way of dress, a way of speech, and the nature of employment, which is conditional upon one's station.

229

The Tongans love their monarchy and treat with great respect all members of the *boake*—the aristocrats. There is no resentment about the superiority of the upper classes. If it should be their lot to serve the *boake*, then they serve with willingness and affection. The Tongans are a loving people, Sir Humphrey told me. They are very proud of their Polynesian heritage and their ancient skills.

"We have a thriving copra industry here, and of course bananas. You'll have to visit the local market and see some of the fine artwork. The womenfolk are particularly skilled at tapa making and mat weaving. Now what about you, young lady. Are you staying long with us, and where are your travels taking you next?"

I was glad to have the information about Tonga and quite flattered to be the subject of his interest, to which I responded eagerly. His hearty laugh over one of my exploits restored my confidence, and when he told me that I had livened up his rather dull bachelor's existence, I began to think I might even be asked to stay to dinner.

Such foolish contemplations were quickly dispelled when he suggested that I stay at the one and only decent hotel in town, and added that they finished serving dinner at eight o'clock. "I rarely eat there myself, actually, unless someone invites me. But the food's not at all bad."

I swallowed my totally unfounded disappointment and decided I had best not overstay my welcome. I hadn't broached the subject of enlisting his aid with respect to meeting the king, and thought to do so before taking my leave. "Sir Humphrey," I began hesitantly, "I'd be glad of your advice, if I may ask you, please?"

"Certainly, certainly. Fire away."

"I had told Mr. Maketti that I would present my credentials for his consideration. I haven't any credentials, and it was ridiculous to have said such a thing."

"Oh, don't worry about that. As a matter of fact, it sounds fine. Just the sort of thing Mr. Maketti would like. Didn't you say you'd sent His Majesty a letter? Do you have a copy?"

"Yes, I do, and a copy of the biographical sketch I enclosed at the same time. I said I was a journalist. Which I am in a sort of modest way."

"Splendid." Sir Humphrey ruminated for a moment. "I suggest you get there long before nine o'clock. Since there's a privy council meeting, Mr. Maketti will be quite busy. Yes, the earlier the better. Very short day is Friday. The king usually goes off fishing in the afternoon. Very fond of fishing is His Majesty."

"Wouldn't a word from you, Sir Humphrey, be far more effective than my bits of paper. If you wouldn't mind, that is?"

"Oh, I don't mind at all, but I really don't think it would help that much. Mr. Maketti has his own way of doing things, and he is the king's private secretary. He's already met you, and I have a feeling that he'll hear all about your visit here. These things have great significance for the people, you know. I'm sure you'll be all right. You seem to have done just fine everywhere else."

"You've been more than kind, Sir Humphrey. I hope you are right. I really would like to meet the king now that I am here in Tonga. I only have until Monday, when I go on to Fiji."

"Yes, well, it does rather depend upon Maketti. I think he'll be cooperative—no promises, mind you. As for the king, he's not a bad old stick; quite a kind person in fact. You being a lady and British and all that . . . The queen was here, you know. Place went wild. It all went off quite well really. The king was as pleased as Punch." Sir Humphrey rambled away as he escorted me to the car. "Pleasure to have met you, I must say. You're quite a traveler, aren't you? Fiji, eh? I think you'll like it—much more developed than here, of course. Let me know how you get on. Er, anything I can do, you know, be a pleasure, a pleasure."

I took his proferred hand. "Thank you, it has been a pleasure for me too."

Mr. Lee whisked me off to the one and only hotel in town. The journey was completed in silence, though I had the feeling that he had been quite impressed by the length of my stay at the high commissioner's residence. Perhaps Sir Humphrey had wisely summed up the situation. Mr. Maketti would hear about my visit and might read into it more than was actually merited.

The street lighting in the parts we drove through was very dismal. I saw little of my environment. What was discernible in the darkness of night looked like a shanty-town movie set. Not quite real and not at all prosperous.

The hotel was more than acceptable, but by no stretch of the imagination could it have been called luxurious. I was shown to a pleasant utilitarian uncarpeted room with shower and toilet. The floors and walls were painted a bilious green. The screens across the windows were intact, water came out of the faucets, and the toilet worked. What more could I expect or need in the tiny Kingdom of Tonga?

The bed was wobbly on its wooden frame, and the mattress very lumpy. The pillow smelled mildewed, and the sheets felt coarse. All this was of little concern to me, my mind obsessed with but a single thought, the absolute conviction of which quickly lulled me to sleep.

Tomorrow I would meet the king.

I slept soundly and awoke to bright sunshine and a fresh breeze coming in from the sea a few hundred feet from my window. It was barely six o'clock, but I was eager to bathe, dress, and go down to a breakfast of pineapple, banana, and papaya—a welcome change from my usual hot drink and Sego Bar. The chambermaids and hotel staff were, without exception, very tall and striking. Smiling faces greeted me wherever I went, and with plenty of time on my hands I set off to walk to the palace by way of the town center. I had been informed that everything was close and that within an hour I could encompass the main street, the marketplace, the post office, and the palace and still be back at the hotel before breakfast was finished being served.

The facial characteristics common to all the Tongans I saw were clearly Polynesian. Light-brown skin, long, straight silky black hair, and softened features. The women and men were quite handsome, and the girls extremely pretty. I noticed that all wore long skirts, the men in their wraparound ones, called *lap-lap*s and the women in their floor-length dresses of brightly colored print cotton fabric. All seemed to favor a sash around the waist, varying in width and material. Some were made from plaited straw; others, from finely woven silkier threads. Everywhere I walked, people smiled and returned in English my "Good morning." I had the impression that they were a happy, contented people who loved their visitors. They were not called the Friendly Islands for nothing.

At eight-thirty sharp I presented myself at Mr. Maketti's office. I gave my name to a tall, pleasant young lady and said that I had some papers for the secretary that I would like to give him personally, please.

Mr. Maketti came out to greet me. He was very polite and with a cordial smile said, "Good morning. I trust you slept well." He took the copies of my letter and biographical sketch and read them over very carefully. He was now quite deferential as he said, "I do not recall receiving any of this, but of course the postal strike in Australia could be the reason."

"Oh, of course, Mr. Maketti. I had quite forgotten about that."

"Well, it is of no consequence now. This seems to be quite satisfactory. I shall have to keep them for a while, and I must ask you to fill out a form. The young lady will attend to you. There may be a long wait. It will probably be after the meeting, not before, but I shall certainly see what I can do."

"Thank you, sir. I understand. I am perfectly happy to wait, and I appreciate your assistance greatly." I found I was adopting his complaisant manner. He had the authority to recommend or refuse permission to anyone seeking an audience with the king, and whereas last evening it had seemed impossible, this morning I felt optimistic.

I used the time to ask the young ladies in the office of the secretary for various phrases in Tongan. I wrote them down and assiduously studied them. I then asked if they would be good enough to listen to me practice, which sent them into peals of laughter over my pronunciation. I eventually won their approval and got down pat the correct way to address the king when first making his acquaintance.

I asked them about the sash I had noticed everyone wearing. I learned that one is incorrectly attired if this is not worn. It is called the ta'ovala for men, and theirs is generally made of plaited straw. The ladies' sash is called the kieke, and can be made from a variety of fabrics, though often one of straw is worn. It is regarded much like the wearing of a tie, and everyone in government service is expected to wear one. I saw very few throughout my stay on the island who didn't.

I wandered around the grounds a little; the offices were set quite apart from the palace, which was surrounded by a low white-painted stone wall. A notice affixed to a tree read: "Please do not climb the trees or jump on the palace walls." I was most amused and took a photograph. The palace itself was worthy of many photographs by virtue of its sweet simplicity. The fresh white wood-frame structure made me think of the fairy-tale style

233

found in Disneyland. The red roofs, white gables, white-slatted shutters, and domed towers had a gingerbread quality. It was small, charming, and looked almost good enough to eat.

I hastened back to the office, which bore a sign over the door saying Office of the Palace; it could not be mistaken for any other kind of office, for there was no other in sight. I was not kept waiting as long as I had expected. The privy council meeting was over by ten-thirty. Doubtless His Majesty's fishing day had something to do with it.

Mr. Maketti came toward me accompanied by an equerry. My pulse beat faster; it looked as if I was going to get my wish. Both men led me across the grounds, and we entered the neat and modest official residence of the king.

Mr. Maketti surrendered me to an aide who stood on duty inside the hall entryway. He requested me to sign the visitors' book. I noticed with quiet satisfaction that my name joined the illustrious company of British and foreign monarchs and other distinguished personages.

All the officials of the palace wore black *lap-lap*s, white short-sleeved shirts, leather sandals on bare feet, and the *ta'ovala* around the waist. The aide wore a scarlet sash in addition to his regular ones. This must have been to distinguish him as one of the king's personal attendants.

I was ushered into the official reception room, one of adequate elegance for state occasions. I seated myself on an upholstered crimson brocade Louis XV chair, one of twenty or thirty that lined the walls of the entire room. A single chandelier hung from the ceiling. The parquet floor shone with a highly waxed finish. There was no other furniture in what seemed a miniature ball-room.

I sat happily rehearsing my Tongan greeting. Literally translated, it meant, "I am glad to find Your Majesty in such good health as to be honored with an audience." Quite a mouthful even in English, but in Tongan it required the greatest concentration. I waited, nervous, excited, and feeling very lucky to be there.

The moment was at hand. The aide beckoned me forward. I was shown into a simply furnished room that seemed to be totally possessed by many chairs and a table of at least twenty feet. At the head, seated in a high-backed elaborately carved wooden armchair, was His Royal Majesty, King Taufʻahau Tupou IV.

He stood at my entrance. I was overawed by the size of him. He not only was extremely tall but very rotund. He wore a long-sleeved frock coat of finely woven white cotton, high of neck with a military-cut collar and buttons down the front, and a smooth plaited straw *ta'ovala* around his waist and midriff.

As I advanced down the length of the room, I sallied forth with my greeting in Tongan. I made an absolutely unqualified botch of the whole thing. Laughter escaped me. I simply could not help myself. Gone were the normal polite phrases. There was nothing for it but to say quite simply, "I'm sorry, Your Majesty. I wanted to express in Tonganese my acknowledgment of this honor. Allow me, sir, to say in English that it is most kind of you to receive me."

He offered me his hand and in faultless English said, "How do you do. Please be seated," indicating a chair placed at his right. He gave not the slightest indication of having heard any of my words, botched or otherwise. His face was smooth, round, and quite imperturbable. He looked like a chubby schoolboy. Standing, he was a man of great height and girth. Seated, he was no less imposing.

With a pleasant smile he asked what I might care to drink. I asked for any bottled soft drink—Pepsi-Cola would be fine if available, but no ice. When it was brought, it was accompanied by a glass of white cloudy liquid that the king drank. I would have loved to know what it was so that I could sample it later at the hotel. I didn't dare ask and kept silent.

The aide left the room and I waited for the king to speak first. "Madam," he began, "my secretary showed me your papers. Very interesting. You have come a long way, I understand, and I am informed you have a lot more traveling yet to do? What places have you liked best?"

"I found India fascinating, but the poverty was most upsetting. Papua New Guinea is a beautiful country, and the people of the interior are charmingly unspoiled. Your Majesty rules over a small island, but the hospitality and friendliness of your subjects is very great, and I shall carry away only the happiest of memories."

The king beamed with the undisguised pleasure of a child. "Everyone who comes to our island loves it. You know, of course, that we entertained Her Majesty and Prince Charles here not so long ago. Charles is a delightful fellow, absolutely delightful." He

235

enthusiastically expounded on all his royal visitors, and then surprisingly turned to political matters and Tonga's economy.

He made no secret of Russia's recent friendly overtures. It appeared that Russia was interested in fishing rights in Tongan waters. This had sparked a host of similar requests from hitherto disinterested countries. The king seemed to be enjoying playing one country off against another.

Speaking of fishing, His Majesty chatted freely away about his love of the sport. "As a matter of fact I am going off fishing this very afternoon. Very relaxing, you know. Very relaxing."

"Yes, Your Majesty, I am sure it is." I was feeling pretty relaxed myself, actually. Everything had gone off better than I could possibly have dreamed. The king had been so friendly, so expansive, so natural, that I found myself saying, "I happen to be fond of fishing myself, but I rarely seem to have the opportunity." My voice was tentative. It was no casual remark; an audacious one, in fact. Still, we had been getting along famously. I had made His Majesty laugh several times. He had even said I was a refreshing change from the usual round of visiting dignitaries.

Was I fishing for an invitation? Of course I was. Alas, His Majesty did not rise to the bait. No invitation was forthcoming, and it was just as well. I am a very poor sailor.

"You say that Fiji is your next stop, madam?"

"Yes, Your Majesty."

"Well, you may find similarities in the artwork and handicrafts, but not among the people. Of course there are Polynesian customs we have in common, but apart from the few British residents, they are quite a racially mixed people and not at all like us here in Tonga."

"I am sure I could not find a friendlier or a happier-looking nation than Your Majesty's subjects. Everyone I have encountered has greeted me with a smile."

"Yes, our people by and large are very contented. We have relatively little unemployment. Work can always be found on our banana and copra plantations. Our womenfolk are very skilled in tapa making and mat weaving. You must visit our markets, but I expect Sir Humphrey will have already extolled all the virtues of our island to you?"

"Yes, thank you, sir. I had a very pleasant meeting with him."

The king stood up and I followed suit timorously, producing my camera.

"Would Your Majesty care for an instant photograph?" I asked.

"Thank you, yes, that would be splendid." I complied with alacrity, glad of the opportunity to then ask for one of us together. The king summoned his aide and we shook hands for the auspicious moment.

"Good-bye, madam, and *bon voyage.*" I was treated to an unexpected and dazzling smile.

"Good-bye, Your Majesty. Thank you for the privilege of receiving me."

King Tauf'ahau Tupou left the room through a door immediately behind his great chair. I walked through the door by which I had entered, now held open for me by the king's aide.

I returned his smile and thanked him. Inwardly my smile remained.

Sir Humphrey's implications had been right. My visit to him had obviously been relayed to His Majesty. Some weight had evidently been attached to it for reasons I could not hope to fathom.

Perhaps my meeting with the king might never have come to pass had I not acted out the little drama of the previous evening. How amusing it all seemed in retrospect.

It would not have been a calamity, of course, had I been refused permission, but going to Tonga would not have been quite the same.

9
Fiji

Suva, the capital city of Viti Levu, the largest island of the Fiji group, is a scant 500 miles from Tonga, but her inhabitants are so multinational that one feels distanced by continents.

White skins and foreigners, for the two seemed inseparable, were the exceptions in Tonga. Here in Suva, every color and nationality appeared to be the rule. Indians, Chinese, British, French, Sikhs, and Australians mingled cheerfully with the Fijians. I felt a little disappointed at the international flavor and decided I would tour the island by bus in the hope of meeting more of the local people in the smaller villages.

I abandoned the idea of hitchhiking, for it was midday and not a time to be standing on a dusty road. The bus that rumbled to a stop as I made that decision had just left the terminus and was almost empty. It welcomed passengers with freshly wiped seats, some visibly the worse for the wear, a clean-swept floor, and a faint odor of disinfectant.

Now, some twenty minutes out of the town and despite the grating clutches, the jerky stops and starts, and the nerve-racking screech of brakes when we careened perilously around the curves, the journey was full of interest.

The road, like an unwinding ribbon, stretched ahead, carved carelessly through the incredibly high and narrow thighs of the mountainsides. The higher the bus groaned and strained to climb, the more the lush green countryside fell away to reveal, on weaving around the treacherous curves, a dazzling expanse of the sparkling blue-green South Pacific waters. A tireless surf fringed the sun-drenched white sandy beaches like a ruff. Farther out, the coral reefs lay like scattered beads across the ocean's breast.

The bus had quickly picked up passengers along the way and was now quite full. Most of the occupants were busily engaged in the consumption of the midday meal. The smell of dried salted fish, salami, bread, garlic, and fruit permeated the air. In the noon-time heat, this tended to depress rather than whet my appetite, which was just as well, for I had no food other than a couple of Sego Bars.

At each stop, scantily clad skinny children offered plates of fruit: tangerines, six for one Fijian dollar (less than twenty cents each), and coconuts for half a dollar. Business was invariably conducted from the paneless windows of the bus. These gaping apertures designed for ventilation rather than protection against inclement weather served most conveniently for the speedier transfer of baggage, small children, and anything else one might wish to pass into or out of the vehicle.

The absence of noise was singularly apparent, as if conversation might disrupt the concentration necessary for eating. I observed no pleasure in this exercise, only a serious application of effort. Old and young, men and women, mother and child, were intent upon the task, oblivious to all else around them. Eating was a ritualistic experience, but one in which I had no part, and my former feelings of relaxation began to dissipate. I felt slightly uncomfortable and certainly conspicuous in not having produced anything to eat. I stared hard out of the window and hoped no one would offer me anything. No one did.

The man beside me hacked open his coconut. First he drank the milk from the holes he had punctured through the top. After gnawing at the white fleshy meat for a few minutes, he nonchalantly consigned the remains to the floor at his feet. He made no attempt to wrap it in paper or conceal the leftovers among his baggage. Such a gesture would, in any case, have been to no avail, for as the bus lurched and reeled, tangerine peels, banana skins, and an assortment of discarded food joined the coconut shells and scuttled and slithered from one side of the bus to the other. These merry ranks of garbage would suddenly roll all the way to the back of the bus when we began a steep incline. When the vehicle took a downward plunge, all manner of remnant edibles would, with increased volume, rush forward to the front.

I conquered my distaste but not my dismay when, soon after, a pregnant woman seated behind me began to retch. I looked around to see if I could change my seat, but the bus was quite full. I had prided myself on acquiring a greater tolerance of foreign customs and ways, but the sound and smell of her vomiting, together with the suffocating heat, abruptly banished all allowances. Without giving much thought as to what I would do later on, I made a hasty descent from the bus and started to walk along the dusty road.

The afternoon sun bore down upon me relentlessly. My backpack seemed unusually heavy. I reminded myself that I had not previously hitchhiked at this time of the day. No wonder; with pack hoisted, it seemed so much more of a trial.

I was glad I was wearing cotton. My T-shirt was sleeveless, my skirt flared, loose, and comfortable. All my underwear was cotton, and I wore no belt or stockings. My sandals were open-toed and, though not ideal for walking, had wedge soles that gave support to my feet. I had no complaints about my choice of clothing. So far it had given me mammoth service. It was my hasty decision to leave the bus that now gave rise to doubts.

I had no idea where I was. The flat road I walked down was quite deserted and hedged in on either side by stubbly banana fronds, palm trees, and dense bougainvillea. I began to feel uneasy.

A few cars went by, ignoring the outstretched hand I raised too late for them to stop. My sunglasses were so dark that until the vehicles were almost alongside, I could not distinguish whether the occupants were male, female, single, or several.

I passed two women standing patiently on the road waiting for a bus, but in the opposite direction. Brightly dressed in long skirts, heads wrapped bandana fashion, they responded to my questions in English, but so sprinkled with dialect I found it hard to understand. It seemed that buses ran less on schedule than on serviceability. They were quite confident that a car or a truck would stop for them soon.

That none stopped for me might be attributed to the comic, and certainly rare, sight I must have presented. A middle-aged, white-skinned woman, with a weird orange contraption rising from her back, plunked in the middle of the road at an hour when the hot sun kept most folk indoors.

After an hour's sticky plodding, it was with great relief that I came across a cluster of thatched roofs—a small village community.

I noticed that a truck was about to pull out. It had a couple of smiling women, three small children, and an elderly man perched in the back. I hastened my pace toward it, casting aside all prior thoughts of seeking a drink and a rest. As long as it was not going in the direction from whence I had come, it would do me fine. I prayed that there would be room and a welcome for me aboard. There were both, and I gratefully accepted the willing hands that helped to hoist me and my pack aloft.

The friendly exchange of conversation was limited by my failure to comprehend all that was said, and soon, in the warmth of a midafternoon sun, heads began to droop, and a quiet somnolence crept over us all.

Two hours later we reached the truck's destination, another small village community, where everyone dismounted. I was advised to take a bus going in the direction of Nandi, which I was assured would pass by within the next ten minutes. Ten minutes turned into fifty, but on its arrival I was relieved upon entering the bus to find its interior to be considerably less filthy than that of the previous one.

Dusk was now falling, and I began to give some thought as to where I might stay the night. To stay on the bus to its final destination would mean arriving too late to be walking around in the dark trying to find somewhere to sleep. Earlier inquiries had not revealed much in the way of small towns along the route where I might have found accommodations.

I was assessing the situation as the bus came to a halt at what seemed to be a scheduled stop, for many passengers began to alight. Were they all leaving the bus? If not, where were they all heading? Perhaps to a toilet, if there was one, and if not, into the bush? I toyed with the idea of following suit, but then noticed some of the passengers returning with bottles of soft drinks in their hands.

I put on my prescription glasses and peered into the darkness. Across the street and partway up a dirt road was a small cafélike place. It bore a sign, barely visible from the few light bulbs around the doorway, that said HOTEL. I made an on-the-spot decision to get off the bus and see if a room for the night was available.

The place did not boast a prepossessing appearance, but as long as I got a clean bed, it would have to do. A bird in the hand, I philosophically reasoned. Later in the night, had I stayed on the bus, I might not even have found this much. I made a firm resolve to accept whatever was going, even though now I felt some dismay as a shabby exterior came clearly into view.

As hotels go, this one looked as if it had gone, as did the bus at that precise moment. I had a fleeting instant regret for the temporary warmth and safety it had offered me. I didn't like the look of the place, but, again, a worse one might have awaited me elsewhere, and where was that anyway?

Whoever should have been around to answer my questions just wasn't. A short while ago I presumed it had been a matter of all hands on deck to sell potables to the bus passengers, but where were they now?

I stood hesitantly inside the square tiled entrance. Straight ahead stretched a long narrow corridor. To my right was a closed door; to my left, one that was hinged in two parts. The upper section was folded flat against the wall; the lower half served as a counter top and closed off a room that had been converted into a store.

A shelf at the back was filled with packets of snack foods and cigarettes. Underneath was a table covered with a red and white checkered cloth. On it, protected from flies, a sheet of thin clear plastic shielded the day's leftover buns and rolls of bread. The insects compromised with this deprivation by feasting on an exposed half-eaten piece of cake and clustering around the neck of an open bottle of Coca-Cola.

Cases of beer and assorted drinks lined one wall. The other was graced by an antiquated but large refrigerator. A fat black cockroach, still and glistening in sleep or fear, now became galvanized into action and sped across its white-painted door.

Farther down the corridor the blue stone wall was relieved by a black iron-frame couch upholstered in flowered plastic. A small wooden table bore an unlit lamp, an ashtray, and a newspaper.

I advanced a few paces, expecting a receptionist, a clerk, or a front-desk person to appear at any moment. What receptionist?

What clerk? What front-desk person? *What front desk?* There was nothing to suggest even the faintest resemblance to a hotel.

"Anyone around, please?" My voice hung limply in the air. It remained unanswered. There was simply no one around. The sound of music coming from somewhere down the corridor explained why no one could have heard me even if they were around. It was clear that once the bus had departed, no further customers for refreshments were expected, the probability of hotel guests considered even less.

Well, girl, don't just stand around waiting. Go in the direction of the noise and obviously that's where you will find someone.

I found plenty. Mostly men and a sprinkling of young women who, by Fijian standards, seemed at first glance to be quite pretty. As my eyes became accustomed to the dimness of the room I had entered, it appeared to be more like a large garage. The colored lights revealed on closer view that the women were not quite so young, or so pretty, as painted. The room was less a room than a bar. Well, most hotels have bars, I thought, only this place hadn't seemed to be much of a hotel either.

The air reeked with tobacco smoke. It began to sting my eyes and irritate my throat. I looked around, trying to spot someone who looked businesslike. The postures of the girls struck me as being a little strange. Few of them were seated among the men; most were draped around the bar in little giggling clusters. It was not until my eyes rested upon one particular woman that the full impact hit me.

She was sitting across the knees of a man whose right arm I thought at first had been amputated at the elbow. When I realized that the rest of it was up the girl's skirt, the full force of my surroundings came home to me.

The heavily made-up girls. The bar. The men. They were all very businesslike. And what a business! It all became very clear to me. My God—now what have I gotten myself into?

I had left my backpack in the hall (stealing was rare among the islanders). Thoughts of my pack and flight were aborted in embryo. There was nowhere to fly to, and, stupid wretch, right now you have to worry more about a hand on your back than a hand in your pack.

I became aware of the stir my entrance had caused. As I had opened the door to step inside, the light from the corridor had streamed into the room, sharply illuminating my appearance. Heads were turned, and I felt a sickening sensation in the pit of my stomach, the gnawings of which were by no means dispelled when an amply proportioned woman of middle years approached me.

It is hard to judge the ages of the women in these parts unless they are quite young. She wore no cosmetics other than heavy eye makeup to enhance a face that struck me as quite attractive. Her eyes were so crinkled with amusement as she spoke to me that I could not detect whether they held friendliness or suspicion.

Stay cool, stay cool, I said to myself. Anyone can see that you're a foreigner. No need to panic—yet.

"Hello, dear," she said. "What can I do for you?"

"Well," my words came out in a frenetic rush to explain as quickly as possible and thus dispel any ideas she might be entertaining about me. It was quite apparent that the word "Hotel" outside was a misnomer. It was also clearly evident that the ratio of men to girls was disproportionate if the business going on here was to be taken care of profitably. All this raced through my head as I spoke.

"Well, I saw the hotel sign from the bus, and since I was feeling very tired, I decided to break my journey and get a good night's rest. I, er . . ." I swallowed hard. "I'd like a room with bath if you have one, please?"

She looked me up and down and she looked me down and up. She actually walked around me to look at me back and front. The smile never left her face; if anything, it increased, as did my consternation.

"Yes, dear, I think I can find you a very nice room."

As she spoke, her eyes traveled toward a group of quite young men, all of whom were animatedly talking and drinking as they sat around a small table.

Her words, her glance across the room, the music, the men; it all spoke volumes. I was in a brothel, and this was the madam, and she intended to do business with me. Her negotiations were to include more than a room, that was abundantly clear. She had more clients than she could accommodate with her services, and it seemed, from her approving looks of me, that she had decided I would be quite a useful addition to her staff of ladies.

"Yes, I think I can find you a very nice room and some jolly

244

company to go with it, dear." She put her arm around my shoulder as she spoke and started to lead me across the floor.

I froze, rooted, appalled. "You're very kind," I said, "but I am really very tired and not feeling too well. I'd be most grateful if you could just show me my room, and I'll go straight to bed."

Steady now, don't panic, keep your head, Sabina. You're in a mess. It's nighttime; you are stuck. You've nowhere else to go and even if you did walk out into the night—to what? And to where? Breathe deeply, put a smile on your silly, frozen face, and *don't look afraid.*

"Yes, dear, but why not join us for a little while and have a drink? It will perk you up fine." (Yes, of course. She doesn't want a half-dead duck on her hands to do "business" with.) "The boys would just love to have your company, I'm sure. All the boys have company here, dear. We're all one big happy family and we love company, don't we, Remus?"

A deep-throated chortle acknowledged this remark. It came from the table behind us. A heavyset man of about sixty years, judging from his crisp, curly gray hair, sat toying with his glass of beer. Crags and valleys, not merely lines, were etched across a face that bore the passage of hard work and a zest for life and living.

"Company," he said. His voice was quite pleasant and not as harsh or accented as most I had heard. "Oh, yes, we all love a bit of company, and the lady looks like she'd be fine company. Stay right here, Jilla. I'd like the lady's company myself."

To my disbelief and despite my panic, I experienced a sudden sensation of disappointment, or was it insult! Was I then to be consigned to distract an older man when but a few seconds earlier I had been considered attractive and suitable enough to please a group of younger ones? Could it be that one is so much a slave of vanity as to feel, even in these circumstances, a sense of rejection at being thus passed over?

The thought, if a conscious one, was so fleeting as to be dismissed before I realized it had been summoned. I was now only desperately aware of Remus's friendly white-toothed grin and a pair of lazy eyes lingering slowly over my arms, neck, shoulders, and breasts.

I forced a smile, praying it would belie the fear locked within jaws I could hardly open.

"Madam Jilla, Mr. Remus." God, my voice was unbelievably calm. "You are both very nice and everyone here seems to be having a wonderful time in this lovely, er, atmosphere. (Lovely? The smoke, the noise, the smell, were damn near suffocating me.) "If my stomach—er, actually it's diarrhea (Oh, what inspiration! Great. Go on, girl, this will surely do the trick.)—were not upsetting me so much, I'd gladly join you in a drink." I raised my hand and slightly covered my mouth while turning toward Madam Jilla, and in a lower voice I added, "I wish you'd please show me to my room, as I am in trouble right now. I feel I'm going to be sick as well."

With an alacrity I would never have dreamed she possessed, Madam Jilla took my arm and led me straight back to the entrance hall. I seized my backpack and followed her swaying haunches through a door that led us into the fresh night air. We crossed a small patch of grass to a flagstone path and a row of little rooms. I guessed there were about six of them, but the solitary light was ineffective in illuminating the low-lying cement construction. We were at the end of the path before I had time to take much into account. I felt such relief at having escaped from the bar scene that all else seemed unimportant.

She opened a door and snapped on the light. Preceding me inside, she beckoned me to enter. She switched on the bathroom light at the right of the door and said, "Here you are, dear. I'll wait." She took the pack from my hands, looking at it with a mixture of disdain and curiosity, and said nothing more. I thanked her and closed the door of the tiny bathroom behind me.

I stayed inside a good five minutes, flushing frequently, although in fact I only used the toilet once.

"Are you all right, dear?"

I knew I could not stay in the bathroom all night; I would have to go out some time. "Yes, thank you," was all I replied.

"Good," she called back. "Take your time, dear. I'm right here if you need me."

I came out wondering how I could get rid of her. Why was she hanging around? Perhaps I should pay her for the room now? Maybe this was what she wanted? Surely she had relinquished any other ideas?

"Well, I'm glad you're feeling better. Let's have a little chat and see what we can arrange."

Thank goodness, I thought. She wants me to pay for the room. I walked toward the bed, my hand already inside my shoulder bag as I groped for my wallet.

"You see, dear, all the girls here have company. It wouldn't be good business otherwise. I get very few visitors in these parts, and you seem like a real nice lady I could do good business with. Now Remus here is very generous, but he gets a little bored with my regular girls. He seems to have taken quite a fancy to you, he does, and it would be very worth your while if you'd give him a little company. Oh, yes, it would be *very* worth your while."

I sat down on the worn chenille bedspread that covered the sagging, thinned-out mattress beneath me. "Madam Jilla." I put my hands across my stomach as I spoke, as if I were in excruciating pain. (Hell, if I wasn't in real pain, this fear in my abdomen was a pretty close second.) I winced as I went on, "You are a charming lady, and as a visitor I love this little island. I am, though, a married woman and have a fine husband. I really do need a good night's sleep more than I need company. I've just taken a tablet in the bathroom because I am in a lot of pain. I'm afraid it will soon put me to sleep. I wouldn't be much use to anyone the way I am right now. You do understand?"

Her eyes were hard, cold, and shrewd. How could I have thought she was attractive? Now she looked mean and calculating. In fact she looked quite ugly, even menacing.

I went on quickly, "Now whatever you get for your room with company, I will pay you the full price. In fact I will pay you double, and it will all be for you."

Regret and avarice marched across her face. She spoke slowly and with great reluctance to give up her intentions. "Very well, but it is a shame. Remus is a very generous man, and it would have been very worth your while. I'd liked to have pleased him. He's one of my best customers you see."

"Yes, I do see," I replied softly. "But I'm sure if you explain my indisposition to him he'll understand. Could you let me have a key to the room, please? And, Madam Jilla, you won't mention where I am, will you? I'd be very grateful."

She turned to face me as she headed for the door. "There is no key. We never need keys. But you'll be all right. I'll remember the room you're in. No one else will use it. You'll not have any trouble —I don't think." She gave me an enigmatic smile and departed.

She doesn't have any keys. She'll remember the room I'm in. They never need keys. I'll not have any trouble. She didn't think —she didn't *think!*

I was thinking plenty. I dragged the nightstand over to the door. It made a ghastly scraping noise and left a big scratch mark right across the painted stone floor. I tried to wedge it firmly underneath the doorknob, but it didn't work. A chair would probably be better, but it would be light and easier to move. No, the stand would be best. I put my backpack against it. At least if the door opened, the pack would topple forward and wake me up.

The pack kept slipping down. Wretched thing, stay still, I cursed. I found the solution by fishing out my sneakers and putting the feet of the metal frame into the shoes. The crepe soles stopped the pack from sliding. Of course, if someone really wanted to force the door open, the nightstand would just push the pack right over, but at least it would make a lot of noise and give me time. Time to do what? Oh, this was terrible.

I sat on the edge of the bed imagining all sorts of situations. I didn't dare undress. What if Remus felt slighted? What if he became drunk and angry and decided he was going to find me? What if one of them got drunk and started to wander around? They must all know the rooms. What was to stop them? (Now it had become plural—no, oh no!) What if Jilla hadn't explained to Remus? Or what if she thought it a good joke to embellish the story and share it with her customers? Oh, horror! I could just see them all roaring their liquor-loosened laughter over me. What if they placed bets as to who should try each door to find the prim English missy?

Prim? I wasn't prim. I was scared out of my silly senses. My stomach did indeed feel queasy. Yes, I was going to be sick. That's all I need now, to start throwing up. I fished around in my bag, looking for a tablet of some kind. Every few seconds I stopped dead, lifting up my head, my ears straining to catch the slightest sound. What was that? Nothing, you are imagining things. Stop being so foolish.

I crept into the bathroom. Heavens, what on earth is the matter with you? You don't have to tiptoe. Walk properly. Stop creeping. There is no one to disturb you. I listened intently. The only sound was the flapping of a moth against the lightbulb. It had come in through the torn screened ventilation grill high up on the bathroom wall. I snapped off the light immediately. No need to advertise where you are. I expect the room is full of mosquitoes, I thought angrily. Well, better meet your death from a million bug bites than from . . . ? Sh! You crazy thing, nothing's going to happen to you. Stop this nonsense.

I closed the bathroom door so that no light would shine out from the bedroom. The window at the other end of the room was half covered with a gay piece of dress fabric stretched taut by a wire across the frame.

I shaded my eyes and peered out into the darkness beyond. There was nothing to see. It was deeply black and quite, quite still. There seemed to be a dense mass of foliage and a blur of tall trees. Nothing moved. There was little to worry about out there. It was beyond my door, across the path and inside where the lights were, where the girls and the smoke and the music and the drink could play havoc with a man's lust—*that* was what I had to worry about.

I looked at the bed with revulsion. I certainly wasn't going to sleep in *that* bed now, not even with my clothes on. I sat down gingerly. How could I sit up all night?

A woman's laughter startled me. Oh, God, there were footsteps coming this way. How could I even *think* of sleeping? A man's voice, thick and hoarse, floated down the corridor. He coughed and spat, obliterating words too mumbled for me to make out. The couple stopped a good distance away from my room, I judged. Was it a couple or more? A closed door muffled the girl's repeated giggles and brought to an end further contemplations.

I found myself straining to catch the slightest sound. Part of me was terrified, part of me grotesquely enthralled. Perhaps there is a certain kind of thrill in acute fear? A psychological theory? A Freudian reality? Mad creature. Are you out of your mind? How can you be thinking, feeling, imagining such things? I shuddered, not caring to dwell upon the frightening complexities of the basic human condition. There was nothing imaginary about the wild beating of the pulse in my throat. I realized I had been too afraid to swallow.

My head felt as if it were bursting. My mind chased one crazy thought after another. Lurid situations possessed my imagination. I was quite beside myself.

The roar of a curse in a male voice reached my ears. It came from across the garden. It was Remus, I felt sure of it. He was coming to find me. One push and he would be in the room. There would be absolutely nothing I could do. Any screams I might make would never be heard with all the din that was going on inside the bar. As for the man and girl in the room nearby, they'd think nothing of it; besides they would be busy making screams of their own.

I was no longer in control of myself. The now-pervading quiet did nothing to restore my shattered nerves. I knew I was distorting every little thing. Each tiny sound suggested calamity. Exaggeration upon exaggeration had piled up. Anything had seemed possible. Fool. Nothing is going to happen, and yet—and yet—how could I be sure?

Sooner or later others are going to be coming over here. If not Remus, it could be someone else. Someone without a girl. Someone who felt like prowling around.

I decided I had better take a tranquilizer to calm myself down. It was utterly ridiculous to carry on this way. Normally I only used a tranquilizer to help me sleep on long plane journeys. Occasionally it enabled me to get a good night's rest and adjust to the varied time differences I had encountered. If the tablet didn't work to calm me, perhaps it would put me to sleep. That would be best of all in the state I was in.

I extracted the pillow beneath the worn bedspread. It was snowy white and clean. I lay on top of the bed, fully clothed, and rested my head on the pillow, closed my eyes, and put my faith in God and the tranquilizer.

Somehow I couldn't get to sleep. I realized I was waiting for the couple to leave the room several doors away. I hadn't heard a sound since they entered and I fuzzily wondered why. Fellows were supposed to have such a great time when they paid for the goods, I had always thought. Maybe a good time is not necessarily consistent with a noisy one. Oh, the heck with it. Who cares? A little persistent devil of curiosity nagged at me. Evidently I did care. I felt a little shocked at myself.

It was an effort to turn my head. It felt heavy and thick. My mind too was drifting from earlier, distressing contemplations to some of the charming sights and attractions I had witnessed in this tropical archipelago of the Fiji Islands.

Just a week ago I had been so happily browsing around Suva . . . the streets with their English names—Queen's Road, Sandringham Road, Queen Elizabeth Drive, Disraeli Road, Edinburgh Drive. How could one fail to feel at home, especially when I had been the houseguest of a young English professor's wife and their two delightful children.

Margaret Porter had sat next to me on the plane coming in from Tonga. With typical British politeness she had apologized profusely for one of her children's exhuberance.

"I'm ever so sorry if the children are disturbing you. They get so restless on long journeys." Then, turning to her little boy, she said, "How many times do I have to tell you to keep your feet off the seat? Oh, look, you've marked the lady's dress. I am sorry."

"Don't worry," I had assured her. "I've been living in this skirt for four months; nothing can damage it now."

"Have you come here from England, then? Peter, keep still for goodness' sake!"

"No, actually I'm from the USA."

"Is it nice out there?"

"Oh, yes." I smiled, temporarily unable to find a better response to a question that conjured up in the mind a strange hinterland of elephants, jungles, and primitive people.

By the time the journey was over, Margaret Porter had offered me the hospitality of her home. I had intended to enlist the help of the Fiji Visitors' Bureau, whose address, telephone, and excellent recommendations had been given to me in Australia.

"My husband is teaching at the University of the South Pacific and will not be back from a course in the Hebrides for another ten days. The children are at school all day, and it will be great company for me to have you stay with us. Please do. I'd love to hear more about your travels."

"And I would love to hear all about your life here in Fiji," I had replied as I gratefully accepted her kind offer of accommodations.

Margaret, an avid history reader, enlightened me that Great Britain had refused a gift of the islands until 1874. From then on, until 1970, they were a part of the Crown Colonies. Fiji then gained its independence with dominion status and was now a member of the Commonwealth. Fervently loyal to the Crown, it had gone wild with joy over the visit of Her Majesty, Queen Elizabeth, some time ago.

"The real Fijians are very proud of their ties to England. Our schools are conducted according to English standards, and we celebrate all the holidays. Of course, the foreign elements here are not so united."

"Tell me a little about your life here," I had said. "It must be very pleasant, but what do you do for entertainment?"

"Yes, it is pleasant, but it gets boring too. We look forward to trips every two years, but we always somehow end up by going home to England, and I would love to see more of the world. You're very plucky to do what you've been doing."

"Just lucky more than plucky," I had replied with a feigned attempt at modesty.

Now, lying on this lumpy mattress, sleep crawling over all my limbs, yet jerking myself awake so as to be alert for the slightest sound, I found myself remembering those words.

Lucky, I had said. Why did I have to push it and end up here?

It had been so attractive in that little town. The quaint stores, the skirt-clad colorful policemen, the bands playing English marches. Talking with the local Fijians in the marketplace—no trouble with dialects in the big town. The song-and-dance outdoor feasts, called *mekes*, where I'd drunk *yaqona* (nonalcoholic) and *kava* (very alcoholic), and the fascination of watching the men perform their fire-walking feats.

Yes, Suva had a lot of charm. The town of Korelevu had been pretty in a sleepy kind of way. And Yanuca Island? What about the sheer luxury of my one night at the Royal Fijian Hotel? An absolutely heavenly bed! And that gorgeous beach, a simply divine view, and my gourmet eating binge!

Fool that I am. No one said I had to punish myself on this trip. No one forced me to stay in YWCAs and guesthouses, sleep in a church on a bench, scurry around looking for pensions, and now this ghastly place.

Lucky, I had said. Some luck now. Why did I have to go traipsing off to see more of the island, to get to know more about the people, and to see rural areas and get away from the big town life? Why? Look where your damnable curiosity has gotten you.

Sh! Stop thinking about that. It's been very quiet for some time now. At least an hour. Maybe your luck will hold and no one will come this way tonight. Of course, it is still very early, not yet ten o'clock. I suppose things (what things?) don't liven up until much later on. Or maybe it just happens to be a quiet night for Madam Jilla.

The pillow smells a bit mildewed and this bedspread thing is so thin. It's no good kicking it around with your feet because there is no warmth in it at all. You're going to be cold later on, you know you are. Don't be stupid. Get underneath the covers or you'll get chilled and then you'll start with your cough. You may not be cold now, but you soon will be.

But I never was. I awoke from a deep sleep to find the sun streaming in so brightly that I had to squint to see what time it was. Six o'clock? I must have slept at least seven hours. Of course you did, even with all the carryings on, most of them in your head.

Well now, seven hours is not at all bad. After a shower and a change of clothes you'll feel just fine. Really, what a fuss to have made about everything last night.

Madam Jilla had understood perfectly. She was a smart businesswoman, and a practical and sensible one. She would not have wanted a a visitor to go away and make any kind of trouble or complaint.

This hitching around and putting up at any old place had just got to stop. After all this traveling I was getting pretty weary. It just wouldn't do to carry on like this anymore.

It had become an obsession with me. Furthermore, false pride and sheer stupidity prevented me from giving in and saying enough already. I didn't have to prove anything to anyone.

There had been some fantastic economies. I had hardly spent a thing. I had denied myself sensible eating, simple comforts, and even a trinket or two. It was not necessary; no one was going to give me any medals for it.

It was one thing to live on a shoestring, but without the shoe, too?

No, from now on it's proper hotels and decent meals, my girl.

Use your American Express card and charge a few expenses. What would Marco say if he knew all about this? He would be furious, and well you know it.

Oh, well, no more rambling. It's time to get up and get moving. Pay your bill and leave this "one big happy family" to those who care more for such "relations."

10
Easter Island

It was always the same. Whenever I needed one of my little traveling aids, I could never find it without upsetting the entire contents of my backpack. This had caused a near disaster on my journey from Fiji to Tahiti, for on arrival in Papeete I was informed that the luggage would not be released until the following day, since it underwent a fumigating process.

Fortunately, I had the barest of essentials in my hand luggage, so I escaped the inconvenience that befell many of the passengers. Now, just as I was about to board the LAN-Chile jet that was to carry me from Papeete to Easter Island, my search for a tranquilizer proved in vain. I ruefully contemplated a wakeful ten-hour journey with regret, for the effects of travel fatigue had, on previous occasions, been quite devastating.

In a mood of philosophical resignation, I settled myself aboard a barely half-full plane. With my own cushion, two blankets, and a full seat upon which to stretch out, I conditioned myself to positive thinking and, to my great surprise, awoke several hours later, realizing that I must have dozed off for quite a while.

The plane was dimly lit; I could barely see my watch. I squinted hard; it looked like five o'clock in the morning—only three more hours to go. Three more hours of stiff neck, aching limbs, and a head as wooly and as thick as a sheepskin rug. I was in a state of apathy. The thought of extricating myself from the warmth of the blanket around me, putting on my shoes, and making my way down the aisle to the toilet was too much of an effort to seriously contemplate. (Drat my wretched bladder; it will just have to wait.) I closed my eyes in defiance, as if to summon a psychological command to end all further thoughts on the matter. An hour later a persistent ache demanded acknowledgment of nature's call, and I reluctantly abandoned all further hopes of sleeping.

The No Smoking and Fasten Seat Belt signs lit up, and I saw the stewardess begin to make her rounds, reminding passengers to comply. Now everyone will decide to go to the toilet, I thought, and abruptly propelled myself along the aisle. The clicking of safety belts being secured in no way seemed to permanently disrupt the slumbering passengers, and I noted with amusement the positions people adopt when deprived of their beds.

Couples lolled against each other for support, singles reclined across empty seats where available, mouths open, heads rolled back, necks near to broken. Hair tousled, ties askew, stockinged feet, bare feet, curled up feet, dangling feet. Hunched up, stretched out, sprawled across, doubled over. An incredible number of unbelievable postures, proving the theory that no matter what conditions are, one will manage to sleep somehow, if tired enough.

It seemed as if I were the only person on board who was fully awake, and I returned to my seat loathe to disturb others by switching on my reading light to glance at my book and pass the time away. I sat against the darkened window and opted to stare out into the nothingness beyond.

As if in some hypnotic state, I watched the blackness give way to grayish hues, and felt a stir of excitement to see the faintest blush tinge the chalky outline of somber clouds.

Now dawn cast its first shining rays at night's feet. Sharp swords of light pierced the drabness of the skies. Like a thief in flight, the darkness sped across the heavens, trailing its shredded robes, caught here and there on clouded rosy peaks. Crimson streaks began to stain the sky; a golden glow lit up the softness of newborn clouds. A bleary red-eyed sun shook off its sleep and rose in all its glory to unite sea and sky in one great explosion of brilliance. A shining path of hot white steel blazed across the ocean. God put aside his paints. He'd made a day.

Never had I seen such beauty. Never had a canvas lived such color. I felt as if a magnet had drawn all breath out of my lungs.

256

I longed for Marco to have experienced this moment of splendor with me.

Suddenly I had the feeling that something was wrong. The craft had been decreasing in altitude for some time, but my attention had been distracted by the glorious break of day. The sea glittered and shimmered below me. It seemed uncomfortably near. I looked around to see if others were awake. None appeared to be. There had been no turbulence to speak of, which I had expected at the request to fasten seat belts. The lit-up sign took on an ominous significance. I began to feel distinctly uneasy. Why were we descending lower and still lower? It was nowhere near time for landing, and anyway, where was the land? At this height surely some land would have been visible? Nothing but ocean surrounded us. Nothing.

The pilot could not possibly be bringing us so low, unless— unless—we were going to crash into the sea. The engines must have failed; we had run out of fuel. No, there would have been coughing and spluttering and we would have clearly heard that something was wrong. Was the craft flying on automatic, the pilot asleep, blissfully ignorant of the failure of complicated instruments? Dramatic scenes from movies flashed through my mind. Something was drastically wrong. Why else were we so low?

No longer did the ocean glow with beauty. It was menacing, dark, and greedy, waiting to claim us to her murky depths. Any second now the captain will announce that life jackets must be put on, and then the screaming will start. Oh, God, so this is it? This is how death is going to be for me? How often had its shadow mentally stalked me? How often had Marco and the boys made fun of me when I would shake out my fears of death into the air of reality?

"Boys, we are not always going to be around, you know. Don't lean on anyone, not even your parents. Stand alone and resolve life's difficulties yourselves. You know we love you, but you can only be responsible to yourselves."

"Oh, come on now, stop all this talk. You're not dying and I'm not dying. Not yet anyway." Marco was always impatient with me. "You've got an absolute obsession with the damn thing."

It was true that I had. For years, thoughts of death and dying had constantly accompanied me. Rare were the nights when I fell asleep free from the thought that I might never wake up. Sometimes, in almost humorous preparation of the certainty, I would not remove a small partial denture. Heaven forbid I should be seen dead without it!

It was as if I had a need to become familiar with death. It was going to happen one day, so why not treat it as a friend? Was it not, after all, the most important part of living? Why should preparation for this major event be neglected?

So many once-taboo subjects are freely broached today. Why, birth itself, the occurrence of which is but the preliminary to death, is now regarded as an almost community event. New schools of thought have reintroduced home delivery, in which family participation is almost obligatory. It has undoubtedly become an everyday feature on television, the exhibition of which, even in its most intimate detail, is now a fashionable trend. But death, who speaks of death?

When it revolves around the aged or the sick, yes, then it surfaces. In hushed and solemn tones, addressed to the air and in third-person plural. The individual has already ceased to exist. It is spoken about, spoken of, and rarely spoken to.

We concern ourselves greatly with the inanities of living, yet assiduously court death on the side. We race to meet it on the highways. Overtake the dumb bastard, blast him off the road for crawling like that. Mow them down as we turn a corner, our haste frustrated by rightfully crossing pedestrians. Out of the way. We've no time. We're in a hurry. The lineups get longer, our patience gets shorter. Move, move, rush, rush. Yes, rush ourselves toward the grave we earnestly dig a little more of each day.

Yet no one teaches us about death. Why? Is it because the certainty of graduation makes a preparatory course unnecessary? We consciously lull ourselves into a false state of security—vanity more like. It won't happen to us, only the other guy. Why was it that *I* never felt this way?

"Look, Marco, I want to know what I should do about insurance policies and documents and money things. Afterward, I won't be able to ask you, will I?"

"What makes you think I'll go first, eh?"

"I don't; I'm sure it will be me, and promise me you'll have me cremated. I'm scared to death of being buried with all that earth on top of me."

"Yeah, Pop. Put her in a little jar and keep her on the dressing table. You'd like that, wouldn't you, Mom?" The boys would roar their heads off when I answered in all seriousness, "Yes, I would like that. It's exactly what I would like and what's so funny about it?"

"Oh, go on, you nut. Why don't you concentrate on living first."

Why not indeed? Why, for the last ten, twenty years, perhaps since the day I got married, has there been this need to be prepared for any eventuality? It has always dominated every plan I made. An absurd expectation, of course, but there had always lurked somewhere in the background of most undertakings the need to anticipate a setback or an unforeseen (though not necessarily unpleasant) circumstance with which I might have to deal.

I would feel comforted, not harassed, by taking such possibilities into consideration. I never thought it odd. I never gave it too much thought at all. It was just there, a part of me. That was all, or was it that the thoughts I gave to living were more enhanced by my appreciation of its value, its frailty a constant reminder of a precious gift never to be taken for granted. Being aware of death was surely the strongest indication of my concern with life and living it fully.

No, Marco, I was not a nut. I wasn't, but now—where had it gotten me? What use was all my talk and philosophical reasoning? I am going first after all. It is not I who will be left alone, but you.

Tears streamed down my cheeks. The pain of regrets was like hot needles stabbing at my breast. Oh, Marco, Marco, how I loved you and missed you while waiting for that time we would spend together. Even now, in all your loneliness, you will never know how sadly I waited and waited and hoped and hoped for your time —like a bird awaiting the crumbs from a shaken cloth. Your time, your touch, even a long sweet look, would have been my embrace. When did I ask for that much more? Unaware of the silent tears that slid into my ears those dark, long nights, you slept and snored, and I lay staring, wide-eyed and lonely, beside your warm body so indifferent to mine.

You said you loved me. In your own measured way perhaps. But your way was not my way, if indeed it was much of a way at all. You loved me as a mother for the comforts I gave you and the convenience of having me there. Did you love me as a wife?

A companion? The best friend you would ever have? Your mind was not an open book to me. Could you not have used more words, so that I could read you better? Oh, yes, you'd take my hand or pinch my cheek in front of others. (My God, how he adores her, they'd say.) If I redounded to your credit, you might speak of me with enthusiasm, but when did you ever praise me to *me*? When did you ever leap to my defense or extol my qualities when I came under attack from those whose opinions you valued more than the outraged feelings of your wife?

Ah, the sadness of it all. The wasted years we could have loved each other more. Those times for talk and opened hearts you swept aside. Not now, not now, you'd say. There never was a now. You did not want to talk or see or know, and met my accusations with hot and righteous anger. Ignoring the gaping holes of truth, you simply closed the door.

What will happen to you now? Will you reproach yourself for the lost companionship you denied yourself? Will you grow into a sad and lonely old man sitting at home and looking at stamps and photographs? Or will you stare at the sea and sigh for what might have been? Will you work still harder and so work your life away? You never gave me answers; no wonder I knew despair and, oh, such utter loneliness.

Good-bye, my dearest. I never ceased loving you, though, yes, it changed as life must change and must go on. I pray God will send another love into your life, one who will not care for the kind of honesty I needed to exact. One whose passions are paler, whose soul is subdued. One with whom the living will be easier though, I guarantee, less exciting. One who will be good to you and make you happy. I only hope you will be happy.

And the boys, what of them? I felt comforted and proud. They would be just fine, I knew it. From the earliest years had I not tried to teach them self-reliance and independence? Surely a parent's major responsibility? Had I been too harsh in standing aside when, groping alone, they had stumbled and cried? I never thought like those parents who always wanted their children to have all the things they never had. No, the boys had shoveled snow, delivered papers, caddied on the golf courses. ("Horse work, that's what 'doubles' are, Mom, horse work.") Their shoulders had been red and blistered, but the working and the waiting had enhanced the value of their pleasures. The instant gratification by doting parents, the checkbook philosophy (peace and quiet and pay the price), were, to my mind, all too quickly taken for granted and, worse, regarded later as a right.

I had given my sons nothing but my time—unstintingly, or it was not given at all if it had to be measured and counted. When we spoke together, they felt I had really heard, not just listened. They knew I loved them fiercely, but not overprotectively.

A bloody nose, a cut knee, a profusion of tears, all compassionately but silently observed. "That's life, boys. Blood, tears, and pain." Perhaps they learned some lessons ahead of time. My concessions were few so that they would be better able to make their way alone.

The only thing I had *really* wanted for them that I felt I *never* had was the freedom from guilt or obligation for anything we had done for them as parents. Heaven spare them a fraction of the guilts that had riddled my own life. This, I felt, could best be accomplished by giving them only that which was needed rather than that which was desired.

I wanted them to know that glorious sense of independence. To grow up secure in the knowledge that they owed not a damn thing to anyone, not even to their parents.

We had given them no more than had been their birthright to have. Their education—the one single burden, of a purely financial strain—we had shouldered on their behalf, and had been our joy to give. If they had by passed the opportunity, it was their loss, not their guilt. If they loved us at all, and we were shown plenty of love, it had been earned, not demanded, not bought. Doubtless the generous, gift-giving parent may well receive a greater show of affection, but has he rendered his child the better service?

The love I hoped for was not the love of gratitude (what a burden that is!) but the love of unbeholden children, who can give to us and the world what they *want* to give, not what they feel they owe and are obliged to give.

Concepts of love and obligation were less tainted with hypocrisy today. Thank God, my sons were unburdened with the notion that telling the truth is rude. Sadly enough, the little lies and falsities that masquerade as excuses and compliments are often preferred and even expected by those whose happiness encourages such deceit.

No, the boys were not so fettered, and I could die proud and grateful that they had been raised to become men. They belonged to themselves, and they were free.

The prayers were tumbling out. My life had flashed by in thickening seconds. My head seemed to be filled with incoherent truths, as if I were on the brink of some wonderful discovery. A bright light felt as if it were piercing my brain, illuminating those dark recesses of enlightenment. The skin of my scalp felt so tight that it seemed at any moment it would burst open and out would spill all the confusion, leaving behind only the crystal-clear beauty of pure truth. Was I going mad, or was this death reaching out for me? Would these last few seconds now reveal the great enigma? Those fleeting instants where, poised and quivering, life and death are united in flight?

Tight bands of steel encased my chest. Terror salivated inside my mouth. I was drenched in perspiration, and panic was robbing me of breath. I felt a scream rise within me, but I was choking and gasping for air. My eyes were tightly closed as I tried frantically for the control of my breathing. Please, God, help me, help me. I am not prepared.

The water will be so cold. I cannot swim. The life jacket will be useless. Why hasn't the captain told us to put them on? Why is there no screaming, no panic, no confusion?

Thump—a roaring noise assaulted my ears. Brakes squealed excruciatingly. I opened my eyes as the plane bounced unevenly on the tarmac. My God, we've landed. It can't be; it's too soon.

You damn fool. Praise the Lord, don't start arguing with Him. You're alive, aren't you? You've landed. He doesn't want you— yet. Isn't that enough? There must be other things He wants you to do with your life. Just say thank you and be still.

A little shaken, I came down the steps to see a sign in Spanish and English that read WELCOME TO EASTER ISLAND. It made me feel good and I took a picture. Before I had walked a dozen paces, an angry-looking official was at my side demanding in Spanish that I hand over my camera. Photographs are strictly forbidden, he said, and it clearly says so "over there." I was suddenly reminded of Chile's grim dictatorial policies not just 2,000 miles away on the mainland but right here as well. This, too, was Chilean soil, and unpleasantness was occurring already.

I made a hasty switch inside my shoulder bag and produced my unloaded 35-millimeter camera; it had been the Polaroid that I had just used. With a smile I was afraid did not look convincing, I replied in English, "I'm sorry, I didn't see the sign, but there is no film in my camera. I forgot it was unloaded. Here, take a look." I offered it to him for inspection.

He looked me straight in the eye and then at the camera, slowly turning it over and flipping open the back. He muttered angrily about tourists ignoring government regulations, and for a moment I felt apprehensive lest he take it into his head to examine my bag. I speak Spanish adequately but could not comprehend his continued, low-voiced monologue.

After an arduous flight and my doubtless disheveled appearance, it must have seemed incongruous to engage in coquetry. Nevertheless, I had to try something to distract him, so I fluttered my eyelashes and said in English, "I don't understand what you are saying, but I am very sorry if I have done something wrong and I do apologize."

My accent was painfully exaggerated, deliberate almost to the point of insult to my mind. It seemed to have been effective, for he raised his hands into the air and, with a less than courteous shrug of his shoulders, turned away and walked back to his post.

Some welcome that was, I thought, and anyway, what the hell are they making such a fuss about? There appears to be nothing here worth taking photographs of. A low-lying cluster of sheds set down in the middle of fields was all there was to the entire airport. Where were the secrets hidden?

Everyone got off the plane. Most were in transit and simply wanted to stretch their legs and breathe a little fresh air. It was fresh enough, and bit into my lungs, raw and cold. I pulled my thin poplin raincoat tightly around me and buttoned it up to the chin as I followed the others trooping into the shed. Just four of us awaited immigration and customs formalities; the remaining passengers were free to pass through the room and outside to where vendors of souvenirs vociferously pressed their wares.

I awaited my turn. There was only one examining officer in attendance, though several others stood around idly smoking and chatting. I watched the man beside me open his large suitcase. His hand contained a much-folded envelope, which he slithered across the top of the lid as he lifted it back.

A snake could not have darted quicker than the customs official's hand in transferring the item to his pocket while brandishing the other hand midair and then plunging it into the contents of the suitcase.

The examination was a farce. The large parcel that the man had placed on the floor was now hoisted up to receive, without a knot untied, the same chalk mark as the suitcase. Approval given, inspection over, it was now my turn.

My pack was placed in an upright position. I held it steady with the top flap already open and laid back to permit easy access to the contents. This did not seem to suit the inspector at all, and he seized the pack and pushed it down flat on the bench. Not satisfied that several items fell out, he thrust his hand inside and began to drag everything out. I stared in shocked amazement at his roughness but said nothing until he started to tackle the side pockets. I attempted to gather up the contents of the larger pouch, but our hands collided and everything went flying to the earthen floor.

I was determined not to speak in Spanish. On other occasions it always seemed to get me into more trouble than out of it. Nevertheless, I could not restrain myself from saying in English, "Allow me to take things out." My remark was ignored if understood, and the wretched man was now shaking things out of my many little plastic bags. My God, what on earth did they think I was bringing into this miserable island? Was I so suspicious-looking because at my age I chose to carry my things around with me in a backpack? What were they looking for? Did I look like a smuggler of drugs or what?

I had had enough and was incensed. A stream of fluent Spanish gushed like a torrent from my lips. "Look here, it's one thing examining the contents of my baggage but another matter altogether to treat them like garbage. There's no need to let them drop on the floor and get filthied up." It sounded much worse in Spanish because I used a word that meant "pigged up" and I accused him of throwing my things on the floor.

His mouth dropped open in astonishment at the colloquial Spanish I had employed and the belligerent tone in which it was delivered. He immediately started to shove things back any old way, but made no attempt to retrieve all that had fallen to the ground. Neither did anyone else, and I was left to grovel about like a four-legged creature scratching around for a bone. I was absolutely furious.

The two other travelers were American ladies. They stood beside me, awaiting their turn. One clucked with sympathy and whispered, "Don't upset yourself, dear, it's not worth it," and added as an afterthought, "and maybe not too wise." Patiently they bore a similar inspection, but as they possessed suitcases, their belongings did not suffer the same fate as mine. I stepped out of the shed with them in hardly the most pleasant frame of mind. "Some welcome to Easter Island that was," I said to the air.

One of the American women hurried to my side. "Are you staying at the hotel? I thought if there was a taxi, we could all go together." There was only one hotel, to the best of my knowledge, and I was not intending to stay there. "No, I'm not, but I'll gladly get you a taxi if there is one about." Only a minibus, two jeeps, and an open truck were parked in the field. There did not seem to be any road into or out of the airport. Dozens of islanders stood around. By what means had they got here? I wondered.

A stocky, dark-skinned man with a peaked cap descended from the bus. "*Señoras, ¿van ustedes al hotel?*" I turned to the women. "You don't need to worry about a taxi. This man is sent from the hotel to meet all guests." I asked him if this was so, and upon confirmation told him that just the two ladies were hotel guests. My conversation in Spanish immediately drew a crowd of women around me. "*Señora, ¿necesita donde hospedarse?*" they chorused. "You need somewhere to stay?"

"Yes—" I couldn't finish my sentence, for they all spoke at once with offers of accommodations.

My first impressions had been thoroughly soured by the treatment of the officials. Now, as I looked at the women, I imagined their faces also bore similar characteristics. Hungry for the tourist dollar, they hovered about me like vultures, greedy, grasping, ready to swoop down on their prey.

I asked how much they charged, to see if prices differed, but none would give me one. Evasively they mumbled, "*No se preocupe, señora, todo se arregla.*" It was all very well their telling me not to worry, that everything would be arranged. I'd heard tales like that before. No, I insisted, I'd like a price, and I'd like to know what the accommodations consisted of.

They turned to each other in annoyance and muttered in a dialect too quick for me to grasp. All except one of them. She had stood apart for most of the time, hadn't even offered. She caught my eye upon her and smiled, whereupon I stepped toward her. She addressed me in a manner quite different from the rest. Her face seemed kinder and her voice less strident. "I live alone, señora. I have a very nice room, and I will not charge you much." I nodded instantly, less concerned with what her charge might be than pleased by her open face and simple direct speech.

The driver of the bus had loaded the luggage of the two American women into his vehicle, and they were now clambering in. My new landlady walked across to him and said something to which he nodded his head and beckoned me over. *"La Señora Carmen me dijo que usted va con ella. Siga Doña, las llevare a las dos."* He had offered us both a ride, and Señora Carmen, for that was her name, and I followed the two ladies inside.

"Oh, I'm so glad you've decided to stay at our hotel; your Spanish is so good, we'd be glad of your help." One of the women beamed away at me with unconcealed delight.

I returned her smile. I hadn't spoken to an American for months, and I felt suddenly homesick for all those wonderful privileges I had taken for granted back home. I felt a temporary warmth just being in their company. We were united by a common language and ways I had eagerly embraced so many years ago. With a faint sense of regret I replied, "I'm not staying at the hotel, but with this lady." I indicated Señora Carmen, who was chatting to the bus driver. "I made inquiries in Papeete and it seemed to be an awfully expensive hotel."

"Oh it is, it is," one of the women responded. "It's seventy-five dollars a night each, and we're obliged to stay four nights, until the next flight out of here. LAN-Chile has the monopoly, you see, and this being a government hotel, it's all part of the deal."

"Of course," the other woman chimed in, "we're very excited about being here, but friends said a day or two would have been more than enough to see the sights. It's turned out to be more expensive than really necessary."

"Oh, well, Doris," the first lady turned to her friend, "after all we've spent, what's another five or six hundred dollars more?"

I smiled, more to myself than to them. I had lived on less than that for months. Not that it warranted any medals; it was just interesting.

We had been traveling along an earthen road, rusty brown and very sandy. The sharp wind had whipped up a fine dust that sprayed the windows and partially obscured visibility. I had glanced out from time to time, thinking that the deserted road would soon give way to busier ones and herald the approach of a town or village. There had been a noticeable absence of trees. In fact, there had been a noticeable absence of everything other than green fields. A few straggly little houses now came into view. They had slanting tin roofs in order to collect the rain water, I imagined. They were all of whitewashed cement and stood well apart from each other in their own little gardens, which boasted low surrounding bushes that fronted on the road. We passed what I assumed to be the post office, if the letter box correctly identified the shack behind it, which was adjacent to the general store. Several bicycles were propped against the painted wooden structure, and half a dozen people stood around chatting. It seemed to be the main gathering place of the village, for I could see little else in the way of other business premises. Children played, two dogs yelped and chased each other's tails, and our driver stopped to deliver a small package to someone inside the store.

A few yards farther along we arrived at a crossroads marked by a small patch of well-trodden grass and an old withered tree. Surely not the center of the town? How dilapidated and soulless the place seemed to be. The bus halted, and Señora Carmen beckoned me to descend. I turned to the ladies. "The island is very small, I'm told. I expect I shall see you again soon, perhaps on one of the tours. I am sure the hotel will take good care of you—it depends upon tourists' recommendations. Don't worry, you'll be well looked after. Good-bye for now."

The bus went off in the opposite direction to the one in which we were now walking. "My house is nearby. We'll soon be there." Señora Carmen set a vigorous pace. By the time we reached her tin-roofed stone house I was quite exhausted. It had been a good twelve-minute walk, and the cold morning air had warmed up considerably more than was comfortable for an early backpack walk.

"I give you the best room," she said as she opened the door. It was a precious remark. There were only two rooms in the house.

Everything was spotlessly clean. The living room had little furniture, but the walls were amply adorned by many photographs and pictures cut out of magazines. The sofa, clearly a bed, was covered with a hand-knit spread. The little coffee table and the one beside the couch had their painted surfaces protected by snowy white crocheted mats. A vase of plastic flowers rested on one, and a large thick book on the other. I took this to be a Bible, as it lay directly beneath a wooden crucifix hanging on the wall and over which a picture of the Virgin Mary was placed.

The kitchen—if it could be called that—was part of the room. A section in one corner was designated for the single-faucet sink. This was surrounded above and below by shelves, of which the lower ones housed cooking utensils barely concealed by a small curtain stretched out on a wire. To the side of this, along the wall, a two-burner hot plate rested on the flat top of a small cupboard. The open shelves beneath housed crockery and miscellaneous kitchen goods. Beneath the only window on the adjacent wall, a table and three chairs were sedately placed. The table top was covered by a gaily printed plastic cloth, in the center of which a small dish held an assortment of plastic fruit. A handsomely carved wooden screen stood in the corner.

My room was the best in the house, without a doubt. It was a proper bedroom, with a large double bed and a splendid brass headboard. A white painted chest of drawers served also as a dressing table by virtue of an oval mirror standing on top. Mounted on a mahogany frame and supported by three legs, it was surrounded by hair brushes and several small pots and jars.

One wall was dominated by a glossy color portrait of Christ. It was glass-covered and elaborately framed in stippled white and gold paint. A large packing crate, partially covered by a lacy cloth, was placed beside the bed. It bore a small lamp, top-heavy with a shade made to represent a crinoline skirt, a book that looked like another Bible, and a photograph of a good-looking young man. An upright cane-bottomed chair standing in the corner completed the furnishings of the bedroom. My eyes swept the room with a quick glance and registered instant approval.

Where was the bathroom? There wasn't one. A back door,

which I had not seen because it lay concealed behind the wooden screen, was now opened by Señora Carmen. She pointed to an outhouse a little way down the path of a flourishing vegetable garden. For washing and personal ablutions of a lengthier nature, the screen opened up to its full dimensions. "I bring in large tin bath, so. It goes here, so. Now you have where to wash. It is very convenient."

I could not imagine anything less convenient, but I smiled, nodded, and said everything was just fine, and indeed it was. This kindly soul and her simple way of living and looking at life had appealed greatly to that ascetic part of my nature to which I paid much lip service but, alas, scant observance.

Señora Carmen bustled about getting water on to boil and producing what I suspected were her best cups and plates. I took my backpack to the bedroom to find a few toiletries and to extract my plastic containers of instant dried milk and tea bags. If she thought my pack strange, she never said so. I had noticed that few in the whole of the South Pacific ever had. Now, when I placed a few food items on the table, her raised eyebrows were the only indication of curiosity. It would have been ungracious to have refused the coffee that she summoned me to share with her. It was bitter and watery. I drank it stoically and seized the opportunity to refer to my packets.

I explained that I would not require any meals. I had a few provisions and intended to supplement these with a visit to the local store. I asked what might be available and how I would find my way there. With my packets of instant soup and coffee I only required the addition of fresh eggs or cheese and perhaps some locally grown fruit and vegetables to adequately meet my needs. I was anxious to assure her that I would not be burdening her with the preparation of any meals and ask if I might boil water whenever I needed it.

Señora Carmen was greatly puzzled by what seemed to her to be meager fare. She protested that it would be no trouble at all to make "proper meals" as she did for any guest staying with her. I realized that the absence of them made a difference to her charge. It was a change to be the one to say *"No se preocupe, señora, todo se arregla."* She was relieved that I only wanted an arrangement with her that would meet her entire satisfaction.

"You must be very tired after your long journey," she said. "I will gladly bring you some things back from the store. I have to go anyway. Why don't you lie down for a little while?"

"Yes, thank you. I would like to rest. It's only nine-thirty and a long way to go before bedtime."

"Oh, no, señora, it is much later than that. You have not changed your watch to our local time."

The mystery of the earlier-than-expected arrival at Easter Island was solved.

I awoke from a deep sleep with a thick head and that strange sensation of still being in a dream. Several moments went by before I could shake off the torpor that claimed my limbs and the languor of my brain. I could not be bothered to think about where I was, why I was lying on this bed in a strange room, and what I was doing here anyway. I idly watched the sunlit patterns on the wall deepen and fade as the brightness came and went until lethargy drained away and the urge to get up and out was too strong to resist.

Señora Carmen was not to be found, so I left a little note explaining that I had gone for a walk and would be back before dusk. The time now being two o'clock in the afternoon, it seemed a certain guarantee that I would be able to fulfill such a promise. I had been told that the island was only about seven miles wide by fourteen in length. Allowing for my stamina to walk two or three hours, I would surely cover a considerable area and not one in which I would get lost. I set off in high spirits, feeling much refreshed from my lengthy sleep.

It did not occur to me until I had been walking an hour that I had not seen a car, a human being, or even an animal since I had left the few scattered houses behind in the vicinity of Señora Carmen's cottage. I reminded myself that the literature I had read about Easter Island had mentioned a mere 1,200 inhabitants in all. Transport was virtually nonexistent, limited to jeep or truck by a few fortunate owners, among whom the military were the predominant proprietors. Horses could be hired for the asking, and scores of wild ones, I was told, roamed freely. Bicycles and homemade pushcarts made up the rest of the transportation facilities. Most people relied on their own two feet, according to the information Señora Carmen had exchanged with me over our coffee.

The few trees that had occasionally softened the deserted dirt road now too had disappeared. All I could see for miles around was open fields and sky until, ah! As I turned the curve in the road, the sea suddenly came into view, abruptly dropping away beyond the tall grasses. Like a giant mirror that lay upon the ocean's breast, a myriad of refractions of light sparkled with the brilliance of diamonds, reflecting the rays of the sun and the blue of the sky. It was a spectacular communion.

Irregular sections of stone walls bordered the fields, the gaps a result of collapsed boulders. My eyes traveled along the uneven lengths and were arrested by a strange configuration of rock. I caught my breath as, with a mild shock of recognition, I realized I had come across one of the great stone effigies on this island of mystery. My reasons for coming to Easter Island in the first place had been to see these gigantic stone men—larger than houses, fashioned with crude tools from natural resources by inhabitants whose origins have been traced back to about A.D. 857.

I had intended to take a properly organized guided tour the next day, but now I approached the many-ton monolith with a quickened pulse heightened by a sense of adventure and the thrill of enjoying my discovery all alone.

It was quite awesome. The gaunt, grim-faced statue's hollow eyes stared out toward the sea and beyond time itself. What manner of people had created him? Where had they come from? How and by what means had they reached this rugged speck of land in the vast expanses of these South Pacific waters? A tiny dot surrounded by one million square miles of ocean.

I tried to remember all that I had read about this unique island's culture, so much beyond my comprehension. Scores of expeditions had been made, and famous anthropologists and archaeologists had advanced countless fascinating theories, some of which later proved to be historically true. Much defied all logical explanation, and many mysteries still remained unanswered. How had the great statues been moved and raised into position? Why did they all bear the same facial characteristics, like no others to be found in the world? Tomorrow I would ask the guide my questions, but for now I only wanted to absorb this solitary moment of being in touch with the past. The architectural legacy bequeathed by these prehistoric people had exercised a subduing effect upon me. It now commanded a silent respect for the eons of a civilization almost beyond belief.

271

My neck ached from craning my head in an upward gaze. The *moai* must have been at least two stories high. I slowly walked around the platform on which it rested. It was incredible that all of it had been fashioned from tools of stone chips. Dark and brooding, did it resemble a people whose identification with a world, too primitive for my mind to grasp, was one where such an effigy represented a god or man? There for protection, or there for appeasement? Perhaps to those who carved these strange figures, it was their assurance of immortality, the transfer to a greater dimension when they died.

It was an eerie moment of centuries in collision. The towering, inscrutable *moai*, a massive stone sentinel of time, and I, a refugee from the twentieth century. I backed away so that once again I could absorb the total impact of its enormous size, and experienced the disconcerting sensation of being suspended between civilizations. The great stone man was a part of the cosmos. I was but an infinitesimal speck of dust in the vast universe. All who had gone and all who would be—pft! No more than atoms to be blown into the air and, but for an elite few, never known to have existed. It was most depressing.

I sat for an unconscionable length of time amid the tall grasses. A phrase by Thomas Carlyle flitted through my mind: "Silence is the element in which great things fashion themselves." It was one of those moments that most of us encounter from time to time, when the senses are stealthily drugged and one has the feeling, albeit unconsciously, that one's form is out there in space, up in the clouds, reunited with shapes that resemble someone dear to us that we once knew.

I sensed the approach of coolness and returned to myself, as it were. The sun's melting rays were slowly draining off into the ground, and I experienced the strangest feeling of weakness pervading my limbs, as if I had empathized with the departure of warmth.

I turned back to the road, the rich red clay glowing in the amber hues of a gradually retiring sun. It cast my shadow, elongated and black before me. On impulse I felt moved to take a photograph and capture the image. Click! It was the moment of my rebirth. In that instant I felt that I had imprisoned my former self on celluloid, never again to be quite the same person. I experienced a sense of loss, as if I had parted from a dear friend whom I would not see again.

I raised my head from the long shadow confronting me. No living thing met my gaze as my eyes swept the barren landscape around me. The stillness was profound, as if nature herself had ceased to breathe. The road, a long, flat red ribbon, stretched out ahead of me. It had no end. Where was I going? Sadness, like a thief, crept over me. I felt hollow and empty inside. It was not the first time I had experienced this lost feeling. It was a feeling less of loneliness than of grief. An inherent longing seems to dwell permanently in one of the secret compartments of my life. It yearns for expression yet knows not the form. From time to time it returns to haunt me and I am filled with an unbearable ache for which neither the cause nor the remedy can be defined.

Geographic location has little to do with the surfacing of this emotional disturbance, but now I linked the present discomfort to the sudden awareness that beyond the subdued horizon of this moment lay my other life. That which belonged to my family and the world from which I had come.

Thus far I had put off dealing with the growing uncertainties that had recently begun to intrude upon my mind. I was aware that changes had taken place within me and recognized, and later dismissed, the ambivalence of my feelings toward the domestic role I would soon be called upon to reassume. What of my husband? What of my children? What of my new country I had been so proud to adopt? Could I ever go back home again? Did I want to? I was not prepared for this personal interview with that inner self now called upon to reexamine motives and equate them with conscience. Later, much later, I had told myself, I can deal with such conflicts. Why was I now being plagued with these disturbing thoughts?

My uneasiness increased and I shivered, though it was not cold. The magnitude of sea, sky, and fields all around me was overwhelming. Slight prickles of terror began to sting the ends of my nerves. I felt not only desperately lonely, but fearful and afraid of my complete aloneness. Those thoughts of home had scudded across my conscious awareness of this utter solitude. They had plunged me into a state of fear and flight in which I groped frantically for the comforting thoughts of the known, the safety of all that was familiar.

Comfort? Safety? What was I thinking of? My God, I told myself, back home you were often afraid. On bustling city streets, on vacant park benches, in crowded theaters, in your own backyard, you knew fear aplenty. Back home, where noise was never absent, where violence was potentially always present, where "civilization" was peopled, of course you were afraid. You heard the term *agoraphobia* and were content to leave it at that.

But here, where never had I dreamed such silence could exist, where solitude wrapped itself around me like a shroud, here no refuge dwelt in which to shelter fear. Here the only fear to fear was the sudden confrontation with my true aloneness, the inescapable human condition. That final lonely crossing into no-man's-land, the truth we all perceive but refuse to face.

My apprehension deepened as it cloaked itself around me. I had come into this world alone, I would walk through it alone, and I would surely leave it alone. My fears, my despairs, my hopes, all were mine alone. Would that I could reach out to share the pain of isolation this knowledge now brought me. Share? A stupid, tiresome word, much abused and practically void of meaning. No one can share anything, much less feelings. If I share an object, it becomes two separate entities. How can one share thoughts, experiences? Can I feel your feelings? Can you feel mine? Can you know the extent of my pain, the intensity of my anxiety, the breadth of my vision, the depth of my sorrow?

I can tell you. You can listen. I can give. You can receive. We cannot share. My aloneness cannot be shared. It is only mine, alas, and I must experience it and endure it if I cannot find my own way to live with it.

Without warning, my apprehension was abruptly punctured by a sudden sense of liberation. Beads of perspiration began to drain away the fear now aborted in embryo. Gone was the panic that had so briefly dwelt within. Relief transcended and dispatched those earlier moments of acute anxiety, the final evaporation of which now found release in the sound of my own voice shouting out loud.

An exhilaration flooded my senses. Like a total eclipse, from which the sun appears the brighter, I felt I had emerged free and complete, released as if from physical bondage. I felt strong. I felt whole. I felt fortified. It was a moment of pure joy.

I had not been unaware these past months of the serenity of

being on my own, but it was only now that I realized the greater dimension of satisfaction that the state of true aloneness could bring. As an enemy, it dwelt as much in idle minds and lonely hearts as it did among the greatest of friends in the noisiest of places. As a companion, it could fill the core and fiber of one's being with comfort if one chose to appreciate its true value.

I had the feeling it could be one from whom, in the years to come, I could draw strength with which to play out the game. Aloneness was to be made welcome. It had to be sought and befriended. It had to be taken home to dwell inside.

Self-reliance and independence were its true companions. This I had discovered in simply being on my own these many thousands of miles. Free of dependence, I found I had acquired new guidelines with which to define love, respect, and trust. I had the time and the freedom to think about the complications of human relationships. Ideally there should be no barriers, no conditions, and no expectations. One should be free of all demands, nor should one make them.

No one lets you down and no one picks you up, for you alone control your own destiny. You should live with others, but not live for them, and you ask that they do not live for you.

You possess yourself and belong to no one. I had relied on no one. There had been no one to ask, nor had I thought to. My decisions had been my own. Good or bad, I had resolved my problems. I had walked alone. Until this moment I had regarded this long, lone journey as an escape to freedom. Now, I realized, it had become a voyage of discovery. Had I found that which I had been searching for so long? My true self?

I set off down the road, now one of challenge and self-realization. As far as the eye could see, no bird, no beast, no man, no moving thing disturbed the mighty stillness encompassed within my vision. It was a scene of unparalleled silence, the indelible memory of which would, from time to time when called upon, calm the troubled heart in search of serenity. Its hypnotic effect slaked my thirst for all further introspective thought. It pervaded my being and took possession of my soul. I sensed the presence of unearthly things. I was at one with myself. I felt at peace.

But for the cross atop the corrugated tin roof, the building might well have been mistaken for the local town hall. The church, stark and simple in its whitewashed cement-block construction, was filled with beauty when the Pascuenses (natives of Easter Island—Isla de Pascua) lifted up their voices in song.

Bare of adornments, its walls ungraced by windows, the church interior was lit by a half-dozen naked bulbs hanging from the ceiling. Early worshippers had claimed the best seats—roughly hewn wooden benches of little comfort and not an inch of space to spare. Children squatted on the stone-slabbed floor or fidgeted restlessly among the standing adults who lined the walls on all sides. At the back, late arrivals crowded around the door and spilled down the steps outside.

Sunday mass was the event of the week and not to be missed. If an event of occasional tardiness for the observant and serious, it was of no little social significance for the young and curious. Girls gathered on the steps in their sabbath finery, inclined toward persuasions of a more ardent nature.

While outside the village boys were being flirtatiously engaged into temptation, the congregants within were fervently being led out of it through prayers and hymns that filled the air with melodic and faintly primitive refrains.

Father David was an American priest. It was not his accent alone that enlightened me as I listened to his sermon; it was the whispered remarks the Pascuenses exchanged as we filed out into the warm sun when the service was concluded. The dialect was unfamiliar to my ear, but the tone of voice and an odd remark I caught now and then were not of an affectionate nature. This in no way impeded my haste to catch up with the priest as he crossed the little square. He had emerged from a back door as I awaited him on the front steps.

"Father David, Father David." The English halted him abruptly. He turned as I drew abreast. "I'm from the States, just visiting the island. I heard you in church and wanted to say hello."

His face broke into a broad smile that produced so many wrinkles around his eyes that, but for small slits, they almost disappeared. He eagerly seized my hand, and in a true Southern dialect, nostalgic to my ear, said, "Well, how about that!"

We warmed to each other instantly, and I accepted with alacrity his invitation to accompany him home, where he had an appointment to keep on his ham radio transmitter. "If you get through to the USA, before you sign off, Father, do you think you could try and get a message through to my husband, please?"

"Sure thing. No trouble at all once I get through—that is, *if* I get through."

He seemed a lonely soul, though I expect his faith sustained him. Whereas the companionship of others might have provided an outlet for conversation and interests, he lavished all that was not directed toward his ministry upon his cat. His tiny house was neglected, dirty, and reeked of his pet. His obsessive devotion to the little creature made me feel uncomfortable. He had a way of crooning endearments to it, stroking it, tickling and even kissing it that was quite disconcerting. This, together with the penetrating smell, made me think of leaving sooner than I had intended. I began to cast about in my mind for an excuse, conscious that I had expressed the wish to make radio contact with Marco. The crump, crump of an arriving motorcycle signaled a visitor, and I saw an opportunity to get away more easily.

"Oh, that will be Arthur Hiatt. He's an American too. He lives here. Don't take too much notice of everything he says, though, he's a bit—" Father David tapped the side of his head with a forefinger. "You know what I mean?"

I nodded, about to inquire further, as Arthur Hiatt walked in. Fair-haired, lean-faced, of wiry build and around fifty, he was dressed in blue jeans and a turtleneck sweater. He looked perfectly all right to me. He sounded all right, too, as he chatted away with the priest, casting a smile and an odd remark in my direction to which neither comment nor reply was awaited.

Father David had by now warmed up his transmitter. For ten minutes nothing but high- and low-range squeals and beeps had issued from the set. The crackles and distortions of airwave interference were less than soothing to the ear, and I decided it was time to leave. Arthur Hiatt's presence would smooth over my unexpected withdrawal from the scene.

"Wherever you are going, I'll take you," Arthur said. "Ever ridden pillion?"

"No, I haven't, and I don't think I want to either, thank you." The thought of riding a motorcycle horrified me. Death machines, that's what I had always said of them.

Father David looked at me reassuringly, "Oh, you'll be all right with Arthur here."

Well, that was some turnabout, I thought. One minute he was telling me that the fellow was a bit touched in the head, and the next minute, that I would be all right with him. Perhaps the priest wanted to get rid of him, but what if, later on, Arthur Hiatt wanted to get rid of me? I had better clear this up right away. "How do you mean 'all right,' Father David?" I smiled to soften the inference while emphasizing the "all right," and shot a glance at Arthur to see if and how he would react. He seemed vastly amused and waited in silent mirth to hear the outcome of this dialogue.

Father David knew at once what I meant but blandly replied, "Don't worry. Arthur has a few ideas upon which we do not agree, but he is a good rider. You'll be quite all right with him."

I did not seek a reference on motorcycle skills as much as on his character, which I had been led to believe was in question. These words, coming from a man of the cloth, had to be accepted as a general recommendation. I took them and took a chance. In so many places I had found myself in situations that had not been to my liking; surely here on Easter Island, where there was hardly a vehicle on the road, the chances of an accident, if confined to that one aspect alone, seemed fairly remote.

Doubts of a more personal nature were hardly entertained at all in view of Father David's assurances, and completely overlooked was my lack of any experience at all with regard to riding pillion on a motorcycle. This only came forcibly home to me as I clung on for dear life the moment we roared away from the priest's house. Other than my terror at being stuck at the back of a death machine, Arthur's conversation and his behavior were both enjoyable and perfectly normal. My confidence that I would be "quite all right" grew by the minute. He was indeed a careful driver, but even the winner of a Grand Prix could not have avoided the very real dangers of the uneven stony roads. While there was no traffic to contend with, for we did not pass one car, the potholes would suddenly come upon us, and Arthur shouted at me to "hold on tight now." To this injunction I yelled back, "I am, but can't you go slower? I'm petrified!"

"What?" was the hollered response.

"Nothing," I screamed hoarsely into the wind, and into my heart, Spare me, God. Why do I do these mad things?

Without Arthur and his motorcycle, I would never have

known (according to him) the scandal of Easter Island. All that I had not seen on the previous day of sightseeing, Arthur now showed me. I was extremely lucky in one way, for Arthur was able to zigzag across the many little roads all around the island to which otherwise there would have been no alternative form of transport.

We had traveled over several miles of open countryside, quite barren of trees or any other foliage. Now we turned into a gently sloping field at the bottom of which clumps of trees came suddenly and surprisingly into view.

Arthur switched off the engine and helped me to totter off the bike. He proceeded to walk with it toward the trees several hundred yards away. In a hushed voice he informed me that we were trespassing on government land but that there was no need for alarm. He took my hand and led me forward into a now thickly forested area, pausing to prop his cycle against a tree and placing a finger across his lips to silence further words. I began to feel uneasy and wondered what it was we were about to see that required such caution.

We walked for several minutes without speaking until we reached a slight thinning of the tall eucalyptus. "Beyond there you can see the clearing," he whispered. I looked between the foliage; it was mystifying. I had expected to see something quite startling, but all that was visible was a large, open circular space, ringed by more trees.

"What is it? What do you mean?" I whispered back.

Arthur again placed his finger across his lips as he mouthed, "I'll tell you later." With this he turned back and beckoned me to follow him. I complied immediately, less from concern about trespassing than from my desire to "get out of the woods" with Arthur Hiatt.

Wheeling his cycle toward the road, he began to explain. "That clearing used to be the corral for the horses. Several years ago there used to be vegetation here. Sugarcane, guava, beans, and many fruit trees. We had sheep, cattle, and the greatest of plans to make the island agriculturally self-sufficient." He picked up a large stone and threw it viciously toward the trees. "Supplies were promised and some came at first. Then they dwindled and eventually ceased. Everything was neglected. What wasn't eaten got bug-ridden and spoiled." He scowled with disgust. "Now we have nothing except visits of the officials from the mainland. They come over regularly in groups, ostensibly to make examinations and recommendations, but I'll tell you why they really come." He paused to make an obscene gesture that set a little pulse of alarm shooting down my arms and into my fingertips.

"They come with cases of liquor and presents. The presents are for the ladies. Oh, yes, we have 'ladies' here. Some of the liquor is for the officials who live on the island. It keeps wagging tongues quiet and friendly. Then the visitors, with the rest of the liquor, and the presents, take the ladies and go and hole up with them over there." He jerked his head in the direction of the trees, and I assumed that somewhere beyond them, some kind of dwellings existed. I was not eager for further clarification. Arthur's voice was angry rather than bitter. "Yes, that's why they come, and everything about this place is as corrupt as anywhere else. The worst of it is that we are all helpless. Wherever we go we are helpless."

His expression frightened me. I made no comment at all and only wanted to get away from this lonely spot. If Arthur Hiatt was beginning to get a bit "you know what," as Father David had said, I preferred it to be in a place that I knew where, but the change of scene was not altogether reassuring either, as he drove me straight to his isolated little house nestled on a rocky hill overlooking the sea.

Tiny though the place was, it had every amenity—a flush toilet and a separate bathroom, an electric stove, and a five-foot refrigerator. I was quite surprised and ventured to say, "My goodness, it's like stateside living." It was the nearest reference I had made to Arthur's life on the island.

"Yes, I expect you have been wondering what a guy like me is doing in a place like this?"

"Mm, I had rather."

"That's all right. I'm not ashamed to tell you. I've escaped." My expression must have registered alarm, and indeed I was already mentally bolting out of the door. "Not from prison. Ha! You thought I was a convict, eh?"

"As a matter of fact, I didn't know what to think," I confessed timidly.

He leaned forward confidentially. We were sitting at the table drinking a very respectably brewed cup of tea. "I've escaped from all that up there." He threw back his head as if the gesture pinpointed the exact geographic location. "The rat race and all those crazy people back home." His voice took on an ominous tone. "Do you realize that this place is just about the only spot left on earth where we can escape annihilation? It's coming, you know."

He rummaged among some papers on his book-lined shelves and offered me a pamphlet. It was entitled *How to Organize for Survival.* "Here, read it. They don't print these things for fun, you know."

I didn't know and I didn't want to know. Up to now Arthur Hiatt had been courteous and, with the exception of his earlier outburst, quite gentlemanly. His bespectacled eyes and fresh complexion had given his face a slightly academic look. He could have been a professor, as his manner of speech had clearly indicated a better-than-average education. At no time had he seemed mentally disturbed. Now, as he spoke, I detected a glitter behind those bifocals that caused me to shiver inwardly. He was embarking upon his favorite topic and one that was his sole obsession—the end of mankind. World disaster was imminent, and only those who had escaped to some remote place would survive.

He went on to tell me that the present administration in the USA was in the pay of the Russians and that the CIA was actually fomenting a nuclear war in the Middle East. He reeled off names of generals in the military, directors in various ministries, and others of high rank whose positions wielded supreme power. It was devastating to hear such wild talk, for while my mind rejected its total credibility, fantasy wreaked havoc with my imagination and plunged me into terrifying contemplations of all that he was saying.

"There is an overall plan of destruction being augmented day by day. I am kept informed by people on the 'inside,' and they estimate that five years from now it will all be over. War in the Middle East will coincide with violent outbreaks in all the Central American countries. You'll see, in five years it will be the end." He lent emphasis to this pronouncement by a wide sweep of his hand, which sent his cup and saucer flying to the floor.

I was thankful for the distraction, and as he bent to pick up the pieces of broken crockery, I asked in as casual a tone of voice as I could muster, "You keep in touch then with friends in the USA?"

"Oh, Lord, yes. I have friends and family back home. In fact, I would be grateful if you could get in touch with them on your return and give them personal messages from me."

"I'd be glad to," I said. I was overjoyed to be given the opportunity, for I had begun to wonder what other traits might begin to surface as his intensity grew. "Why don't you give me the names and telephone numbers," I continued. "I'll write them down right now in my notebook."

"Fine," he said. "Let me get my address book." He disappeared into the back room, and I immediately began to scribble down all the names of the people he had mentioned who were part of the terrible scheme to destroy the world. Even if the fellow was quite mad, there would be no harm in mentioning all this to the FBI or at least inform some newspaper about it. Wasn't that how the Watergate affair started? If it was all a hoax and no more than a lonely, unbalanced man's fantasy, the worst that could happen to me was to feel a little ridiculous. Vanity seemed a paltry price to pay, and my feverish imagination ran its usual riotous course as I tried to remember and jot down the details. I flipped over to a clean page as Arthur reentered the room, a much-thumbed notebook in hand.

He gave me names and addresses not only of people in the States but also of one in Paris and one in Monaco. Perhaps the fellow was not mad at all. Why would he have addresses in Europe? Maybe I should take some of this seriously after all.

He must have been reading my thoughts, for as I mumbled something about leaving, he produced a cassette tape. "Here, take this and play it when you get back. I receive them regularly—they are news bulletins. I don't need it anymore. If you want to get them, you only have to write or call one of the names I gave you."

Anxious to extricate myself from a situation that so far had been manageable, I pleaded to take photographs. At the back of my mind I thought this a necessary adjunct when passing on the information to whatever source would listen to me.

Arthur complied readily enough and even fixed up my 35-millimeter camera, by use of the time-delay feature, to take a photograph of both of us together. I took an additional Polaroid of him, just to be sure, I said to myself. The roll of film could be damaged or the photograph badly taken; one never knew, and it was best to be sure. I felt like a female Sherlock Holmes who had lured the unsuspecting victim into a trap. I also felt just a trifle foolish in the projections of my imagination, but was not the truth often more bizarre than fiction? No, I had lost nothing with such precautions.

I was returned to my lodgings none the worse for my outing, for Arthur had been pleasant and polite right up to the moment of parting. He thanked me profusely for my company and my offer to contact his friends. With a courteous greeting to Señora Carmen and an odd militarylike salute to me, he revved up his motorcycle and ripped off down the road.

"*Ese gringo está loco, señora.*" My landlady was convinced that he was quite mad and clearly relieved that I was unharmed and in one piece. I assured her that I had met him under the most respectable of circumstances. What could have been more proper than an introduction by Father David?

She needed no encouragement to discuss the priest's tenure and confirmed my earlier impression that few returned the affection and concern he so anxiously wanted to bestow upon his congregants.

"He is not one of us and never will be," Señora Carmen confided. "No one can ever replace our beloved Father Sebastian." She shook her head sadly and went on to tell me that times were not at all what they used to be on the island. "Once our visitors would be greeted with flowers and necklaces. Our girls would wear the grass skirt and sing and dance for them. Now, well, you have seen for yourself how it is. Everything is different now."

When it came to settling my bill, I asked if there were any of my belongings she might like as part payment. I was running very low on cash, and she had fingered my raincoat longingly as she explained how difficult it was to get anything brought in from the mainland, and even then at a prohibitive cost. My suggestion was met with great enthusiasm. So delighted was she with the prospect of replenishing her wardrobe that she offered me the entire four-night's stay gratis in exchange for as much as I could spare of my possessions.

With reckless abandon I gave her the three-piece matching outfit that Nina had given me in Australia. I threw in the slacks I had worn only once and added two T-shirts, one nightgown, a half-slip, and a brassiere.

Of my toiletries, Señora Carmen chose a lipstick, a pressed-powder compact I had never used, a half-finished bottle of deodorant, and a quantity of bobby pins. An assortment of safety pins, rubber bands, ballpoint pens, and a variety of miscellaneous travel aids I had lugged around for emergencies that never arose were eagerly accepted as items of great store. Parting with my raincoat occasioned some misgivings. It was not the cost of the garment as much as the use for it. On reflection I remembered the little protection it had given me against rain and even less warmth against the cold. (Oh, throw the thing in as well.) My change purse changed hands, and a pair of pantyhose was consigned to encase shapelier legs than mine. Aware of Señora Carmen's eyes dwelling longingly on my acrylic "fun" watch, I unstrapped it from my wrist and included it as a part of the deal. She was overjoyed and warmly embraced me.

"*¿Está conforme?*" I asked her. "Is everything to your satisfaction?"

"*Ah, sí, sí. Estoy muy contenta. Muchisimas gracias. Usted es muy amable. Todo está bien arreglado, señora, muy bien arreglado. Que Dios le bendiga.*"

The trade had been highly successful. Señora Carmen was content. My backpack was infinitely lighter, and I had God's blessings thrown into the bargain as well. It was not a bad deal at all.

I had encountered little on Easter Island to endear it to me, yet on leaving, I felt quite sad. It was a strange feeling. Elsewhere in the South Pacific I had experienced a warmth of welcome; I had witnessed spontaneous gaiety or displays of native charm. People had smiled; they had been friendly, interested, concerned.

The Friendly Islands had rightfully earned their appellation. If tourist prosperity had motivated an attitude, it was a pardonable cultivation, for hospitality was generously given and offered with charm.

Here on Easter Island, the Pascuenses had made not the slightest attempt to capture my affections. I had tried to engage their interest, but the few with whom I had spoken were but polite but no more. They had been indifferent to my efforts, their insularity and sullen mien a barrier that defied penetration. Thus discouraged, I had ceased to try further. I was puzzled.

Could it be the extreme remoteness of their geographic location, flung into the ocean thousands of miles from the nearest neighbor? Did parent Chile treat them like outcast children in disgrace? Did they feel rejected by the world? Was this why they clung so tightly together, scorning the prying eyes of visitors only tolerated by the jingle of coins? Did the awesome presence of the *moai* burden them with a history they were ill-prepared to shoulder now that strangers came to prod and stare?

What *was* the reason the Pascuenses seemed so resentful, so unloved perhaps. And why did I care anyway?

Leaving the island was almost as mystifying an experience as arriving had been. One moment it was there, the next it had vanished. I strained to glimpse the spot where I had stumbled across the world asleep. Those quiet green fields where I had trembled on the threshold of infinitely new beginnings, where serenity had possessed my soul. It was not to be. Barely had the plane lifted its wings, when Isla de Pascua had disappeared into the shimmering satin of the sea.

A profound sadness swept over me. I knew now why I was so deeply affected. There, among the sentinels of a civilization marooned for all eternity, I felt I had been born for a fragile moment of magnificence, and there a part of me would remain behind forever.

11

Homecoming

Was I really walking down the concourse at Miami's International Airport? I felt numbed. Was it excitement? Nerves? Apprehension? How would Marco look? How did I feel about seeing him again? Why was I asking myself all these silly questions? I bet he won't even notice I'm thirty pounds slimmer.

I changed my dark sunglasses for clear ones. I still couldn't see anyone at the exit who looked like Marco. Maybe he hadn't been able to get away. Maybe some emergency had cropped up in the office. Where were the boys, then? Surely one of them would be here to meet me? After all this time away, what, no one?

That's how it looked as I approached the group of people hovering around the entrance of the concourse. I scanned the eager faces. Glasses or not, there was no one there of mine. I felt a great lump of disappointment in my throat but turned philosophically toward the battery of telephones. There must be a good reason. I'll call the office before passing judgment.

"Darling!" Someone grabbed hold of me. It scared the life out of me even though I realized instantly it was Marco. His arms were around me and my head went back at a ninety-degree angle to take in his full six feet one inch.

"Oh Mong, Mong." I was gulping and sniffing. "I thought no one was coming!" He was kissing my forehead, my nose, and then —the sweetness of his mouth on mine.

It was a very long moment from which I had to pull away most reluctantly. I couldn't swallow, and my neck felt as if it was about

286

to snap in two. We both laughed and kissed again. I felt warm and safe and very much loved.

"Honey, I had a terrible time trying to park. I went around and around the damn place for twenty minutes. I was getting desperate until some guy pulled out. I was afraid I would miss you. Let me look at you. Where've you gone? You've shrunken to nothing."

He'd noticed. "Don't you like how I look? I thought you'd be pleased."

"Well I am, I am—but I don't know if I like you this skinny just the same."

I decided to adopt a positive stance. "Well, I think I look gorgeous, so there."

"You look great, darling, great. I've missed you."

We walked hand in hand to the baggage claim, stopping every so often just to look at each other and smile. Our conversation was like one of those transatlantic calls made yearly as a Christmas treat for the family at home, limited to inquiries about health so as to avoid lengthy involvement with matters requiring detailed explanations.

"So how are you?"

"Fine, fine."

"So what was it like?"

"Fantastic. Just marvelous."

"You look terrific."

"You look a bit tired, Mong."

"Yes, I am a bit. But never mind me, what about you? So how've you been?"

We were back to the beginning, and we laughed and embraced all over again. I kept saying to myself, You're home now. You are no longer the single roamer of the world but a married woman. You belong to this tall, handsome man beside you. And he *was* handsome, too. His hair a little thinner and grayer, a few more lines on his face perhaps. But he was my husband, and once again I was accountable to another human being.

It was a strange feeling and a disturbing one, and I hastened to brush it aside. Recognition of this brought further turmoil. How could it be? How could I feel the greatest of joys at being reunited with the ones I loved and yet experience a vague sense of—what?

Misgivings? About what? I quickly asked for news of the boys and of the business.

"Is that all you have?" Marco picked up my pack with one hand and carried it with ease.

"Yes, I traded most of my things for accommodations on Easter Island."

"You *what?*" He looked at me incredulously. "I can't get over this whole thing. My wife. My missis. To think you actually circled the whole damn globe on your own like this. You are the most, to say the least."

"Oh, Mong, do you really think so?"

"Of course I do! Don't you think so too?"

We stepped out of the cool terminal to be enveloped by a blanket of thick, moist air. I had forgotten how sticky Miami's heat and humidity could be. The dampness seeped into every pore. Within minutes of walking to the car, my clothes began to cling to my body. It was an uncomfortable reminder of how life can be here for nine months of the year.

The next jog to my memory was the ever-present lineup of angry-looking motorists, all honking and jockeying for the best way to get out of the airport precincts. It is never a pretty sight at best, but after so long an absence it seemed especially ferocious. I began to feel quite dismayed.

As we whizzed along familiar expressways I told myself that such reactions were to be expected and natural. But was it natural to feel suddenly trapped? I was caught in the snare of a modern world where transistor radios filled the air and pollutants filled the lungs. The full impact struck more forcibly here, for in other cities where similar conditions existed, I had been only a visitor.

Now I was finally home. This was where my real life was. The life of a homemaker. The shopping, cooking, cleaning, and caring were all awaiting me, and (please God, forgive me) I just did not look forward to it one bit.

The doorman relieved us of the car as we stopped in front of the apartment building. There was no greeting. He was a new man and either did not know I had been away for quite a while or did not care. The lobby had been renovated and recarpeted, and there were several large plants that had not been there when I left.

"Looks as if they decided to smarten up a bit," I commented.

288

"Have they painted that mildewed patch on our ceiling and is the air conditioning working better now?"

"Neither. They're not going to do a thing. It's rumored that they may go 'condo' and that's why only the lobby's been done."

We emerged from the elevator and walked down the long corridor to the very end. Our fifth-floor apartment was the last one and looked directly over the ocean. The brilliance of sun and sea flooded the room as Marco opened the door. The white-painted walls and mirrors reflected the dazzle beyond the windows, and involuntarily I gasped, "Oh, it's so beautiful, Marco." I turned, put my arms around his neck, and kissed him. "It's wonderful to be home. Thank God for everything and that all of us are safe and well."

I looked around at my little palace. Sure enough, the damp patch on the ceiling was still there. The carpet had been recently vacuumed. It all looked so neat and fresh that it struck me as being quite new and attractive. "My goodness, who's been doing the cleaning? Where are the boys? I'll bet it wasn't always as tidy as this?"

"Far from it. We all set to last night, but there are plenty of skeletons you'll come across soon enough. The boys won't be in till much later. It was quite amusing the way they looked at me and said, 'Guess you and Mom will want to be on your own for a while.' "

Marco's tone of voice was light and jesting, yet I found myself blushing like a new bride. I didn't know what to say or how he might expect me to react. I only knew that I felt suddenly shy and strange.

I got up immediately from the couch on which we were sitting and, with a declaration that I was dying for a cup of tea, busied myself in the kitchen to hide any display of nervousness.

Marco followed me in and kissed the back of my neck. "It's all right, darling. I know how you feel. It's the same for me too."

My sons were gorgeous. How else can a mother describe her children? My husband was as dear to me as ever, if not more so. What else could I wish for? When the euphoria began to fade, I felt wicked and guilty for asking myself "Now what?"

At first it was hard for me to accept that the period of adjustment could be so difficult. I felt in limbo. Utterly disoriented. I was devastated by my inability to function. Nothing seemed real, and I performed little tasks like an automaton. Often there were moments of traumatic confusion, such as awakening in the night petrified that someone was lying beside me. Or, on a nocturnal visit to the bathroom, puzzled as to which hotel, home, or country this bedroom was in.

As is perfectly natural and proper, the novelty of having me back again soon wore off, and for Marco and the boys it seemed as if I had never been away. Michael decided to go to Oklahoma, where he had been to college, had friends, and "real people" lived. Tony took a small place of his own. Both boys felt that the apartment was too cramped now that I was home. They were right, of course. I, too, found that my world had shrunk.

Had I made the effort to stir out of the apartment, I might have picked up the threads of my old life a little sooner. I had no desire to. I rarely ventured out, not even to the beach below, but sat at the window staring at the sea and thinking of those faraway places I had been to so recently.

I discouraged the few friends I had from visiting. The neighbors I skillfully avoided. I felt I simply could not be bothered with idle curiosity or gossip-seekers. No two ways about it: my homecoming was an anticlimax—first class.

Marco came home from the office burdened most nights with as much work as ever. He chided me for expressing my dismay that nothing seemed to have changed.

He was chiding *me* that nothing had changed. Little did he know that for me many things could have drastically changed had my love and loyalty not brought me back to him.

My return home had taken me through Los Angeles, Chicago, New York, and Washington. The last was the capital of the country, but for me New York was the heart and soul of America, and I loved the city with a passion.

Those towering edifices reached up, up into the sky, and with them soared all my frustrated dreams and ambitions repressed or sublimated during all those many years of mothering and housekeeping. How I longed to be a part of those intense, curious, garrulous, helpful, pulsating, enquiring, *alive* people who walked those wide, heady Manhattan blocks. All carried newspapers and *books!* They knew what was going on, and if they didn't, they made it their business to find out. Questions, smiles, nods, arguments, refusals, but *involved*, not like some of the phoney, pol-yurethane puppets I had come across elsewhere in my travels.

If only Marco *knew* how I had secretly entertained ideas about working out a "commuting marriage." One where I could be an independent, working woman for five days a week and a loving wife and housekeeper at weekends. I knew such an unconventional lifestyle would be totally unacceptable to him. He would laugh at the very idea. No, my life was in Miami, that pretty, palm-treed picture-postcard place where Marco was evidently carrying on in the same old way, yet complaining that nothing had changed. It was for *him* to change, not me. I had changed so much I was even afraid to broach some of the issues that were now affecting the harmony between us.

Adding to the growing conflicts within me was the apparent lack of interest Marco showed whenever I spoke of my trip. One Saturday morning I received a large package from the Polaroid Corporation. They had been absolutely marvelous to me and had developed all my slide photographs gratis. Now, holding them up to the light, I asked Marco to take a look.

"Honey, I looked at all your instant pictures when you first came home. I really haven't time now to start squinting at slides. The accountant is coming in next week and I've just got to get the books done. I'll look at them some other time."

No time was ever the right time, and the weeks went crawling by. I threw myself into a frenzy of housecleaning to right the neglect most evident in the kitchen. It was neither satisfying nor rewarding. The results were not even noticed. I slammed cupboard doors and banged pots and pans around, determined that my efforts should at least be recognized if not appreciated.

"You really are going to be impossible to live with if you carry on this way," was the only acknowledgment Marco gave me. I was furious, and smoldered inwardly. How could he be so insensitive to my feelings of helplessness at being back in the same old rut? I had traveled the world, I had seen wonderful and terrible things, I had a million experiences I wanted to share with him. If not with him, who else? Did he resent all the adventures I had had? Did he feel just a little threatened by them?

I decided he must sense that I felt differently about everything, including my role as a housewife. I was not the same person and knew that nothing could be as before. Maybe Marco feared this subconsciously, for he did not seem to know who I was anymore, and I found myself unable to relate to him. We always seemed to be at cross-purposes.

Friction between us was occurring with regular monotony. The episodes were trivial in nature, but our disagreements generated an immediate hostility that colored our interaction with each other on almost every level.

A letter from one of my sisters, addressed with humorous intent, no doubt, to "Ms. Marco Polo," triggered his evidently much repressed anger.

" 'Ms. Marco Polo,' indeed. It's a lot of rubbish, this Ms. stuff. I've no patience with it. You're a middle-aged married woman. You're not Ms. anything. You are Mrs. Marco Shalom, or has all this traveling given you ideas that have turned your head a bit?"

I was stunned, as if I had received a blow. Tears sprang to my eyes and I turned away and went into the bedroom. Why was he so sharp with me, sarcastic even? I felt destroyed. Is this what my "marriage sabbatical" had come to? A wasted experience? Two strangers no longer able to relate to each other? I began to fear that an erosion of our marriage was taking place with an alarming rapidity that neither of us knew how to halt.

A torpor claimed my body. An all-too-familiar pattern was slowly being manifested. I felt too indifferent, too tired, or just too lazy even to take a walk. An insidious stagnation paralyzed my mind, quite obliterating all former intentions to make changes in my life. It was as if I had slipped on my old skin the moment I entered my home.

The door seemed firmly closed now against that creature who only functioned on a different level when removed from the familiarity and responsibility of living with her family. The implications were devastating, and I consequently blocked them from conscious recognition. Alas, impetus in any direction was also blocked. I found myself confining my remarks to the minimum rather than risk arguments that could possibly widen the chasm I felt had opened between us.

This ploy was neither healthy nor effective. One Sunday morning as I was clearing away the breakfast dishes, resigned to Marco's immersion in his papers, he suddenly surprised me by taking the plates out of my hand and putting them back on the table. He led me toward the couch and gently pushed me down onto the cushions. I knew I was in for a lecture and I was glad. He hadn't shown this much interest in me since the first week or two after my return.

"Now listen to me. It's no use us carrying on this way. First of all, you just have to stop resenting my work habits. It has never been any different. That's the way I am and you know it. Secondly, you must stop looking to me for your distractions. I realize it's hard for you to settle down again after all you have done. You will simply have to find some way of being creative for yourself. Something different from your voluntary work, something that offers you some self-expression. Only you can do it, you know."

"Oh, Marco, I want to and I'd like to. It's just that I feel so stifled here. I can't explain. I just do, that's all."

"Well you had better 'undo,' then. We've been bickering away at each other lately, and it's got to stop. I don't like it and I know it's making you unhappy. Your sisters and friends have written to you. Answer them. They've asked you about your trip. Tell them. Better still, write it all down in a book."

"A book!" I stared at him. "Oh, Mong, I haven't been able to write to anyone at all, and you say write a book?"

"Why not? You used to write excellent articles, and your letters have always been a pleasure to read. Anyway, I'll tell you something now to get you going and I'm sorry if you don't like what I'm going to say. I'll never really know about your trip until I can read it in a book. When you start to tell me in bits and pieces during meals or after them, my mind wanders back to the office and all the unfinished work I've brought home. To be honest, I haven't really heard what you've said. I'm sorry, honey, but it's the truth."

I knew it was, but hearing it was painful. Seeing the look on my face, he tried valiantly to soften the blow. "Darling, try and make the effort; it will help bridge the gap between the trip and being home again. Make a start. All right?"

And it *was* all right, for writing became my salvation. Indeed, it became a catharsis. As I wrote of events and happenings, I began to live them all over again. Not only did I re-create feelings that had gone to sleep, but with their awakening I realized that my journey was far from over.

It was the beginning of the journey into myself.

*   *   *

293

Those rays of self-awareness that had pierced my deepest consciousness on Easter Island now took on a more realistic dimension when juxtaposed against the background of my day-to-day existence. I had known then, and firmly told myself now, that a second chance at life and living is there to be grasped, especially for those of us in later years when we can call upon emotional maturity and life experience to help us reach our full potential.

I had proven to myself that I was capable, self-reliant, and independent. I had managed on my own and had not been afraid to deal with the loneliness and the many fears that had often beset me throughout those many months in unfamiliar surroundings.

I had made peace with that other aloneness and could now more serenely accept that quiet sanctuary within, and which, when terms are made, can only bring the greatest comfort. It was there, on Easter Island, that I had felt complete and whole, and I wanted now so badly for Marco to understand and feel the same. Only then could I feel that the love between us was a free exchange and not a barter.

I wanted love for love's sake. Not love for power, love for convenience, manipulation, or need.

Obligation, duty, and service in love is not a tenet with which I quarrel, but there comes a time when these aspects become imperative for all but the stagnant mind to examine. If one's life is being lived out to the exclusion of one's own purpose and the very reason for being on this earth at all, then with the diminishing years left to us it is time to take appropriate measures.

Marriage, of all relationships, is a partnership the successful management of which is the fair and honest division of effort and interests. The give and take in equal measure.

I had never given too much thought to the feminist movement, but now I began to realize how vastly our roles in life had changed over the past decade or two. One could no longer deny that women had at last won their rightful place alongside men. Whether in the home or in the workplace, the basis of success should ideally rest upon a foundation of equality.

Society had granted approval for those too timid to have otherwise freed themselves from the self-imprisonment of their cocoons. This unique phenomenon now augured well for personal growth and achievement. Why should this not apply to me also? No longer was there a need for guilt about my expectations of self-fulfillment. We all have the potential within us to make change and to improve our lives. There is no situation on this earth that does not have an alternative—not always a palatable one, but an alternative. With one exception. Life itself. And this is what I had to get on with.

The more I wrote, the more I perceived that the time of reckoning had come. It was now or never that I must begin to clear away the rubbish that had cluttered up the garret of my mind.

Writing became an all-consuming passion. My love affair with my typewriter claimed every spare moment I had. Four or five o'clock in the morning often found me sliding out of bed obsessed with thoughts and ideas clamoring for expression. Dishes and beds were unattended to, laundry was left until the very last moment, or rather the last shirt. The spare room in which I wrote was strewn with an unbelievable mess of papers. The chaos I created together with my frenzied writing habits led to an almost humorous reversal of the entire domestic scene.

It was now Marco who ambled in to inquire, "Haven't you done enough for tonight? I thought we might take a walk or watch the news. It's nearly eleven o'clock, honey."

We both laughed at such times. "Ahah!" I smiled. "The shoe is on the other foot these days, isn't it? How about all those times when I used to wait up all night for *you* to say a few words to *me?* Besides, who told me to write a book?"

A much greater harmony existed between us, but my lighter heart and my laughter turned to heaviness and tears when I heard that Audrey, my youngest sister, a beautiful, talented woman in her forties, was gravely ill in England, where all of my own family still lived. I immediately called my brother and begged him to get her on a plane to come here to the States for medical consultations.

She came, but it was too late. The prognoses the doctors gave me privately was that she had not long to live. I had to summon up every ounce of strength to hide my anguish from her. In innocence she was able to enjoy the sun, the rest, and the wonderfully happy month we spent for the last time together.

We had been seeing each other almost every year lately. Our phone calls were frequent, and ten-page letters were not uncommon in the regular exchange of correspondence between us. Even living on the opposite side of the world, she was all I had as my closest and dearest friend. When she died several months later, I felt as if my own life was once again grinding to a halt. Nothing seemed to matter anymore. I withdrew into myself. I was unconsolable. Work on my book stopped completely.

I have always had a very deep faith in God, even during times like this when I became most bitter and angry with Him. Without friends or my remaining two sisters and brother in England to turn to for comfort, I felt utterly alone and abandoned. There was a limit to which my husband and sons tried to console me for the loss of one who, for them, had been little more than an occasional visitor. I consequently shut them out of my mourning, silently harboring a protracted dwelling of my grief in a lost and unloving heart.

God eventually came to my rescue. I knew He would somehow understand that His presence was still an essential part of my life and always daily acknowledged even when I felt He was absent from my side. Slowly, at first imperceptibly, but assuredly with His help, my sorrow lightened. I found relief in voluntary work with the Hospice movement.

This wonderful organization provides a nonprofessional supportive addition to the doctors and nurses who care for the terminally ill at home. The training I received gave me an invaluable insight into the needs of the dying. Emphasis is placed on the necessity for the patient to receive loving care in his or her own home surroundings, rather than be left to die in the hospital and denied the very quality of life in those last few weeks. It was this experience that made me realize that loneliness is truly not a part of living. It is all of dying.

Contrary to my family's concern that the work of Hospice would depress me more, it brought me considerable comfort. I was able to give to others what I had been unable to give to my sister. The experience added a new dimension to the rebirth of feelings that were now enabling me to pick up the pieces and return, as it were, not only to Marco and the boys, but to a more normal life.

I resumed my work with the American Lung Association, chaired a committee, and was later honored as a representative director. I continued to read for the blind, escaped the solitary confines of my four walls more often, and thanks to an empty office put at my disposal by an absentee landlord and without obligation of any kind, the desire to work on my book was rekindled.

I wrote as one possessed. Feelings, thoughts, and viewpoints poured out of me with such intensity that, alas, deeply rooted as they were and inspired as I was, often the written results became bogged down, obscuring comprehension. My wastepaper basket was filled with these discarded attempts.

Such trials nevertheless began to produce a much clearer delineation of the new "me" that was slowly beginning to emerge. I saw myself as a creature who was highly susceptible to the social atmosphere in which I lived, its influences more powerful than I could ever have suspected.

There was one social pressure, however, that was more the exercise of society's influence of the times. This, together with my fundamental upbringing and the traditional role of wife and mother that I freely chose, had pulled me along on my journey toward that which had become, after a quarter of a century, a powerful relationship with one other human being. My husband.

He had become the most important part of my life, but he had also become a habit. Unflattering though such a portrait was, I had to face the truth about him and, more important, about myself if I were to function as a whole human being and no longer walk in his shadow.

I felt it was vital to establish a pattern of living that would nurture further intellectual growth and greater emotional freedom in order to reach my later years with a feeling of fulfillment. I could not leave this responsibility in my husband's hands, and he must relieve me of the same responsibility to himself.

It was not to be an introspective exercise. We had to feel secure in ourselves. It was a matter of self-preservation, for one day one of us would be in sole control. We had to make the effort to be prepared. For the present, and while together, we could only hope to be truly united when we could function separately and feel independent of each other. I knew that the habits of thirty years of marriage would not be easy to discard, but our commitment had been fashioned from sturdy fabric and I felt sure it could weather a thorough dry-cleaning.

There were issues to be faced and differences to be resolved, and each of us had the right to go his or her own way. Nevertheless, the paths could be parallel if differ they must.

I made firm resolves. I would discard all previously held notions about the way things and people ought to be and are not.

Marco was my only concern. I loved him dearly and the boys too, but they were no longer my responsibility.

Marco is as he is, and it was now high time for me to relinquish all immature expectations of him. He cannot think as I do, much less feel the way I feel. And why should he? He will never be the kind of husband I would have liked him to be, for, as I now recognized with dismay, it was in some aspects traits of my own character that I sought to find in him. Other qualities I felt he lacked were those which would have made him more like my father.

I had to rid myself of both the vanity and the need.

If I had been guilty in the past of trying to influence his choices, I would no longer, for I found I now had no wish to. He would make his own choices. He would learn to free himself *for* himself. Nor was I to be a consideration in his choices. I needed to be freed from that burden. It was one from which *I* had freed *him*.

By the same token, he would have to learn to accept me the way I was *now*. That I did not conform to the pattern others expected of me as his wife had often embarrassed him. There was no need for us to be apologetic for each other. Neither of us is responsible for the other's words or actions. There is never any need to tolerate—one just terminates—the presumptious criticism of one's spouse. It is quite as simple as that.

For my part, I had long since made a decision about those insufferable busybodies who have had the arrogance to dictate the terms of my behavior as Marco's wife. It was now up to my husband to risk, if need be, their disapproval and society's frown if he wanted to preserve what existed between us. Was not the harmony of our marriage all that really mattered? It was his choice. Would he not also gain an emotional freedom from the blackmail of narrow thinking that had exercised an unhealthy influence over him for far too many years already?

That, too, was his affair. I vowed to stop trying to live his life, as I had learned to stop living the lives of my children.

It was time I got over the need to try and please everyone. I never could. I was not Super-Wife or Super-Mom, and I didn't want to be, either.

I found I had acquired a less complicated way of looking at daily situations. Once, they had surfaced as problems; worse, calamities. Now it was only a matter of outlook. Everything appeared much simpler. Even the dishes and domesticity I no longer regarded as thwarting, but rather a matter of decision. These, together with other situations, were either to be accepted or rejected. Sometimes a solution presented remedies that were not to my inclination, and I would be obliged to search for the most effective alternatives that were available. If these were not to be found, the matter would just have to stay unresolved until a more propitious time.

Not everything was so straightforward, of course. For all the steps I felt I was taking in the right direction, there were many that led me into the wrong one. Nor was it easy to hide my true feelings from Marco, for I knew he would be wounded to know that neither he, the boys, nor my home any longer represented the sum total of my existence. I had to acknowledge the truth at least to myself, or else I would go to the grave afraid of it forever.

The master had taught the pupil well. For so long the life we had shared together had, in some respects, been a life apart. I had been a willing victim of Marco's habits. I was my own worst enemy. The guilt had been mine. All those years of unspoken words and feelings that had lain between us would now forever remain unsaid.

I had my typewriter and my thoughts. The need was no longer a necessity.

Perhaps I had finally grown up.

My lonely sojourn had completed a training that, until now, I never realized I had been well prepared for so many years ago. Until quite recently I had been riddled with anxieties, many of which I now knew stemmed from the sole desire to constantly please my husband. For years I had tried to hide those aspects of my personality that were sometimes undesirable and unacceptable to Marco. Always concerned to win his approval, I saw now that it was I who contributed the greatest to my feelings of low self-esteem.

Of late and through my writing, I felt much more at peace with myself. My mind belonged only to me. It was as if I had reclaimed my soul.

Marco did not take kindly to my new ways. The changes were hard for him to accept. I had always fostered the image for the children, and believed myself, that he was the Head of the House. "Whatever Daddy says goes." Now that the boys were grown and gone it was no longer a matter of disputing authority. I simply asserted my own preferences. My direct answers of just "yes" or "no" were quite disconcerting to him. He was too used to my former "maybe's" or "if you like's." The "if's" and "but's" of a year ago were less in evidence, if in fact they were employed at all these days.

I was not aggressive and I was not angry. I was just different. Either I did or I didn't. I was or I wasn't. I would or I wouldn't. I made every effort not to say "I couldn't," for I readily acknowledged that I always could if I really wanted to. Generally I did, and was glad and thankful to be able to. There was no resentment and no resignation. Whatever I did was done with good will, or I simply spoke up and said I preferred not to. This was not always accepted with good grace, of course, and on the occasions when I knew I was being taken for granted, I minded now much less. After all, is that not a happier situation than never being taken for anything at all?

Poor Marco, he did not know how to relate to himself in regard to me. His irritations and complaints were but a reflection of the uncertainties he felt with his no longer compliant and acquiescent wife. He blamed it all on the book.

"How long is it going to take you to write the damn thing?" and sometimes, when standing in the doorway of the spare room where I wrote, surveying the chaos I had created, "Is there always going to be this mess of papers now that you've decided to become a writer?"

It was true, of course. Papers on the floor, papers on the spare beds, clippings, boxes, pages used and pages unused, dictionaries, reference books, typewriter ribbons, overflowing wastebaskets and such an abundance of miscellaneous materials as to prohibit more than two paces into the room without causing a major disaster.

I swung around from the typewriter and answered softly, "You were the one who suggested it, remember?" Without thinking, I added, "Look, Mong, if this is going to be a source of discontent between us, it is simply not worth my carrying on. Do you want me to give it all up? Is that what you are really saying?"

As the words hung in the air I felt a sense of anger. If he were to say "yes" I knew in my heart I would not, could not, comply. Writing had now become a very part of me. It was all I had as a substitute, or perhaps a release from all my sublimated ambitions that I could have unknowingly harbored from the very day I decided to change careers and get married.

Marco alarmed me by his hesitation to reply. I felt that maybe this time it was I who should deliver a lecture. I stood up and said, "Let's go into the living room and talk."

We sat on the couch. I took a deep breath. "Darling, you have to try and understand once and for all that I am no longer just "Marco's wife." For too long I have felt relegated to the same category as Marco's house, Marco's dog, Marco's book, Marco's business—and incidentally—just by the way, as it were, there's "Marco's wife." I am not saying this is your fault. Not at all, though in your business life, despite being well known to all your clients, I'm simply a nothing. At best, and if I'm *ever* referred to at all, it's 'How's your wife' or 'Regards to your wife.' What would be wrong with 'How's Sabina?' or 'Regards to Sabina'? Any time at all I have attempted to be personalized, both you and they have virtually disclaimed my existence. Now, and perhaps for the first time since we've been married and certainly as a result of writing, I have come to see that while I am proud and happy to be Mrs. Marco Shalom, I am also Sabina Shalom. I am a person in my own right and I have every intention to remain so. Furthermore, it is time that you see for yourself how vital it is to both of us that we seek and preserve our very own identities especially now at our age."

Marco looked at me both shocked and puzzled. "Oh, so now I'm going to have to put up with one of these liberated women, am I?"

"Don't be so close-minded about liberated women," I answered him with some asperity, for this had often been an issue between us. "There are many distinctions between what you call liberation and I call self-realization, and there is nothing wrong with any of it depending upon the person and the degree. As far as I am concerned, a truly liberated soul must embark upon a course that generally brooks no division of interests, and to my way of thinking such a pursuit has the potential for ultimate isolation. This is not for me or the stability of my emotional comfort."

"That's all very well," Marco interrupted, "but I'm not comfortable with this new and independent woman you seem to have become lately, either."

"Oh, Mong, it's not a matter of being like that at all. I just feel I must try to preserve the inner strengths I gained all those months away from you. I have to have a strong and healthy identity of my own, just as you need to have, and I think you do have, in fact. This is why it's important for me to feel free to follow creative pursuits of my own choosing. It would be foolish and unnecessary for me to immerse myself in the kind of alternatives that only you might like, and I'm certainly not going to rush around in all directions simply to make a statement of my own independence."

"Why do you feel you need to be independent anyway?"

I could see Marco was at loss to understand. "Darling," my voice was low and I looked seriously at him, "you know how difficult it has been for me since Audrey died. During the time I worked with Hospice, I realized how important it is to give some hard thought to that time when one of us will be alone. One goes through a period of 'letting go,' as they called it. One has to face up to the hard facts of life again, and for many it is a life alone. I'm not being morbid, I'm trying to find a way of saying to you that it is not too soon to encourage ourselves to think and act independently of each other in many aspects of our life together so as to be better prepared to face as best we can those times of anguish alone."

"All right, I see your point, but there are plenty of years ahead of us, God willing. Why this sudden rush for all this independence stuff now? You can do your thing, as they call it, without being so liberated, can't you?"

"Oh, Mong, you are being purposely obtuse. You are likening my words to those kinds of liberated souls of both sexes who cling leechlike to their independence with such tenacity that they diminish their capacity and their opportunities to love and be loved. Surely you see the difference between that and what I am trying to explain?"

Marco pursed his lips and thought hard for a few moments. "Yes and no. I suppose there is a need to change and grow and think about the years ahead. Life does go by so damn fast, and I suppose that if we stand still, all the tomorrows are suddenly today and it's too late. The changes I see in you are, if I can be honest about it, disturbing to me because I am beginning to see how necessary it is for me to make changes in my own outlook on life. The daily hassles of the business leave me little time to think about these things. I have to make changes, it's true. Not just for you but for myself and our life and the way we have been living it together."

Marco's words quite thrilled me for he had never spoken like this before. In fact he rarely spoke about anything but the business or the boys. I was thankful that at last he had begun to understand and see the mutual desirability of an "independent-dependency." That is, recognizing and enjoying the need for each other while appreciating the necessity, at our time of life, to stand alone.

"I was beginning to feel that your writing was taking you away from me."

I took his hand. "No, darling, it's just the opposite. I'm learning things about myself and in relation to you that ultimately can only bring us closer together."

"Like what, for example? Go on, teach me something about myself."

"You will have to learn this for yourself, Mong, but for my part I've stopped berating myself for falling short in my expectations. I have learned to recognize and accept my limitations. You must try to do the same or you will never be at peace with yourself."

"What else?"

"I know that nothing is as precious or as important to me as our happiness, but that is only possible if you can learn to see me as I really am, not as you want me to be. This might be hard for you, Mong. It wasn't easy for me to learn to accept and love you just as you are either, but," I hastily added, "I did."

"You already are everything I want you to be; I just didn't want to lose you, and I was afraid you might be discovering *I* was not all you wanted *me* to be. If it makes you happy to write your book, then go on writing it. Your happiness is my happiness."

"You are deluding yourself, Mong. I said I loved you as you are because I found you were *not* all the things I wanted you to be. I now suggest that you forget about me being what you *want me to be*, and learn what I am or am *not*. Then you can love me as you please. Anyway, for now would you mind loving me enough to let me go back to my room and get on with some more work?"

Over the next few weeks I saw changes in Marco that such a short time ago I would never have thought possible. His first declaration of independence was announcing that he had decided to play bridge again. Not only in clubs, but he had also enrolled in night school for a refresher course. I was delighted. I did not play the game and welcomed this new outlet for him. It also left me free to work away late at night undisturbed.

There now seemed to be a new honesty between us. We were able to work out our differences in a complete and more wholesome fashion. I was thankful that we had triumphed over the pitfalls that had threatened to pull us apart and which had first beset us on my initial return home.

Another surprising change was his clear indication that our personal lives no longer required the approval of others to influence our conduct. He also showed less inclination to bring work home. It was as if he was anxious to make up for lost time. There was time now for walks and talks and holding hands.

The intimacy between us reached deeper levels. Desire needed no fostering. The love that we gave to each other was at last unfettered and free.

My journey had come to an end, though I knew it would never be over.

I gathered up my papers and stacked them in a neat pile. I put the cover on the typewriter and then looked around the room in which I had spent so many hours. Here, in all its untidiness, was where I had found order in my life again.

I turned off the light and went to find Marco.

The soft glow of the lamp cast shadows across his face as his head lolled in sleep against the cushions of the couch.

The newspaper lay on the carpet, its pages in disarray.

The crossword puzzle rested in his lap. His glasses had slipped down his nose. The pen was still in his hand.

I stood for a long moment, just looking at him.

A tight constriction gathered slowly in my chest. He looked so vulnerable. He was my child, my lover, my friend.

He opened his eyes. His look was one of discomfort and surprise.

"You were spying on me?"

"No. I was loving you."

"Have you finished for tonight?"

"No."

We Can Learn

"Learn" is the word. We might say that for the first three or more years of life a person can say, "I am what I am given." In the next few years, probably to about eleven or twelve, he is characterized by the words, "I am what I will." In the third period, adolescence, he says, "I am what I imagine I will be." Then, in the fourth period, which may extend to the grave, "I am what I learn."

The last of these is probably the most important and, in a way, goes back to childhood. Jesus expressed this idea in the words, "Unless you turn and become like children, you will never enter the kingdom of heaven" (Matt. 18: 3 RSV). Children grow in their ability to get along with people. Unless we adults retrace our steps and unlearn some of our bad personal habits, open our minds to new patterns of conduct, there is no hope for us. That is what Jesus was saying, for one thing. Growth is not only "adding to" but also relearning. I have seen people sixty years of age "turn" and learn how to follow Jesus in dealing with people.

Lewis Mumford called man "the unfinished animal," and says,[2] "Unlike other organisms, the final stage of growth is not determined by his biological past: it rests with himself and is partly determined by his own plans for the future." Jesus said, "Come unto me and learn of me." It is precisely because we are not animals that this is possible.

Let us not suppose for a moment that getting along with people means being namby-pamby or just good natured, like the amiable alcoholic, Elwood, in the play *Harvey*. In one of his speeches Mary Chase has him say: "Dr. Chumley, my mother used to say to me, 'In this world, Elwood, you must be oh, so smart or oh, so pleasant.' For years I was smart. I recommend pleasant. You can quote me."[3]

Such relating to people is about as realistic and about as useful as that of another drunk who wandered into a saloon with
a long list in his hand. When questioned about the list of
names, he said, "Here, I have written all the names of the
fellows in this town I can whip."

A burly chap asked, "Got my name on that list?"

"Yes, I have."

"Well, you can't whip me," said the man, drawing himself
up to his full height.

"Okay," said the drunk, "I'll take your name off." Come
to think of it, that was the result of some social learning!

One of the ways of improving our relations with our fellows is to look at some of the faulty techniques we use. The
interesting thing about them, too, is that they all are dealt with
in the New Testament. There never has been such a valuable
book on human relations.

Scapegoating

There is the bad technique of "scapegoating." This expression comes from the ancient Jewish practice of laying hands
on a goat, confessing all the sins of the people over him, and
then sending him away into the wilderness (see Lev. 16:20
ff.) on the Day of Atonement. It was as if he were the one
who was at fault, the one who had sinned.

In modern times the term "scapegoating" has come to mean
calling attention to the faults and evils of others in order to
distract attention from our own. A scapegoat is anybody we
blame for the trouble we are in. Hitler blamed the Jews for
all of the deprivations he forced upon the people as he built
up a war economy. As the Roman Empire crumbled, the
Christians were blamed. In the Old Testament, Ahab said to
Elijah, "Art thou he that troubleth Israel?" (See 1 Kings

18: 17 ff.) When Paul came to Thessalonica the Jews shouted, "These that have turned the world upside down are come hither also" (Acts 17: 6). It is hard for those who are failing to honestly analyse the reasons for failure and to change what is wrong. It is so much easier to blame someone else.

The Halo Technique

Closely associated with scapegoating is the "halo" technique. This is the practice of being perfect. One of my friends illustrated this perfectly in the words, "I am not the least bit conceited, but I don't know why I am not." Jesus pointed out this type in the person who says, "Let me help you get that speck out of your eye" while all the time there was a whole beam in the speaker's own eye. He dramatized the technique by telling of a man who stood and prayed, "God, I thank thee, that I am not as other men are . . . even as this publican." Pardon me while I adjust my halo! "Confess your faults one to another and pray for one another" (James 5: 16).

The Throne Technique

A third error in interpersonal relations, and one that is equally destructive to the self, is the "throne" technique. This is the method of individuals who regress to a childhood state of mind, or who never grow up. They need a master, a teacher, a leader, an adult to whom they can look and whom they honor. They have renounced their own God-given right of individuality and allowed someone else to stand on their feet. They want a church which calls itself "Mother Church," and they insist on calling their religious leaders "Father." This is a form of projection, as the psychologists would say. It seems never to occur to such people that they are really in love with themselves—projected like a picture on a screen, onto an ideal person—and they live a life of fantasy imagining that they are like the person whom they worship.

The idol, or the person they have placed on a throne, may be a movie actor or actress, a millionaire, a college professor, a minister, or a gangster. The unfortunate thing about this type of a person is that his hero is just as likely to be inferior as not. Except in the case of those who worship Christ, the idol is bound to be inadequate. If something happens to shatter the image of such a hero worshiper, his own ego is shattered. That is why such people are so unrealistic; they have to be in order to hold on to their idol.

Jesus struck at the religious idols when he said, "Call no man your father upon the earth: for one is your Father, which is in heaven" (Matt. 23:9). He meant exactly what he said. For grown people to place one person on a throne and look up to him as one who can do no evil is disastrous to the growth of the soul. It is an easy life but a wrong one. In some social circles you see these characters and hear them gush, "Isn't he just divine?" Or "He is the smartest man I have ever seen; he speaks seven languages." Admiration for those who are worthy is desirable, but it is easier to admire a great man than to become one. God calls us to become valuable people, not to worship them. And genuine people do not want to be put on a pedestal, much less on a throne.

LABELING

Another method which often destroys good human relations is the "labeling" technique. All of us hate to be called names. And some people seem never to realize that they can get just as bad results as a "cusser" without being profane. A man may not slap you for calling him narrow-minded, prudish, naive, or old fogy, but he won't like you. The trouble with labels, you see, is that they are used to describe individuals as if that were all there is to the person. For example, "Smith is a neurotic." Is he neurotic all the time? And just wherein is he different from you or me? Smith may be honest, industrious, religious, and unselfish too.

Labels are devices used by talkative people to save them the trouble of thinking. Jesus warned against this hateful manner of speaking, "Whosoever shall say to his brother, . . . Thou fool, shall be in danger of hell fire" (Matt. 5:22).

IN THE DOGHOUSE

One of the most common ways of losing friends and hurting people is the "doghouse" technique. You make a mistake with some people, and they are off of you for life. The religious people in Jesus' day had tax-collectors and sinners in the doghouse. Most of us can understand how they felt toward tax-collectors, especially as we get nearer to March 15 each year. The sinners were not moral degenerates, but, according to the best Bible authorities, they were in general simply "nonpracticing Jews, ignorant or careless of the scribal laws." Jesus was known as "a friend of publicans and sinners."

It is common to find people who have whole classes of people who, to them, are in the doghouse. Sometimes they differ from them economically, sometimes racially, sometimes socially, sometimes religiously. But to them they are ostracized. They will not associate with them, even if they try to grow, even if they make an attempt to cross the barriers they have erected. To them they are a different kind of human being, and the more they magnify the difference the greater becomes the gulf between them. "The Jews have no dealings with the Samaritans."

I'll-Take-My-Dolls-and-Go-Home

There is one other antisocial technique which all of us have practiced at one time or another; in childhood, if not since. It is the "I'll-take-my-dolls-and-go-home" technique. Our feelings are hurt, and we resign. We get a divorce. We quit the job.

Even in church this pattern of conduct is sometimes seen. I have known people to drift from one church to another because in each new group they got their feelings hurt and form deep injuries. We sometimes criticize them as "church tramps," but the facts are that it is easier to move on than it is to grow up. Sometimes, of course, there are real reasons why people ought to change churches. However, it should be said that the only reason for anyone's joining any church is that he feels directed by God's Spirit.

Divorces are oftener than not the result of this "I'll-take-my-dolls-and-go-home" technique. A large per cent of couples who separate could learn to live together if they did not resort to this revenge method. It is the easy—though childish —way. And as long as society adds its blessings to the "incompatibility" and "mental cruelty" types of divorce, people will be encouraged to remain immature.

Principles of Good Human Relations

Now let us look at the positive side of getting along with people. What are the principles of good human relations? How do we grow in this very important matter of living together? We Christians ought to be interested in this. Our religion stands for good relations, and none of us is perfect in this matter. "If it be possible, as much as lieth in you, live peaceably with all men" (Rom. 12:18).

But let it be said that good relations does not mean always living at peace with everyone. Jesus said: "I came not to send peace, but a sword. For I am come to set a man at variance against his father, . . ." (Matt. 10:34-36). We cannot always please man, if we are to obey God. Evil must be driven out, at times, just as Jesus drove the money changers out of the Temple. "Yes-men" and "me-too" Christians are not strong Christians. Jesus exposed the hypocrites of his day and rebuked them publicly. Paul withstood Peter to his face at Antioch "because he was to be blamed" (Gal. 2:11). Communism must be resisted, and the criminal must be locked up. Even the church must withdraw itself from some who walk disorderly (1 Cor. 5:9-13; 2 Thess. 3:7; 2 John 10-11).

Most of our troubles arise from our not being unselfish and big enough to practice the principles of love and good will. We either will not use our imaginations enough to understand how the other fellow feels, or we do not love enough to relate ourselves to him. Some of us have learned in childhood to relate to people only on the basis of domination or cold justice (legalism), and we have not grown since. To some, we must be in the role of leadership; to some, we must be followers; and, to most, we must relate as equals and sharers of responsibility. But in every case we are interdependent. We must interact. Isolation and segregation are dangerous, We need the love and acceptance of others as they need us. This requires flexibility and constantly strengthening our ties with those about us.

COMMUNICATION

A primary principle in getting along with others is *communication*. When relations get bad between nations they "break off communication" and recall their ambassadors. It is just as true within family circles. I have known husbands and wives who would not speak to each other. At the breakfast table the father would say, "Jimmie, tell your mother to pass me the bacon." Sometimes we become so mad that we do not trust ourselves to talk. A man will say, "I would have gone to see the man and tried to talk it out with him, but I was afraid I would say something I would regret."

About the meanest sort of refusal to communicate is to refrain from the common courtesy of speaking to people. "I am through with that guy for life," a person says. Or as one man said to another, "I want you to promise me that you will never speak to me again as long as you live." The other replied calmly, "Well, I won't speak to you if I can remember it, but I may forget." One of the shrewdest statements the late George Bernard Shaw ever wrote was: "The worst sin towards our fellow creatures is not to hate them but to be indifferent to them. That's the essence of inhumanity."

Of course, talking is not always communicating. Some people talk to cover up their real anxieties, their real feelings. And the most polite people are often the most hostile. But by words, looks, smiles, gestures, we tell people how we feel about them. If we get too emotional with anger our words become "snarl" words. We show our lack of respect and block real communication.

Jesus placed communication as the basic means of good relations. "If thou bring thy gift to the altar, and there rememberest that thy brother hath ought against thee; leave there thy gift before the altar, and go thy way; first be reconciled to thy brother, and then come and offer thy gift" (Matt. 5:23-24). "If thy brother shall trespass against thee, go and tell him his fault between thee and him alone; if he shall hear thee, thou hast gained thy brother" (Matt. 18:15). The common factor in settling differences, whether one has offended

or has been offended, is to talk it out. The Christian is to re-
new communications, whether the difficulty is in the church
or between labor and capital, husband and wife, father and
son, or business associates. I have known Ph.D.'s on university
campuses who would not speak to each other. So regardless
of education or social class, the principle is the same; communication is a prime essential in good human relations.

GROUP AUTHORITY

A second principle of good relations is *group authority*. Let
the group decide.

This is precisely what Jesus said. In the passage in Matthew
18 we are to talk first to the offender alone; then take one or
two more; the third step is to "tell it to the church." The two
last steps involve a very understandable fact, that individuals
need the counsel of the group. A concensus of opinion as authority is inherent in the very meaning of democracy.

Let us look at an opposing viewpoint. Some would assert
that the few are better equipped to instruct or to govern or to
judge us than the many. Perhaps this is so. But I agree with
C. S. Lewis that democracy is necessary because fallen men are
"so wicked that not one of them can be trusted with any ir-
responsible power over his fellows." Authority must be exercised over small children, the mentally deficient, the insane,
and criminals. But when fairly normal adults, however bright
or saintly, claim to have authority over their fellows, real
harm is done.

If the authority is accepted, immaturity on the part of both
the dominated and the dominator results. If it is rejected by
those being dominated, conflict arises. This is true in both
politics and religion; and no amount of appeal to "divine
right," the Scriptures, inspiration, or special revelation can

justify one individual or a minority group dominating others.

The jury system in jurisprudence rests upon this need for a consensus. Congregational government in churches is the same. In politics it is the representative form of government. In intellectual matters the technique of discussion is based upon this principle. Of course, the majority opinion will not always represent the truth—perhaps seldom, in some fields—but it must be recognized if people are to get along together.

"I want your advice" or "I should like to discuss a matter with you" are words of humility. We need to check our opinions on morals, religion, politics, and any other subject by discussing them with our fellows. As we come alive in Christ we will know that only the group which has a similar experience will be able to counsel us on matters pertaining to the kingdom of God. In some situations only God can guide us in the true way. Sometimes, to be in such a situation seems precarious. That is, ideas of such divine guidance sometimes seem close to certain insane delusions to non-believers. "We ought to obey God rather than men" is a true Christian attitude, but the men who said that were closely knit into a Christian group.

PERMISSIVENESS

A third principle of good human relations is *permissiveness*. This is the opposite of domination and criticism. It applies to normal relations between adults. Actually, it applies to nearly all affairs where one human being comes into contact with another. The permissive attitude says: "I accept you as the unique person you are. You may chart your own course, make your own mistakes, say what you really feel, and you will not be frowned at or criticized unless you attempt to hurt or destroy someone."

Permissiveness requires that advice be given, if at all, only in a circumstance where it may be rejected without punishment. Suggestions are proposed with perfect freedom for them to be rejected. All attempts at coercion are carefully avoided. In this setting, teaching and preaching become the imparting of knowledge, the testimony of personal experiences, or the description of reality and the invitation to or offer of a particular advantage or blessing.

Nothing but faith in individuals and in God can undergird this attitude. It expresses great respect for individuals and great faith in their ability to make valuable decisions.

Jesus gives us many examples in the way he dealt with people. The rich young ruler "went away sorrowful" when the demands of discipleship were made plain; most of us would have followed him and brought pressure to bear on him. Peter was warned but not browbeaten concerning his denial. The Pharisees were exposed and told of their destiny because they were destroying life. But Jesus was so permissive toward tax-gatherers and sinners that they "drew near to hear him" —and the religious leaders murmured, saying, "This man receiveth sinners, and eateth with them." He also dined in the home of Simon the Pharisee and welcomed an interview with Nicodemus. And did any leader ever show as much patience and acceptance as he did toward Peter and other erring disciples? Jesus' method was exactly the opposite of the "doghouse" technique.

TRICKS OF DOMINATION

Attempts to dominate have left a long trail of blood and human misery across the centuries. Besides the Spanish Inquisitions there have been many little private "trials of heretics" in homes, churches, and schools. We have used pressure methods all the way from ridicule to promise of eternal bliss. Most of these methods have not been due to our conceit and immodesty but to a more vicious motive of will to power or desire for omnipotence.

Tricks of dominance are often subtle and appear as very noble virtues. *Shame* is one of these. "Aren't you ashamed of yourself for even thinking such a thing?" a parent may say. Then the real feelings are driven underground, and the ugly emotion continues to operate. *Pity* is another. "Look how much I have done for you; surely you are going to do what I ask you" may be merely a method of enforcing demands. *Fear* is an equally effective one. "God will punish you if you neglect your duty" has been used to whip people in line. *Offer of approval* also is used to coerce. "People will not like you unless you learn to co-operate." All of these and many more daily are used by human beings, but they do not produce growth. Jesus never used these on his disciples. He appealed to love and voluntary loyalty. Threat of hell or hope of heaven were used more as the description of reality than as incentives or means of control.

For example, the words "Ye will not come to me, that ye might have life" are sad words—William Lyon Phelps once said that they are the saddest words in the English language —but they leave the individual free. "What does it profit a man if he gains the whole world and loses his own soul?" is a searching, disturbing question, but its force is in the reality principle back of it. All of us must feel the pressure of reality.

FORGIVENESS

The last principle in getting along with people is *forgiveness*. This handles situations where injuries, real or seeming, have occurred. And occur they will. When you meet a person who is hard to hurt, you see one who does not love deeply. It is no compliment to be able to say, "No one can insult me; I just don't pay any attention to them." The finest people in this world are sensitive people who are hurt deeply when they are misunderstood, who really want to love and to be loved.

Under the spell of some evangelistic services a very fine woman in a small town began to worry about her neighbor. They had "fallen out" over a milk bill. There were no ugly words. Both were courteous but cool. As they had gone along each had secretly harbored a grudge against the other. The revival had caused some self-examination.

The first woman finally got up nerve to go to the second and say, "I feel awful about that misunderstanding we had last year, etc." The second was a Christian also. She accepted the apology of the first woman and then admitted that she had been wrong. She sought forgiveness, too. There was a joy in their hearts which they had been deprived of for many months.

We remember that Jesus said that we must be willing to forgive an unlimited number of times (Matt. 18:21-22). Furthermore, he said that we can be forgiven our sins only as we forgive others (Matt. 6:14-15). If this is true, some people whom I know have been wasting their time praying for forgiveness of their sins. They may have withheld punishment from those who have hurt them, but that is not forgiveness.

WHAT FORGIVENESS MEANS

Forgiveness involves three things. First of all, the person who has been injured accepts the injury. He bears a cross. In order to do this, he must be mature enough to be honest about his injury and mature enough to accept suffering. In the second place, forgiveness means helping the sufferer bear the burden of his sin. Joseph said to his brothers who had sold him into slavery, "Be not grieved or angry with yourselves." When a person really forgives, he gets under the load of the offender, and their former fellowship and understanding is restored.

All of these examples are illustrated in the cross. In accepting forgiveness through the cross we come to see that God accepts the injury of our sin, relieves us of our feeling of guilt, and brings us into a close relationship with himself. The same process occurs in human forgiveness. Fellowship is rebuilt. Each person involved actively shows good will toward the other.

People being what they are, forgiveness is a very important part of getting along with one another. Those who never seek or offer forgiveness either relate to others on a very superficial basis or never obey God in rebuilding broken or disturbed relationships. Some husbands and wives drift apart and never get close again because they do not forgive. And we are such sinners that church members must again and again ask one another to forgive. Only in this way can the full power of God be fully experienced in human life.

A control operator in a radio station had a misunderstanding with another operator. Some deep feelings were involved. The first operator heard a sermon on the Matthew 18 passage about how to straighten out difficulties; the preacher insisted that it would work. He tried it, and to his pleasure he and the other operator became good friends. It was the first operator's initial step to Christ. He had felt himself a failure in getting along with people. Now he had found a real help. "I thought to myself," he said, "If Jesus Christ knew what he was talking about in that matter, I would try him in others also. That's how I came to be a Christian."

YOU'LL GROW IF YOU PRAY RIGHT 8

I WAS visiting a twenty-five-year-old man in a hospital recently. He was sick both physically and emotionally. His doctor had asked me to see him but had told me how frail he was mentally. We talked about his condition, and I encouraged him to trust his doctor and be patient. As I was about to leave, he said, "I wonder if you could bring me a book of prayers the next time you come. I want to pray, but I don't seem to know what to say."

"Suppose you don't do much praying right now. God knows how you feel, and he understands that you have a hard time finding the right words. If I may suggest something to you, I would say that you ought to pray very calm prayers for the time being. Sick people often try to pray too strenuously. Just say, 'Lord, you know how I feel. I need your help, and I know that already you are helping me through this hospital. I trust you to give me patience, and I want your will to be done.' Then just leave it up to God. You don't have to pray long prayers. And don't pray too often."

The next time I saw him I explained a little more to him about prayer. I told him that if he needed some written prayers I would bring him some, but there were some things about prayer that I wanted him to know. Prayer is not "saying prayers" but telling God exactly what we feel and want. God wants us to be simple and natural and honest. He prefers truthfulness to skill in phrasing our wishes. God wants us to be sincere.

It seemed that he understood. As he recovered he told me that he prayed less often but that his prayers seemed to satisfy. It is a delicate and important task to teach an emotionally sick person to pray—or to teach a child to pray. Often the wrong kind of praying will work against recovery, and too much praying may actually make the person less susceptible to accepting help. Anyone who has ever worked in a mental hospital or with nervous and disturbed people knows what this means.

It seems strange for a Christian minister to tell anyone not to pray too often. Most of us pray too little and too seldom. But prayer can do harm as well as good. It may make us feel self-righteous, or confirm us in our errors. In Aldous Huxley's novel, *Eyeless in Gaza*, he has one of the characters, Dr. Miller, say: [1]

> As for prayer . . . I've never really liked it, you know. Not what's ordinarily meant by prayer, at any rate. All that asking for favours and guidances—I've always found that it tends to make one egoistical, preoccupied with one's own ridiculous self-important little personality. When you pray in the ordinary way, you're merely rubbing yourself into yourself.

G. A. Studdert-Kennedy has written of standing one day by a giant sergeant, a friend of his, while on the other side of him was a chap who had lost his nerve and was whining for protection. Here is what he was saying: "O God, keep me safe! . . . O God, save me!" The sergeant, however, was busy thinking of his men as he shouted out his orders. But the cries of this frightened chap were getting on his nerves. Finally, turning to Kennedy, he said: "That chap's saying his prayers, isn't he, sir?" Kennedy replied, "No, he isn't, sergeant; that's not prayer, it's 'wind.'" Studdert-Kennedy adds: "Now that may sound hard, but it is true. They were not prayers, those whinings of his. Why? Because there was none of Christ's spirit in them. He had only one thought in his mind: his own skin. It was purely selfish prayer, and selfish prayer is not prayer at all." [2]

There are few things in a man's life which reveal his real self as fully as his private prayers. They tell how large his heart is, how deep his sympathies are, and whether or not he is growing. If he prays only when he is in trouble—called, by some, "fox-hole praying" or "successful raft praying"—his religion is merely an escapist, cowardly type. If he prays only the Lord-keep-me-safe type, he is still on a childish level of religious living. In fact, you can tell a good deal about a man if he will tell you when he prays. When you hear a man say "I say my prayers every night before I go to bed," you may know that he is spiritually in the childhood stage of development. But if he begins the day with prayer, he is likely to be on an entirely different level.

WHY PEOPLE PRAY

Every Christian ought to ask himself why he prays. *Why* is probably more important than *how*. If he prays for the right reasons he will grow. If not, his prayers may actually stunt his growth.

Some people pray as a kind of atonement. There is something in every human being which makes him feel that he ought to punish himself when he does wrong. It is a kind of automatic justice-maker which says that for a given wrong you must receive a given punishment. We may not always know, or be able to admit, what the wrong is, and we often do not know what an appropriate punishment is. But usually we expect a penalty, sometimes we even bring on the sentence in the form of accidents, sickness, depressions, or even just plain unhappiness. If someone else does not punish us, we punish ourselves.

Many religions capitalize on conscience troubles by having the individuals who are suffering say certain prayers. Some have them repeat prayers over and over or even pay money or do penance. This is the origin of the practice of repeating so many "Pater Nosters," for example. Fasting is often in the same class. The individual feels better after he has punished himself; he has atoned. Every religious person has experienced the desire to pray atonement prayers when he feels guilty. "They think that they shall be heard for their much speaking," is the rationalization, but the real, emotional reason is a feeling of guilt and a desire to atone.

But what do such prayers accomplish? Do they make the person better? On the contrary, they actually make one weaker. He says prayers in order to make himself feel better without facing his sins, and thereby he is kept from God. Furthermore, the individual actually runs a bargain with his conscience by which he secretly promises himself that when he sins again he will accept the punishment and thereby resolve the conflict. Conscience pain is accepted as a kind of bribe so that he can repeat the sin.

Christianity, in the New Testament form, is the only religion with which I am acquainted, which does not endorse some kind of self-punishment as a recompense for sin, at least a recompense for guilt feelings. Offerings, weeping, self-sacrifice, and prayers are the usual prescribed atonements. Even some modern forms of so-called Christianity prescribe these. If a person can weep and mourn for his sins, he feels holier. Asceticism is glorified as a means of accumulating merit for the salvation of other souls as well as one's own.

Christ, however, discouraged such atonement in his death for our sins. He requires confession (the admission of guilt), repentance (decision to renounce autonomy and relate oneself properly to God), and faith (the recognition of acceptance) as the conditions of forgiveness. Paul made clear in 2 Corinthians 7 that repentance is not the same as remorse and self-punishment. Christ and his immediate followers knew that we are no more capable of judging and sentencing ourselves than we are of judging our neighbors.

> Could my tears forever flow,
> Could my zeal no languor know,
> These for sin could not atone;
> Thou must save and Thou alone:
> In my hand no price I bring,
> Simply to Thy cross I cling.

Yet deep within everyone of us is the impulse to punish ourselves when we feel guilty. And saying prayers is a favorite method, but it really keeps us from God.

Another common reason for praying is to get God to perform magic for us. A woman whose son was in an automobile accident told the doctors that she had prayed and God had told her that her son would not die. The doctors looked at her a little sadly and said, "We hope you are not disappointed." They knew that her son was very badly injured. He died. Six months later the woman had a nervous breakdown. She said, "God let me down."

Of course, God could have restored her son. Miracles occur all of the time, if you mean by miracles that things occur which cannot be explained by natural laws. But the woman's prayers were wrong. She did not say, "Nevertheless, not my will but thine be done." Her seemingly answered prayer probably came out of her unconscious, out of her wishful thinking. No one can blame her for wishing for her son's health with all of her soul. But we must learn that prayer is not a magical means to get what we think we want.

Nor is it a means of warding off evil. A man who has a great deal of trouble with food allergies, as well as obsessions of death, had been accustomed to asking God to prevent these. But God, for some reason, did not do it. Later the man said, "Now I have learned to ask God for courage and strength and my death fears are fading." He still has some of his allergies, but he is a happy, effective man. Perhaps God will remove his allergies later. Who knows?

Sometimes praying is a kind of swapping prayers and love for protection and help. If we pray enough God will love us so we will not be hurt, is the way such reasoning runs. Of course, no one quite admits that he is praying to secure "protection" from God. But fear is so strong in human life and our souls so frail that we develop compulsive rituals to ward off evil or to get peace of mind. Dr. Ralph W. Sockman said of prayer a few years ago, "Some people have the slot-machine attitude toward God. We put in a prayer or a decent act, and expect to take out a prosperous business or an eternity of bliss." We expect to hit the jackpot. Prayer is much more than this.

Prayer Not Vague Wishing

One of the most misleading conceptions of prayer is that it is "a wish turned Godward." Most praying of that sort is too vague to do any good. Often, we are like naughty children who ring door bells and then run away before an answer comes.

The classic expression of this view of prayer is in James Montgomery's little poem, "What Is Prayer?" [3]

Prayer is the soul's sincere desire,
Uttered or unexpressed;
The motion of a hidden fire,
That trembles in the breast.

Prayer is the burden of a sigh,
The falling of a tear;
The upward glancing of an eye,
When none but God is near.

Is that all prayer is? Or is that prayer at all? If we give a little thought to the matter we will see that Montgomery wrote some pretty words but some equally erroneous ones. Desiring and sighing and a falling tear are a good prelude to prayer but not prayer itself. Prayer may begin with a tear or a lump in the throat. Or it may begin with a feeling of joy and deep gratitude for what God means to us. It may even be born out of an awareness that we are subjects—servants—of God and should talk over with our Lord the life he has entrusted to us.

PRAYER NOT AGONIZING

There is a very common belief abroad that if we are to get results in prayer we must "agonize with God." To such people, we must "pay the price" of answered prayer. We ought to beat our breasts and pound at heaven's door, else God will not think that we are serious. We need not try hounding God until he gives in. I admit that there are times when we will cry to God out of our desperation. Jesus had a Gethsemane. But, as Dr. Paul Scherer says, "Every once and a while life stops for a moment and looks around and shudders; but after that the band strikes up again." And we ought to pray during such times. To act as if the struggle is due to God's reluctance is contrary to all we know about him.

What kind of a God do we have? Is he a father? I could not respect myself if I made my child go through a long process of begging before I granted her requests. If she begs me for something, it is because, in her childish stage of development, she is trying to dominate me or because she does not trust me. We often, in a childish frame of mind—for most of us are not as old as our birth certificates show us to be—try to move God to do our way. I have found myself saying on occasions to individuals, "Don't tear your hair when you pray; God is not impressed. He loves you and wants to give you what is good for you."

What, then, is the right kind of praying? If we do not have to reach the boiling point before we can pray, how do we go about it? We must not allow our human frailties to keep us from praying as best we can. A woman, who attended church quite regularly, once said, "It takes me about two weeks to get back to praying normally after I hear a sermon on prayer." This should not be. Prayer is a very simple and natural form of communication between an individual and his God.

BE HONEST WITH GOD

It is easy to forget that sincerity is a prime essential of true prayer. We must be really talking to God and not have an eye cocked to the response of someone who may be listening. That is why we close our eyes when we pray. We do not want to be distracted by what we see, but neither do we want to pray "to be seen of men." Personally, I deplore the habit of some modern clergymen of keeping their eyes open when they pray. Jesus said, "But thou, when thou prayest, enter into thy closet, and when thou hast shut thy door pray to thy Father which is in secret" (Matt. 6:6). The old story about a man who, upon being criticized for not praying loudly enough to be heard when he led in public prayer, replied, "I wasn't talking to you," is not without point. Of course, public prayer should be followed by the group as they say "Amen" in their hearts, but prayer must always be addressed to God.

This throws some light on the question of reading prayers. It seems to me that reading prayers to God cuts down on their sincerity. Personally, I would no more read a prayer to God than I would read a proposal of marriage to a woman. Does God require a special elegance of language when we talk to him? Is he worried about our grammar or our sentence structure? And if we pray for things which at the time would not rise normally in our consciousness, is that sincere? Are these things we ask God for, or thank him for, what we really feel?

The habit of hypocrisy is a very subtle one, and at no point is it more likely to lay hold upon us than in our prayer life. Even the Lord's Prayer is probably not given us as a ritual to be repeated again and again. It serves better, some believe, as an outline and an example, rather than exact words to be said in either public or private prayer. The Lord's Prayer, as other written prayers, may be of real value to the individual if used in the right way. They serve as a phrasing of what the individual would like to say but has not found just the right words for. When we come to the time of prayer we may do well to say what is in our hearts in the words that are on our lips at the moment.

Have you heard someone say, "Oh, I think so-and-so is sincere, but . . ." When we say that a person is sincere, we have paid him about the highest compliment possible. At least, from a religious standpoint. He may not be as clever or as well educated or as strong as we could wish. But there is no excuse for a man's not being honest with God. Therefore, when we pray, we must tell God the truth. "The Lord looketh on the heart."

TELL GOD YOUR NEEDS

Prayer is telling God exactly what you want. The new
Phillips translation of Philippians 4:6-7 states this very
clearly: "Don't worry over anything whatever; tell God every
detail of your needs in earnest and thankful prayer, and the
peace of God, which transcends human understanding, will
keep constant guard over your hearts and minds as they rest
in Jesus Christ." It was the Master who said that "what things
soever ye desire, when ye pray, believe that ye shall receive
them, and ye shall have them" (Mark 11:24).

Many times we ask for things that we do not need. God
knows best. We even ask for things which we really do not
want. And not infrequently we just assume that we have
asked for something because we had an awareness of a vague
wish for it. But when we ask for our needs, in detail, we are
preparing ourselves for an answer from God. Elizabeth Bar-
rett Browning expressed it:

> God answers sharp and sudden on some prayers,
> And thrusts the thing we prayed for in our face,
> A gauntlet with a gift in't.

Dr. Theodore F. Adams tells of a little boy who explained
to the visiting minister that he did not say his prayers every
night because "some nights I don't want anything." Is that
not like us adults, too? We want something, but we do not
want anything which would especially interest God. We just
want our own way, and we know that such motivation is unworthy of God. So we do not pray. When religion is a cross
between a fire-escape and a Christmas tree, prayer becomes
weak and even harmful.

Yet we should never forget that God accepts our humanity.
He must feel very sorry for us at times, when we fixate (or
stop growing) on a certain level and say the same prayers over

and over. There is actually not much place for prayer in a life that is not growing. To go round and round in "saying prayers" is a poor substitute for the kind of praying which pushes us out of our ruts and starts us up hill.

Prayer is closely associated with work. Carlyle was wrong when he said that "work is worship." But they are twins. A saintly Negro maid was questioned about her method of prayer. "I ain't got no method," she replied. "While I wash de clothes, I asks de Lord to wash hearts whiter than snow. While I irons 'em, I reminds him of de troubles and problems that need ironing out. While I sweeps de flo', I jest asks him to sweep out fault-findin' from the hidden corner of mah heart, so he can bless—an' he always does!"

In an ancient parable on prayer two boys were sent into the field to dig for hidden treasure. All day they toiled in vain; and at evening, coming home weary and disappointed, they were met by their father. "After all," he said to comfort them, "you did get something—*the digging itself was good exercise.*"

Prayer is more than spiritual gymnastics. It gets results! Prayer changes things! It changes people! I refuse to get involved in any philosophical speculation about how God answers prayer or why prayer is necessary. Jesus taught us to pray, and prayer works. That is good enough for me. The best proof of prayer is that those who pray find that God uses them and their prayers are answered.

Douglas Steere has an illuminating story of a man who promised his pastor never to drink again. Later, that man returned to say he must have a drink or die. The wise pastor quietly told him to go home and die. The next morning the man came back and said, "I died last night." He did die. His childish self died, and he became a new person in Christ.

This leads to the significant fact that prayer, in addition to asking, is listening and reporting for orders. Dr. George

Buttrick has said that when we pray "we expose ourselves to the promptings of God."

A young man was having a terrific struggle with himself. He was converted when he was young and had received what seemed to be excellent religious instruction. But he was failing. Some vicious habits had laid hold upon him while he was in the army. He was desperate. Prayer had not seemed to help him much.

He turned to a Christian friend and laid his case before him. How could he live the victorious Christian life. His friend said, "Your trouble is that you are trying to run your own life. You are praying, but you are not listening for God to tell you what to do." Then he explained to him that he must start every day with God, to get up early enough to have time for Bible reading and prayer, and then to listen.

The suggestion was simple. He was to sit down with a notebook in hand and ask God to give him his orders for the day. Sometimes there would come to his mind the faces of people who would give him trouble or need his help. He would write down his "guidance" in the matter. If God told him to witness to a particular person, he would write that down. If he was tempted, he was told what to do, and his word from God was recorded. Sometimes he merely thanked God for a consciousness of his presence. That, too, was recorded.

The young man found an amazing victory and real growth. Some may object to the method of using the notebook, but Christian biographies record the successes of many people who start off the day with God. Jesus spoke of prayer as being closely related to listening to his words: "If ye abide in me, and my words abide in you, ye shall ask what ye will, and it shall be done unto you" (John 15:7). "If"—that makes the difference. If we live in him, prayer is more like a member of the armed forces reporting for orders than like someone trying to order God around. I like reporting for orders better than any definition of prayer I have ever heard.

When we come face to face with our duty to pray, however, we sometimes wonder what we ought to pray about. "We know not what we should pray for as we ought," even Paul said. We suggest four prayers which, it would seem, fit all lips anywhere in the world.

First, prayer for the Holy Spirit. "If ye then, being evil, know how to give good gifts unto your children: how much more shall your heavenly Father give the Holy Spirit to them that ask him? (Luke 11:13). When Paul came to Ephesus (Acts 19), he found some professing Christians who were powerless. Something was wrong with them. In his usual straightforward manner he said, "Did ye receive the Holy Spirit when ye believed?" (ASV). They admitted that they did not know about such a person. Paul presented him to them, and they were not only changed but expressed that change in baptism. All a person has to do to receive him is to pray to God for the gift of the Holy Spirit.

Second, another type of successful prayer is for forgiveness. "God be merciful to me a sinner" (Luke 18:13). Such a prayer not only becomes all men but all men every day. We must never forget that we are sinners and always will be sinners. It is a prayer which shows that we accept our responsibility. This does not mean that we beg God to forgive us as if he were a whimsical, pouting, peevish old grandfather who has to be persuaded. We need to admit that we are guilty, indict ourselves, and call sin by its real name. Else how can we ever grow? For sin is anything less than our best.

If this prayer of honest confession does not become a part of our daily practice, we will soon turn away from God. It is the agony of unresolved guilt which drives men from heaven's door. Hear King Claudius, in Shakespeare's *Hamlet:*

O, my offence is rank, it smells to heaven;
It hath the primal eldest curse upon't,
A brother's murder. Pray can I not,
Though inclination be as sharp as will:
My stronger guilt defeats my strong intent;
And, like a man to double business bound,
I stand in pause where I shall first begin,
And both neglect . . .

. . . .

In the corrupted currents of this world
Offence's gilded hand may shove by justice,
And oft 'tis seen the wicked prize itself
Buys out the law: but 'tis not so above;
There is no shuffling, there the action lies
In his true nature.

                                        Act III, scene 3

Third, the prayer of Isaiah, "Here am I, send me," is both a stimulus to growth and an evidence of growth. Isaiah volunteered for work, and God assigned him a hard job. He was not afraid to trust God to do right by him, so he did not "fight the call." We are so prone to forget that God's will is always a good will. This is the kind of praying which is appropriate for every Christian. It is the only hope of the church.

Finally, under all circumstances, we can pray the words of Jesus in Gethsemane: "Nevertheless, not as I will, but as thou wilt"; or, as expressed in the Lord's Prayer, "Thy will be done on earth, as it is in heaven." This is praying at its highest. There is no more meaningful prayer. It is not a sickly resignation to something which we call the inevitable. It equips us to change the evil about us with a cross of love and self-giving. It often means struggle, hardship, bitter decisions, and deprivations. Sometimes, it means great privilege and exhilerating joys. But it is the only good way to live.

REAL FOOD FOR GROWTH 9

IT IS an obvious fact of science that one of the indispensable aspects of physical growth is eating. Life, whether plant, animal, or human, cannot get along for an extended period without food. Some living beings may go for several weeks without food and several days without water, because they live out of their own storage system. To live we must eat. The biologist will tell you that food for us serves two purposes: (1) to supply the energy necessary for the maintenance of proper body temperature, and (2) to supply the material to rebuild against the wear and tear of tissues. Some chemicals speed up growth while others retard it, but growth depends on what we eat. In a very real sense, I am physically what I eat.

This furnishes a very appropriate analogy for the mental and spiritual life. The way the personality functions in using the bits or bulk of spiritual sustenance is, of course, very important. But to make available for ourselves the right kind of food is wise for our souls as well as our bodies. Sometimes we need to be on a soft diet; again we have mental indigestion and need to look for its cause. We may even be undernourished and not know it. We can learn how to nourish ourselves spiritually as well as physically.

Not By Bread Alone

Jesus made one of his most profound remarks when he said to Satan: "Man shall not live by bread alone, but by every word that proceedeth out of the mouth of God" (Matt. 4:4). This bit of wisdom is quoted from Moses. Neither he nor Jesus meant to belittle food but to place an importance on our dependence upon God. Too many people are still trying to live on that which they can provide: art, science, recreation, business, or even a purely human religion. But to try to get along on the merely human is like trying to grow a rose in a dark, dank cellar.

Another striking passage on food for growth, in the New Testament, is in 1 Peter: "Wherefore laying aside all malice, and all guile, and hypocrisies, and envies, and all evil speakings, as newborn babes, desire the sincere milk of the word, that ye may grow thereby: If so be ye have tasted that the Lord is gracious" (2:1-3). The writer urges these Christians to "yearn intensely" for the pure milk of the Word. Most commentators say that "the Word" refers to Christ. It is the adjective form of the word which John used when he said that "the Word became flesh." It often meant reasonable or spiritual but, in this case, evidently refers to Christ and the whole revelation of God which climaxed in Christ.

At least, Peter refers to the food for the soul which we find in God's revelation. Paul had the same thing in mind when he wrote to the Corinthian Christians that he had fed them with milk (part of the revelation) rather than solid food because they were infants in Christ (1 Cor. 3:1-2). Apparently they were not willing to digest the more severe thruths which would lift them out of the "church politics" stage of development. Their "factionalism" needed to be challenged, and Paul was doing that very thing.

The Bible holds a unique place in the history of religions. Many religions have their sacred writings, which usually consist of moral codes or worship rituals or both. That is all many people get out of the Bible, except, perhaps, some history which they try to say is folklore. They overlook the fact that the New Testament Christians look upon the writings which they had, and came to have, as sacred.

SEARCH THE SCRIPTURES

"Search the scriptures . . ." Jesus said, "and they are they which testify of me" (John 5: 39). All one has to do to see the close relation between Jesus and his teachings is to read the Gospel of John. Whoever would receive him must receive his words. So he took care to promise his disciples that when he went away he would, by his Spirit, cause them to remember all the things he had said to them (John 14: 26). When we read the New Testament it is not hard for us to believe that there was divine aid in its production.

There is no question but that the early Christians relied greatly upon the written Word. Paul wrote to young Timothy and reminded him that he was made "wise unto salvation" by the Scriptures. Then he says: "All Scripture is inspired by God, and useful for teaching, for reproof, for correction, for training in doing what is right, so that the man of God may be perfectly fit, thoroughly equipped for every good enterprise" (2 Tim. 3: 16-17 Williams). This does not mention growth or food but it is very close to these concepts. Jesus called himself "the living bread which came down from heaven"; if a person ate of that bread he would never be hungry again or ever die. By the Scriptures, we come to know God in salvation, and, by them, we learn to do his will—this is spiritual growth through the use of the Word.

We must not overlook the fact that Paul considered the Scriptures adequate without the traditions of men. The man of God was to be made "perfectly fit" by them. Jesus had already met the problem of the relative value of the accumulated religious traditions which had been put alongside the inspired Word. He had said, "You have transgressed the commandment of God and made it of none effect by your traditions." There was no compromise with him. The traditions were only the opinions of men (sometimes very clever ones). The Word of God was the inspiration of the Holy Spirit (2 Peter 1: 19-21).

Someone may ask, "How did these early Christians decide which writings were Scriptures and which were men's traditions merely?" This is an honest and fair question. The answer is a long story, but it can be given briefly by saying that a primary consideration always was whether God was speaking through the particular writing. This could be checked by the oral teachings in the early days of Christianity. It can be checked today by both the authentic record of the Gospels and by the very Spirit of Christ. If it is God's Word, he still speaks through it and recreates us by the "renewing of the Holy Ghost."

This brings us to look intently at the Word of God. What does that mean? When Jesus said that we must live by "every word which proceedeth out of the mouth of God," what did he mean? Not every voice which speaks to a man's inner soul is divine. There is the voice of the unconscious, the voice of Satan, the voice of culture, even the voice of false religions. All of these appeal to man because they feed his pride and encourage his desire to be autonomous. They make man a god and propose to save him by letting him lift himself by his own bootstraps. But the Word of God holds a mirror to man's weakness and, at the same time, offers a goal and guidance.

THE WORD OF GOD

The concept of the Word of God has depth that is often overlooked. As used in the New Testament, it means the written Scriptures, but it also means much more. It is the creative Word that spoke the world into being (Gen. 1). It is the message of God which came to inspired prophets, from Noah to John the Baptist. It is primarily the truth about Jesus Christ who was the very Word become flesh. The writer of the Hebrews summarized the whole history of God's revelation when he said, "In many and various ways God spoke of old to our fathers by the prophets; but in these last days he has spoken to us by a Son, whom he appointed the heir of all things, through whom also he created the world" (Heb. 1: 1-2 RSV).

Just what is the Word of God? It is God making himself known; not his will or his laws or his wisdom, but himself. Other religions, Islam and Judaism particularly, claim to have a message from God, but not in the same sense. Christ is the final, unique, complete manifestation of God. When we know him we know God. This is not claimed by any other religion on earth.

Many seem to have overlooked the greatness of the Christian idea of revelation. God speaks to us! He is not telling us simply how to behave or where we are going or even where we came from. He is telling us about himself and his relation to us. We are made in his image—"God is our nearest relative." He speaks to us! This leaves us free. He does not coerce, overwhelm, or browbeat us. He does not sneak in the back door of our minds. He respects us and, therefore, comes to us in sincerity and straightforwardness.

He speaks to us! The very idea demands a response. We may ignore, doubt, deride, or accept him, but the Word implies a human response. When Jesus was here on earth men had to take sides. Which side they took, for or against him, revealed themselves. John put it very clearly:

He that believeth on him is not condemned: but he that believeth not is condemned already, because he hath not believed in the name of the only begotten Son of God. And this is the condemnation, that light is come into the world, and men loved darkness rather than light, because their deeds were evil. For every one that doeth evil hateth the light, neither cometh to the light, lest his deeds should be reproved. But he that doeth truth cometh to the light, that his deeds may be made manifest, that they are wrought in God (John 3: 18-21).

There we have it. We are not sent to hell because of ignorance, but because we reject the Light which we are given.

How do we know that God is speaking? How would you know whether a person you meet in the park is a genius or a lunatic, or is feeble-minded? The Christian holds that when Christ is properly presented to men, they know that they have met God. Their pride may keep them from admitting it; self-deception may cause them to postpone responding to him. But they know, deep in their hearts, that God has spoken. There are some puzzling aspects to his revelation, but this is probably intended. Perhaps it is a hurdle that tests our intellectual humility. We must find God where he chooses to be found.

This brings us to the part that the Word of God plays in our lives. The claim made here is that its place is unique. Earlier quotations in this chapter point this out. We cannot be saved without the Word, and it is all that is needed. By it we are confronted with the all-powerful, all-loving, all-forgiving God. By judging ourselves and by coming to him (repentance and faith) we experience life. "Faith cometh by hearing, and hearing by the word of God" (Rom. 10: 17). "He that heareth my word, and believeth on him that sent me, hath everlasting life" (John 5: 24). Each conversion is a creative act of God.

But after a person has become a child of God by faith, how is the Word used to grow him?

The Bible Is Real Food

I should like to point out some of the ways in which the Bible becomes food for growth. Life is one thing, but health is another. The Christian life is similar to the natural life in this respect: yesterday's food will not sustain good health for tomorrow. Malnutrition may occur in the spiritual realm as well as in the physical. For instance, a woman once said, "All that you can hope to get out of life is what you can eat and what you can wear." The same woman also said, "We have never let any of our children go to any church; then they are free to join whatever church they marry into." We all are dependent on God for good health as well as for the new birth.

The Bible is our guide for doctrinal truth. Some people try to make the distinction between practical and doctrinal religion, but the whole truth—as revealed in Christ, for example—was written down because it was essential to spiritual life. To cut out the parts which seem not to agree with our tastes is hardly an act of humility. The early Christians contended "for the faith which was once delivered unto the saints" (Jude 3). Jesus himself said, "Heaven and earth shall pass away, but my words shall not pass away" (Matt. 24: 35).

Today, there is a return to what is called biblical theology, in both Catholic and non-Catholic groups. It is a good sign. When people turn to the Bible in search of truth, they stand a good chance of hearing the voice of God. Whether they heed or not will depend on openness of mind and humility of heart.

Another function of the Bible in the believer's life is that of overcoming doubt and fear. The two are mentioned together because they are of the same cloth. Both stem from a feeling of rejection which grows out of our own sense of guilt. When little children are afraid or expect to be rejected, we talk to them and reassure them. What we actually do is to communicate our love to them. This is exactly what God is trying to do to us.

The history of the Bible is the record of God's action in trying to redeem men. One look at the life of Christ, for example, and we see a divine person, "full of grace and truth" (John 1: 14). Our whole confidence in the resurrection and in immortality is based upon the power of God as manifested in the living Christ. No mysticism can bring man the assurance which God can speak through his Word. "These things have I written," said John, "that ye may know that ye have eternal life" (1 John 5: 13).

GROWTH IN LOVE

Similar to the overcoming of doubt and fear, perhaps even the other side of it, is our growth in love. The primary method of teaching love in this world is to love. No lessons explaining it will take the place of genuine acts of love. In the Bible we have every possible approach to love. There are examples given, direct commandments, explanations of how love works. But, most of all, when I read the Bible I feel that God is loving me; I feel secure in his love. That is why the Bible is spoken of as "God's love-letter to man."

When the love of God is really accepted two things happen. First, the person who really enters into this experience can no longer be cowed by fear. Most religious rituals are merely insulation against fear. Saying affirmations to yourself every morning is not fundamentally different from the pagan beating tom-toms to ward off evil spirits. But when love comes in fear goes out the window. It would be futile to try to build a world of love if the "ultimate reality" is either cruel or indifferent.

The second effect of God's love is to cause us to love others. "This commandment have we from him, That he who loveth God love his brother also" (1 John 4:21). When people read their Bible regularly and allow God to speak through them, love grows. It is a book of love. It rebukes our small hearts. God becomes very real to us. When one of the disciples asked Jesus how he would make himself known to them (after he went away) without the world seeing him, he said, "If a man love me, he will keep my words: and my Father will love him, and we will come unto him, and make our abode with him" (John 14:23). Notice that "keeping his words" is both the result of love and the condition of greater love.

THE BIBLE AND REALITY

Finally, the Bible is a constant challenge to us. That is why it is so difficult to read; it makes demands on us. Someone has said, "The part of the Bible which bothers me is not the part I do not understand, but the part which I do understand." We either turn our backs on our sins if we study the Bible, or we, sooner or later, turn our backs on the Bible. A good note for the fly-leaf of any Bible is: "This Book will keep you from sin, and sin will keep you from this Book." Many of us are like the little boy who wound up his prayer, "And please, Lord, put the vitamins in pie and cake instead of spinach and cod-liver oil." The Bible forces us to face reality even when we are reluctant.

There is a very revealing conversation in the play *Harvey* where a character has sunk so low that he thinks he has overcome reality: Sanderson says to Elwood P. Dowd,[1] "If you'll begin by taking a cooperative attitude—that's half the battle. We all have to face reality, Dowd—sooner or later." And Elwood, in reply, says, "Doctor, I wrestled with reality for forty years, and I am happy to state that I finally won out over it."

A study of church history will reveal that each generation of Christians tends to major on certain portions of the Scriptures and forget entirely other portions. This is true of various churches also. Of course, we know that all portions of God's Word are not equally usable or equally needed at all times. We believe that it is all inspired but not equally inspirational, for instance, compare Ahab's story with Paul's career.

But where the Bible has been read, preached and studied, it has produced results. Individuals are convicted of their sins, revolutions are inspired, Christian witnesses are called out, and revivals are initiated. Simple, humble people have become great, valuable, forceful people. That is why it has inspired so many notable testimonies. William E. Gladstone wrote: "I have known ninety-five great men of the world in my time, and of these, eighty-seven were all followers of the Bible." And Douglas MacArthur said: "Believe me, sir, never a night goes by, be I ever so tired, but I read the Word of God before I go to bed."

How and when should this "bread of God" be taken? The answer to this should be simple, but apparently it is not. I would certainly say that the Bible ought to be read every day, but there are very few of us who actually do that—many only pronounce a few words from it daily. It seems to be a fact that great Christians are always great Bible readers. Biographies of Christian leaders will bear that out. What we seem to have overlooked is that it is absolutely impossible to be the right kind of a Christian unless we take time regularly to expose ourselves to the Word of God.

How to Use the Bible

I wish I could establish a formula for Bible reading which would guarantee understanding, but that is hardly possible. A more important factor seems to be the "how" of Bible reading and study. Some study the Bible and some even teach it without much observable influence on their lives. All of us have known some village skeptic who could argue the Bible by the hours, really knew the words, but who was not affected by it. There is a very good reason. He refused to allow God to speak through it. Our ears are never forced to hear. "He that hath ears to hear, let him hear."

It is at this point that our understanding of the Bible is made plain. If we admire it as a collection of ancient, wise, and true statements, we hold the viewpoint of a scholar. If we revel in its beautiful and touching stories, we yield to our artistic nature. If we see in it the record of dogma and moral codes which God demands that we accept, we express the immaturity of a religious fanatic. If we claim it is the invention of men seeking God, our attitude is a very natural one of human reason and of science. All of these frames of mind are natural and reasonable, except for one thing. They do not account for the power of the Word. It is like describing everything about the atomic bomb, its history, size, reason for invention, and possible uses, and at the same time overlooking the secret of its explosive power.

Even devout people read the Bible with a degree of admiration and accept it as authority without really listening to it with their hearts. They may follow its thoughts yet personally hold themselves aloof from the Author. The great Harvard scientist, Agassiz, used to begin an experiment by saying, "Gentlemen, we shall now seek to know God's thoughts after him." Many think that this is what needs to be done in Bible study. But there is more. When we open the Bible we must say, "Now what is God trying to say to me." We need not read the Bible as a sort of spiritual daily-dozen, but as a conversation with a superior Being—the other side of the dialogue is prayer. Without this "conscious listening" study, the Bible never becomes the Word of God to us.

Preaching and Growth

Preaching has its meaning and power only if it is the personal word of God. We may have deep insights into the thought content of the Bible or trace clever relationships between one passage and another. We may be thoroughly sound in our theology. But unless the sermon is a personal challenge, a confronting of our own souls and the congregation's with the living Christ who is our contemporary, it is not the word of God. No lecture on religion is of itself a preaching of the Word. The power of the Spirit is more essential than logical or dramatic organization or presentation.

Paul deals with the powerful content of preaching in his first letter to the Corinthians. He says that he was sent "to preach the gospel, and not with eloquent wisdom, lest the cross of Christ be emptied of its power" (1 Cor. 1: 17 RSV). He then shows that preaching is the divinely ordained means of saving the world. There is no other. One sincere, living witness faces others with what he believes to be the Word of God. It is God's method. Catechisms, Bible teaching, religious lectures, worship, none of these will take the place of the preaching. The sermon confronts man with God's call and even with God's comfort. Paul describes his own preaching as "not in plausible words of wisdom, but in demonstration of the Spirit and power, that your faith might not rest in the wisdom of men but in the power of God" (1 Cor. 2: 4-5 RSV).

Dr. James Denney has said, "No man can give at once the impression that he himself is clever and that Jesus Christ is mighty to save." Those who want a funny, showy, or clever sermon are usually those who have never received the Word of God. They have closed their minds to the method and message of God; therefore, they are not impressed with the real Christian message.

Even after a genuine conversion there remains the fact of Christian preaching as a means of growth. If we do not receive the Word with proper concern and obedience, only starved, stunted souls can be the result. The parable of the soils is applicable here, for each type of soil represents a class of people who "hears the word" in a certain way. There is another group in our churches today: those who never hear the Word because they never attend the preaching service or, if they do, it is only at Easter. Such people are a living affront to God. Even private reading will not take the place of public proclamation of the Word.

There is a surprising spiritual effect in the real preaching of God's Word. It is a spiritual tonic. Even when the sermon is tainted by a large element of the human, God often speaks through it to the hearer. Worship may be stultifying and deceptive, but when the Word is spoken reality becomes more real and truth, in deed and in thought, becomes important. When a man faces another with a message about the very meaning of our existence, it is the most significant experience in life. Significant in the sense that it signifies the constant human situation, that we are face to face with God whether we like it or not. No wonder there is deep prejudice against "preaching."

A well-known pharmaceutical laboratory recently published a study which had been made of some school children in a fine suburban community in Ohio. These young people were from homes of the high income group. They had every reason, at least from an economic standpoint, to grow normally. However, the study showed that one third of these boys and girls were suffering from "growth failure." The researchers were piling up evidence that the occurrence of "simple growth failure even among children of high-income areas had been, and continues to be, on the increase." They were experimenting with adding vitamin B_{12} supplements to the diet.

Growth failure! What a meaningful phrase when applied to the spiritual life. We cannot grow as God intends us to unless we feed often and bountifully on his Word. "Man shall not live by bread alone but by every word which proceedeth out of the mouth of God."

CONSIDER THE LILIES 10
HOW THEY GROW

CONSIDER the lilies of the field, how they grow" were just words to me for years. Of course, they were beautiful. Fields of beautiful flowers waving in the breeze, wilting in the hot sun; standing dew-laden, fresh and crisp in the early morning; these images make us warm with delight. But the relation between lilies and everyday life was not clear.

It was not too difficult to "spiritualize" such a passage and draw analogies between the growth of a lily and human existence. Matthew Henry talked about the fact that a lily is "frail"; it is "free from care"; it is "fair and fine." These similarities do not impress me. Of course we are frail—so what? We do not have to live long before we learn that human beings cannot remain "free from care." It does not seem to be even intended for us. And few of us are fine or fair. We are deformed, ugly, deficient, inadequate—at least, some of us are. Jesus must have meant something by these words which would apply to all of us at all times, to both the fine and the disfigured.

Then, one day, I noticed that I was saying to individuals who came to me for counsel, "Consider the lilies how they grow." At first, they looked puzzled. Then, there was a look of I'm-beginning-to-catch-on.

Here is a case in point. At a given place in a series of interviews, a man said to me, "I see now what caused me to have this trouble, and I want to overcome it. What do I do next?" I could outline a way of life for him or tell him a lot about how to "think positively" about his circumstances. Not only would such suggestions do no permanent good, but they would actually do harm. To act as a father to another human being usually prolongs his state of immaturity. And there are no trick mental methods to produce growth. So I said, "Consider the lilies how they grow."

An explanation was in order. For one thing, I told him that he was trying too hard. Such attempts at growth do not produce the desired result; they block it. He was very emotional. "What do I do next?" meant to him that he must do something in a hurry. He was prepared to put forth a great effort. My feeling was that "easy does it."

WHAT JESUS MEANT

Let us look now at what Jesus really meant by this remark. It is in that passage in the Sermon on the Mount which deals with worry. Many people who read books on how to stop worrying would do well to save their money and read Matthew 6: 25-34. It is the divine recipe for handling normal worry. I say normal because many people who are emotionally sick need psychotherapy, just as cancer patients need X-ray treatments.

Jesus gave his disciples six distinctive approaches to the problem of worry: (1) Life, or the real person, is more important than the "things" we are worrying about; we must value our true selves. (2) It does no good to worry—which of you by worrying can add one cubit to your stature? (3) You must learn to trust God your Heavenly Father, "O ye of little faith." (4) First things must be put first—"Seek ye first the kingdom of God." (5) Each day has its own troubles, and only its own (v. 34)—so, live one day at a time. (6) He has divinely ordained means of growth and daily provision for us, just as he does for the birds and the flowers.

The Williams translation expresses the thought of this passage very beautifully:

So I tell you, stop worrying about your life, as to what you will have to eat or drink, or about your body, as to what you will have to wear. Is not life worth more than food and the body worth more than clothes? Take a good look at the wild birds, for they do not sow or reap, or store up food in barns, and yet your heavenly Father keeps on feeding them. Are you not worth more than they? But which of you by worrying can add a single minute to his life? And why should you worry about clothes? Look at the wild lilies and learn how they grow. They do not toil or spin; but I tell you, not even Solomon, in all his gorgeous splendor, was ever dressed up like a single one of these. Now if God so gorgeously dressed the wild grass which today is green but tomorrow is tossed into the furnace, will He not much more surely clothe you, O you with little faith? So never worry and say, "What are we going to have to eat? What are we going to have to drink? What are we going to have to wear?" For the heathen are greedily pursuing all such things; and surely your heavenly Father well knows that you need them all. But as your first duty keep on looking for His standard of doing right, and for His will, and then all these things will be yours besides. So never worry about tomorrow, for tomorrow will have worries of its own. Each day has evil enough of its own (Matt. 6: 25-34).

It is the expression, "Consider the lilies how they grow," or as Williams says, "Look at the wild lilies and learn how they grow," that especially interests me. Why did he not say, "See how they stand"? Or "See how they surpass other flowers in beauty"! Instead he said, "How they grow." This may mean nothing more than "See how they normally become the admired flower." In any case, he took the flower as an illustration of the kind of individuals we may become.

It is of little consequence to us that the word translated lily probably referred to the red anemone which dots all of the hillsides of Galilee in the spring. Actually, no species of the lily is a conspicuous feature of the flora of Palestine. This word may merely refer to "wild flowers" and is so used often, the scholars tell us. Jesus' use of it is merely that. He takes the beautiful flower and says, in effect: "Look at how it grows naturally. All of the robes of Solomon were not as beautiful." How does the lily get that way? By struggling? By effort? By trying hard? "No," he says, "it simply expressed the life within it and became what God created it to be."

Then Jesus draws a further analogy. If these plants, beautiful as they are, lasting only for a brief season, are so well taken care of, what about you, O you who have such little faith? These are striking words. He has a real point; perhaps several. But most of the world seems to have read right over them.

If I wished to spiritualize this famous quotation I could draw many analogies to the tender, beautiful plant. Growth for the flower and for us is very slow. We must depend on external nourishment, especially sunlight. We must suffer an environment which is often adverse and hostile. Sooner or later we will be cut down. But these are not the lessons Jesus had in mind. Tennyson was nearer the spirit of this passage in his little "Flower in the Crannied Wall" lines:

> Flower in the crannied wall,
> I pluck you out of the crannies,
> I hold you here, root and all, in my hand,
> Little flower—but *if* I could understand
> What you are, root and all, and all in all,
> I should know what God and man is.

Both Tennyson and Jesus felt that the life of the flower and the life of the human spirit are closely related to the Living God.

The Christian, like the lily, grows naturally, unfolding the life that is within. The Christian, mind you, not the unsaved person. "He who has the Son has life; he who has not the Son has not life" (1 John 5: 12 RSV). The Sermon on the Mount, in which Jesus suggested that the lilies be considered, was spoken to disciples, to believers. It is as natural for a Christian to grow as it is for the heart of a living person to beat. In this day of "activism" such an outlook on life must appear dead wrong. But it is not.

Did you ever see a person really grow by *trying*? "We can do nearly anything if we try hard enough," we have all heard. I will go so far as to say that clinching your fist, putting out your chin, and tensing your body for a struggle will not help you to grow but will definitely hinder your growth. Every Christian who is a careful observer, of himself and others, knows this to be so.

The first requirement of growth then is in being somebody to start with. Becoming is preceeded by being. By this we do not mean simply the popular idea of self-acceptance. Rather, we must form a concept of ourselves as the unique persons which God made us to be. We must become individuals. The "I" must be the true "I", not the sham self or the mask or the idol which we imagine ourselves to be. This is what modern psychologists call "ego-identity." It is self-consciousness in the best sense of the word. It is the way the "I" thinks of the "me."

Your Picture of Yourself

What kind of a picture do you have of yourself? Perhaps we have different pictures hanging on different walls in our lives. Some of them may be caricatures. Are you smart, ugly, kind, conceited, cowardly, sissy, weak, flexible, or a dozen other adjectives which might be used? Unfortunately, many people think of themselves solely in terms of the "tags" which society places on them, determined usually in terms of their "market value." From kindergarten to college, we try to educate a person to become "marketable." Our only concern seems to be in producing people who can make "big money," be the top man on the totem pole, be the best of something or other. A few hours before a TV set will prove that. We are alienated from our true selves, so we have to try to live up to the false selves which we have created. Harriet Beecher Stowe records that she went to a party where "everyone seems to have left themselves at home."

If self-acceptance means settling down to live with this "sham self" I do not want any part of it. The prodigal son was pursuing the sham self when he demanded his property so that he could "have a good time." But later he came to himself (Luke 15: 17). He then started to grow from the core of the personality God had given him. He could not deal with the "ought" until he came to grips with the "is" of human existence. The painful reality of the real self must be faced before growth can take place.

Imagine a lily trying to be a violet. Or for that matter, imagine one kind of lily trying to be one of another species. That is no more absurd than for one human being to try to be like another. "Solomon in all of his glory" was not supposed to be superior to a lily. It is this everlasting rejection of God's creativity which brings us worry and waste. To wish that we were like someone else, or superior to them, is downright insolence to God. The beginning of all spiritual growth is the will to be unique.

Christian growth, then, consists not only in a man coming to himself but in a constant revision of our self-concepts. It is the divinely ordained means of growth. If we allow anyone to prescribe for us the kind of self which we are to be or if we refuse to think about our true selves, there is no hope for us. To grow we must stay conscious. Some people think that we grow toward our ideals, but this is too intellectual. Actually, we grow toward the picture of the selves we are in love with. This loved image may be secret and unconscious. It may have come from a parent, a movie, a book, a neighbor, or even be a creation of our own; but, once we are in love with it, the control over our lives is automatic. Therefore, we must constantly revise it in line with the self which God created.

Nowhere does the rejection of the real self become more noticeable than in the treatment of children. A noted psychiatrist, Dr. Robert W. White, of Harvard University says:

Rearing and guiding children can best be represented by the metaphor of raising plants. This should be encouraging, because raising plants is one of mankind's most successful activities. Perhaps the success comes from the fact that the husbandman does not try to thrust impossible patterns on his plants. He respects their peculiarities, tries to provide suitable conditions, protects them from the more serious kinds of injury—but he lets the plants do the growing. He does not poke at the seed in order to make it sprout more quickly, nor does he seize the shoot when it breaks ground and try to pull open the first leaves by hand. Neither does he trim the leaves of different kinds of plants in order to have them all look alive. It is the children who must do the growing, and they can do it only through the push of their own budding interests! [1]

Another aspect of considering the lilies, which Jesus may have had in mind and closely related to the meaning of the whole passage, is this: a lily must grow where its bulb is planted. Or in the case of many flowers, where the seed is sown. The environment is not always favorable. Jesus in this passage on worry referred to the birds in this manner, "Yet your heavenly Father feedeth them." In other words, all of

God's creation, even plants that spring up for a season and then perish, are under his "providing eye"—we call it providence.

I shall not attempt to prove that

> There's a divinity that shapes our ends,
> Rough-hew them how we will.
> SHAKESPEARE

Most of the attempts to prove providence leaves me cold and unconvinced. I do not believe that we can prove chance, mechanism, or providence. To me pantheism, with everything being God, and deism, with its far-off God, seem to me to be a blinder faith than a belief in a God who looks after the sparrow and numbers the hairs on our heads. Philosophy cannot answer the question of happenings. Faith must step in and show us that the God who revealed himself in Christ causes all things to "work together for good to them that love God" (Rom. 8:28). This is a faith.

SPIRITUAL FIXATION

For this discussion the important point is that growth depends on our taking the right attitude toward our environment, physical or human. If we do not, growth stops. The psychologists speak of this as "fixation." A person has a very painful experience, one that produces anxiety, and growth (at least in an area) stops. A lily can stand just so much cold weather, for example; and a human being can stand just so much anxiety, insecurity, and frustration. Every person has his "tension capacity." Beyond that capacity, he will develop protective symptoms, become stereotyped, withdraw, become belligerent, or perhaps go insane. These extreme reactions are much more complex than I have indicated, but they are reactions to stress and strain.

All of us have seen people who were "spiritually fixated." "My mother made me go to Sunday school when I was a boy, so I made up my mind that if I ever got big enough I would stop." This is easy to see when a person talks about it, but it is equally operative in those who are not that honest. Sometimes a disagreement with a friend, loss of a job, a death, an illness, a handicap, a few nights of insomnia, or even confusion over an intellection problem, may stop us from growing.

Somerset Maugham, in *The Summing Up,* gives us an illustration of how a very threatening situation caused him to lose faith in God: [2]

> I had not been long in school before I discovered, through the ridicule to which I was exposed and the humiliations I suffered, how great a misfortune it was to me that I stammered; and I had read in the Bible that if you had faith you could move mountains. My uncle assured me that it was a literal fact. One night, when I was going back to school next day, I prayed to God with all my might that he would take away my impediment; and, such was my faith, I went to sleep quite certain that when I awoke next morning I should be able to speak like everybody else. I pictured to myself the surprise of the boys (I was still at preparatory school) when they found I no longer stammered. I woke full of exultation and it was a real, a terrible shock, when I discovered that I stammered as badly as ever.

I have seen people stop growing, sometimes for a short time, at various ages. The most critical periods seem to be adolescence, middle age (from forty to fifty-five particularly), and later maturity (beyond retirement age). The environment becomes difficult, the individual loses hope, and soon he turns within himself.

The way we look upon events has a lot to do with continued growth. Did you ever turn over a thin rock, laying lightly on the top of the ground, and see there a plant which the sunlight had never touched? The seed sprouted and the tender shoots pushed hard against the severe stone, to no avail. Then the shoot just grew around, crooked and pale, and that is the way winter found it. Some lives are like that. They are underprivileged lives, we often think. But are they?

My faith tells me that there are no underprivileged lives except those which reject the privileges which are offered. Each life has grace for its grind and comfort for its circumscriptions. Some insecurity and blockings are undoubtedly ordained of God to make us walk by faith. When the outlook gets bad we often are forced to an upward look. Unhappiness, tension, frustration, crosses, are a part of the Christian life just as the blasting heat, the twisting wind, and the footsteps of animals are a part of the lily's environment. We must grow where God plants us.

Getting Off Balance

Finally, real growth takes place, in the lily or in the human being, as a process of getting off balance and on again. This may seem a little odd at first. But growth is possible because there is in all living things some kind of automatic self-regulator which keeps the organism functioning. The scientists speak of it as "homeostasis." When we eat too much food, it is stored in the body; when we eat too little, the storehouse is raided. When germs attack, the whole system is mobilized to throw them off. A biologist writes: "Every organism is so built, whether by mechanical principles or not, that every deviation from the equilibrium point sets up a tendency to return to it."

The biologists and botanists know that all living things are in a constant state of adjustment. For impersonal living organisms this adjustment is regulated by such growth factors as catalysts, hormones, light, temperature, and many others. But in human beings this matter of balance is, in addition to its being influenced by the physical, largely a matter of consciousness. Just as our bodies get hungry, tired, "keyed up" (or tense), and then come back to normal, so our souls get out of kelter and have to be brought back to equilibrium.

Many Christians seem to feel that they should never experience any anxiety or tension or temptation. And some almost achieve that state, but they are not growing Christians. Elton Trueblood is correct when he says: [3]

It is not the poise of perfect balance that moves mankind forward on his zigzag path, but the glorious immoderation of those who see something so clearly that they are willing to live and die for it. Such abandon seems tumultuous, but it actually produces a species of inner peace, for it helps to overcome crippling anxiety. The only way in which a man can move forward in what we call walking is by always being slightly out of balance, since the perfectly balanced man stands still. History moves forward as the balance is recurrently broken and restored.

Life moves along a zigzag course. Our moods even swing like a pendulum. "Sometimes I'm up, sometimes I'm down, O yes Lord," says the Negro spiritual. Like Simon Peter walking on the water we cry, "Lord save me, or I perish." We feel as if we are going to pieces. Actually, the mind and soul of man are both very tough.

Of course, real character consists of a "steady" state. The great Christian may have turmoil within, like milk beating about in a churn. He may have inner conflict and psychic (soul) pain, but that does not prove that he is a weakling. The strong soul puts one foot in front of another and does the will of God until it becomes easier to do it. Or he says, "No" to temptation even when it is most alluring. This is the end of the Christian life, and to be perfectly frank, is never fully attained in this world.

In the meantime, growth consists of trial and error, effort and failure, but also attempt and attainment. In home life we all see illustrations of these unbalanced states. The tender-minded become disturbed and seek a divorce. The tough-minded realize that the person who is "off center" needs two things; someone to associate with him who is strong and patient and loving, against whom he may bounce; and, second, time. God gives us both. "Like as a father pitieth his children, so the Lord pitieth them that fear him. For he knoweth our frame; he remembereth that we are dust" (Psalm 103: 13-14).

Perhaps some of us would like to claim that we never get off balance; our opinions are never colored by our prejudices, and our decisions are never entirely bad. A few people may convince themselves of that, but most of us know better. The best of us get off balance at times. In fact, growth depends on imbalances. We may even go further and say, as Trueblood hinted at, that the will to grow is so strong in a living Christian that if he is balanced he will deliberately find a way to be unbalanced.

I have seen this over and over in churches. If a church does not have a creative program which requires adjustment, the real Christians will be very frustrated because they feel the need of growth and challenges. But those church members who are not growing, while the monotony will bore them some, have learned to insulate themselves by maintaining a kind of "peace of mind." To the living, monotony may be as disturbing as change. The dead are perfectly balanced.

MAINTAINING EQUILIBRIUM

By now, it is obvious that what we are aiming at in Christianity is not returning to any former state of equilibrium but the "steady state" of successful change and the speedy change to the right track when we find ourselves astray. "Let any one who thinks that he stands take heed lest he fall" (1 Cor. 10: 12 RSV). Counselors often find themselves saying to individuals, "You will just have to walk a tight rope for a while." What Jesus was trying to get across in the passage in Matthew was this: you may be walking a tight rope—in fact, you always are, from a human standpoint—but there is a mysterious aid that is always present. We are never alone, and hands greater than our own are holding us.

It is our faith that makes us veer back into the narrow path when we have gone astray. We never retrace our steps or take up where we have left off. What we do is to regain our spiritual balance.

The old-fashioned Bible terms for this process are as new and up-to-date in meaning, when properly understood, as the morning newspaper.

We must confess our sins, the Bible says. At a given point in therapy the psychiatrist or counselor must lead the individual to give up old "defense mechanisms." What is the difference? Perhaps there is more of the unconscious in the latter; but, sooner or later, the individual must say, "I have failed."

Then there is repentance. It is a "change of mind," the theologians say. But they also see more than that in it. The Bible speaks of it as "repentance toward God." Growth in human beings involves growth in interpersonal relations. The blocking in this sphere is, primarily, wrong attitudes. When we repent we renounce our independence, shed our insulations (that shut us from God), and acknowledge our status as subjects of God and fellow workers with men. Every sin is a denial of God's rights and an assertion of our own. Therefore, repentance is a part of growth, the divinely ordained means of maintaining spiritual balance.

Faith is also a part of the growth process. Trust is perhaps a better word, and its opposite is mistrust. Erik Erikson applies it to young children by saying that trust "implies not only that one has learned to rely on the sameness and continuity of the outer providers, but also that one may trust oneself and the capacity of one's own organs to cope with urges; and that one is able to consider oneself trustworthy enough so that the providers will not need to be on guard lest they be nipped." Erikson makes the point that "basic mistrust" of others goes back to infancy and that growth consists of learning that sense of belonging which means security. Without it we do not grow.

Jesus was trying to inspire that basic trust for growth. "Now if God so gorgeously dresses the wild grass which today is green and tomorrow is tossed into the furnace, will He not much more surely clothe you, O you with little faith?" (v. 30 Williams).

> Lord of all growing things,
> By such sweet, secret influences as those
> That draw the scilla through the melting snows,
> And bid the fledgling bird trust untried wings,
> When quick my spirit grows,
> Help me to trust my wings.
>
> AUTHOR UNKNOWN

KEEP MOVING! 11

THE *Ladies Home Journal* carried the story a few years ago of a child who never developed mentally. It was written by the famous novelist, Pearl S. Buck, and was about her own mentally retarded child.

When the child was born the mother said to the Chinese nurse, "Doesn't she look very wise for her age?" She was then less than an hour old. "She does, indeed," the nurse declared. "And she is beautiful, too. There's a special purpose for this child." She did not know then that before long they would discover the truth about this tragic little life. Her body grew, but her mind did not. It remained on about a three-year-old level.

Mrs. Buck recounted the months spent in going from one clinic to another to discover what was wrong and to secure aid. Finally they came to Mayo Clinic in Rochester, Minnesota, where every test was given. In reply to her question, "Is it hopeless?" the doctor was too kind to tell her the truth and responded, "I think I would not give up trying."

But a worker at the hospital gave the mother some sound advice. He said, "You will wear out your life and beggar your family unless you face the truth. She will never be normal—

do you hear me? I know—I have seen these children. She will never be able to speak properly, or read or write . . . Find a place where she can be happy and leave her there, and live your own life. I tell you the truth for your own sake."

But the mother was not able to give up. She took the child back to China with her. Some little American neighbor children were giving a party. One of them chattily remarked, "My mama says I can't have your poor little girl to my party next time." She realized then that she must find another world for her little daughter, which she did. By then, the child was nine.

This heartbreaking story was published to give encouragement and guidance to other parents who might be faced with similar situations. I have told it here to remind myself and others that if God is like Christ said he was, he must be concerned over our growth. He must be even grieved over his children who, somewhere along the way, become cases of arrested development.

What Spiritual Growth Means

Spiritual growth would be much simpler if it were possible to inject in our arms some magic substance which would speed up growth. Some "grower" which would act as a kind of inner policeman who, when we slow down, would shout to us "Keep moving!"

Thomas Mann in *Doctor Faustus* says:[1] "There is at bottom only one problem in the world, and this is its name. How does one break through? How does one get into the open? How does one burst the cocoon and become a butterfly?" This sounds impressive, but it is an oversimplification. A little child has an intense desire to grow up. There is not anything that he normally wants more. This is because our world is an adult world. The rewards come to adults. Adults marry, make money, have children, take trips, receive honors, whip their enemies, etc. So to just be grown physically is the greatest ambition of most youngsters. But to "become a butterfly" is only the beginning; we must then fly and fly. Life, in other words, is not one act of getting into the open.

Mental growth which has to do with remembering, knowing, and thinking is hardly so simple. Emotional maturity is concerned with feeling right about ourselves, getting along with others, making decisions, and being able to stand up to any emergency. These are slow processes also. Spiritual growth involves the whole person in all of his relationships. It especially designates such matters as finding the meaning to life, coming to know and serve God, living in a Christian manner with our fellows, and learning to manage our own lives in the most acceptable manner. In a way, then, spiritual growth includes mental, emotional, social, and religious living. It even includes the physical, inasmuch as the body is "the temple of the Holy Spirit," and because our whole being is constantly affected by the body. Yet spiritual growth is snail-like too.

GROWTH AND THE BIBLE

There is an expression in the Revised Standard Version, in the passage in Ephesians 4 on growth, which sets this matter of growth in bold relief. "Grow up *in every way* into him who is the head, into Christ" (Eph. 4: 15 RSV). The "into Christ" is not such a good translation. It does not mean "grow into a Christian." Anyone who reads the New Testament even casually knows that it teaches that you can no more grow into being a Christian than a monkey can grow into a human being. Thayer, the Noah Webster of Greek dictionary makers, says that this preposition translated "into" may be translated "towards, for, even to, with respect to," and in other ways.

Paul had just said that their standard of spiritual maturity was the "fully grown Christ." Dr. W. O. Carver says that this is "the most daring concept of the New Testament"—that Christian growth should aim at producing a church which is perfect like Christ. Then Paul says that we are to aim definitely at "growing towards" Christ. He may even intend the additional meaning of "in" Christ as saying that each of us who is a Christian is a part of Christ and therefore should grow proportionately just as cells in a living body. A perfect body, to continue the figure, must have perfect units or organs. So we as units in the body of Christ are to be perfect, full grown, mature.

Paul's phrase is that we grow up "in every way." "In all" is a literal translation, but apparently he is saying, "in all points in which we grow." This seems to be important because it is so difficult to become a well-rounded Christian. Some of us are kind but covetous; others are active but unwise; others are ignorant but zealous; some are, as a friend of mine expressed it, "abidingly ignorant and devoutly glad of it." It is hard to grow in Christ "in every way."

There is a passage from Peter's inspired pen which emphasizes the continuous aspect of growth. It is at the end of his second letter. He writes, "Grow in the grace and knowledge of our Lord and Savior Jesus Christ" (2 Pet. 3:18 RSV). The verb "grow" is continuous action. He says, actually, "Keep on growing." There is no time and no place to stop growing.

He names two components or aspects of this growth: grace and knowledge. Grace is the unsolicited, undeserved, and unlimited love of God. Grace implies that the gracious one has the advantage of the receiver, in some respect is superior. In some cases, say injury of some kind, the offender is "over the barrel." It always implies unselfishness. Jesus was spoken of as being "full of grace and truth." And Paul illustrated grace by the life of Christ. "He was rich, yet for your sakes he became poor, that ye through his poverty might be rich" (2 Cor. 8:9). That is real grace. It is the graciousness of God in Christ. Peter said, "Keep on growing in that kind of living."

"Knowledge of Christ" is the other sphere of growth which Peter mentions. Man is an educable being. He is born ignorant and with less instinctually controlled behavior than most animals. He is in a state of either learning or abnormality all of his life. Many people think that they are growing intellectually because they are acquiring facts, becoming acquainted with new phases of reality, or enjoying new art experiences. I have no word to say against art, science, philosophy, literature, history, or any other branch of human learning. Rather, it seems to me that a Christian should be more interested in the creations of both man and God than others. As the hymn has it, "This is my Father's world . . . He speaks to me everywhere."

But of all the knowledge available to man the knowledge of Christ is the most spiritually stimulating. It is inexhaustible too! For parents to suppose that a few hours in Sunday school will equip their child for life is pure stupidity. If a person thinks that he can learn enough about Christ in one year to suffice the following year he is simply deceiving himself.

PRACTICAL RELIGION

I suppose that the best single demonstration of the religious superficiality of our age is a remark such as, "I'm not interested in doctrine; I just want to learn about practical religion." The village atheist of fifty years ago, who sat on a cracker barrel at the general store and argued Scripture, was a gentleman and a genius compared to such a critic. It is childish to think that knowledge of Christ can be contained in a catechism, and at the same time ignore such a treatise as the Epistle to the Romans or the Gospel of John. Such popular, modern critics of religion may not like the modern, readable translations of the Bible that are coming off the press every day. They may not like some of the theological jargon and the religious clichés. That I can understand, but to throw out the baby with the wash, and turn their backs upon truth is puerile if not infantile. Religious doctrines and theology have lived for the very reason that they are practical. Nothing is more practical than the atonement, forgiveness, repentance, and faith.

We must not forget, however, that knowledge of Christ is always personal knowledge. Literature and death are not the only things people must experience alone. Their real knowledge of Christ may be aided by group study, preaching, teaching—in fact, it ought to be—but individual learning at the feet of Christ is necessary to growth. And God expects every one of us, as long as we live, to grow individually in our knowledge of Christ.

RESTING ON OUR OARS

"Keep growing!" This would make a good slogan for all of us. Toynbee, the contemporary English historian has said:

Nothing fails like worldly success. My study of twenty-one civilizations has convinced me that cultures are healthy only when they are creative. The civilization that solves its problems and rests on its oars has a sad future if it does not respond to the next challenge with a different answer.

This is true for individuals as well as nations. Growth is so much a part of life, the urge to grow is so strong, that when they stop growing some real trouble begins. It may show up as grouchiness, discontent, a kind of deadness and lack of motivation, overt acts of sin (usually secret), and many other symptoms. They are signs of death. Unhappiness itself often results from the suppression of the good impulses of our lives. We cannot ignore growth and remain healthy.

Robert Browning stated it this way:

> I say that man was made to grow, not stop;
> That help, he needed once, and needs no more,
> Having grown but an inch by, is withdrawn:
> For he hath new needs, and new helps to these.
> This imports solely, man should mount on each
> New height in view; the help whereby he mounts,
> The ladder-rung his foot has left, may fall,
> Since all things suffer change save God the Truth.

It seems to be easy to stay on the beaten paths, not to take chances, to play it safe, to avoid the risks. But this is not the way for us human beings. Especially is this true of our souls. Christ calls us to "launch out into the deep." We hear a voice saying, "Get thee out . . . into a land that I will show thee." Beaten paths are for beaten men. A prominent St. Louis businessman said, "Stagnant minds are the world's greatest obstacle to progress." We would say that stunted souls produce stagnant minds.

On the wall of a cowboy's bar, in the wide-open West, hangs a saying, "I ain't what I ought to be, I ain't what I'm going to be, but I ain't what I was." That must be some consolation, that our reach exceeds our grasp, and we "feel like travelin' on." We find the idea in folk material and in classic literature. But regardless of where we find the growth concept or its opposite, we must hold doggedly to the belief that we can grow as long as we live. George Bernard Shaw expressed this hope, after a fashion, in one sentence: "The only man who behaves sensibly is my tailor; he takes my measure anew every time he sees me, whilst all the rest go on with their old measurements and expect them to fit me."

Shaw did not grow spiritually, in the Christian sense, but he did change mentally as long as he lived. We Christians need to place a primary value on spiritual progress, as the world does on mental advancement. We need to pray to that end, to expect ourselves to grow, to place ourselves in stimulating environments. Most of us feel that if we do not grow, it will not matter too much because we can at least mark time. The truth is, however, that this is not the way human life behaves. When we do not grow, we regress or go backward. It would seem that life could stand still, but I doubt that it can.

How, then, can we insure our growth? To put it differently, what is a person to do to encourage growth of soul? What are the spurs to keep us moving on in our spiritual progress?

SPIRITUAL ANTIQUES

The first one which I would suggest is that of continuously getting rid of our "spiritual antiques." An antique, in the furniture world, is a piece of furniture which belongs to another period. At one time it was modern, up-to-date, but now its value consists of the fact that it does belong to another time. "It is an authentic Louis XIV bed" is enough to raise its value in the eyes of many people. But not so in matters of the soul. What was valuable in one period, say childhood, is usually a very bad pattern of behavior at forty or sixty.

In literature critics speak of "anachronisms." It would be an anachronism to write of a clock striking in the New Testament times, for there were no clocks until around 1000 A.D. We are sometimes cluttered with anachronisms of the inner self. For example, saying "I don't feel good" to keep from doing something that is unpleasant is a very normal pattern of behavior for a child from six to ten years of age, but it is an anachronism if it is used by a person twenty-six years of age.

Paul gave the classic expression to the growth process when he said, "When I was a child, I talked like a child, I thought like a child, I reasoned just like a child. When I became a man, I laid aside my childish ways" (1 Cor. 13: 11 Williams). Many of us have seen people become emotionally sick and begin to put on the ways of childhood, but every one who has been very close to emotionally sick people has also seen them, in the recovery period, lay aside the clothes of childhood. Under some good, kind treatment the patient seals over his delusions, or begins to associate with his fellows again, or learns ways of handling his tension other than "blowing up," or even begins to value his real self.

My primary concern is not emotional illness but spiritual retardation. Many of us are not as good Christians as we were ten years ago. Everyone seems to recognize our "spiritual antiques" except ourselves. Let us list some antiques that we have seen or heard of in our neighbors' homes. Paul's statement may help here: "I talked like a child." Children, normally, tell falsehoods to gain some end, call each other bad names, tease and bully, say extremely cruel and cutting things; and, in one way or another, try to get by with a domineering pattern of speech. "I thought like a child." A child thinks selfishly. "Can I go?" or "Give me some" are perfectly natural ways of thinking. When a child is frustrated or "blocked," revenge seems to him to be the most appropriate response.

"I reasoned like a child." Here we come into the realm of truth. A child believes what he is told. So do most of us adults, especially in religious matters. When any church says "give me a child until he is five or seven, and then you can teach him what you please," it should remember what a dastardly insult that is. If the statement is true, it tells us much more about the immaturity of the communicants than it does about the truth of the religion. And most people who hold to the fixity of childhood ideas also count it a sin to attend groups (even universities) where opposing ideas are presented.

Another example of putting away childish reasoning occurs on the college level. I am thinking of two pronounced illustrations. One is the student who "loses his faith" in college. The very expression is misleading. Usually he does not lose his faith. He exchanges it. My experience in counseling college students leads me to believe that 90 per cent of those who give up their childhood religious faith accept the faith of their rationalistic professors just as blindly as they did that of their parents, merely exchanging one dependency for another.

But there is another reaction of college students which illustrates Paul's statement. Many students revise their religious ideas, think for themselves, search for truth, but do not give up one set of ideas until they can find a better one. Instead of reacting with fear and prejudice when opposing ideas are presented, they accept their limitations in seeking certainty and walk by faith. If the creation of the world may have taken millions of years, they still have a great God. The magic of praying changes into a more mature kind of praying. Such stupidities as "all roads lead to the same place" are discarded for a healthy search for religious truth.

In intellectual, as well as social matters, we must lay aside our out-of-date patterns. Spiritually, we must go beyond even our own egocentric reason, which is a spiritual antique, and learn to walk daily (though trembling at times) by the revelation which God gives us. Faith requires growth. Reason often drops anchor and stands still.

REJECTING OUR "OUTS"

A second guarantee of growth is that we *reject our "outs."* The term "outs" comes from those who have made a specialty of dealing with "alcoholics." They say that as long as an alcoholic has a fairly satisfactory "out" he will never stop drinking. An "out" may be the geographical escape (moving to another city), changing the type of work he is doing, getting in a hospital for treatment, getting a divorce, or even "sitting tight" and denying that he has a drinking problem. As long as he has one person who will pull him out of a hole when he gets drunk, he will never quit drinking. When he sees that he has exhausted his "outs" and has hit the bottom, there is more hope for him.

But is not this precisely the problem of all struggling saints as well as sinners—I use the words loosely. Jesus told of some people who were invited to a feast (Luke 14: 15-24). "They all with one consent began to make excuse." One man said that he had bought a farm, another a yoke of oxen, and another had recently married a wife. The one who was giving the feast decided to invite the less busy people who would appreciate his invitation. All of us have, at times, been so busy about the good things of life that we did not have time for the best things. To do good is often the greatest obstacle to doing God's will. Decency may easily breed decay, because it seems so right that we are not aware of our smugness. Families degenerate, churches stand still, individuals stagnate because they find an acceptable rationalization for doing nothing.

This is perfectly illustrated by the words of Simon Peter on the Mount of Transfiguration. He said, in substance, "Let us just stay right here forever." For the moment, he had forgotten the people in the valley who needed Jesus' message and healing power. "It is good to be here" were his words. Yes, but the next stage in life may be just as good in a different way. Browning wrote,

> Grow old along with me,
> The best is yet to be.

Halford Luccock has a very interesting sermon on the transfiguration, entitled "Keeping Life Out of Stopping Places." He tells of taking a little six-year-old girl for a ride on a merry-go-round one afternoon. He had thought that surely five rides would dull the appetite of anyone. But he was wrong. The little girl exclaimed, "I'd like to live on a merry-go-round."

This reminds us of the Negro wife who greeted her delinquent husband after he had spent the dollar they had saved. The money, a large sum for them during the depression, was for the pleasure of both of them, but he had used it all for his own childish enjoyment on the merry-go-round. Shamefacedly he started to explain how much you get for your money on the merry-go-round. She interrupted, "Rastus, you sho' don' ride a whole lot but where's yo' bin?" That is something of the futility of a person who is not growing. Even the most progressive of us feel at times like we are going round and round and coming out nowhere.

The "outs" for the Christian are sometimes very attractive. I have mentioned doing good instead of doing God's will. Often we find time for such church projects as recreation, administration, money raising, music—and all of these are important—but never get around to making disciples or presenting the Word. Too many civic projects or lodges or clubs are "outs" from the work of the church of Jesus Christ. Even relatives, sometimes, take the money or energy which belongs to the homeless or to those who know not Christ. Sickness or old age are sometimes "outs" to escape from doing the best we can.

Moses sought an "out" when God called him to lead the Israelites out of Egypt. He said that he was not important enough, but God promised to be with him. He said that he did not know God well enough, but God gave him additional revelation of himself. Moses said that the people would not believe him, but God performed some miracles for him—he always does when they are needed. Then he said that he did not have the special talent needed for that particular job; God offered to increase his ability as the occasion demanded. Finally, Moses said, "Don't ask me to do it; just get someone else." No wonder God became angry!

There is a difference, however, between our "outs" and those of the story of Moses' call. It was one great event in which he was confronted by the opportunity of a lifetime. To most of us our challenges come without any burning bushes and appear to be unimportant, therefore our "outs" seem like good reasoning. We refuse to live in a state of constant decision.

It is more comfortable in the rut than out of it. Lot's wife tried to go back but turned to a pillar of salt. Jesus said, "Remember Lot's wife." The rich young ruler would not move on into another and better kind of life. Oliver Cromwell once said, "A man never mounts so high, as when he does not know where he is going." And Jesus said to a man who gave an excuse for not following him immediately, "No man, having put his hand to the plow, and looking back, is fit for the kingdom" (Luke 9:62). Hal Boyle, the newspaper writer, said: "Most people would rather look backward than forward for a very simple reason: It is easier to remember where you've been than to figure out where you're going."

ACCEPTING OUR CROSSES

There is one other, at least one other, essential to a progressive life, *the ability and the willingness to accept crosses*. This may be put in secular or religious vocabulary. Fritz Kunkel, in secular language answering the question "How does one achieve maturity?" makes the following two-fold statement: [2]

It means first, "How can I increase my capacity for tension?" or, to put it into more simple terms: "How can I learn the art of swallowing bitter medicine?" And secondly it would ask, "In my efforts to cope with the difficulties of life, how am I to prevent myself from forsaking an objective attitude for an egocentric one?" Primarily this means, "How am I to prevent unpleasant and dangerous behaviour patterns from being formed. If egocentricity, with its rigid behaviour patterns, is already a feature of my character, what way must I take that I may return most quickly and completely to an objective attitude."

This capacity for tension is what other psychologists call the ability to suffer anxiety. Dr. O. Hobart Mowrer says that pain is not always bad but is also good. To him "anxiety is a sign of strength within the personality and that it is something to be used as a basis for further personal development and greater maturity, rather than something to be analyzed away." [3] This, of course, could be carried to extremes. Children, sick adults, and all of us to some extent should be forced to face only as much anxiety as can be tolerated without serious injury. We can stand just so much. But it would seem that this facing of anxiety is a greatly needed emphasis in our day.

Peace of mind seems to be the goal of life. "Give me happiness or I want to die" is the request of so many. Kunkel, in another book, *In Search of Maturity,* speaks of the false religious voices today which are saying: [4]

There is no evil! Look for the positive value which is to be found within every one and everything. Do not countenance negative thoughts or feelings, they are wrong. Everything is beautiful. We are not fettered by the past, nor by sin, nor by diseases, nor by wrong social orders. There is no darkness; just believe in the light.

While such voices are being heard, he points out, cities are raided, thousands of women and children are maimed, soldiers are killed. Then he says that a religion which does not have a thorough study of sin as well as "individual and collective darkness, evil and deviation, is not religion but blind idolatry." These are the words of a psychoanalyst!

The very heart of this matter is that those who grow must be willing to worry. I would not give a dime for a church member who refuses to worry about his relationship to his church. He may call it concern or interest or even thinking, but he has to be willing to tolerate a "stirred up" state in which he is motivated to amount to something for Christ.

Jesus expressed it this way: "And he said to them all, If any man will come after me, let him deny himself, and take up his cross daily, and follow me. For whosoever will save his life shall lose it: but whosoever will lose his life for my sake, the same shall save it. For what is a man advantaged, if he gain the whole world, and lose himself, or be cast away?" (Luke 9: 23-25).

The emphasis in this passage probably ought to be placed on the word "daily." The crosses Jesus speaks of are not the "inevitables" of life. A man loses his health or money, or is mistreated by someone, and he says, "Well, I guess that is my cross; I will bear it the best I can." But the crossess Jesus was talking about were those we could take up or leave alone. They are the things we can do or refrain from doing which make us more unselfish, more mature. Through them we die to self—a cross is to die on—and become the more mature self.

Of course, the events in life which stagger us are challenges to growth too. Dr. Paul Scherer says, "Every once and a while life stops for a moment and looks around and shudders; but after that the band strikes up again." I have seen cases where the band seems not to strike up again, but even then God's grace is sufficient (see 2 Cor. 12: 7-10).

> The plant cut down to the root
> Does not hate.
> It uses all its strength
> To grow once more.[5]
>
> ELIZABETH JANE COATSWORTH

Elton Trueblood tells of a college president who was asked how he was able to keep his composure in the face of continual shots fired at him from students, professors, alumni, and from the general public. He replied, "Oh, I just keep moving and let the shots drop behind me."

We Must Keep Moving

It is the ability to keep moving which constitutes growth, but let none of us think this is easy. A clinical psychologist tells of a little girl who said, "Why can't you be born grown up or stay little always? It hurts so to grow up." How can I grow up? How can we figure that out? It certainly is not an easy problem, but the "dailyness" of it is really the hardest part. A friend of mine said, "I get tired of fighting, of struggling. Is there no other way to live?" In a way, yes. But even the lilies have to bear the chill night wind.

Homer Rodehaver used to tell the story of a little freckle-faced, cross-eyed, red-headed, big-eared, tough boy who came to Sunday school. The teacher knew how tough he was and decided to talk one Sunday about the devil. She laid it on. When she got through, the fierceness, viciousness, and all the other qualities of Satan were clearly portrayed. This might be the only chance she would have with some of these boys, especially the new, tough one. Finally she turned to him and asked him what he thought of the devil now, wasn't he afraid of him? "Yes, I guess I am afraid of that old, big devil, but if you will bring in one my size I'll give him hell for a little while."

That is all we ever meet, the enemies our size. God sees to that. If we do not turn our backs but willingly accept the crosses which we see, we will grow. The writer of Hebrews describes the life of Moses in these words, "By faith Moses,

when he was come to years, refused to be called the son of
Pharaoh's daughter; choosing rather to suffer affliction with
the people of God, than to enjoy the pleasures of sin for a season; Esteeming the reproach of Christ greater riches than the
treasures in Egypt" (Heb. 11:24-26).

Measure me, sky!
Tell me I reach by a song
Nearer the stars:
I have been little so long.

Weigh me, high wind!
What will yon wild scales record?
Profit of pain,
Joy by the weight of a word.

Horizon, reach out!
Catch at my hands, stretch me taut,
Rim of the world:
Widen my eyes by a thought.

Sky, be my depth;
Wind, be my width and my height;
World, my heart's span:
Loneliness, wings for my flight! [6]

LENORA SPEYER

NOTES

Chapter I

1. *Lives in Progress* (New York: Dryden Press, 1952), p. 4.
2. *How to Help Your Child Grow Up* (Chicago: Rand McNally and Co., 1948). pp. 271–272.
3. *Our Inner Conflict* (New York: W. W. Norton and Co., 1945).
4. *Personality: A Psychological Interpretation* (New York: Henry Holt and Co., 1937), chapter 8.
5. "Man-Making," *Poems of Edwin Markham*, ed. C. L. Wallis (New York: Harper and Brothers, 1950). Used by permission.

Chapter II

1. *Cell and Psyche* (Chapel Hill: University of North Carolina Press, 1950), p. 16.

Chapter IV

1. *The Chain* (New York: Doubleday and Co., Inc., 1949), p. 64.
2. *The Divine Imperative* (Philadelphia: Westminster Press, 1945), pp. 157–158.
3. *Eyeless in Gaza* (New York: Harper and Brothers, 1936), p. 320.

Chapter VI

1. *The Struggle of the Soul* (New York: Macmillan Company, 1952), p. 1.

Chapter VII

1. *New York Times*, April 14, 1945, p. 7, col. 1.
2. *The Conduct of Life* (New York: Harcourt Brace and Co., 1951), p. 36.
3. *Harvey* (New York: Dramatists Play Service, Inc., 1950), p. 64. Used by permission.

Chapter VIII

1. *Eyeless in Gaza* (New York: Harper and Brothers, 1936), p. 423.
2. Author's reconstruction of passage from G. A. Studdert-Kennedy, *The Hardest Part* (London: Hodder and Stoughton, 1919), pp. 99–103.
3. *Masterpiece of Religious Verse* (New York: Harper and Brothers, 1948), pp. 406–407.

Chapter IX

1. *Harvey* (New York: Dramatists Play Service, Inc., 1950), p. 49.

Chapter X

1. *Lives In Progress* (New York: Dryden Press, 1952), p. 363.
2. *The Summing Up* (New York: Alfred A. Knopf, Inc., 1938), pp. 153–154.
3. *The Life We Prize* (New York: Harper and Brothers, 1951), p. 163.

Chapter XI

1. *Doctor Faustus* (New York: Alfred Knopf and Co., 1948), pp. 307–308.
2. *What It Means To Grow Up* (New York: Charles Scribner's Sons, 1947), pp. 25–26.
3. *Anxiety*, ed. Hock and Zubin (New York: Grune and Stratton, 1950), p. 29.
4. *In Search of Maturity* (New York: Charles Scribner's Sons, 1951), p. 203.
5. Used by permission.
6. "Measure Me, Sky!" Used by permission of author.

TAPROOTS

for

TALL SOULS

R. Lofton Hudson

TOWERING sequoias have a secret in resisting quake and storm. Taproots anchor them in the depths of the earth.

Christians must grow tall in spirit, ever seeking to attain their potentialities as children of God. But emotional growth does not come easily, for the mind plays tricks to keep one satisfied with his own immaturity. Even the conscience can be shaped to fit a selfish pattern.

Dr. Hudson makes use of the findings of practical psychology to uncover forces in the unconscious which keep us self-satisfied. At the same time he uses the basic Christian teachings to give guidance and energy for growth in Christian living.

Taproots for Tall Souls is the book for those who are honestly interested in reaching toward their full possibilities.

The striking chapter titles hint at the unusual approach of this book.

"Ah! What a shame."

"I've finished. Period."

"Honestly?"

"Yes, honestly."

"Oh, honey, that's wonderful. At last I've got you back again. Come here; let me give you a big kiss."

We sat together on the couch, our hands entwined. It was one of those moments when the eloquence of silence fills the heart with serenity and the soul with golden peace. I was loathe to spoil the magic of the stillness that lay between us.

"Darling," I murmured softly. "While I was so far away from you, did you ever think that I might never come back? I don't mean because of an accident or anything, but because I might not want to come back to you?"

"Never."

"How come?"

"Because, my precious, adorable, nutty wife, our marriage has been made from the strongest of bonds, but there have never been any chains."